Non-Being in Ancient Thought

Non-Being in Ancient Thought

DMITRI NIKULIN

OXFORD
UNIVERSITY PRESS

Oxford University Press is a department of the University of Oxford.
It furthers the University's objective of excellence in research, scholarship,
and education by publishing worldwide. Oxford is a registered trade mark of
Oxford University Press in the UK and certain other countries.

Published in the United States of America by Oxford University Press
198 Madison Avenue, New York, NY 10016, United States of America.

© Oxford University Press 2025

All rights reserved. No part of this publication may be reproduced, stored in a retrieval system, transmitted, used for text and data mining, or used for training artificial intelligence, in any form or by any means, without the prior permission in writing of Oxford University Press, or as expressly permitted by law, by license or under terms agreed with the appropriate reprographics rights organization. Inquiries concerning reproduction outside the scope of the above should be sent to the Rights Department, Oxford University Press, at the address above.

You must not circulate this work in any other form
and you must impose this same condition on any acquirer.

Library of Congress Cataloging-in-Publication Data
Names: Nikulin, D. V. (Dmitriĭ Vladimirovich), author.
Title: Non-being in ancient thought / Dmitri Nikulin.
Description: 1. | New York, NY, United States of America :
Oxford University Press, [2025] | Includes bibliographical references and index. |
Identifiers: LCCN 2025004420 (print) | LCCN 2025004421 (ebook) |
ISBN 9780197781616 (hardback) | ISBN 9780197781647 | ISBN 9780197781630 (epub)
Subjects: LCSH: Nonbeing. | Nothing (Philosophy) | Ancient philosophy.
Classification: LCC B187.N66 N55 2025 (print) | LCC B187.N66 (ebook) |
DDC 111.5—dc23/eng/20250304
LC record available at https://lccn.loc.gov/2025004420
LC ebook record available at https://lccn.loc.gov/2025004421

DOI: 10.1093/oso/9780197781616.001.0001

Printed by Integrated Books International, United States of America

The manufacturer's authorized representative in the EU for product safety is
Oxford University Press España S.A., Parque Empresarial San Fernando de Henares,
Avenida de Castilla, 2 – 28830 Madrid (www.oup.es/en).

Contents

Preface vii
Acknowledgments xxv
Permissions xxvii

1. Parmenides: Being and Nothing 1
2. Democritus: Non-Being as the Void 42
3. Plato: Non-Being as the Other of Being 73
4. Diogenes: Non-Being as Convention 116
5. Aristotle: Non-Being as Thought in Many Ways 148
6. Plotinus: Non-Being as the One 187
7. Simplicius: Non-Being Voided 231

Conclusion 257
Bibliography 259
Index 269

Preface

τὸ γὰρ αὐτὸ νοεῖν ἐστίν τε καὶ εἶναι.

For thinking and being is the same.
Parmenides[1]

οὐθὲν μᾶλλον τὸ ὂν τοῦ μὴ ὄντος εἶναι.

Being is no more than non-being.
Democritus[2]

Being has always been at the forefront of the philosophical debate, while non-being has been considered a nuisance for thought, which thinking continually tried to get rid of once and for all. Yet, as this book intends to show, non-being is crucial for the constitution of being, without which being can neither be nor be thought. *Being.* Being is. Being cannot but be and be what it is, and it is therefore nothing but is. Yet, being *qua* being is not a thing and thus is not an object of thought as a particular object. Hence, being

---

[1] Parmenides. DK28B 3. All references to Parmenides are taken from Hermann Diels and Walther Kranz, Eds., *Die Fragmente der Vorsokratiker.* Vol. 1. Berlin: Weidmann, 1996; reprint of the sixth edition of 1951. Henceforth, I will omit the author number (28) and "B" (fragments), and I will only indicate the fragment and line number, except for references to the "A" group (testimonies of Parmenides' life and work). See also Leonardo Tarán. *Parmenides: A Text with Translation, Commentary, and Critical Essays.* Princeton, NJ: Princeton University Press, 1965, 7–172; A. H. Coxon. *The Fragments of Parmenides: A Critical Text with Introduction and Translation, the Ancient Testimonia, and a Commentary.* Rev. ed. Trans. and ed. Richard McKirahan. Las Vegas: Parmenides, 2009; John A. Palmer. *Parmenides and Presocratic Philosophy.* Oxford: Oxford University Press, 2009, 362–87; and Daniel W. Graham. Trans. and ed. *The Texts of Early Greek Philosophy: The Complete Fragments and Selected Testimonies of the Major Presocratics.* Pt. 1. Cambridge: Cambridge University Press, 2010, 206–33.

[2] Democritus ap. Aristotle. *Met.* 985b8.

defines thought and becomes identical with thought when it is thought.

This is the understanding of being from the beginning of thinking about it. One needs to find a language and a way of saying being—of saying the logos of being, which is expressed by a verb that stands for an act of the *is* that is not a thing and thus remains indefinite. As indefinite, it is a substantivized infinitive (*einai, esse, to be*)—an in-finite form of the verb that stands for an action that can only be defined concretely in a concrete case but is never as such before the action. So being is defined each time in a particular case as the being of this particular object while not being itself a specific object of thought. As such, being can also be expressed as a participle (*on, ens, being*), a non-finite verbal form derived from the infinitive that can be used as a noun without itself standing for a thing.

Both the infinitive and the participle—to be and being—are linguistic compromises of the logos that needs to grasp being within language and logical thought. Yet, as the source of such linguistic expression and argumentative thinking, being remains elusive for logos because logos speaks and thinks, and thus expresses and structures itself, through distinctions. The primary logical distinction is between the act and that to which this act extends, or between being and thought, predicate and subject, saying and the said, thinking and the thought. But being *is* thought, or being and thinking is the same, as Parmenides tells us.

Another solution that the logos comes up with in its attempt to approach being is the distinction between *to be* and *to be something* or *being* as different from *being-of*. For anything that is, its *is* differs from *what* it is. For that which is grasped by and expressed in logos, the existential meaning (A is) is different from the essential meaning of the "is" (which, in an elementary way, can be rendered as a tautology, A is A, or in general as A is B). Similarly, for the logos "being is" is different from "being is being," where the former presents the existential claim that being (somehow) is; and the latter that being is something. But because being is not different from *is* in "being is," being is tautological with itself in its "is" and "what" when it comes to being.

This means that being is simple and thus prior to the logical distinction of the existential and essential, which it makes possible. Being is such that it simply is, without any reference to any particular act or subject, and it is neither an object nor a thing. This makes the thinkers of being wonder if being (or the unconditional is) *is* at all, what it is, and whether there is something other than being that makes being be.

Being and history. If being is and is what it is, it always is and is the same. Hence, being does not change, and it is always thought as the same being. This seems to suggest that being cannot have a history. Being is commonly thought of as opposed to becoming, since being always is, and becoming attempts to be and reach being without ever becoming being. Thus, Plato takes being to transcend becoming, since being surpasses the flow of things that strive to being but can never properly be. Yet, in a sense, it is becoming that is transcendent to being because being has literally *no idea* what becoming "is" and becomes. So, becoming becomes, yet it is without a beginning or an end, since becoming cannot *be* in its own becoming, and thus it is a happening that is never complete and has no meaning in the present. Hence, becoming is never present, cannot be traced or detected, and is elusive in its present absence. Therefore, becoming leaves no trace and thus has no history. And if non-being is not, it cannot have any history either.

And yet, there is a history of our understanding and misunderstanding of being and non-being that can be considered as establishing the pattern for the history of human *res gestae*, which originates in an attempt to resolve the dramatic tension between our temporary existence and non-being, in the face of which our historical being is constituted. In this sense, history always presupposes an ontology. This book is an attempt to trace a history or genealogy of non-being in its relation to being.

Speaking about being. When philosophy realizes that it is entrusted with the task of thinking being and clarifying its meaning(s), it looks for being everywhere. If being is that which is and cannot be otherwise, then nature can be the locus of and for being as exemplified in the ever fluent, yet incessant, self-reproducing living beings. From its inception—in Parmenides, Democritus, and Aristotle—thinking being is related to nature as being *in* nature, and even as the being of nature as that which always is and underlies the visible transformations of things.

Yet, thinking being also implies speaking about being. Hence, on the one hand, the thinkers of being need logos as language and reasoning about that which is. But, on the other hand, they realize the inadequacy of logos to adequately grasp that on which it itself depends, and thus it becomes necessary to adjust logos and find new ways and means within it to speak about being.

The main obstacle for such an undertaking is that being as that which is and only is, is simple. Therefore, it needs to be grasped in a simple act of speech and thought. Yet, logos is complex, discursive, and structured as a process of speaking and reasoning, where that which is in need of being said and thought comes at the very end, provided that we are capable of following all the intricate logical moves and turns along the way. By reasoning and argument, logos intends to come to a conclusion that will stand on its own logical grounds against possible objections and counterarguments.

This logical self-justificatory process implies a distinction between discursive and non-discursive thinking, between logical thinking, *dianoia*, which is a reasoned process, and the intellect, *nous*, which thinks and is what it thinks—being—in an act. This distinction is already established in Parmenides, accepted by Plato, recognized by Aristotle, and refined by Plotinus and Simplicius. The *nous* is capable of thinking being by *being* being. In its thinking, the *nous* requires no mediation with the thought and is what it thinks. The dianoetic logos, on the contrary, presupposes a distance between thinking and the thought, and thus has to overcome it in orderly thinking. Such thinking, as Plato suggests, can miss its target in many different ways but can get it right in just one way, by providing the right understanding and definition of the thought—in this case, of being.

This means, again, that logos lives off, speaks, and thinks by making, establishing, and justifying the distinctions needed and appropriate for its thinking and expression. A logical way of approaching being, which for logos appears indistinctly and as nondistinguished, is through distinctions—as many distinctions as the logos can come up with within its linguistic use. So everything is thinkable and sayable *in many ways*. This program was first formulated by Prodicus and then adopted in one way or another by all thinkers: to think philosophically means to make distinctions and then choose the right one(s). Logos is inescapably plurivocal, and everything that is said and thought discursively is said and logically thought in many ways; thus, the same—being—can always be expressed differently and in another way.

Thinking being. Being as thought. While thinking by way of logos moves discursively in a number of steps toward a conclusion, it attempts to abandon itself and become non-discursive, a thinking that would overcome a well-laid-out process of reasoning and thus become—be—being. If thinking can think being in an act, it is being, and being is thought.

When logos moves along and with an argument, it changes itself along the way. But the act of thinking that has already thought what it thinks does not undergo a transformation. It is already there by thinking that which is and cannot but be. This means that the thought that thinks being and is being by thinking has to be reflective, or be thinking that thinks itself.

That being, *einai*, and thought, *noein*, do not differ in the act of being thought is the fundamental insight of Parmenides and becomes the leitmotiv for all later ontology, which either accepts—as with Plato and Plotinus—or rejects it. The coincidence of being and thought does not imply that thought exists independently on its own, but rather that if being and thought are not the same, then being cannot be thought. Therefore, being and thinking is the same. This means that only being can be properly thought. So when thinking thinks without presuppositions, it is being.

Yet, the thought that is being is not a concept. Today, the concept has become central to philosophy because modern subjectivity considers the world to be an object of thought at its disposal, to which reason has attached the required conceptual tags that make the thought intelligible. It is striking, therefore, that ancient thinkers of being do not have a concept of the concept. Neither the *idea* of Plato nor Aristotle's *ousia* is a concept of a thing but *being*, that which is, the real, thinkable thing itself.

Being and non-being. Being is. But it also is not because being is not what is not being. So negative determination has to be included in being.[3] Hence, non-being has to be accounted for by the thinking of being. But if thinking and being are/is the same, then the not-being as the other of being cannot be thought. And yet, it should be because being as the same and always identical to itself cannot be thought and be without its other.

Therefore, without non-being, being cannot be. Being is the other to non-being. Without non-being, being is only a "given," an object of thinking as any other thing but not thinking itself, and hence it escapes thinking and, contrary to Parmenides, it is not being thought. In this way, not only being but also non-being escapes being thought.

This is the case for much of philosophy throughout its history, which posits that only being is and is the subject of predication and an object of thought, whereas that which is not being is not. Such a philosophical approach concludes that non-being is not absolutely and privatively and is forever absent from the order of being and as

---

[3] On the importance of negation and negative language in Parmenides, see Scott Austin. *Parmenides: Being, Bounds, and Logic.* New Haven, CT: Yale University Press, 1986, 11–43 et passim.

such is unthinkable. That which strives toward being, then, never becomes being.

And yet, as I intend to show, without non-being, being is not and cannot be. And if we take a closer look at the ancient thinkers of being, from Parmenides through late antiquity, they agree, one way or another, on *meontic primacy*: being is rooted in non-being.

Non-being as the other of being is an utter negativity that, however, is not a mere privation of being or its positive expression but the elusive origin of being, without which being cannot be. Yet, such an origin itself is not, and therefore it is a not properly thinkable nothing. Non-being itself does not have an origin, and hence the origin of being is not an origin or is unoriginal.

So on this interpretation, being is thought, and yet being has an origin or is original without having a properly identifiable or thinkable source, which is opaque, not transparent, and not provided in and by thinking or in self-reflection of being about itself. Being can neither be nor be thought without non-being, but because non-being is not, it is not the, or a, beginning of being. Therefore, being does not, and cannot, have a beginning. And yet, without non-being, being could not be.

Because non-being is the other of being, non-being needs to be thought *differently*, which makes logos struggle with non-being and even abdicate its attempts to approach the unapproachable and say the unsayable. An attempt at a logical thinking of non-being leads either to contradiction or to the recognition that, as being, non-being is said in many ways. The ontology that takes non-being seriously might appear strange and unusual, but ontology is always such because what it has to grasp and account for—being—is the unordinary that transpires among the ordinary and yet is not a thing and thus no-thing.

Beyond being: the other ontology. Non-being as the other of being is not a mere privation or lack of being, as it is in Aristotle, but an *otherwise* than being or a *beyond being*. Already Parmenides calls it "beside," *parex*, being"; Plato refers to it as "beyond being," *epekeina tēs ousias*, as do Plotinus, Proclus, and Simplicius throughout their voluminous works.

But if non-being is beyond being, it is thereby beyond thought, thus disrupting the congruence of being and thought. Hence, non-being is not thinkable, sayable, or graspable in any way, even if it is considered the source of being. However, one might also say that that which is beyond being is not beyond thought but is thinkable, though in a different way.

The modern thinking of being is that of first-person thinking that stresses *that* I think,= rather than *what* I think, since I may be mistaken in *what* I think, but I cannot miss the *is* of thinking, that I *am* thinking. So this is the thinking that is non-identical with the thought and thus thinks being as an object. But the negative ontology that originates in the thought of Parmenides and Plato and accepts, on the one hand, the coincidence of being and thought and, on the other hand, non-being as the beyond-being that is constitutive of being, is the *other ontology* that is obliterated and actively suppressed by the ontology of object-thinking. Object-thinking takes things or substances as existing on their own, accessible in and by mental representations, which stand between, both separating and connecting, things and the mind.

Via negativa. The Parmenidean goddess warned us long ago not to speak and think non-being because of its utter impossibility, yet we still do not listen and probably never will. As systematic reasoning about being, ontology can be considered a heteroreflection, since it reflects on something that does not belong to its thinking but is radically different from such thinking, on that which is other than thought. Ontology, then, thinks about the improper, about that which cannot be thought. But then it has to come up with new means of speaking about the unspeakable, naming that which cannot be named, and thinking being as identical with the thought as grounded in the unground of the beyond being.

At the level of a methodical argument, ontology uses the language of refined dialectic and nuanced logical reasoning. Yet, thinking about non-being requires a different thought, and language, that goes beyond thought and language, which philosophers attempt first as poetic (Parmenides), then as dialogic (in Plato), then as logical (Aristotle), and then as apophatic (in Plotinus and the Neoplatonists). The negative approach is a productive clearing of the space of thought in order to approach the same in another way because the same—of being and thought—always depends on its other of non-being as beyond being. The negative determination of being can be expressed as: not this but that (from the perspective of the other) and as: not that but this (from the perspective of the same). But non-being that determines being in the absence of any determination can be expressed as: not this and not that. It is the negative, or apophatic, approach that is the way of heteroreflection, of speaking by abstaining from speech up to the point of its silent evaporation, of thinking by suspending the discursive order of reasoning.

The protagonists. The *dramatis personae* of this book are Parmenides, Democritus, Plato, Diogenes, Aristotle, Plotinus, and Simplicius, along with many other supporting actors, who span the history of ancient Greek philosophy, philosophers who wrote in awareness of the work of their predecessors to which they directly or indirectly responded. The extant tradition of thinking about being and non-being is remarkably consistent over the thousand years that separate Parmenides from Simplicius, and yet it is equally innovative, since each thinker attempted to find their own way while building on the thought of their predecessors. The temporal—but not philosophical—gap between Aristotle and Plotinus spans the vicissitudes and diversity of Hellenistic thought, which deserves a separate discussion. But the density of thought and the extent of writings of these seven thinkers—who are not the seven "wise men" but rather philosophers in search of the truth about what is and is not—more than suffice for an original genealogy of being and non-being in ancient Greek thought.

Parmenides. Being announces itself in philosophy through Parmenides' poem as *being*. In doing so, the poem thinks by narrating and narrates by thinking as *being is*. Being becomes a problem for thought in that it asserts itself in and as thinking, for *being and thinking is the same.* Hence, thinking thinks being and being is thought. If being is identical with thinking, it thinks itself and thus is itself in the same act of thought as *being is one.* Therefore, not being distinct from itself, being is being.

So mere being not even is and is thus nothing without being identical with nothing because nothing is *not, is* nothing, and is *nothing.* Mere *being,* then, is to be thought apophatically, as not the other of and to itself. But in *being is,* the being of being is already established, and thus the *is* that is yet can be thought in its existential (that being is) and essential way (as the copula in being is being). Only when *being is being* can being be thought in its "is" and "what."

And yet, being cannot be thought without its other, non-being—as being that is not non-being. Non-being, therefore, is not and is many.

If being is thought, its thinking establishes an important distinction between two ways of thinking being, which becomes crucial for all subsequent thinking of and about being. One form of thinking being is the philosophical discursive narration that asks—or gives—reasons for being as being what it is. This is logos, which is propositional and which in its elementary form is set by the thinking of *being is being.* The structure of logos is that of predication, which makes possible an ordered, successive telling or explanation of the thought. The other form of thinking being is reason or intellect, *nous* or *noos,* which is complementary to, yet distinct from, logos. This form of thinking is non-discursive, and grasps being as *being is* in an act of thought without a sequence of steps of propositional reasoning and is thus that very thinking that is identical with being.

Democritus. The "laughing philosopher," Democritus originated an innovative interpretation of being in ancient philosophy as a critique of its Parmenidean understanding. In Democritus' own concise formulation, "in reality—atoms and the void."

Whereas for Parmenides being is one and non-being is many, for Democritus, on the contrary, one (the void) is non-being and many (the atoms) is being. So, for Democritus, being is full and discrete, and non-being is empty and continuous. Being comprises the entire multiplicity of indivisible atoms, imperceptible because of their smallness.

So while for Parmenides being is thought and is thinking, for Democritus being is body or many bodies, and thus is non-identical and opposite to thought. Moreover, being is infinite in number, and non-being is infinite in divisibility and extension. In their plurality, atoms are the elements of being, or letters in the infinite alphabet of the infinite book of nature. Even the worlds are infinite in number. Yet, the infinite is not thinkable, even if it is essential to being. Democritus' seemingly simple ontology yields an understanding of being that in its bodily indivisibility, minuteness, and numeric infinity is elusive from thought and is rather a subject of imagination.

Since non-being is the void of non-embodied extension, it provides the possibility for the movement of atoms and their very being as being located in the void. Hence, non-being allows being to be. In this sense, non-being *is*, as is being. This leads to a striking conclusion, that being is no more than non-being. But because being is full, there is no non-being *in* being. Yet, being is *in* non-being. Therefore, being (atoms) cannot be without being, although non-being (void) can be without being.

Plato. Plato's *Sophist* is central to his dialogical and dialectical reasoning about being and non-being. Here, the interlocutors discuss and attempt to refute Parmenides' claim that non-being is not. In order to do so, Plato makes the Stranger from Elea establish an account of being that would then justify and corroborate an account of non-being. Plato accepts Parmenides' insight that being is thinkable and is thought. Thinking-being is the reason-*nous*, which differs from the dialectical, discursive logos that unfolds itself throughout the dialogue, making turns and twists of the pros and contras through the dialogue's speakers. The *nous* thinks itself as and in many different forms or ideas, each of which *is* and is being as being thought. Yet, since all forms are being and are thinkable and thought, they are not mutually isolated but instead comprise an entire intelligible, beautiful cosmos of beings where they always actually, and not potentially, communicate and reflect each other and thus connect into a system of forms.

Therefore, being is one but also against Parmenides, not-one, or many. Being is a synthetic unity of one and many, or one-many. Or being is not just one but also many. And contrary to Democritus, beings as forms are many but not infinitely many, because being is primarily defined, or defines itself, through limit. Being for Plato is one-many as an interconnected plurality of forms, where each form is one and yet each is not, and cannot be, without others. In this way, being is always beings, and beings are being.

Hence, being is because of the other, which comes as the other of being. In the constitution of the categories that characterize being in the *Sophist*, where being is approached through the mutually opposite categories of motion–rest and other–same, the negative category of the other takes priority by way of deduction to the positive one of the same. However, there is no opposite of and to being: being is and is what it is in the plurality of its forms. But because being is the other to that which is not being, being has its other, which thereby is not being and yet is indispensable for being's being and its understanding.

This other of being is non-being. Thus, against Parmenides, Plato establishes that non-being *is* in its contradistinction to being. And yet, non-being is not opposite to being because non-being is not and being has no opposite. Non-being is being's elusive and not properly thinkable other, which does not belong to being and thus has no form that could be thought. Non-being stands for negativity without which being as one-many, being as beings, cannot be and cannot be thought. Other to everything that is, non-being is the *other* of being.

Diogenes. Contrary to his forerunners, Diogenes does not think being but *enacts* it. From his perspective, Plato's dialectical and dialogical method of achieving being is useless for living well in accordance to being. So Diogenes invents his own method of enacting being, not through an argument but in and by an *ergon*, which is neither an act of theoretical reasoning nor a practical moral action nor a productive activity aimed at creating a desired outcome. *Ergon* is a deed that shows the *what* of being by enacting *how* it is in the life worth living, performed in public and corroborated by Diogenes' own life. From this perspective, being cannot be thought or realized once and for all but needs to be enlived again and again, always anew, in a strenuous exercise or *askēsis* of the body and the soul.

The non-theoretical knowledge of being, then, is the enacting of being as well-being and as such an exercise—*askēsis*—of living well in the *erga* of one's life. Being is therefore embodied in the good life, which for Diogenes is the life according to that which is, or by nature. Non-being, then, is the unnecessary conventions that go against nature and stand in the way and deny being as being enlived or living well. In this way, non-being is constitutive not of being but rather of the effort of the *ergon* to gain being in and of the good life.

Hence, the "ascetic" exercise of being also means critical reflection on, suspension, and rejection of non-being, which is encrypted into social and political life in many ways. Diogenes' audacious denial of non-being in public is often accompanied by scandal, which, as the exercise of free speech, confronts, criticizes, and transgresses the implicit and explicit legal and habitual norms of thought and action. By publicly enliving the being of the good life according to nature and by rejecting the non-being of the conventional in his *erga*, Diogenes therefore demonstrates the possibility of liberation from non-being and freedom for being in the self-containment and simplicity of the good life.

Aristotle. Before coming up with his own account of being, which becomes decisive for later ontology, Aristotle begins with a careful critical discussion of the doctrines of his predecessors, including those of Parmenides, Democritus, and Plato. For Aristotle himself, being is sedimented as substance, *ousia*, as that which is on its own and does not need any other in order to be and is thus independent of other beings. Being is always the being of a *this one*, *tode ti*, one among many, all mutually ontologically independent, and has a unique *is*, *esti*, and an identifiable *what*, *ti*. As such, being is primary to that which exists due to another, and as such it is a substrate, *hypokeimenon*, that which underlies all transformations, while not being transformed itself. As substrate, being bears properties and is the ontological and logical subject defined by its predicates. In reality—in nature—being is present in substance, that is, is on its own independently of another substance and is thinkable and definable. This further means that there is no void, which seems to be a place in which nothing is, which is non-being or something that is non-existent. Since nothing is not, void only appears to be where there is no body and no defined and definite being.

Being is and always is what it is. As such, it is perennial. Yet, this does not mean that being is atemporal, residing in a present beyond time. Rather, being is *to ti ēn einai*, or being that *was* being at all times. Being is not characterized by eternity but rather by limit: Aristotle is preoccupied with boundary, edge, limit, in a constant effort to draw and think a thin line that separates being from being and from the abyss of chaos and the infinite. So, in a sense, his entire philosophy is a struggle against non-being, which he has to take seriously since non-being has no limit and is therefore indefinite, defying attempts at its definition and thinking. At a certain point, in an unpreserved— and thus not really existing—Aristotelian dialogue, Silenus even claims that it is best not to be born, so to die is better than to live.[4]

---

[4] μὴ γίγνεσθαι μὲν . . . ἄριστον πάντων, τὸ δὲ τεθνάναι τοῦ ζῆν ἐστι κρεῖττον. Silenus to Midas; Aristotle. *Eudemus*. In *Aristotelis fragmenta selecta*. Ed. W. D. Ross. Oxford: Oxford University Press, 1955, fr. 6.

By turning to the principles, the starting points that allow the existent to be and be understood, Aristotle rethinks not only being but also non-being, which becomes thinkable as a principle. The three principles are form, matter, and privation, which stand, respectively, for being, relative non-being, and absolute non-being. Being and non-being, then, are taken as the opposites, those of form and privation, which as principles of being and thought are considered not only as ontological but also as logical categories. By way of logical expression, both being and non-being are plurivocal: not only being but also non-being is said in many ways.

So non-being is further tamed by being split into two: into matter as relative non-being, which is defined in three aspects as substrate, possibility, and indefiniteness; and into non-being as such, which is privation as the lack of being, or never-being. Privation is thus a principle of the existent that, however, stands for non-being as not properly accountable and not definable and hence not knowable, or perhaps knowable only analogically and negatively.

Plotinus. Realizing that he was at the outer edge of the entire tradition of philosophy but in fact originating a new one, Plotinus considers himself to be a humble commentator on the works, deeds, and thoughts of his predecessors, attempting a synthesis of Plato and Aristotle, even if giving a clear preference to Plato as well as to Parmenides in his ontology. Similarly to Parmenides, Plotinus takes the one to be the principle of the existent; yet, contrary to Parmenides, the one does not belong to the realm of being. With Democritus, Plotinus takes the one as non-being; yet contrary to Democritus, the one is not the extended, immense emptiness of the void. With Plato, Plotinus takes the one to be beyond being. Yet contrary to Plato, the one is not a constitutive principle of sameness within being but surpasses being and so cannot even be thought on its own. As does Aristotle, Plotinus believes that being possesses a thinkable and determinable essence. Yet contrary to Aristotle, being is univocal, whereas non-being is said—even if not properly thought—in many ways.

So in fact Plotinus thinks about being in a new and most original way. Being for him *is* original, or it has a source and an origin in something other than being. The origin of being surpasses being. The principle of being is not being, and thus it is not or is beyond being. It is the one, the only one, without and before any multiplicity, that to which nothing (literally) can be added or subtracted. As such, the one transcends thought and cannot be thought or represented in any way. As the origin of being, the one is the other of being, other than being, and yet its trace is in anything that is one because the one is productive of being and is the source and beginning of everything that itself has no beginning. The origin of being is itself unoriginal. So the source of being is beyond being and therefore is non-being or, strictly speaking, nothing. Yet, this is not the nothing of privation but the possibility of being, the power for being to be, which, however, itself is not. The one is *the good* because it gives the gift of being without itself having what it gives. It is the good beyond being. So the origin of being can be approached only negatively, as not this or that and not even being, as not properly sayable or thinkable.

Being, then, is not one but the other of the one, and hence it is one-many. Being cannot be one without many because then it would not be being but beyond being. But being cannot be many without one either because without unity it would be dispersed and thus not be and not be thought. So being is and is thought as one-many, or, with Parmenides, being *is* thought.

By being thought, being is, and by being, being is thought. It the intellect-*nous* that thinks being and is and becomes being by thinking it. The intellect *is* by thinking and is what it is by thinking itself, which is being as. But because being is one-many, the intellect as thinking-*noēsis* thinks itself as its thought(s)-*noēta*, which form the intelligible cosmos in which the noetic objects or forms stay in mutual communication and reflect each other in their being by and as being thought. In this way, the intellect is reflexive, or is thinking thinking itself that always comes, or has come, to itself. In its thinking, the intellect thinks being in an act and thereby is the non-discursive reason that thinks without a logical step-by-step reasoning or has always already thought itself.

So the one as the origin of being is beyond being and hence is not being. As the power to originate anything that is, including being, the one is the first in the order not only of the existent but also of the non-existent that lurks at the end of this order as the utter lack of power to originate anything, which thus is not an un-origin of non-being. This is matter as a receptacle for everything existent, which is non-being and nothing, unlimited, indefinite, and deficient in all respects. As such, it is not thinkable, and it is ever elusive to thought. But how can the one and matter be distinguished if neither is nor is thinkable on its own, and yet both are necessary for the constitution of being and thought? The one and matter are not properly distinguishable, and yet there is an absolute difference between them in that the one is beyond being and matter is "below being," or that the one is the not yet being and matter is the utter privation of being. Most importantly, the one is the good while matter is evil, so the grand order of being and the existent begins with the non-being of the good and dissolves into the nothing of evil, being ultimately granted by the above-being of the good.

Simplicius. Simplicius stands at the very end of the ten centuries of philosophical inquiry into being and non-being. A learned commentator and the keeper of the wealth of the textual tradition, he is also a thinker in his own right who contributed his own insight to the discussion.

Central to Simplicius' interpretation of non-being is the concept of the void, which comes with an inherited Aristotelian conceptual apparatus but here is more finely tuned and systematically elaborated. Since, as Aristotle argues against Democritus and the Atomists, void does not exist, one can only have a "common opinion," *doxa*, about it. But for Simplicius, in order to be able to discuss the void, one has to begin with a "common conception," *ennoia*, which is a vague and not properly formed thought. In the case of the void, *ennoia* refers to a non-existing thing that thought inevitably misses. Such *ennoia* of the void, or that which the void is thought to be, is an interval or a place devoid of body. Accepting Aristotle's understanding of place as the limit of the surrounding body, Simplicius argues that without a body there is no place, which means that void is impossible, either as that between and outside the bodies or as an empty interval within them. The non-existence of the void can also be demonstrated from motion: against Democritus, void is the condition of the impossibility of motion because a body cannot move through nothing inasmuch as its speed and location will be indefinite and thus lose the name of action. As non-being or nothing, void has no definable or thinkable relation to anything existing, including a body that might be contained and move in it. Hence, any attempt at thinking being in nothing implies a contradiction. So not having a proper concept and not being a particular describable and thinkable entity, void is non-being or "altogether nothing." Therefore, the void is out of place in the cosmos ontologically, mathematically, and physically. Nothing is the void by not being there.

With Simplicius, being finally wins in its struggle against non-being. Non-being is voided from being and the order of the existent, and it loses its role as the constitutive origin of being. But the other ontology, the one that asserts the importance of non-being for the constitution of being, still remains and keeps returning as an often overlooked, yet powerful, alternative in thinking and understanding being.

Acknowledgments

I want to thank Eyjólfur Kjalar Emilsson, Christoph Horn, Krishna Boddapati, Matteo Burrell, Gwenda-lin Grewal, Nickolas Pappas, Samuel Yelton, and Elena Nikulina for their most helpful comments on the manuscript.

Permissions

Chapters 3, 4, and 7 of this book are reworked versions of previously published papers: "Plato on Non-Being." In *Praxis e interpretación. Un homenaje a Alejandro G. Vigo.* Ed. Patricio A. Fernández, Luis Placencia and Gabriela Rossi. Baden-Baden: Georg Olms, 2023, 73–104; "Diogenes the Comic, or How to Tell the Truth in the Face of a Tyrant." In *Philosophy and Political Power in Antiquity.* Ed. Cinzia Arruzza and Dmitri Nikulin. Leiden-Boston: Brill, 2016, 114–33; and "Simplicius on the Void." In *Körperlichkeit in der Philosophie der Spätantike/Corporeità nella filosofia tardoantica.* Ed. Christoph Horn, Daniela Patrizia Taormina, and Denis Walter. Baden-Baden: Academia, 2020, 231–55. I want to thank the publishers for permission to reproduce these texts.

1
Parmenides
Being and Nothing

ἔστιν ἢ οὐκ ἔστιν;

Is or not is?[1]

Being is at the center of Parmenides' poetic saying and thinking. Being is one and simple, and so it seems to be simple to tell and understand. And yet, an attempt to approach it by way of narration or reasoning risks going awry. After Parmenides, being is reinterpreted and rethought in many different ways, thus becoming indispensable and central for the entire tradition of western philosophy, which comes out of thinking about being. Being[2] becomes both the point of departure and the point of return for a complex and elaborate account of what is, of the world in its multiple representations, some of which, however, will remain deceptive, ambiguous, and indeterminate out of the necessity of being.[3] Without being, nothing.

---

[1] Parmenides. fr. 8.16.

[2] Parmenides expresses being as a finite form of the singular (impersonal) third-person present (is), a present participle (being), or an infinitive (be). The verb "to be" in its various forms is used throughout the entire poem, standing both for being and copula: ἔστι(ν): fr. 2.3, 2.5, 6.1–2, 8.2, 5, 9, 16, 20, 34, 36, 47; ἐστί(ν): fr. 3, 5.1, 8.11, 24, 34–35, 42, 46, 48, 54, 9.3; ἔσται: fr. 8.39; εἰσίν: fr. 8.54; εἶναι: fr. 1.32, 2.3, 2.5, 6.1, 7.1, 8.18, 40; ἔμεναι: fr. 8.38; ἔμμεναι: fr. 6.1; πέλειν: fr. 8.18; πελέναι: fr. 8.11, 8.45; ἐόν: fr. 2.7, 4.2, 6.1, 8.3, 7, 12, 19, 32, 35, 37, 47; ἐόντα: 7.1. Cf. Charles Kahn. *The Verb 'Be' in Ancient Greek; with a New Introductory Essay.* Indianapolis, IN: Hackett, 2003, 221, 369.

[3] See: Gemelli Marciano and M. Laura, Trans. and ed. *Die Vorsokratiker.* Vol. 2. Berlin: Akademie Verlag, 2013, 48.

Without being told about and understood, without another as the other, being is nothing. However, being not only is but is also the beginning of everything that is for us, of the world as a whole. Everything that is has to be said, thought, rethought, and fit into a system of thoughts tightly woven together. But why should being be thought at all? Because being is also thinking that thinks, and therefore is thought and does not leave us a choice of not thinking it, thus eventually thinking itself.

(1) *Being.* The point of departure for Parmenides is *is*, ἔστιν (fr. 8.2).[4] But of what is the "is"? There is nothing but *is*, so it is not an "is" of anything.[5] Just *is*, and because there is not a thing except or besides *is* at this point, it is not an indicator of anything being there, not an *a* or a *the*, and hence it cannot be thought at all. As such and on its own, ἔστι, a mere being and not a being of something, is literally nothing. In this sense, the *is* is nothing, and therefore it cannot be and cannot be thought.

This sheer being, ἔστι, is the elusive being as absent present. As such, it is a challenge because it cannot be, and yet must be, addressed, held, or thought. But thinking that which is and is simple is difficult, if it is even possible, since the thinkable has to be referred to the other than it is and in this way it has to be thought as it is. So in order for anything at all to be and to be thought, ἔστι has to be referred to something else, which will then become its other and thus be something, anything at all, as existent and as thinkable. This other, then, is the negative as the possibility of negation, in both saying and thinking.[6]

---

[4] For the analysis of fr. 8, see: Patricia Curd. *The Legacy of Parmenides: Eleatic Monism and Later Presocratic Thought.* Las Vegas: Parmenides Publishing, 2004, 75–94.

[5] Mourelatos argues that the "is" in Parmenides stands for both predication and identity: Alexander P. D. Mourelatos. *The Route of Parmenides.* Las Vegas: Parmenides Publishing, 2008, 79–80.

[6] This is the meaning of negation, ἀπόφασις, or moving away from the posited or asserted as said, which then becomes equalized by moving toward the said as the assertion, κατάφασις, as its opposite. See Plato, *Crat.* 426d1; *Soph.* 263e12; Aristotle, *De int.* 17b16–18a27. All references to Plato's dialogues are to John Burnet, Ed., *Platonis* Opera. 5 vols. Oxford: Clarendon Press, 1900, repr. 1989.

This other of the *is* is something, grammatically and linguistically simple and unchangeable, and only indistinctly does it point to the other of the simple *is*, the other that still cannot be thought because it is *not*. This *not* (μή or οὐ) is a simple negation of *is*, which, however, cannot yet be thought in logical propositional terms or in its properties, and hence at this point remains an arbitrary particle.

Therefore, *is* requires *is not*, ἔστι needs οὐκ ἔστι, but neither is yet thinkable on its own because neither is yet the other of the other, is not referred to the other or another, and is not mediated by anything else. "Is," as well as "is not," is therefore not thinkable on its own, and neither is or is not of itself or of another.

(2) *Being is*. However, being, *is*, ἔστι, is to be and to be thought. For mere *is* is nothing just as *is not* is nothing. There is nothing yet, and nothing is—is not—thinkable.

In order to be and be thought, being should be itself. But for being itself or what it is, there should be the other. The other is introduced by the application of the simple *not*, which is not yet a negation and cannot even be thought by itself because there is nothing to be negated. The *not* is an unthinkable and inexpressible nod of being toward being. Only then *is*, ἔστι, is set against or opposed to *not is*, οὐκ ἔστι. The opposition of *is* to *is not* is yet without mediation, and so *is* and *is not* are inconceivable on their own. However, they can be brought together as unmediated by being juxtaposed by *and* or *or* (which are indistinguishable at this point), *is* or *is not*, ἔστιν ἤ οὐκ ἔστιν (fr. 8.16). *Is—is not. Is not* is then the other of *is*, but because *is* is not thinkable on its own, it is nothing (of its own).

So being is only when and once it is not. The *is not*, which not really is but is negated by *not* and is nothing (of its own), is thus the other, but also the same, of *is*. Only once the other of the other to being is set, still not thinkable to the extent that it "is" non-being, is there the first sayable, thinkable, and meaningful being. This being is: *is is*, or *being is*, which also thereby means that *not is*, which up to this point could not be said or thought, *is not*. Therefore, *being is*, only and because being is and non-being is not (ἐὸν ἔμμεναι· ἔστι γὰρ εἶναι, μηδὲν δ' οὐκ ἔστιν, fr. 6.1–2). Only then and thus being is. Nothing else is at this point because non-being is not. In this sense, being is by simple repetition or doubling of itself as *is is* or *being being*, which means *being is* once being becomes the other of itself through the elementary act of negation or through application of the *not*.

At this point, we already have a number of ways of conceiving being and non-being. (i) *Being is*. In its very form, "being is" or "*is is*" is also already a simple multiplicity. Therefore, *is* is the other of itself and thus *is not*. The otherness here comes in the form of *not*, which makes being, ἐόν or ἔστιν, the other to itself, μὴ ἐόν or οὐκ ἔστιν (μὴ εἶναι, fr. 2.3–5). Applied to both constituents of "being is" (which are now still the same), it becomes (ii) "non-being is not."

Because now only "being is" is, even if it is not anything in particular and is still nothing, it is to be true because nothing else is and can be conceived. This is what truth or ἀλήθεια now is and looks like as unmediated and unreflective, and thus is not properly understood, a pure form for anything that can be thought and said to be true later. The power of negation, of *not*, which is that of a simple gesture of spacing, distancing, or othering by another, of being coming close to itself, approaching itself without ever yet (reflectively) reaching itself, separated only by a space, _, which is literally nothing, in *is_is*, cancels itself out when applied to itself in both of its constituents as other to each other. Hence, "non-being is not" is equally true and should be conceived as such (fr. 6.1).

But applied to itself once again, or only once, to one of its constituents only, being cancels itself as being and true. Therefore, (iii) "being is not" (or: "*is is not*" or "being = non-being," εἶναι μὴ ἐόντα, fr. 7.1) is not true, or false. And such is also (iv) "non-being is" (fr. 6.2).

At this point, truth is simply established by being as "is is," or "being is," and as the application of the negation to itself that cancels itself out. The non-truth or falsity, then, is the simple negation of truth.

These are the four possible expressions established by the very form or way that being comes close to itself and thus clarifies itself as "is is". These are not yet statements or propositions properly, which are of the structure of subject–predicate, S–P, connected by the copula. For, first, there are no predicates yet, since "is" is not a predicate of "being" but rather is an expression of sameness as non-distinction of being to itself as simple *is*. And second, "is" is not *yet* a copula, which appears only when the propositional structure becomes possible and meaningful; so "being is" is not a proposition.[7]

Of these four expressions, two should be considered as true ("being is" and "non-being is not"), to the extent that they are necessary or cannot be otherwise, and two should be viewed as false ("being is not" and "non-being is"), to the extent that they are impossible (οὐ γὰρ μήποτε τοῦτο δαμῆι εἶναι μὴ ἐόντα, fr. 7.1).

Modality of being and double negation. The negation of being can also express the modality of the necessity that comes with being and its negation. The necessity, expressed with χρή, comes up in Parmenides in "it should be said and thought that being is, for being is and nothing is not."[8] Modality in Parmenides is grounded ontologically.[9] The violation of necessity is an act of ignorance, not will: when we mortals, not knowing being, name non-being as if it were being, which should not be named (οὐ χρεών ἐστιν (scil. ὀνομάζειν), fr. 8.54). "It is necessary" equals here "it is not to be that non-being is," or "it is not possible not to be." The modality of necessity, then, is not of an arbitrary established obligation to be

---

[7] So "is" is not primarily a copula, contrary to the view defended by Luis Andrés Bredlow in "Parmenides and the Grammar of Being." *Classical Philology* 106:4 (2011), 283–98.

[8] χρὴ τὸ λέγειν τε νοεῖν τ' ἐὸν ἔμμεναι· ἔστι γὰρ εἶναι, μηδὲν δ' οὐκ ἔστιν, Parmenides, fr. 6.1–2.

[9] Graham translates χρή as "it is right." *The Texts of Early Greek Philosophy*, 215.

followed and respected but is the expression of being itself.[10] It is not only that being is and non-being is not but that being is and non-being is not cannot be otherwise.[11]

This understanding of the modality of being further suggests a double negation: non-non-being not only is but has to be being and cannot be other than being. However, the double negation is not arbitrary, but its very form comes from *is is* as the elementary repetition that cancels itself out because in (2) being is the other of nothing, and nothing is the other of being. It thus establishes the form of negation, which, applied to itself, becomes the double negation.

But the double negation is not a reflexive procedure because when the negation first applies to being—in non-being—being is not at all reflexive, and even in its negation it cannot be distinguished from non-being. Once being and non-being are juxtaposed, but not yet opposed as contradictory, as being *and/ or* non-being, the negation allows for the possibility of repetition. Therefore, *not not*, ~ ~, is first a mere *repetition*, which reproduces the structure of *being being* or *is is*, which allows for establishing being as not-not-being. It might be for this reason that Greek does not have a double negation, and neither does Parmenides, who uses οὐ μή only for emphasis and strong prohibition (against the judgment of mortals, fr. 8.61).

Nothing. The decisive moment of going from *being* to *being is* (*is is*, or *being being*), from ἔστι to ἔστι εἶναι (fr. 6.1), is the indefinite otherness of the same to the same, of being to being, which is still the same but not identical to itself and "is" (or, rather, is) beyond discernment in its simple *being* or *is*, which cannot be even conceived or thought on its own. This otherness is expressed by negation, which at this point is not the negation of anything definitive

---

[10] On the modal use of being as that which is and must be, see Palmer. *Parmenides and Presocratic Philosophy*, 133–36 et passim.
[11] ὅπως ἔστιν τε καὶ ὡς οὐκ ἔστι μὴ εἶναι, . . . ὡς οὐκ ἔστιν τε καὶ ὡς χρεών ἐστι μὴ εἶναι, Parmenides, fr. 2.3–5.

and thus is the negation of nothing. This first indistinct distinction, which does not distinguish between two clearly distinct terms but functions as the first opposition of and within being, is a simple *not*, which cannot be considered on its own. It is the negation-of, but it is the negation-of not anything definite, of being that is not defined and not definite on its own without being, and thus of nothing. As such, the negation is named rather enigmatically, if not arbitrarily, with a single syllable of οὐ, which can be substituted for a non-distinguishable non-other of μή.

Conjoined to being, it becomes non-being, οὐκ ἐόν or μὴ εἶναι. This non-being is not yet properly opposed to being because there is no possibility of discerning between the two, and no propositional structure is there yet. Therefore, this non-being is not yet thinkable and does not exist. In other words, non-being (is) nothing, where *is* is not yet a copula, or: non-being—nothing, οὐκ ἐόν—οὐδέν or μηδέν (cf. fr. 6.4, 8.10, 9.4). But nothing is not, μηδὲν δ᾽ οὐκ ἔστιν (fr. 6.2). Or, in the later reconstruction by Simplicius, "not being— nothing" (τὸ οὐκ ὂν οὐδέν, DK 28A28 = *In Phys.* 115.12),[12] which intentionally and understandably omits "is" as a copula.

Says Parmenides: "for nothing other [than being] is or will be beyond being" (οὐδὲν γὰρ ἔστιν ἢ ἔσται ἄλλο πάρεξ τοῦ ἐόντος, fr. 8.36–37). Beyond, except, and beside (πάρεξ) being, there "is" but nothing (οὐδέν), or, in Simplicius' reinterpretation, "besides or beyond being—non-being" (τὸ παρὰ τὸ ὂν οὐκ ὄν, DK 28A28 = *In Phys.* 115.12–13). Nothing is neither identical with nor different from non-being because neither is on its own. Therefore, being cannot be because of non-being, come to be, or begin in nothing (fr. 8.10). From non-being, ἐκ μὴ ἐόντος, nothing can come (fr. 8.12).

Nothing is the other of being, and yet, because it "is" nothing and because no distinction of opposites can be made yet, this other *is not* and cannot be properly said or thought. But nothing is equally

---

[12] Simplicius. *Simplicii in Aristotelis Physicorum libros quattuor priores commentaria*. Vol. IX of *Commentaria in Aristotelem Graeca*. Ed. Hermann Diels. Berlin: Reimer, 1882.

not the other of being. And while nothing is not, nothing is indistinguishable from being, and hence, in a sense, nothing is being without being. This conclusion coincides with the previous one in (1), that *being*—or *is*—is not, and as such is unthinkable. Only *is is*, or *being is*, is thought as being. Mere being is beyond and beside itself without being itself. Being nothing, it can neither be identical nor different form itself. Being cannot be being without nothing or being nothing. Just *being* (is) *beyond*, or rather, *being*—beyond being and thought.

Negation(s) as asynonyms. Non-being "is" nothing, μηδέν. But nothing is nothing, so it is not (fr. 6.2), and as such, as was said, it is neither distinguishable nor identical with being before being can have the other or stand in opposition to non-being as *being is*.[13] But non-being does not have an "itself," αὐτό; it is only and always an indefinite "beside itself," τι παρ' αὐτό (fr. 8.13). Nothing is *not* the same, μὴ τωὐτόν (fr. 8.58), non-identical to itself or anything other because nothing is other to non-being. But because nothing is not, nothing is not other to non-being. Nothing can be opposed to non-being as its other. So non-being is to be *posited* in opposition to being, as *is* vs. *is not* or *is*—*is not* (ἐστιν ἢ οὐχί, fr. 8.11; εἶναί τε καὶ οὐχί, fr. 8.40). At this point, the vs. can both mean "or," ἢ, and "and," καί, since the two conjunctives are indistinguishable before the opposites can become propositional. Non-being, then, is the "not," pure negation, or ~. As such, the *not*, οὐχί, is not a negation of anything; it *is* the negation, not the negation of being as being negated but as non-being.

As such, negation is not graspable or meaningful on its own, as it also is in the case for non-being. The "not" is not the *not* of this or that but the not of non-being which "is" non-being that is nothing. Nothing, literally. Inevitably, the linguistic expression of the "not" is always a problem, which leads to an unavoidable, and in a sense

---

[13] See Leonardo Franchi. "Parmenide a l'origine della nozione di nulla." *Giornale critico della filosofia italiana* 7:14 (2018), 247–74.

welcome, confusion. The "not" cannot be expressed unambiguously and unequivocally, which leads to proliferation of the ways of negation in the language and to a plurality of negatives or negative constructions. In ancient Greek, οὐ, whose origin is obscure, is usually taken grammatically (by Goodwin, for example et al.) as "objective" or "non-intentional" contrary to and against μή as "subjective" or "intentional.[14]"

When referring to non-being, Parmenides uses both negative particles with the verb: οὐκ ἔστι(ν) (fr. 2.5, 6.2, 8.9, 8.16, 8.20; cf. fr. 8.5) and οὐκ εἶναι (opposite to being, τὸ πέλειν, fr. 6.8) as standing for non-being. But μὴ εἶναι also refers to non-being (οὐκ ἔστι μὴ εἶναι, fr. 2.3, 2.5). Both μή and οὐ are equally used with the participle: non-being is expressed both as οὐκ ἐόν (fr. 8.46) and as μὴ ἐόν (fr. 2.7, 8.7, 8.12; μὴ ἐόντα, fr. 7.1).

One could make a distinction in Parmenides' use of μή and οὐ in that μὴ εἶναι might stand for non-being *simpliciter*, whereas οὐκ εἶναι—as qualified with reference to being. Similarly, μὴ ἐόν could be taken as unqualified non-being, whereas οὐκ ἐὸν could be seen as qualified when making a distinction of "there is neither non-being...nor being, such that..." (οὔτε γὰρ οὐκ ἐὸν ἔστι...οὔτ᾽ ἐὸν ἔστιν, fr. 8.47).

Yet, one cannot properly distinguish non-being from non-being because it is nothing and does not have a "self." Hence, as pure negatives, μή and οὐ are indistinguishable twins, which are still linguistically distinct when referring to non-being as nothing. The two are not different because pure negation cannot be distinguished either from itself, because there is not self to the pure negation, or from the negated, because the negated is non-being and cannot be distinguished from anything either, especially from non-being. But the two are not identical either because there is not a self or self-identical itself to negation, so *not* (οὐ) cannot be identical with *not*

---

[14] William Goodwin. *A Greek Grammar*. Boston: Ginn and Company, 1892, chs. 1607ff.

(μή). As pure negatives, οὐ and μή are mutually non-other before otherness, and mutuality can be established and thought and thus are distinguished in a non-distinguishable way. Hence, if μὴ εἶναι is not different from οὐκ εἶναι but is not identical either, then μή and οὐ can be taken as indistinct without distinction, or as *asynonyms*.

(3) *Being is being.* Mere *being*, ἔστι, not even is without the other because there is nothing but being and is thus nothing. *Being* as mere *is* is a possibility of *being is* when it *is*, which cannot even be called a possibility because as *is is* it is a possibility of being that is not anything—and thus nothing. In *being is, is is*, or *being being*, being is nothing to itself. There is no self to being when it is, and thus there is no reflectivity. But only when being is, it is being, and as such can be thought—but not as a being-of, or the being of something.

Being is is not even identical to itself because an act of identification, E = E, presupposes a distinction and discernment of the identified with itself as itself (E) as also the other of itself (on each side of the identification). But *being is* already establishes a basic opposition, an indefinite duality or otherness as a possibility of multiplicity. Being other to itself without a distinction to itself, being is *nothing* to itself as its negation in *is is*, which establishes the form of otherness in which one term functions as an elementary negation.

Once the otherness is there, then another, or something else, can be and can be thought. Being then can be the other to itself as distinguished in its being and is thought not as nothing, but rather as that which now hides, or contains, a plethora of properties and meanings.

The elementary form of *multiplicity* thus comes in and with the unmediated opposition of *is—is, being—being*, or *being—is*. But the elementary form of the *plurality* of another (and another, and another...) comes with the mediation of the two terms of *being–being* by *being*, or *is–is* by *is*, the mediation that is neither being nor nothing but a mediating connective relation, or copula. Copula is the "downfall" of being.

Hence, the third decisive step on the way of being is being reflectively referring to itself, that is, through mediation. This can only be the mediation of being by being, which is now itself reflected by itself. Since *is* is the only one that is, it can be mediated and come into a relation with itself as *is is is*. And *is is is*, or *being being being*, means *being is being*. Now being is reflectively identical to itself and thus can also be discerned from itself as a subject that is what it is by being what it is. From the simple yet incomprehensible *being* or *is*, which is non-distinguishable from nothing, being becomes self-established and thinkable. But being what it is also means being endowed with properties that are meaningful in a relation to what is and thus to each other. Not only being but its being as another, or the whole world, is now possible as fully distinguishable and discernible.

The application of the "not" to each of the three constituents in *being is being* generates eight different versions or "hypotheses" of the primary statement "being is being." These are: (I) being is being; (II) being is not non-being; (III) non-being is not being; (IV) non-being is non-being; (V) being is non-being; (VI) being is not being; (VII) non-being is being; and (VIII) non-being is not non-being.

The unreflective truth of *being is* was discussed in (2), which came from the non-reflective relatedness of being to itself before any "itself," in and as *being is*, which is posited as being true, and its negation as not true, or false. This truth can be called *noetic*. But now, with being mediating between itself and itself, distancing from itself as *being is being* in the "is," and thus establishing itself, which is properly itself and thus not itself as reflected in itself as the other and mediated and thus connected by itself as itself by the copula, truth is established as predicatively related. This truth can be called *logical*.

Of the eight "hypotheses," the first four, (I–IV), can be considered logically true, and the last four (V–VIII) are logically not true, or false. Again, as with the noetic truth, the true and the not-true in the logical truth are related by the application of a negative, *not*, οὐ or μή. The single application of the negative turns the true into its unmediated opposite, not true or false, while the unmediated application of the negative to itself, or double negation, returns the true to itself, while another negation, or triple negation, again makes the true false. This working of the negative, originally rooted in the non-being as the negation of being, which is neither true nor false, works in the same way in noetic and logical truth.[15]

Contradiction and opposites. The *being* and *non-being* that come in the first act of being (1) are not opposites as being–non-being since they are not opposed to each other in any way, for being is *not yet* and non-being is not yet either. *Not*, οὐ or μή, in and of non-being, οὐκ ἔστι, is not yet a negation of an existential expression, but a hint at something other than *is* before *is is*, and thus before the other can be thought. Yet, on its own, as mere *is*, being is nothing, and thus cannot be distinguished from non-being. Hence, being as such is not thinkable. Being is not the other to and of non-being. Hence, the two are neither identical nor distinguishable and thus cannot be opposed. Being cannot be thought.

Simplicius observes that Aristotle has demonstrated that in Parmenides' attempt to get rid of non-being and for that reason making the assumption that being is one, he not only introduced some kind of non-being but, because beside being nothing is, proved that being itself is non-being.[16] Indeed, if nothing is beside being, being is nothing and thus is non-being.

---

[15] If E stands for "being," εἶναι or ἐόν; ε for "is," ἔστι; and ~ for "not," οὐ or μή, then the three acts of being can be presented as:

(1) E, ~E: being; non-being. Neither is true or not true.

(2) (i) E ε, (ii) ~E ~ε: being is; non-being is not. Both are noetically true.

(iii) E ~ε, (iv) ~E ε: being is not; non-being is. Both are noetically not true, or false.

(3) (I) E ε E, (II) E ~ε ~E, (III) ~E ~ε E, (IV) ~E ε ~E: being is being; being is not non-being; non-being is not being; non-being is non-being. All are logically true.

(V) E ε ~E, (VI) E ~ε E, (VII) ~E ε E, (VIII) ~E ~ε ~E: being is non-being; being is not being; non-being is being; non-being is not non-being. All are logically not true, or false.

[16] βουλόμενος τὸ μὴ ὂν ἀνελεῖν καὶ διὰ τοῦτο ἓν τὸ ὂν ὑποτιθέμενος, ἐπειδὴ τὸ παρὰ τὸ ὂν οὐδέν ἐστιν, οὐ μόνον εἰσάγει τι μὴ ὂν διὰ τῆς ὑποθέσεως, ἀλλὰ καὶ αὐτὸ τὸ ὂν μὴ ὂν εἶναι δείκνυσι, Simplicius. *In Phys.* 126.3–7.

Only when *being is* is established along with *non-being is* in the second act of being (2) is the opposition established as contradiction. Since in *being is* or *is is*, being is identical to itself without being itself, or without reflection, then *non-being is* and *being is not* are distinguishable yet identical in their non-truth. The elementary opposition as contradiction is then between *being is—being is not*. Such an opposition is a contradiction because it is set as unmediated, where *being is* and *non-being is* cannot be together and cannot be thought together.

But when *being is*, then being can be thought. Only now being as "itself" can be established as meaningful. *Being is* in the contradictory opposition to *being is not*. Then being, εἶναι, is itself, αὐτό, is now itself to itself, which is reflected as thinking, νοεῖν (fr. 3). For "itself" is the coincidence with itself as not itself, or the other. Opposition comes as an act of immediate opposing of the same–other, of identification–othering, with the application of the *not* to itself. This establishes the distinction between the unmediated yet now (barely or non-propositionally) thinkable same and other as: same as not-other, and not-other as same, and hence, by application of the *not* to each of the two, of same as not-not-other, and other as not-not-same. The coincidence of the unmediated opposites comes from a contradiction in being as mediated by nothing, that is, as not mediated by itself or thought.

It is only when *being is being* (being *qua* being) is established in (3) that the opposition is appropriated into saying and thinking as discursive and accountable on the way of truth and is already capable of both recognizing and avoiding contradiction between the contradictory opposites of the propositions "being is being" and "being is non-being."

Logos. We thus find two different senses of being's relatedness to itself, as not itself and then as itself, as non-reflective in *being is* and reflective and mediated by itself as "is" in *being is being*. This distinction is translated in Parmenides into two distinct cognitive attitudes toward being: those of νόος and λόγος.

Since for the most part we, the Parmenidean mortals, are logical beings who live, act, think, and go astray within the discursively mediated realm in which we attempt to support our claims by logically justified reasons and to avoid contradiction, or the direct coincidence of the opposites, we might begin with λόγος.

(α) Λόγος tells. *Being* is simple and *being is* is not propositional and does not refer to another, so neither can be properly told. Hence, λόγος tells *about* being, narrates the way of, toward, around, and back to being. In this sense, the entire poem is a λόγος about being. Moving around being, it can also turn away from it and become lost on the way of the uncertain and multiple opinions, or beliefs, of mortals (fr. 8.50–51).

(β) Being narrative, λόγος is propositional. A proposition of and by λόγος is complex, or has the structure of multiplicity, where parts of the told can be distinguished. Such a distinction, then, becomes *logical* and is then translated into the grammatical structure of the subject–predicate distinction, where "is" figures prominently as the copula in "S is P." Hence, "being is being" or "being being being" establishes the elementary form, or structure, of the λόγος, which is that of predication and thus of the possibility of an ordered telling of the thought. Here, however, we need to distinguish between, on the one hand, a statement (A is), which is either true or false noetically, when applied to *being is* in (2), and, on the other hand, a proposition (A is B), which can become judgment, γνώμη, which is either true or false logically, or is an assertion or negation when applied to *being is being*.

Therefore, λόγος is propositional—what Aristotle calls λόγος ἀποφαντικός (*De int.* 17a8–37). When the *not* is applied to any of its three components, it becomes cataphatic and apophatic, or it can generate a whole variety of the types of assertions and negations as in (3), and then generate even more by the repeated application of the *not* in the double negation.

(γ) Implying multiplicity in its very predicative structure, λόγος can tell many things, or it can narrate differently. For this reason, λόγος can tell differently about the same. Or, as Prodicus, Socrates, and Aristotle suggest, everything can be said or predicated in many ways, even if told about one thing, πρὸς ἕν (*Met*. 1003a33). But primarily, being is said in many ways (τὸ ... ὂν λέγεται ... πολλαχῶς, *Met*. 1003a33, 1026a33, 1030a17–18, 1089a7; cf. πολλαχῶς τὸ ἕν λέγεται, *Met*. 1004a22). Λόγος is thus many-voiced, and so it is fundamentally ambiguous and capable of being told otherwise, which the λόγος tries to rectify by disciplining itself through the accepted logical procedures that should establish it as true or false. However, Parmenides chooses only one λόγος, that of the goddess, because it is meant to tell about being, which cannot be otherwise.

(δ) Being propositional, λόγος is logically and narratively *extended*: in its pronouncement, and it spreads throughout narration and reasoning. It runs through them, unable to present what it intends to in one single word or act. Λόγος thus has to be discursive, transiting through reasoning, or dianoetic. In Plato's rendering, the dianoetic λόγος is a silent conversation of the soul in itself with itself (διάλογος ἄνευ φωνῆς, *Soph*. 263e3–5). But Parmenides does not—and cannot—recognize the interiority of the λόγος because for him it is the speech of being that is not internalized until it becomes fully reflective, and as such has to be told by the other of us humans, personified in the goddess.

(ε) As propositional, λόγος can either assert or negate, and hence it can argue, justify, and judge, κρῖναι, even contentious refutations (fr. 7.5; cf. fr. 8.15). It thus can make a judgment and a decision, γνώμη, about the told, especially when the said is uncertain, coming from humans (fr. 8.53, 61). As such, λόγος can be right or wrong. It is capable of proving, of providing a *logical truth*, which we are obliged to recognize and either accept or reject (fr. 7.1), to the extent that it is justified according to the rules of engagement that are implied in and then are explicitly clarified from within the λόγος. Such a λόγος becomes not just narrative but also discursive reasoning that aims at attaining the conclusion through a number of steps that strictly follow immanent logical rules. Such a λόγος, then, becomes a certain and self-assured one, πιστὸς λόγος (fr. 8.50).

Therefore, λόγος not only narrates but also investigates what it submits to itself in the form of a proposition, and thus it can become engaged in inquiry, διζήσιος (fr. 2.2, 6.3, 7.2; cf. fr. 8.6). Λόγος is inquisitive. It is curious, sometimes inappropriately, which can make it err. Capable of achieving truth and being variegated and multiple, the λόγος can be truthful in various ways or, literally, it can exercise many methods in pursuing truth (μέθοδος comes from μετά and ὁδός, following along a way). It can put itself under its own scrutiny, and, in case it finds itself impassable, it can provide its own refutation and thus become a judgment and proof about a logically justifiable and justified statement.

(ζ) Finally, in its very act and activity, λόγος both complements and opposes itself to reason or mind, νόος. Whenever λόγος happens or dares to express itself in narrating and reasoning, there should be reason. The decisive difference is that the activity of logical thinking, λέγειν, is discursive, whereas the act of noetic thinking, νοεῖν, is not, or is without logical mediation. Hence, it is difficult for λόγος to think and tell about νόος.

Noos. Reason is thus first considered negatively in its complementarity to, and distinction from, λόγος. Reason is that which has to process and realize what the goddess tells along the way of λόγος. The discursive ("digital") activity of the said is to be transformed and converted into the ("analogue") act of spectacle for the mind or reasoned seeing. It is not by chance that the reference to goddess, θεά (fr. 1.22), differs in name only by an accent from spectacle, θέα. Reason is not a faculty of νοῦς, as Plato (*Rep.* 511d) and Plotinus (*Enn.* V.1 [10]) later posited: it is that which exercises thinking, that which thinks.

What does νόος think about? The said and the told. When the heard of the said is guided by helplessness, ἀμηχανίη, in the heart of the mortals, then reason wanders around and is clueless, πλακτὸς νόος (fr. 6.5–6). But when reason is kept on the way of being by the λόγος that does not veer off from the way, then νόος thinks what is has to think.

On the way of being, it is impossible for the two not to accompany each other, and thus the two have to complement each other and appear together: it *must* be *said* and *thought* that being is (χρὴ τὸ λέγειν τε νοεῖν τ' ἐὸν ἔμμεναι, fr. 6.1). Λόγος can tell many things about being, but reason should think one thing only, being. Λόγος is the fox, but νόος must be the hedgehog, unless it wanders off its only thought.[17] Reason thinks being.

And while the sheer being as *is* cannot even be thought, *being is* already can and must be thought. Hence, unlike λόγος, which is discursive and always runs through the said and logically conceived, reason is non-discursive because being as *being is* is non-propositional and thus simple in its immediacy. Being remains unknown on the convoluted and unsteady ways of us mortals, and yet it is always already there. The "must" of reason is not a normative moral task but is the translation into action of what reason is in its contemplating or looking steadily at *being is being*, in which the absent transpires as present (ἀπεόντα νόωι παρεόντα βεβαίως, fr. 4.1). Reason makes the unthought thought and apparently absent palpably present. Reason thinks being firmly, constantly, and without distraction. It cannot be and think otherwise.

Reason is there at every moment but becomes explicit when the journey of the narration about being halts for a moment along the way of being—just to be resumed at any moment in the suspension of the moment.

The activity of the νόος as thinking, νοεῖν, is defined by being and becomes definite in the act of thought, νόημα. In thinking, reason is thought. Νόημα, thought or, rather, *the* thought is what is and cannot be otherwise. Hence, νόος is; νόος is νοεῖν; νόημα is

---

[17] Cf.: "A fox knows many [things], while a hedgehog one [but] great," πόλλ' οἶδ' ἀλώπηξ, ἀλλ' ἐχῖνος ἓν μέγα, Archilochus. In *Iambi et elegi Graeci ante Alexandrum cantati*. Vol. 1. Ed. By M. L. West. 2nd ed. Oxford: Oxford University Press, 1989, fr. 201.

what is; νόος is νόημα. Therefore, thinking is the same as thought (ταὐτὸν δ' ἐστὶ νοεῖν τε καὶ οὕνεκεν ἔστι νόημα, fr. 8.34). The "same," ταὐτόν, means that thinking and thought are not two different terms of an equation that come to coincide in reason as a result of a thinking process. The "same" means that thinking and thought already always coincide or are non-distinct, are the same and one reason. Thinking and thought are distinguished only when reflected in reason, which then takes itself (thinking) as the other (thought) while still being the same—or when thinking and thought are distinguished in discursive reasoning and narration in the works of λόγος. In logical thinking, the thought is always discursively removed from the propositionally expressed thought and needs to be achieved through correct reasoning. Such reasoning has to respect the law of non-contradiction because λόγος cannot grasp the opposites at once and without mediation: they appear as contradiction for the πιστὸς λόγος, which asserts logical truth by avoiding contradiction through thinking that properly connects a subject with a predicate. But in noetic thinking, the thought, νόημα, is thought as immediate, as *palpable*, as if being touched by the reason-νόος. This coincidence without a mediation of intermediary reasoning or narrative is the noetic truth in the thought-νόημα.

Because reason attends to its thought without mediation and without movement through opposing statements, the νόος is capable of, if not altogether disregarding, then at least suspending the opposites, which play a regulative role for the thinking of the λόγος. Both the correct discursive reasoning and the always right, non-discursive act of thought turn toward and around truth (πιστὸν λόγον ἠδὲ νόημα ἀμφὶς ἀληθείης, fr. 8.50–51), but they do it differently: the former needs to be achieved, whereas the latter needs to be recognized. The λόγος can be mistaken; the νόημα cannot err (cf. Aristotle. *De an*. 430a26–27). The reason-νόος cannot miss what it thinks, and thus it does not judge. When it thinks itself in thought-νόημα, it knows.

Being-thinking. Hence, reason-νόος has truth and *is* truth, and thus *is being*. By thinking, it is. Thus, reason *is*. And in its being, it thinks. When thinking, there is nothing else to be thought, which means that it thinks itself without a gap, immediately, without mediation. Reason cannot think and be otherwise, which is the truth of being.

This is why, γάρ, says Parmenides, being and thinking is the same (τὸ γὰρ αὐτὸ νοεῖν ἐστίν τε καὶ εἶναι, fr. 3). Thinking-νοεῖν *is* and is being-εἶναι; being-εἶναι *is* and is thinking-νοεῖν, without mediation. It is one and the same, not distinguished by the copula—only by "and," τε καί, which is an indication of the same without difference. Or, rather, it is non-different to itself, since in order to establish differentiation and difference, one needs a third, mediating term.

The *it* itself, αὐτό, is the coincidence, or non-distinction, of being and thinking. The non-distinguished *it*, τὸ αὐτό, of the same does not mediate. So, strictly speaking, it is not yet *itself* but just *it*. The opposition between being and thinking, εἶναι and νοεῖν, is then reflected *in* the same *it* but not *by* the same *it*, which makes being and thinking coincide without mediation. Being and thinking thus are (or, strictly speaking, is) the same, remaining the unreflected and not yet realized other to and of each other. The distinction between ontology and epistemology cannot be established once the (only) thought, νόημα, of thinking is being.

When thinking is not reflective, it is indefinite, and such is also being, which then does not have any essence except for *being is*. Thinking is not the "what" of being until thinking and being become reflective and mediated by *being is being* in *being is thinking*, by the *is* of the copula of the logical connective. Because in mediation there is the "same" of "itself," τὸ αὐτό, being is immediately reflected as thinking, and thinking is reflected as being. Being and thinking, then, are *not* the same, but the unreflected same is being-thinking. To be recognized by itself as being, being needs to be mediated, or recognized by itself as being, which then is *not* thinking, or by thinking that is *not* being. And since being *is* thinking, to be recognized by itself as thinking, thinking also needs to be mediated, or recognized *by itself* as thinking, which is *not* being, or by being that is *not* thinking. The unmediated reflection has to be mediated and thus become proper reflection. As such, it can only be a mediated thinking that travels on and by the way of reasoning or λόγος in Parmenides' poem.

In this way, thinking without a thought becomes *itself* that *recognizes* itself as thinking thinking itself as being, or as thinking that can be told about or logically accounted for. As Parmenides explains, without being about which the thought, νόημα, is told, predicated, or spoken, πεφατισμένον, you will not find thinking (οὐ γὰρ ἄνευ τοῦ ἐόντος, ἐν ὧι πεφατισμένον ἐστιν, εὑρήσεις τὸ νοεῖν, fr. 8.34–36). Only then does being become reflected being, τὸ ἐόν, is *itself*, recognized and reflected in thought. And thus, being and thinking are now not only the same but also other to each other: thinking as reflected by thought and thought as reflected in being. Thinking now properly thinks itself as thought that is and reflects being, and being is realized and thought as *being is being*, which is thinking and thought.[18]

What being is. What we have reached so far along the way of the poem is as follows: mere *being* (1) not even is and is thus nothing without even being identical with nothing because nothing is *not*, *is* nothing and is *nothing*. So no identity can be established at this point because identity requires identification with itself as the other. *Being* is now not the other to itself. But in *being is* (2), the being of being is established, and thereby the *is* that can be thought, although in its "is" and not in its "what." Only when *being is being* (3) can being be thought in its "what." In later, Aristotelian terms,

---

[18] Cf. Plotinus, *Enn.* V.9 [5].5.29–30. All references to Plotinus' *Enneads* are from *Plotini Opera*. Ed. by Paul Henry and Hans-Rudolf Schwyzer. 3 vols. Oxford: Oxford University Press, 1964–1982.

being is opens a possibility for existence and *being is being*—for essence.

So what exactly is being? It is *being*. As such, it is tautological in the exact sense of the word, is ταὐτόν, or itself, is *it* and the self of it in being, and is the thought and the thinking of it on itself (fr. 8.34), when the self of itself reflectively becomes self, or what it is when it already is. Being the indistinguishable same self in its mere *being*, which is nothing (1), being has to become the other of and for the self as being in *being is* (2), and then again has to become reflected, thought, and understood as the same in *being is being* through the mediating *is*, which logically functions as the copula. Now, once being is other to itself, it is possible for being to be understood as not mere being but as another. Now, the entire world can be thought and wandered through.

Univocity and plurivocity of being. Being is is one and unique. In Simplicius' interpretation, for Parmenides "being is said in one way," τὸ ὄν μοναχῶς λέγεσθαι (fr. 2; *In Phys.* 116.25–117.1; DK 28A28). However, for Simplicius as for Eudemus, this is a shortcoming of the Parmenidean account because both accept the Prodican and Aristotelian program of making as many logical distinctions between various meanings of being, or any other concept, as possible. In Eudemus' account, Parmenides presented unreliable arguments (ἀναξιοπίστοις λόγοις) because he did not yet know of the plurivocity of being, which appears in Plato, who was the first to distinguish being in two ways, as being itself and accidental being, which was discovered through dialectical disputations with reference to theses and antitheses (in Socrates and Plato) and through syllogistic logic (in Aristotle). No wonder, then, that previous thinkers, Parmenides included, presented their claims without proof.[19]

---

[19] οἱ δὲ πρότερον ἀναποδείκτως ἀπεφαίνοντο, Eudemus apud Simplicius. *In Phys.* 115.25–116.4, as related by Alexander.

Yet, this objection is beside the point because for Parmenides being in "being is" *is* univocal because in *being is,* or *being being,* being is its only singular, unique, and as yet unreflected other, and there is no other other to it. Rather, it is non-being that is to be said in many ways because it is not, and thus can be rethought, missed by thought, or non-thought differently but never in a finalized way.

This is why the thinking of the *is* of being, which is that done by reason-νόος, is univocal. But in *being is being,* being is already a reflected other to and onto itself, which is an other other to itself and thus can be another to itself in a logical proposition built by the conjoining and separation of the *is* as a copula. Here, being ceases to be being but becomes a mere possibility for establishing a relation between the same and the reflected same that was the other to itself. It is first the relation of being and being through being as the copula. However, the form of its thinking through as a subject–predicate relation in which the predicate inheres in the subject establishes for being another of and in being. Hence, the thinking of the "what" of being by λόγος in a logical proposition is inevitably plurivocal. "Being is" is univocal, and, once it is said or narrated by λόγος, it is *the* one that is told about.

In other words, for Parmenides being in *being is* is noetically univocal but becomes logically plurivocal in *being is being.*

Therefore, when being *is* being, being can be said to be "being," or ἐόν. What then is being as ἐόν? It is plurivocal, and thus the same being can be *logically* said to be many or to have different denominations or "signs" (σήματα, fr. 8.2).

Being one. Primarily and uniquely, when *being is being,* in its "signature" being is *one,* ἐόν is ἕν (fr. 8.6).[20] Why is being one? It is one because there is nothing else, no other for being itself when it is itself, from which being could possibly originate or come from (fr. 8.6–7). There is nothing opposite and opposed to being when

---

[20] See: Jonathan Barnes. "Parmenides and the Eleatic One." *Archiv für Geschichte der Philosophie* 61 (1979), 1–21.

it is being, so it is one (cf. Plotinus. *Enn.* VI.6 [34].18.39–43). Such a logical account of being as one becomes possible once being is being can reflectively turn to itself in order to provide an account of itself.[21]

Since it does not come to be from anything else, one being is one-being that is atemporal or pre-temporal, a being that is altogether now (νῦν) and never was or will be (fr. 8.5). In other words, in Parmenides' earliest formulation of the principle of sufficient reason, there is *no ground* and no way to think and explain what the other of being except being itself could be. When being is being, it is thus one.

However, because being is reflective, it is the same that is also other to itself, or being is the other same to itself. Hence, being now can be thought as one that is not one, or many, or as one-many. In Plato's interpretation, this understanding of being generates many (eight) different possible relations between one and many in being (*Parm.* 137c ff.).

As was argued in (1), being as mere *being* has no other, and thus (is) nothing, beyond being and thought. But in (3) when *being is being*, it is one. In the already mentioned account of Simplicius', "That which is different from being is non-being; non-being is nothing; therefore, being is one" (DK 28A28; Simplicius. *In Phys.* 115.17–18). When *being is being*, it has the other, which is being, or itself. Once it has the other, it can also be distinguished from, and opposed to, non-being. Yet, non-being "is" nothing. But since nothing is not, nothing both is and is not nothing without violating the principle of non-contradiction because there is no identity of the subject in this case. So non-being (is) nothing, "not being— nothing," or not being (τὸ οὐκ ὄν)—not one (οὐδέν; literally "not one"). Non-being is not one. So being is one, which, again, is meaningless for the mere *being*, and yet is meaningful for *being is being*,

---

[21] This is why, for Aristotle, Parmenides provides an account for his understanding of the one, τοῦ κατὰ τὸν λόγον ἑνὸς ἅπτεσθαι, *Met.* 986b18–19.

once the distinction of the other and the opposition becomes only possible.

There are other "signs" of one-being, which still make it thinkable as one through a plurality of predicates inherent in the same one logical subject that is now also other to itself. Being is unoriginated (ἀγένητον, "unoriginal"), indestructible (ἀνώλεθρον), stable (ἀτρεμές), continuous (συνεχές), fulfilled (τελεστόν, fr. 8.4, p. 82 Tarán; τέλειον, fr. 8.4, p. 216 Graham), complete (τετελεσμένον, fr. 8.42), not unfinished (οὐκ ἀτελεύτητον), not in need of anything, or self-sufficient (οὐκ ἐπιδευές, fr. 8.32–33), not divisible (οὐδὲ διαιρετόν), self-similar (ὁμοῖον, fr. 8.22), whole (οὖλον),[22] immovable (ἀκίνητον, fr. 8.38), inviolate (ἄσυλον, fr. 8.48). This, however, is not, and never can be, a full list: what has been said in one way or univocally about being can always be said or "signed" in many other ways.

Being and beings. Being is, τ' ἐὸν ἔμμεναι (fr. 6.1). Being is one: it is one being. But does it mean that one being is the *only* being or *a* being, one among many? Being almost always comes as a singular in Parmenides, as εἶναι or τὸ ἐόν, yet he also speaks about being in the plural, as beings, ἐόντα. The goddess tells the youth that one cannot cut being off being or from holding on to being (οὐ γὰρ ἀποτμήξει τὸ ἐὸν τοῦ ἐόντος ἔχεσθαι, fr. 4.2). One could interpret this claim as suggesting that although there is one being, stable and indestructible (fr. 8.3), there are also beings that include individual things in the one, continuous, all-embracing being (ξυνεχὲς πᾶν, fr. 8.25), which is all and everything and as such is the sphere of the world.

Yet, since nothing is not, nothing can—cannot—separate being from being, so nothing does separate being from being,[23] so being will not be atomized into many without still being one. Only the

---

[22] Untersteiner argues that wholeness, rather than unity, is the primary characteristic of being: Mario Untersteiner. "L'essere di Parmenide è 'ΟΥΛΟΝ', non 'ΕΝ'." *Rivista Critica di Storia della Filosofia* 10:1 (1955), 5–23.

[23] οὐ γὰρ ἀποτμήξει τὸ ἐὸν τοῦ ἐόντος ἔχεσθαι, Parmenides. fr. 4.2.

entire sphere of the things is and as such did not come to be and is unborn, while the plurality of things, or beings, is not. Properly speaking, beings, ἐόντα, are not in the way being is and do not exist on their own. This is why beings come in Parmenides as a negative, as μὴ ἐόντα, as that which cannot be, εἶναι (fr. 7.1). The impossibility of beings as being of the many or many beings then becomes central to Zeno's philosophical project, which demonstrates, already by logical means, that the assumption of being as plural leads to unthinkable and unsolvable aporias (Zeno, frs. 1–3).

Apophatic reasoning. Contrary to Eudemus' objection that "previous thinkers" did not use arguments, Parmenides does argue that since being is one, it does not need anything other than being. In doing so, he proceeds by negation. It is not by chance that many "signs" of being as being one are negative inscriptions, often marked by the alpha privative. Yet this is not a dialectical argument as used later by Socrates and Plato, which moves by questioning propelled by the unmediated, and thus contradictory, opposites that show themselves in questions implying univocal "yes" and "no" answers that move toward a logically justified conclusion but more often a refutation of the thesis. Thinking about being is *apophatic*, since it cannot avoid the negation of a suggested signification or "signing" of being while pointing to the other of being, which then transpires in a negative form.

The pure form of apophatic thinking about being is expressed in Parmenides as "neither . . . nor . . . since . . ." (οὔτε . . . οὔτε . . . ἐπεί . . .) (cf. Heraclitus. DK 22B93: "neither . . . nor . . . but . . ." [οὔτε . . . οὔτε . . . ἀλλά . . .]). Thus, there is neither non-being that . . . (would hinder being from attaining to the same), nor being that . . . (would be more here and less there than being), since . . . (in its entirety being is inviolate), (οὔτε γὰρ οὐκ ἐὸν ἔστι . . . οὔτ' ἐὸν ἔστιν . . . ἐπεὶ πᾶν ἐστιν . . ., fr. 8.46–48). The three parts within the argument (. . .) can be filled in many ways, yet one being in *being is being* transpires, as a result of this apophatic procedure, as the one beyond the interaction of unmediated, contradictory opposites.

So for being one to be said in one way means following one form of negative apophatic argument. However, this one form of the apophatic presentation of being can become many, and thus it may be said in many ways, depending on a particular signification of being, which can always be chosen otherwise, pointing or converging toward one being that can be thought univocally by the reason-νόος but cannot be pinpointed in the reasoning of λόγος.

Being is same in its otherness and other in its sameness, and so it is never a fully, logically thematizable ultimate and utmost limit of itself (πεῖρας πύματον, fr. 8.42) that reaches its own limits (fr. 8.49), since non-being is not, and thus nothing can delimit being other than itself. Being is therefore finished, fulfilled, everywhere the same, and as such it is similar to a sphere because there is neither non-being nor being that could make being-one more or less than it is (fr. 8.42-49). Therefore, being-one is *all*, τὸ πᾶν, or the entire existent, one and unchangeable, the world that is and is what it is.

Therefore, Eudemus' contention that Parmenides reasoned "without proof" misses the Parmenidean way of thinking about being, since Eudemus' own thinking is driven by the λέγεται πολλαχῶς dialectical approach that keeps multiplying logical distinctions about one-being within multiple justified propositions. For Parmenides, being is univocal because it is being-one, or one-being, which is present to itself through its multiple "signs" or significations, when *being is being* for itself as ἐόν. Being-one, it is being-many as other to itself as one without any other being that could be one. Or being the same to itself, being is the other to itself that has become the same without ever ceasing to be it.

The way. Thus, since nothing *is* (is not) beside being, and *nothing* is (is not) beside being, being is one, simple. Hence, being is pre-propositional or is not fully grasped by a proposition or any number of them, since a proposition is complex, first established in and by *being is being*, which is already thought noetically but yet has to be achieved logically in narration and thought.

Therefore, one has to come to being. Parmenides' poem *is* such a way, or the way of and to being. Because of the univocity of being, for Parmenides, understanding being is not a dialectical game of questions and answers but a journey. Its narrative form is an epic, paradigmatically represented in the *Odyssey*, which depicts a long and dangerous journey, marked by encounters with colorful characters and splashed with elaborate descriptions of things and places. It is no surprise, then, that Parmenides' poem is written in hexameter, the epic meter of choice, which allows him to progress steadily and also provides a vibrant description of the gates on the way to being (fr. 1.11–20).

One can say that the poetic description of being in Parmenides and the later prosaic accounts from Plato differ in the form of the narrative. The poetic presentation of being is distinctly rhythmically organized, selecting synonyms (εἶναι, ἔμεναι, πελέναι) based on the meter rather than making subtle logical distinctions of meaning within muddled, prosaic speech interspersed with ironic hints and erotic allusions. Yet, Parmenides does not choose the form of narration. Rather, the poetic speech chooses him as its rhapsode because the speech of being is not only about being but also comes from being.

Behind the epic story is the voice of the Muses, who know everything and are repeatedly invoked by the poet (*Il.* 2.484–85) who relies on their knowledge; thus he never speaks in the first-person singular, of and for himself. But Parmenides' poem is told in the *Proem* in the first-person singular, with reference to *me* (με, fr. 1.1–3), which is that of the speaker-writer who is retelling what the goddess tells the youth (fr. 1.25 ff.). Yet, this is not an expression of the author's subjectivity because the story is about him as the one chosen by the goddess to testify to the truth of one-being, which does not depend on individuality and unique subjectivity. Each "me" is many. The singular of the "one" in one-being does not have a plural, even if it shows itself through multiple attributions on the "myth of the way" (μῦθος ὁδοῖο) by the "signs," tokens, or marks (σήματα) that need be told, interpreted, and translated (fr. 8.1–2). Being is only pluralized in *being is being*, still remaining being but also becoming the "is" of the copula that holds the parts of the enunciation. The one of being is the only one that does not have the plural and thus is the *singulare tantum*. The only one in the poem is being. Everything and everybody else, including the narrator and the poet, are ones. We as "ones" are not the plural of the one, but we are already and forever many, the *pluralia tantum* who hope to become unique and choose by the δόξα of fame.

Most importantly, the time of the first poetic thinking and singing about being and the being of the world is also the time when history becomes an established genre. Parmenides' contemporary, Hecataeus, is the first to use prose for writing history.[24] Yet, elaborate prose is not a "natural" way of telling about the world, but, as Strabo later argues, it is an *imitation* of poetry.[25] For the epic, prose is unsuitable and unthinkable because the epic's solemn progression needs a regular and steady rhythm that enchants the narrator and enthralls the listeners, making them imagine the seen and hark to the heard. But for history, which is the description of the known and inhabited world, as is Hecataeus' *Periēgēsis*, prose is most suitable because it allows the narration of the "knowing or learning much," πολυμαθία, of small and seemingly unimportant details of the narrator's personal testimony and observations on his travels (cf. Heraclitus. DK 22B40, Herodotus 2.35 ff.). This is why Hecataeus is called πολυπλανής, "roaming far and wide," the one who has journeyed far and wide.[26]

---

[24] Dmitri Nikulin. *The Concept of History*. London: Bloomsbury, 2017, 21–23.
[25] ὁ πεζὸς λόγος, ὅ γε κατεσκευασμένος, μίμημα τοῦ ποιητικοῦ ἐστι, Strabo. *Geography*. Vol. 1. Trans. by Howard Leonard Jones. Cambridge, MA: Harvard University Press, 1917, I.2.6.
[26] Hecataeus. In *Genealogie und Mythographie*. Vol. 1 of *Die Fragmente der griechischen Historiker*. Ed. by Felix Jacoby. Leiden: Brill, 1957, fr. T 12 = fr. XXXIV. In *Hecatei Milesii Fragmenta*. Ed. by Giuseppe Nenci. Firenze: La nuova Italia editrice, 1954.

Therefore, Parmenides metrically follows Homer but conceptually is much closer to the new genre of history that tells about the wanderings, encounters, and events along the way of being in thought, based on the personal experience of seeing the new places (in the celestial realm, before and behind the threshold of the gates) and listening to others (to the maidens and the goddess) on the way of and to being. In this sense, Parmenides' poem is a history of being.

Female guides. Being is complete and has no origin or birth, whereas we mortals are immersed in that which is born and comes to an end (fr. 19); thus we are ontologically not commensurable to being. Driven by opinions, we are torn between the opposites that we doxastically take to be independent principles, and we miss the simplicity of being that in its absent presence is nothing for us and even for itself. Hence, we can neither come to being on our own nor direct each other toward it. We need a mystagogue, a non-human divine guide to lead us on the way of and to being.

It is remarkable that in his journey toward the truth of being the youth is helped, and sometimes hindered, exclusively by female personifications and goddesses.[27] The world of the mortals is dominated by self-asserting, heroic males who are cluelessly wandering around, deaf and blind, with unstable and split personality and thus of "two heads" (δίκρανοι, fr. 6.4–7), senselessly fighting each other in epic battles, shortening their already short lives. They are driven by the illusory lure and deceptive promise of mnemonic immortality of and in fame or glory (κλέος or δόξα; cf. Plato. *Symp.* 208c), which is the δόξα of unreliable opinions or beliefs that reign supreme among mortals (βροτῶν δόξας, fr. 1.30). Misguided by the roaming or confused reason (πλακτὸν νόον, fr. 6.6), the courageous fighters are incapable of attaining the path of being and of discerning between being and non-being, and thus they keep to the way that always turns sideward and leads them astray.

---

[27] I am grateful to Mitchell Miller for this observation.

In opposition to the confused humans, who in their blindness prefer to represent themselves as valiant male warriors, these divine female guides keep and steer those who dare to think and thus get engaged in a long and dangerous journey of discovering the truth of being, which is preserved in its unity by mighty Necessity (κρατερὴ Ἀνάγκη, fr. 8.30–31; cf. fr. 8.16). These divine guides in female personifications are the maidens, κοῦραι (fr. 1.5, 15), the daughters of the sun (Ἡλιάδες, fr. 1.9), and the goddess, θεά, who readily greets the traveler who comes to her home and tells about being and non-being (fr. 1.22, 25). And it is not evil fate (μοῖρα κακή, fr. 1.26; cf. Μοῖρα, fr. 8.37) but Right and Justice (Θέμις and Δίκη, fr. 1.28; cf. severely punishing justice, Δίκη πολύποινος, fr. 1.14, 8.32) who send the youth on the way of learning the core of the unchanged Truth (Ἀλήθεια, fr. 1.29; 2.4), as well as the opinions of the mortals, in which there is no true assurance, equally female (πίστις ἀληθής, fr. 1.30; cf. fr. 8.51). Plato later represented the female guide to the truth by the invented character of Diotima (*Symp.* 201d), a priestess who leads mortals to being by way of love.

The mystagogues of being are thus all female, and it is the goddess who tells and guides us on the way of truth.

The truth of being. The way of the truth of being and non-being related by the goddess is not a philosophical one, as Eudemus and Simplicius already notice, because philosophical truth, from the Sophists and Socrates on, has to be arrived at dialectically by establishing a proposition that starts with accepted premises, moves by way of reasoning through questions and answers that tend to avoid contradiction, and hopefully ends in a conclusion that discloses the essence of thing in its definition—if only we happen to find the way through the maze of reasoning. Only then does the justified conclusion become knowledge, or ἐπιστήμη. The dialectical way is prosaic, long, uncertain, frequently confused, and often boring, since for the most part reasoning does not lead us anywhere, but it provisionally stops in puzzlement and aporia, and therefore has to be resumed and repeated again and again, as Plato famously portrays it in his Socratic dialogues.

The Parmenidean way is different. As Socrates says, in order to demonstrate what they want, some people prefer long speeches, and others, like Parmenides, whom Socrates heard when he himself was a youth, use questions in their beautiful speeches (Plato. *Soph.* 217c). Yet, although Parmenides might have used dialectical questions and answers in his oral disputations, now he addresses us in a long speech on the way of and to being. It is the way of the deity, along which one is driven by very wise (πολύφραστοι) horses in a chariot that goes as far as our striving spirit, θυμός, can reach (fr. 1.1–5, 25). This way is that of an anonymous youth, and yet this way is not impersonal as in philosophical reasoning: in Plato's elenchic dialogues, dialectical reasoning is staged as a spectacle in which the actors' voices enact the argument and the questioner usually wears the mask of Socrates, while the responder is not anonymous but still is always disposable and can be substituted for anyone else. On the Parmenidean way, the youth (κοῦρος, fr. 1.24), who stands for each and every one of us, is guided by the maidens (κοῦραι, fr. 1.5, 9) in the flight from darkness into the light. This journey is poetic, written in verse, because, before the prosaic wandering of mostly confused dialectical thought, this path is a unique way to being, straight and incapable of being otherwise. This means that the way of the truth of and to being is *not* deductive: it is neither a momentary noetic leap to being nor a logical dialectical argument.

Truth as the truth of being *is* the way—not a Hegelian way, where the end is already inevitable and necessary from the beginning, but the way from which we mostly wander away, and yet by which, when guided by those who are already on the way, we reach being by being brought there where it always already is.

There are many distinct directing marks and guideposts on this way (σήματ' ἔασι πολλά, fr. 8.2–3). Parmenides therefore uses a number of different terms for the path, road, track, or way: ὁδός (fr. 1.2, 1.27, 7.2, 8.18; in plural, fr. 2.2); πάτος (the trodden path of people, ἀνθρώπων, fr. 1.27); ἀταρπός (the utterly unknowable path of "is not," fr. 2.6); ἀμαξιτός (traversed by wagons, fr. 1.21); and κέλευθος (the road of Night and Day, of Persuasion, fr. 1.11, 2.4, 6.9). Most importantly, one has to step, or be brought onto, the way that is the "famous, or much spoken of, way of the deity" (ἐς ὁδὸν...πολύφημον...δαίμονες, fr. 1.2–3), which can also be understood as many-voiced, abounding in what is said.[28] Guarded by mighty necessity (fr. 8.29–31), it is the way of being, complete and completed and yet testified to by a plethora of voices and attended by many characters, of which the goddess is the one who entrusts Parmenides with relaying its truth to us who otherwise go awry.

Because being is one, the way of being is one. However, precisely because of its uniqueness, it can be gone through, thought through, or told in any order. This is why "it does not matter where I begin because I will come there again" (ξυνὸν δέ μοί ἐστιν, ὁππόθεν ἄρξωμαι· τόθι γὰρ πάλιν ἵξομαι αὖθις, fr. 5.1–2). We always begin *in medias res* because, in a sense, any beginning for us is always in the middle, where the end is always present and yet has to be achieved.

The way of being is not the way to truth but of truth, which is why it has no beginning or end. It is its own beginning and end. One can begin anywhere and return to the same, when the same of being has its other and is itself. There is no beginning of being except for itself, which thus has no beginning. Only for us logical and mostly confused beings the story has to be told as a "myth," with the beginning, middle, and (missing) end of the poem.

The inquiry or investigation, δίζησις, about the way is a speech, story, tale, or "myth" (μῦθος, fr. 2.1–2) and not a reasoned, logical argument because truth is the way and not an abstract proposition or a principle of reasoning. This way is traversed by and in an oral

---

[28] We find many superlatives in Parmenides' poem, conveyed by πολυ-: πολύποινος, much-retributing (justice); πολύφραστοι, supremely wise (horses); πολύφημον, much spoken of or many-voiced (way); πολύπειρον, much experienced (habit, fr. 7.3); and πολύδηριν, most contentious (refutation, fr. 7.5).

word, in the speech by the goddess, the transcription and transmission of which she entrusts to Parmenides' unavoidably seductive and deceptive order of verses (κόσμον ἐπέων ἀπατηλόν, fr. 8.52). These verses inevitably betray the beauty and truth of the said and thought about being in its simplicity. However, they still guard it against the dissection of and by the prosaic, boring argument of dialectical reasoning, which, in the end, even if it is correct and fully self-justified, remains—paradoxically—truly deceptive and unable to communicate and reach the simplicity of being.

On the way to the truth of *being* there is nothing to be reached because *being is*, is always and already there, noetically thought even before and without having been thought. The divine, poetically related "myth" of and about being is a narrative in which the opposites can *coexist*, though not necessarily coincide without mediation. Myth thus can both violate the principle of non-contradiction and violate its violation. Therefore, the truth of the "myth" about being lies not in its ordered, logical justification but in being itself, which in this way becomes *the* way.

Hence, on the way of being there is *nothing* to be reached. One can start with *being* in any place because, by *being is*, one will come there back again, arriving to *being is being* without having ever left the beginning in being led through all things by being itself, encountered as the divinity (δαίμων, fr. 1.3).

Two ways. The truth about the unchangeable being does not change: the heart of truth is unmoved (ἀτρεμὲς ἦτορ, fr. 1.29). It does not beat. Because the truth is the way of and to being, and because being is one, the truth of being is also one and unique. Hence, the way of truth is one and unique.

It is *the* way. But there is *another* way—the path of the many opinions of mortals (δόξας... βροτείας, fr. 8.51; cf. fr. 1.30–32, 2.2) rather than of appearances.[29] In a sense, it is not a way at all but

---

[29] See Néstor-Luis Cordero. *By Being, It Is.* Las Vegas: Parmenides Publishing, 2004, 151–63.

rather a confused wandering once we have followed to an end the path of the certain reasoning and thought about being (fr. 8.50–51). This is the unknowable sideway of non-being assumed inevitably to be being (fr. 2.5–7).

However, this other way cannot be gone through: the contradiction of the unmediated juxtaposition of being and non-being is not—literally—pervious in thought, and thus it always has to turn back: it is the crooked way (παλίντροπος...κέλευθος, fr. 6.9) of the wandering and lost mind (πλακτὸν νόον, fr. 6.6). The way of persuasion and truth is the way of patient and solemn epic narration, which moves slowly, and yet it is the shortest way because it is a straight one, whereas the other way is impatient and hasty, and thus is always a long and convoluted one. Unlike the way of truth, this other path, which is meant to be a shortcut, never returns to itself, as does the way of truth (fr. 5), but it never leads anywhere and is thus altogether unknowable (fr. 2.6). In wandering along this way, one has already always and forever gone wrong and can never get to the right way without the help of truth itself.

Prohibition of thinking non-being. If only being is, nothing is besides and beyond being: nothing is not. As has been argued, since in *being* there is nothing besides being, being nothing; in *being is*, non-being is nothing; and in *being is being*, being is the other of nothing. So in *being, being is* and in *being is being*, non-being is not. If only being is and can be thought, then only being is and can be known, while non-being as nothing cannot be told about, and thus, strictly speaking, cannot even be said to be not known.

Since the being-thinking, εἶναι-νοεῖν, is, it is thought noetically or non-discursively by reason-νόος and logically and narratively by λόγος. But can non-being be thought at all, and what can be thought about it?

The narrator of and on the way, or the historian of the way, is the goddess because she knows what she is talking about to the extent that she *is*. In her narration, the goddess leads along the way by assertion (being is) and negation (being is not), which can be considered equally an assertion but in negative form. Yet, there is another form of negation, that of prohibition, which, however, is not a moral demand but a warning to reason not to wander off being, which is its main and only thought. This is a prohibition that comes from being itself: not to think that being is not and that non-being is, because it is unthinkable and untraversable in thought. Thinking has to keep away from the way of non-being, which is unthinkable, unnamable (ἀνόητον ἀνώνυμον), and not true (οὐ ... ἀληθής), and go the other way, the only way of being and truth (πέλειν καὶ ἐτήτυμον, fr. 8.17-18).

But what exactly is that which cannot, and should not, be said (φάσθαι) and thought (νοεῖν)? That being comes from non-being (ἐκ μὴ ἐόντος, fr. 8.7-8): as the goddess says, you could not know (γνοίης) or tell (φράσαις) non-being (μὴ ἐόν), for it cannot be accomplished (οὐ γὰρ ἀνυστόν, fr. 2.7-8) because being already and always is, and non-being is not. Hence, non-being cannot be said or thought (οὐ γὰρ φατὸν οὐδὲ νοητόν ἔστιν ὅπως οὐκ ἔστι, fr. 8.8-9). Or, being is not, the *is is not* or the *not is is*, is impossible. There can be neither knowledge nor opinion about non-being, and thus it cannot be expressed. The "non-being" is only a mark of that which cannot be thought and thus inevitably misses the said.

Hence, the goddess will not allow (οὐδ'... ἐάσσω, fr. 8.7) one to say or think that being comes from non-being because non-being is not and is unthinkable. The future tense here, ἐάσσω, stands for prohibition as the intention of not allowing the impossible rather than for a description of a possible future event, which is not an event at all because being can never be non-being or come from it. In this sense, this prohibition comes from being itself and becomes the origin of the way and thought about being or about itself. This suggests, once again, that for Parmenides being is not the opposite of non-being because being is and is one, and non-being is not and "is" nothing. Being can never be non-being. This is why we have to shut our thought in, out, and from the inquiry about non-being and ultimately refrain from it.³⁰

Once being and non-being become thought by the discursive reasoning-λόγος as opposites within statements marked by the copula and its negation, then this ontological prohibition becomes the principle of non-contradiction, the most fundamental and maybe even the sole beginning-ἀρχή of both being and thought. Yet, for Parmenides this is a mistaken judgment, γνώμη, of us mortals who think of ourselves as solely logical beings, capable of apprehending the truth only through λόγος and taking *is* to be the "is" of the copula of a logical statement. For this reason, we came to name (ὀνομάζειν) two forms (μορφαί), one of which—non-being—should not be named at all (τῶν μίαν οὐ χρεών ἐστιν, fr. 8.53–54). We do not listen to the warning of being about being.

Once we start thinking within the opposites, then any attempt to think logically being and non-being (in Aristotle, ὑπάρχειν and μὴ ὑπάρχειν) at once in the same respect and with reference to the same is impossible and amounts to contradiction, thus failing.³¹ The contradiction arises when the now established opposites of being and non-being are impossible to be co-thought because Parmenides (and later, Plato) did not allow for the existence of a mediating opposition-neutral *same*, τὸ αὐτό, or substrate.

This is what discursive thinking cannot grasp because it thinks in terms of the opposites as mutual. This means that contradictory statements cannot be thought and are thus logically false, in particular, that being is not (2.iii); non-being is (2.iv); and that being is non-being (3.V); being is not being (3.VI); non-being is being (3.VII); non-being is not non-being (3.VIII).³² Exactly half of the

---

³⁰ οὐ γὰρ μήποτε τοῦτο δαμῆι εἶναι μὴ ἐόντα· ἀλλὰ σὺ τῆσδ᾽ ἀφ᾽ ὁδοῦ διζήσιος εἶργε νόημα, Parmenides. fr. 7.1–2.

³¹ τὸ γὰρ αὐτὸ ἅμα ὑπάρχειν τε καὶ μὴ ὑπάρχειν ἀδύνατον τῷ αὐτῷ καὶ κατὰ τὸ αὐτό, Aristotle. *Met.* 1005b19–20.

³² In our notation, the statements that cannot be gone through, or are logically false, are: (2.iii) E ~ε, (2.iv) ~E ε; (3.V) E ε ~E, (3.VI) E ~ε E, (3.VII) ~E ε E, (3.VIII) ~E ~ε ~E.

statements in each case are contradictory, and thus they cannot be logically thought or gone through by λόγος. This occurs in all the cases when the statement has either one negation or three negations, which, if the double negation logically amounts to affirmation, also has the value of single negation.

Where does this impossibility come from? From the prohibition of thinking *non-being* (in 1), before it can be said to be (*non-being is* (in 2), and before it can be said to have a "what" (*non-being is being* (in 3). Non-being is always unthinkable, but only in half of the cases in (2) and (3) does it amount to contradiction. Non-being as such is not contradictory in itself and to itself because there is no other to it and thus no predicative statement in which a contradiction can arise, not even "is not." In (1) non-being cannot be said or thought either to be or not to be, and hence it is not opposite or contradictory to being when only being is posited without "is." So the logical impossibility of saying correctly or thinking logically the above cases comes from the very impossibility of non-being, which is not logical. It is the impossibility for the thought-νόημα of the reason-νόος to think or grasp non-being, μὴ εἶναι, or not-is, οὐκ ἔστι (fr. 2.3), in a single act.

The sheer impermeability in thought, the bar across its way, and the gate that can never be open thus come with and from non-being that has the power of negation. The negative, *not* (~), blocks any movement of thought and arrests thinking. The sheer negation is blind and even turns against itself as its double (οὐ to μή and μή to οὐ), without having any way of distinguishing between the two because there is no other at this point. Just being. Only *is*. *Nothing* cannot even be, and neither it is not. Only *not*. And this *not* cannot be distinguished from being. So ultimately, the power of negativity or negation resides in being, but it cannot be thought by νόος or accounted by λόγος. The *not* cannot be different from being as mere *being*, but it cannot be identical with being either. All distinctions can be made, thought, and told about only when *being is*, and they become distinguishable when *being is being*. Hence, the way of negation is regulated by mere or only being as the only being, being-only, or one-being as being negative or nothing before being is itself (τὸ αὐτό) and is reflective to itself in thought. *Being*—just being—is pure negation without negating anything, even itself. The very prohibition of thinking non-being, of being as non-being (ἔστιν ὅπως οὐκ ἔστι, fr. 8.9), comes then from the performative contradiction coming from being because in order not to think non-being, we have to somehow already think it. If thinking non-being amounts to non-thinking of being not as being, then one has to be silent. Yet, the goddess speaks. She keeps talking on the way of being and then she keeps talking off the way of being. So despite the prohibition of not going the way of not being, the youth—each of us—will still have to learn about the opinions of the mortals from the goddess (fr. 1.30–32). This happens for Parmenides when the way of being turns into the way of opinion (fr. 8.51), which is not that of being but not altogether the way of non-being either.

Two principles of the diacosmos. Here, we follow those things, τάδε, that, according to opinion, κατὰ δόξαν, came to be, are, and will come to an end, for which we humans have established a name distinguishing each one (τοῖς δ' ὄνομ' ἄνθρωποι κατέθεντ' ἐπίσημον ἑκάστωι, fr. 19). Here, we humans are immersed in the diacosmos, the probable ordered arrangement of things (διάκοσμον ἐοικότα, fr. 8.60; διακόσμησις, fr. 19, apud Simplicius. *In de caelo* 558.8), which becomes disclosed along the rugged way of opinion. Here, all things in their entirety, τὸ πᾶν, are embodied as one being, which is single, continuous, indivisible, complete, and whole, and as such is a sphere equal to itself in all its aspects and sides. Here, we are within the realm of the totality of the doxastic distinctions of everything from everything, of all things that appear as ultimately distinguished, each appearing on its own, each one a being for the time being.

As has been argued, the opposites are posited by the act of thought of reason-νόος, which is unconditioned and therefore is not bound by any previously imposed limitations, including the prohibition of positing the opposites as immediate or not mediated by anything else, as A and ~A, or A ~ A, where negation is not a mediation. Reason thus thinks them without mediation and is not afraid of contradiction. But the λόγος already regulates itself by respecting the principle of non-contradiction. Thus, in order for its discursive reasoning to be correct, the opposites should be mediated and their immediate confluence or coincidence has to be avoided at all costs as impervious and false by refining the argument and logical thinking ever further. But in the diacosmos, we meander along the path of opinion, which, however, is still not without consistency, even if it is presented in the deceptive order of the goddess' verses. This order is deceptive (fr. 8.52), and yet it is still an order or κόσμος (fr. 4.3) and is thus defensible against the arbitrary judgment of us mortals (βροτῶν γνώμη, fr. 8.60–61). Here, the opposites, τἀντία (fr. 8.55, 8.59) are distinct and yet are embodied, acting within all things and within each one.

The opposites in the things of the diacosmos are thus accountable by correct reasoning, πιστὸς λόγος, and they are narratable by the way of opinion (fr. 8.50–51). They appear and act in all things, τάδε, as two principles-ἀρχαί that are assumed to exist and act independently and separately from each other (χωρὶς ἀπ' ἀλλήλων, fr. 8.56) in their bodily constitution and signs (δέμας καὶ σήματ', fr. 8.55). Because the opposites as principles of things are considered apart from each other, they are present in all things as their elements, στοιχεῖα, which are understood as the things' productive cause, τὸ ποιητικόν, and matter, ὕλη (Simplicius. *In Phys.* 39.12), which stand for being and non-being in the diacosmos. In the ordered world, the two opposing elements are doxastically distinguished as the bright and the dark (τὸ λαμπρὸν καὶ σκοτεινόν, fr. 10), Day and Night (fr. 1.11), flame (φλόξ) and night (νύξ, fr. 12.2), light and night (φάος καὶ νύξ, fr. 9.1), ethereal fire of gentle and light flame (πῦρ) and dark, dense, and heavy night (fr. 8.56, 59). In the order of all the things, each of the two opposing principles is everywhere the same to itself but not same to the other (ἑωυτῶι πάντοσε τωὐτόν, τῶι δ' ἑτέρωι μὴ τωὐτόν, fr. 8.57–58). And yet, everything equally participates in both principles because nothing, or no single thing, is filled with only one of them (ἴσων ἀμφοτέρων, ἐπεὶ οὐδετέρωι μέτα μηδέν, fr. 9.4). Everything in this one world, including the aether, the sun, the stars, the earth, the moon, and the sky (fr. 10–11), is powered and moved by the opposite principles, which are mixed in all things in different proportions (fr. 16) to the entirety of things, which mediate the opposites and allow them to be thought without contradiction.

Speaking the non-speakable. But back on the ever returning to itself way of being, how does one speak about the non-speakable and think the non-thinkable, which is pure being that, as we found, amounts to the sheer *not* or negative, and thus cannot be distinguished from non-being, yet cannot be identified with it either? Parmenides does not explore apophatic expression and thinking, probably because the *via negativa*, despite denying the possibility of saying or thinking anything about the ineffable, still denies or negates the *via positiva* of the discursive logical or dialectical account that moves along, around, and by arguments and counterarguments, λόγοι and ἀντιλογίαι, in propositional statements and their contradictory opposites,[33] propelled by the power of contradictory opposites. Instead, Parmenides chooses the solemn, unrushed rhythm of epic narration, which he turns into an unadorned, dry, and clear form,[34] the one in which we should be able to hear the unheard through the repetitive and boring monotony of the hexameter lines, which will put the listener into a position of opening up to being in the said beyond the said, to thinking as non-thinking of the thought. Non-being cannot be thought, but mere *being*, ἔστι, just-being cannot only be thought when the other is indistinguishably co-thought. Only *being is* can

---

[33] ἐκ τῶν λόγων καὶ ἐκ τῶν ἀντιλογιῶν ἐθεωρήθη καὶ τὸ συλλογίζεσθαι, Simplicius. *In Phys.* 116.2.

[34] τὸ ἀκαλλώπιστον καὶ ἰσχνὸν καὶ καθαρὸν εἶδος, according to the judgment of Proclus, himself a prosaic dialectical thinker. Proclus. *In Parm.* I 14–15.

be thought. It will transpire to the reason-νόος as yet unthought through the texture of the poem and its carefully arranged logical narration.

Since truth is about being that only is and is not in time (fr. 8.5), the truth itself is atemporal. Opinion, on the contrary, is about those things that move, as the moon around the earth (fr. 14), or that change in the mixture of the elements in bodies (fr. 16), which, however, remain in their transformations within the same one being of the sphere of the diacosmos. So opinion is shaky but also constant, everlasting, because such are the things about which it is the opinion. And such is also the δόξα of temporal fame that preserves the memory of people and their deeds as everlasting in the lore of the epic, in the poetic narrative told by the poets and preserved by us in our commonly shared memory.

Hence, the way of opinion is not really different from the way of truth; it only is such in the account for us mortals. Now, at the end of Parmenides' story, we know that in opinion the ordered existent is, *that* it is. We also know in knowledge the truth of *being*; that *being is*, even if we do not know *why* it is, only that it is what it is and cannot be otherwise; and for *being is being*, we know *how* it is. Yet ultimately, the *that* and the *why* are—*is*—the same if asked about being because being is one. The straight way of the thought truth continues as the crooked way of the meant opinion, which then turns back to the beginning, which is always there and thus ever in the middle of things. It does not matter which way we start because we will come back again to that which can never be abandoned, to being that never leaves us. Being cannot be thought without negation and therefore without non-being, and non-being is thus the non-thinkable precondition of truth and being.

2

Democritus

Non-Being as the Void

Δημόκριτος ὁ Ἀβδηρίτης ἀρχὰς ἔθετο τὸ πλῆρες καὶ τὸ κενόν, ὧν τὸ μὲν ὂν τὸ δὲ μὴ ὂν ἐκάλει.

Democritus from Abdera established as the principles the full and the void, of which the former he called being and the latter non-being.[1]

τῶν ἀνθρώπων αἱ ἐλπίδες ὅσον τὸ κενόν!

How void are human hopes![2]

Laughing philosopher. The ancient doxographic tradition testifies that Democritus was a laughing philosopher (DL 9.41).[3] Unlike Heraclitus, who wept, Democritus was always laughing, rejoicing in being and non-being as always entangled and at play in the constitution of the marvel of the world and of human affairs. It is reported that Democritus' joyous curiosity about how things are impelled him

---

[1] Simplicius. *In Phys.* 28.15–17; see also Solomon Lurie, Ed. *Democritea*. Leningrad: Nauka, 1970, fr. 147; henceforth L, followed by fragment number. All fragments of Democritus are taken from Lurie's edition. See also "Democritus" (68). In *Die Fragmente der Vorsokratiker.* Vol. 2. Trans. and ed. by Hermann Diels and Walther Kranz. Berlin: Weidmann, 1996.

[2] Scholia to Persius. *Saturae* (I 1, L 799): "O curas hominum, o quantum est in rebus inane!"

[3] Democritus "laughed at everything, as all things human are worth the laughter" (οὗτος ἐγέλα πάντα, ὡς γέλωτος ἀξίων πάντων τῶν ἐν ἀνθρώποις, DK 68A40). Cf.: τοῖς δὲ σοφοῖς ἀντὶ ὀργῆς Ἡρακλείτῳ μὲν δάκρυα, Δημοκρίτῳ δὲ γέλως ἐπῄει, Stobaeus II.20.53; *Heraclitus . . . flebat . . . Democritum . . . numquam sine risu in publico fuisse*, Seneca. *De ira* II.10.5; Cicero. *De or.* II 58,237 = L LXI-LXIII; Aelian. *Varia historia* IV.20.

to travel widely and sail around,[4] studying the ecumene (*oikumene*) through personal evidence, as Hecataeus and Hellanicus, the first historians, did before him. Journeys through the inhabitable and natural match and reflect Democritus' travels around the thinkable, which made him a universal thinker, who wrote extensively on many different topics, including physics, ethics, politics, mathematics, agriculture, poetry, and art (DL 9.37). Thus, Democritus was the first to determine the volumes of a cone and pyramid, but he only formulated the result without proving it, which Eudoxus did later.[5] Democritus was a good writer: clear and almost poetic.[6] Of his numerous works, none have been preserved, only the ancient lore, often dim and obscure.[7] And yet, from Democritus we have one of the most sizable sets of fragments, which come mostly from Aristotle and his later commentators, although they often do not make a clear distinction between Democritus and his teacher, Leucippus.

Democritus and other thinkers. Democritus was born around the end of Parmenides' life and was a contemporary of Socrates. When he came to Athens, at first without being noticed at all (DL 9.36), the philosophical talk of the town was of the Eleatics. Various attempts at their refutation (by Socrates in the form of philosophizing, turning to definitions and prioritizing ethics over cosmology), as well as appropriation (by Plato's critical account of the one and the many). Diogenes Laertius, in his *Vitae Philosophorum*, speaks about Leucippus and Democritus right after the Eleatic thinkers Parmenides, Melissus, and Zeno, and he reports that Democritus refers to Parmenides' and Zeno's teaching about the one, a topic that was much discussed at the time (DL 9.21–29, 30–49). This suggests that ancient understanding of the relation between the philosophers and of the procession of thought is very different from our contemporary view, which is

---

[4] περίπλους, L 407 = Agathemerus 1.1.2; DL 9.35.
[5] L 125 = Archimedes. *Meth.* 428.26ff.
[6] L 826 = Cicero. *Orat.* 20.67 *Acad. priora* II 23.73.
[7] See DL 9.46–48.

philologically and chronologically oriented. At the outset of the 4th century BCE, Democritus was perceived in ancient Greece as disputing with and responding directly to the Eleatic thinkers, and thus as their successor. This perception explains a certain animosity toward Democritus by Plato, who could not have missed Democritus' writings and teachings and yet *never* mentions Democritus in his dialogues. Rather than criticizing Democritus directly, Plato chose to be silent about him, while Aristotle, equally critical of Democritus, mentions him dozens of times. We learn from Diogenes Laertius' doxography that Aristoxenus, a pupil of Aristotle, affirms that Plato even tried to burn Democritus' writings (DL 9.40). And even if contemporary philosophers were usually not mentioned by name, Plato's abstention from a direct debate with the Abderite philosopher might suggest that his own reappropriation of the Eleatic doctrine of the one and the many ran contrary and opposite to its refutation by Democritus, thus making the two bitter philosophical rivals in thinking being and non-being.

Being and non-being. As Simplicius tells us, for Democritus' predecessor Leucippus, whom Democritus appears to follow closely, *being is no more than non-being*, and both equally are the cause of that which comes to be.[8] This suggests that the Eleatics and the Atomists came up with two different and opposite ontological approaches.

Democritus's own concise formulation was "in reality—atoms and the void" (ἐτεῇ δ' ἄτομα καὶ κενόν).[9] *Both* being and non-being are in reality and truly are. This is what reality is: atoms and the void.

---

[8] οὐδὲν μᾶλλον τὸ ὂν ἢ τὸ μὴ ὂν ὑπάρχειν, καὶ αἴτια ὁμοίως εἶναι τοῖς γινομένοις ἄμφω, L 147 = Simplicius. *In Phys.* 28.11–12. See also David Furley. *The Formation of the Atomic Theory and Its Earliest Critics.* Vol. 1. of *The Greek Cosmologists.* Cambridge: Cambridge University Press, 1987, 115–22.

[9] L 79–80 = Galen. *De medica empiria* 1259.8; L 85 = Sextus. *Pyrrh. hypot.* I 213; L 90 = Galen. *De elem. sec. Hipp.* I 2. Another formulation is: ἀληθὲς δὲ ἐν τοῖς οὖσιν ὑπάρχειν τὸ ἀτόμους εἶναι καὶ κενόν, L 55 = Sextus. *Adv. math.* VII 135; also L 93 = DL 9.44; L 95 = Aetius IV 9.8. According to Galen (L 90), ἐτεῇ is Democritus' own term, which he made from ἐτεόν, taken as an adverb, "truly."

(1) This means that, contrary to Parmenides, for Democritus non-being *is* no less than being. *Being cannot be without non-being*.
(2) Being and non-being are opposite to each other and are ontologically equal. As opposites, however, they do not allow for mediation and thus are contradictories.
(3) As unmediated opposites, being and non-being are many and one. Many is full and one is empty.

Put succinctly, while for the Eleatics (Parmenides and Zeno) one *is* and is being, whereas many *is not* and is non-being, and for the Atomists (Leucippus and Democritus) one (the empty or the void) *is* and is non-being, while many (the full or the atoms) *is* and is being.

Many and one. So contrary to Parmenides, being for Democritus is many and non-being is one.[10] Ancient tradition associated Democritus with the Pythagoreans, who considered the one and the many as the two main principles of their ontology (DL 9.38). The two ontological principles are mutually irreducible and non-deducible from each other. Such are also the one and the many for Democritus, for whom, according to Aristotle, neither the many comes from the one nor the one from the many.[11] The distinction between the Pythagoreans and Democritus lies in the ontological status of the principles: for the Pythagoreans, the one and the many are both the principle of being and are in being: one of the definite and the limited, and many, or indefinite dyad,—of the indefinite and the unlimited. For the Pythagoreans, and according to the view ascribed to Eurytus, numbers are generated from the one (τὸ ἕν)

---

[10] For Zeno's arguments regarding the plurality of bodies as continuous and thus infinitely divisible, see Christoph Rapp. "Zeno and the Eleatic Anti-Pluralism." In *La costruzione del discorso filosofico nell'età dei Presocratici*. Ed. by Michela Sassi. Pisa: Edizioni della Normale, 2006, 161–82; 171–80.

[11] οὔτ' ἐξ ἑνὸς πολλὰ γίγνεσθαι οὔτε ἐκ πολλῶν ἕν, L 292 = Aristotle. *De caelo* 303a6–7.

(in their unity and definiteness) and from the indefinite dyad (responsible for the multiplicity of the numbers), as if from place and an infinite void.[12] But for Democritus, the many *is* being and being is *many*, represented by the plurality of the atoms.

So the many is the atoms, and the one is the void. As for the Pythagoreans, the many for Democritus stands for non-finite or infinite. Being is infinite in number, which is contrary to both the Eleatic and the Pythagorean understanding of being. And yet, each atom as being is one and is indivisible, whereas the void is one and is divisible. This means that the opposition between the one and the many is blurred because the many of being is also one (as an indivisible atom), and the one of non-being is also many (as indefinitely or infinitely divisible). The opposition between the many and the one as that between being and non-being is, then, between the *discrete* and the *continuous*.

Therefore, being is discrete and non-being is continuous. And yet, the discrete, as exemplified in numbers that number different beings or atoms, is many-one, where each number is a distinctive multiplicity of indivisible or atomic monads. And the continuous is one-many as an abyss of indistinguishable nothing, where the one is the continuous extension, the void of and for being, infinitely divisible into ever further divisible parts. As we will see, in Aristotle number and magnitude behave very differently with respect to division, since number cannot be infinitely divided (for the one as monad is indivisible) but can be indefinitely increased, whereas magnitude is divisible indefinitely (for there is no discrete, indivisible constituent to limit it) but cannot increase indefinitely beyond what they are (*Phys.* 204a2–7). Hence, the one and the many of being and non-being as one-many and many-one are represented and opposed to each other without mediation as numbers and the continuum.

---

[12] ἀπὸ τῆς ἀορίστου δυάδος οἷον τόπος καὶ κενὸν καὶ ἄπειρον, DK 45B2 = Theophrastus. *Met.* 11.

Full and empty. As Aristotle and his commentators report, Democritus considered the principles (ἀρχαί) or elements (στοιχεῖα) of the existent as the full and the void, where the full is being and the void is non-being.[13] Being is thus the full, and non-being is the empty or void.[14] These two originary ontological principles suffice for the production of the immeasurable complexity of the existent: from the intertwining and combination (συμπλοκή) of the empty and the full come all the things.[15]

Since the full is indivisible whereas the empty is divisible, the two principles of the existent, being and non-being, are again unmediated. This means that, since being is many and indivisible, it has to be atoms—many and indivisible—while non-being is the void. Exactly as is the case regarding the opposition between the many and the one, the opposition between the full and the empty is that between the discrete and the continuous. The full is thus discrete and the empty is continuous. Even if it is non-being, the void is continuous or is divisible ever further and further. Non-being as void is thus devoid of an ultimate limit. It is a non-distinguishable, infinite abyss.

That being is full implies that many beings cannot be in the same place at once.[16] One being is topologically exclusive of another. Or beings are mutually impenetrable. Put otherwise, being is material, if being material means being in a place exclusive of another material being. Even gods are material "images" (εἴδωλα).[17] All beings-atoms, therefore, have the same substance (ὁμοουσίους τὰς ἀτόμους), the full (τὸ πλῆρες), which is one nature (μία φύσις),

---

[13] τὸ μὲν πλῆρες καὶ στερεὸν τὸ ὄν, τὸ δὲ κενὸν... τὸ μὴ ὄν, L 173 = Aristotle. *Met.* 985b6–7; L 8 = Aristotle. *Met.* 1009a27–30; ἀρχὰς εἶναι τῶν ὅλων ἀτόμους καὶ κενόν, DL 9.44; τὸ πλῆρες καὶ τὸ κενόν, ὧν τὸ μὲν ὂν τὸ δὲ μὴ ὂν ἐκάλει, L 147 = Simplicius. *In Phys.* 28.15–17; L 178 = Alexander. *In Met.* 303.34–31. The full is also called ναστή, Simplicius. *In Phys.* 28.13; L 264 = Asclepius. *In Met.* 33.9–11.
[14] ὂν μὲν... τὸ πλῆρες, μὴ ὂν δὲ τὸ κενόν. L 262 = Alexander. *In Met.* 303.34.
[15] L 246 = Philoponus. *In Phys.* 116.21–23.
[16] L 45 = Aristotle. *Phys.* 213b6.
[17] L 472a = Sextus. *Adv. math.* IX 42.

one matter (μία ὕλη), one substrate (ἓν τὸ ὑποκείμενον).[18] Being solid, material, and mutually impenetrable, such beings or atoms are impassible and unchangeable[19] because, being the only one, the substrate is not open to modification by anything else—since it is the only nature or substrate in existence.

As impenetrable, full, and material, being is thus *being in place* or is placed being, exclusive of another being in the same place. To be is to be situated in the empty extension, in non-being or the void. Contrary to Parmenides, being for Democritus not just is but also *moves* through the unmovable: being moves through non-being or the void. As we will see, for Aristotle as well as for Simplicius void means the *impossibility* of motion, but for Democritus, on the contrary, motion is impossible without the void as the condition of possibility not only of motion but indeed of being itself.

This means that being and non-being equally *are* but are *not equal*, for non-being can be without being (there is void without atoms), yet being cannot be without non-being (atoms are and can only be in the void).

Knowledge. Because being is many but not infinitely divisible, its limit is the one single and singularly indivisible being. So being is an *atom*, which literally means "indivisible." Because there is one substance to being, and it is material, atoms are the smallest primary, indivisible bodies, ἄτομα σώματα.[20] As small and indivisible, they are imperceptible[21] and thus they are apparently only thinkable. Our perceptions are related to things as constituted

---

[18] L 228 = Simplicius. *In Phys.* 44.3; L 230 = Philoponus. *In Phys.* 398.11; L 368 = Simplicius. *In de caelo* 693.9; L 261 = Aristotle. *De caelo* 187a1.

[19] ἀπαθῆ καὶ ἀναλλοίωτα, DL 9.44; ἀπαθῆ, L 112 = Galen. *De elem. sec. Hipp.* I 2; L 113 = Simplicius, *In Phys.* 925.10. Atoms are indivisible and impassible because they are solid and have no share of void (ἀτόμους καὶ ἀδιαιρέτους ἐνόμιζον καὶ ἀπαθεῖς, διὰ τὸ ναστὰς εἶναι καὶ ἀμοίρους τοῦ κενοῦ, L 214 = Simplicius. *In de caelo* 242.15; cf. L 215 = DL 9.44; L 217 = Aetius). See also: Gemelli Marciano and M. Laura. Trans and ed. *Die Vorsokratiker.* Vol. 3. 2nd ed. Berlin: Akademie Verlag, 2013, 498–501.

[20] τὰ ἐλάχιστα πρῶτα σώματα, L 111 = L 508 = Simplicius. *In Phys.* 36.1; τὰ φυσικὰ καὶ πρῶτα καὶ ἄτομα σώματα, L 196a = Simplicius. *In Phys.* 1318.33–34.

[21] L 204 = L 227 = Simplicius. *In de caelo* 295.5–6.

by the atoms, which, however, can appear differently to different people under different circumstances.²²

There is no clear explanation of the smallness of being(s) in Democritus. Still, one can think of two different, though not mutually incompatible, accounts.

Simplicity. The first explanation is a peculiar version of Parmenides' claim that being and thinking is (are) the same or that only being can be thought. Being is simple and thus can be thought. This should also mean that the explanation of being should be simple, unambiguous, and clearly expressible: there is being and non-being. There are only atoms and the void. So beings, or atoms, should not be sensibly perceivable but only thinkable. The beauty and power of this account lies in its simplicity. This is recognized by later thinkers—tacitly by Plato and explicitly by Aristotle—as logically consistent yet contrary to sense-perception.

Obscurity and truth. The second explanation for the minuteness of the indivisible being(s) is that nature conceals itself in plain sight. Already Heraclitus famously claims that nature likes to hide (κρύπτεσθαι φιλεῖ, DK 22B123). As Plutarch relates—or rather as he interprets the extant tradition—for those who study nature theoretically for the sake of truth, knowledge of the existent (μετιόντι) is not the purpose but the beginning of the ascent toward the first and the highest.²³ So we start with appearances, with what is first for us, and then we move toward the first principles, to that which is first by nature, as Aristotle will later tell us (*Phys.* 184a16–18). For Democritus, sensible qualities (such as hot and cold) are thus the matter of perception and opinion, but in reality they are determined by being as atoms and by non-being as the void, which themselves are not sensibly perceivable.²⁴ Or, atoms have no sensible

---

[22] L 441 = Theophrastus. *De sensu* 63–71; L3 = Theophrastus. *De sensu* 69.
[23] τῷ δὲ φυσικῷ, θεωρίας ἕνεκα μετιόντι τἀληθές, ἡ τῶν ἐσχάτων γνῶσις οὐ τέλος ἐστὶν ἀλλ' ἀρχὴ τῆς ἐπὶ τὰ πρῶτα καὶ ἀνωτάτω πορείας, L 506 = Plutarch. *De primo frigido* 8, 948b.
[24] L 51 = DL 9.72; L 71 = Theophrastus. *De sensu* 60–61, 69.

qualities.[25] So our perceptions refer only to complex appearances and not to simple being(s) or atoms, and they do not tell us about how things are in themselves. Hence, knowledge of how things are is difficult.[26] Why? Because non-being *is*, no less than being.[27] Because of the present absence of non-being as the unfathomable and yet ubiquitous void, nature keeps its principles simple and yet inconspicuous and non-evident.[28] Nature for Democritus hides reality in the depths and obscurity, so reality is inconspicuous and lies in a bottomless well.[29]

Therefore, nature, which itself has no reason (φύσει δέ τινι ἀλόγῳ),[30] is not immediately accessible but needs to be studied through logos as inquiry (ζήτησις)[31] in an attempt to grasp how things are, hidden in plain view from the direct gaze of reason.[32] However, Democritus does not distinguish between reason or

---

[25] L 433 = Philoponus. *In de gen. et corr.* 17.16.
[26] καίτοι δῆλον ἔσται, ὅτι ἐτεῇ οἷον ἕκαστον γιγνώσκειν ἐν ἀπόρῳ ἐστί, L 48–50 = Sextus. *Adv. math.* VII 137.
[27] τὸ δὲ μηδαμῇ μηδαμῶς ὄν... περὶ οὗ ὁ Δημόκριτός φησι μὴ εἶναι ἐπ᾽ ἔλαττον τοῦ ὄντος, L 177 = Asclepius. *In Met.* 33.9–19. Cf. Plato. *Rep.* 577a. Yet, there is no need to assume that Democritus accepts another kind of non-being, absolute non-being, τὸ μηδαμῇ μηδαμῶς ὄν, distinct from the void, as Voelke takes it. André-Jean Voelke. "Vide et non-être chez Leucippe et Démocrite." *Revue de Théologie et de Philosophie* 122:3 (1990), 351–52.
[28] Hence, when studying nature, "one should study the non-evident and not the absolutely evident" (περὶ τοῦ ἀδήλου τὴν ζήτησιν ποιητέον καὶ οὐ περὶ τοῦ φανερωτάτου), L 102 = Michael of Ephesus. *De partibus animalium.* In *In libros de partibus animalium, de animalium motione, de animalium incessu commentaria.* Vol. XXII.2 of *Commentaria in Aristotelem Graeca.* Ed Michael Hayduck. Berlin: Reimer, 1904, 70.13–14).
[29] *in profundo veritatem... penitus abstruserit,* L 51 = Cicero. *Acad. priora.* II 10.32; Lactantius. *Inst.* III 28.13
[30] L 589 = Aetius I 25.3.
[31] L 102 = Michael of Ephesus. *De partibus animalium,* 70.10–14; L92 = Sextus. *Adv. math.* VIII 6; λόγῳ δὲ θεωρητά, L 209 = Eusebius. *Praeparatio Evangelica* XIV.4.
[32] In Sextus' reconstruction of the logic of Democritus' interpretation of being, there are two kinds of cognition: by senses and by thought (τὴν μὲν διὰ τῶν αἰσθήσεων, τὴν δὲ διὰ τῆς διανοίας, L 83 = *Adv. math.* VI 138). Since the criterion of research or the search for being is thought (ζητήσεως δὲ τὴν ἔννοιαν, L 81 = *Adv. math.* VI 140), all sense perceptions are false because they are concerned with phenomena or appearances, which do not exist in reality, while thinking investigates that which is *hidden* (ἀποκεκρυμμένα, L 83 = *Adv. math.* VI 138; L 54 = *Adv. math.* VII 369) from the senses.

intellect (νοῦς) and the soul (ψυχή).³³ And because everything that is is being, and being is atoms, and atoms are bodies, and the soul itself is body, it (the soul) is perishable and consisting of the smallest round atoms, which are the atoms of fire.³⁴ So if the soul is material, so, too, is reason, and when we think and know being, we conceive atoms by atoms in us, or being by being. This means that being and thinking is (are) the same for Democritus as for Parmenides, but, contrary to Parmenides, they are not immaterial but atomic and bodily.

So atoms are only thinkable. Yet, on the other hand, since being as atomic is full, it is impenetrable, which means that it is impenetrable for thought. Being full and material, being is mutually exclusive of another being and cannot be located in the same place in the void. This means that being cannot be placed in place of another— or one being cannot be thought by another. Or, being as atoms is in fact not only imperceptible but also not thinkable, and thus only imaginable. So even if Democritus does not explicitly develop this conclusion, his ontology might be in fact the ontology of imagination, where multiple disparate, mutually impenetrable beings are located and move in the imaginary extension of non-being.

Being, then, hides in its imperceptible minuteness, and non-being—in unfathomable darkness. Since the reality is concealed, the *clear* (the perceived things) is *false* (as the appearances), and the *obscure* (the reality of the atoms) is *true* (as the principle of being). Therefore, Democritus' account of being and non-being implies, first, their simplicity and, second, their obscurity. In other words, being and non-being are thinkable, and yet this thinking is non-evident, or both distinct (in that there are indivisible beings) *and* obscure (in that these beings are imperceptible yet thinkable).

---

³³ ταὐτὸν ψυχὴν καὶ νοῦν, L 67–68, 452 = Aristotle. *De an.* 404a28; ταὐτὸν γὰρ ὑπελάμβανον εἶναι ψυχὴν καὶ νοῦν, L 69 = Philoponus. *In de an.* 71.20–21; L 463 = Aristotle. *De respir.* 472a6–8.

³⁴ L 460 = Theophrastus. *De sensu* 58; L 466 = Aetius IV 7.4; L 443–451; L 443a = Aristotle. *De an.* 403b28; L 463 = Aristotle. *De respir.* 471b30.

Imagination. This rather paradoxical conclusion follows from Democritus' insistence on the simplicity of reality, of being and non-being, which should be easily accessible and understandable in the mental visualization of the atoms as situated in and moving through the void. And yet, the truth of reality beyond appearances turns out to be distinct but obscure. This means that in fact being is neither sensibly perceptible nor thinkable but rather *imaginable*.[35] It also means that in fact the first principles in Democritus—being and non-being, the many and the one, discrete and continuous, full and empty, atoms and the void—are not thinkable but rather imaginable concepts. All of Democritus' ontology, then, is based on *imagination*: it is easy and convenient to imagine atoms moving in the void, but it is difficult, or even impossible, to think the atoms as imperceptible and physically indivisible and non-being as the void of an empty extension.

Being. Being *is*. Being is many and full. Being is atoms, or atoms are (is) being. Yet, besides being, there is non-being. Non-being is there. It is one and void. Because atoms can only be in the void, non-being equally *is*. Being is *in* non-being. But *in* being there is no non-being.

Indivisibility. Because being is full, it is impenetrable. Because being is impenetrable, it is indivisible. Being is thus unique, singular, and individual, or atomic. This is what atom means: "indivisible."[36] So atoms are indivisible because they are full. Being is many, divided into the indivisible atoms, which are indivisible in their magnitude and not only in their form.[37] Everything, then, consists of atoms, whose coming together results in the birth of things, while their dissolution results in their perishing.

---

[35] κατὰ φαντασίαν, L 53 = Epiphanius. *Adv. haer.* III 2.9.
[36] Usually, ἡ ἄτομος but also τὸ ἄτομον and ἄτομα in plural, Simplicius. *In Phys.* 36.1–2.
[37] κατὰ μέγεθος ἀδιαίρετα τὰ στοιχεῖα, οὐ κατ' εἶδος μόνον, L 114 = Alexander. *In Met.* 355.14–15.

Democritus' account of being and non-being becomes a powerful heuristic device for explaining the phenomena of and in the world, which is recognized but not shared by Aristotle and his followers, who equally intend to build an ontology that would explain how and what nature is. The main reason for their rejection is Democritus' major claim—which he postulates and thus neither proves nor deduces—that being is many and indivisible in its simplest constituents, or atoms. Aristotle even praises Democritus for postulating his principles not just logically or mathematically but also on the basis of physical arguments, reasoning, and investigations (φυσικοῖς λόγοις, *De gen. et corr.* 316a19–21). In this respect, Democritus' approach is more consistent for Aristotle than that of Plato, who erroneously built his ontology on principles derived from both Eleatics and the Pythagoreans, taking mathematics as the model for ontology and thus establishing indivisible planes (triangles) as the foundation for bodies.[38] Atomism for Aristotle is a powerful theory, and yet it contradicts his own main postulate that the world consists of infinitely divisible magnitudes. The continuous magnitude for Aristotle cannot be made up of indivisibles because indivisibles cannot touch each other and thus cannot make up a continuous and extended magnitude. For a point does not touch a point (οὐκ ἔστι στιγμὴ στιγμῆς ἐχομένη)[39] and does not follow immediately another point (Aristotle. *De caelo* 300a14; *Phys.* 218a18–19). Therefore, the line does not consist of points, which thus are not parts or constituents of the line but are its indivisible *limits* that do not belong to the line but make it definitive and knowable in its being.

Aristotle resolves the aporia that each physical body is divisible (διαιρετόν) in any point and at the same time is indivisible (ἀδιαίρετον) by pointing out that magnitude is divisible *potentially* (δυνάμει), yet is indivisible *actually* (ἐντελεχείᾳ, *De gen. et*

---

[38] L 101 = Aristotle. *De gen et corr.* 315b28–32; Plato. *Tim.* 54a–b.
[39] L 105 = Philoponus. *In de gen. et corr.* 39.23.

corr. 316b19–21). This means that Democritus' "divisibility every way" (πάντῃ διαιρετόν) should be self-contradictory because it is based on a wrong assumption.[40] In other words, the indivisibility of atoms contradicts the fundamental presupposition of mathematics (geometry), that of the infinite divisibility of geometrical and physical magnitudes.[41] Later writers explain the introduction of the concept of the atoms as arising from Democritus' study of mathematical indivisibles, particularly from consideration of the sections of the pyramid as adjacent and yet neither equal nor unequal to each other.[42]

Yet, Democritus takes it that atoms are extended *and* indivisible, and hence that every divisible magnitude, be it physical or geometrical, should consist of the atomic constituents that are continuous yet indivisible.[43] That a magnitude as an atom—be it a body or a line—can be ultimately indivisible *and* extended can only be postulated. Defying Aristotle's objections, this claim, then, is the subject of a distinct yet obscure, and thus deeply paradoxical, knowledge that has great explanatory power for the constitution of being that ultimately might be only imaginable.

Atoms as letters. As indivisible constituents of everything that exists and comes to be as a temporary congregation of many indivisible beings, atoms are elements of all things (στοιχεῖα πάντων).[44] Atoms are the elementary, simple constituents that generate compound bodies (συγκρίματα).[45] But the elements are *letters*, στοιχεῖα, of being and its expression.[46]

---

[40] L 105 = Philoponus. *In de gen et corr.* 35.10.
[41] L 109 = Simplicius. *In Phys.* 512.34; L 126 = Aristotle. *De caelo* 306a26; L 127 = Syrianus. *In Met.* 143.16.
[42] L 126 = Plutarch. *De comm. notit.* 39, 1079d–e.
[43] For the discussion of mathematical indivisibles, see Dmitri Nikulin. "Indivisible Lines in Ancient Philosophy and Mathematics." In *Neoplatonism in Late Antiquity.* Oxford: Oxford University Press, 2019, 205–30.
[44] L 277 = Alexander. *In de sensu* 68.24; L 494; L 121 = Sextus. *Adv. math.* X 252.
[45] L 271 = DL 9.44.
[46] *Littera, pars minima, atomus est nec dividi potest*, L 565 = Isidore. *Hisp. etym.* XIII.2; *litterae per simile dicuntur elementa*, L 565 = Beda Venerabilis I.2.

Yet, as letters are the elements of words but are *not* words themselves, so atoms are the components of bodies and, while being bodily, are not bodies as perceivable and divisible. So, contrary to the claims that Democritus came up with his atomic understanding of being while studying nature or geometry, the study of language might have been the origin of the doctrine of atoms as elementary constituents of the perceivable, and it is thus logical rather than physical.

The "book of nature," then, is written in an alphabet in which atoms are its letters. But the alphabet consists of a finite number of letters. Yet, if the number of different atoms is infinite, then the text of the world is written in a language whose words are transcribed by an infinite alphabet. If the number of letters is infinite and all the letters are used, then such is also the number of the words. The dictionary of the world, then, comprises an infinite number of vocables. But how can we read a book that consists of an infinite number of words made up of an infinite number of letters?

The infinite

Infinity of the atoms. According to Aristotle, the Atomists took atoms to be infinite in number while indivisible in magnitude.[47] The number of atoms in a body should be finite because otherwise a body would be infinitely divisible, whereas, according to Democritus, atoms are precisely the limit of the divisibility in a body. Atoms are small but not infinitely small. Democritus does not explain why this is the case, but one might assume that infinitesimal bodies can be neither perceived nor thought, and thus the concept of the infinitely small yet indivisible body is logically impossible and self-contradictory. Atoms are similar to minute pieces of dust or motes in a sunbeam (ξύσματα), which, however, are not further divisible.[48] In this respect, the properties of the atoms are contrary

---

[47] εἶναι τὰ πρῶτα μεγέθη πλήθει μὲν ἄπειρα, μεγέθει δὲ ἀδιαίρετα, L 109 = Aristotle. *De caelo* 303a4–6; L140a = Aristotle. *De an.* 404a1–2; L 240 = Aristotle. *De gen. et corr.* 314a21; L 225 = Alexander. *De mixt.* 213.14.
[48] L 200 = Aristotle. *De an.* 404a3.

to those of Aristotle's magnitudes, which are finite (for an infinite magnitude cannot be thought and traversed), yet infinitely divisible (in which respect they differ from numbers, which are divisible down to the not further divisible monad). But atoms are also infinite in number. Moreover, not only is the number of atoms infinite, but such also is the number of their forms, shapes (μορφὰς καὶ σχήματα), and sizes.[49] Thus, fire is made of the smallest spherical atoms, while the other three elements are made up of atoms of different size.[50] And because atoms are being(s), they cannot change, and therefore they cannot change their size.[51] The grand total of the world, then, is made by and from the combinations of atoms, which differ in their shape (σχῆμα, as Δ and N), position (θέσις, as Z and N), and order (τάξις, as ZN and NZ).[52] These examples refer to letters and thus to the alphabet of the world, which further supports the hypothesis of the linguistic and logical origin of the doctrine of the atoms.

An aphoristic formulation of Democritus' doctrine, according to a scholiast, is "all in all" (πάντα ἐν πᾶσιν); that is, all the atoms in their infinite variety of shapes and sizes are found in, and contribute to, the constitution of the world.[53] In Aristotle's and Philoponus' interpretation, Democritus' atomistic doctrine replicates that of

---

[49] τὰς ἀτόμους δὲ ἀπείρους εἶναι κατὰ μέγεθος καὶ πλῆθος, L 271 = DL 9.44. See also L 140a, L 200 = Aristotle. De an. 404a1–2; L 222 = Aristotle. De gen. et corr. 325b24; L 145 = Aristotle. Phys. 203a19; L 204 = L 227 = Simplicius. In de caelo 295.7–8; οὐ μόνον τῷ πλήθει ἄπειρα, ἀλλὰ καὶ τῇ τῶν σχημάτων διαφορᾷ, L 141 = Philoponus. In de gen. et corr. 12.2–5.

[50] L 231 = Aristotle. De caelo 306b32–33; L 275 = Aristotle. De caelo 303a14; Simplicius. In de caelo 610.18–19; Themistius. In de caelo 178.32–33.

[51] *Magnitudine transmutationem non admittat*, L 275 = Themistius. In de caelo 180.17–18.

[52] L 240 = Aristotle. De gen. et corr. 314a21; L 244 = Simplicius. In de caelo 242.22–23; Philoponus. In de gen. et corr. 12.30; L 241 = Aristotle. Met. 985b4. In his native (Ionian) dialect, Democritus also called shape ῥυσμός, position τροπή, and order διαθιγή (Aristotle. Met. 1042b11; L 247 = Simplicius. In Phys. 28.18–19).

[53] L 144 = Wilhelm Frommel, Ed. *Scholia in Aelii Aristidis sophistae Orationes Panathenaicam et Platonicas*. Frankfurt: Broenneri, 1826, 225B; 356.

DEMOCRITUS: NON-BEING AS THE VOID 57

Anaxagoras' panspermia, according to which various forms comprise physical things.[54]

But if atoms come in a variety of different sizes, there might be (very) large atoms. According to one late testimony, there can even be an atom the size of the world (κοσμιαίαν).[55] The atom the size of the world might still be imperceptible because it would have transcended the limits of perception, but it would not leave room or place for any other atoms because it would have occupied the entirety of the world. Yet, as said, atoms are very small, full, indivisible, and, as such, imperceptible. Large atoms contradict this condition, which means that the infinity of shapes and sizes should be the infinity of imperceptibles.

Why are atoms not finite but rather infinite in number and shape? Simplicius' answer is that atoms are infinite in their number and form because of their smallness and fullness (διὰ σμικρότητα καὶ ναστότητα ἀτόμους).[56] This explanation seems to be rather perplexing because one can think of a world consisting of bodies made up of a finite number of atoms of a finite number of shapes. That is, a world book can be written in the language that consists of a finite number of words comprising a finite number of letters, as it is for Galileo.[57] Then only if the world is infinite or the number of worlds is infinite can the number of their constituent atoms be infinite. But this still does not explain the infinite variety of the shapes and forms of atoms. Only if we assume that there is *no reason* why the atoms should be limited in number and shape can they be unlimited or infinite in both respects, for the ontological structure of the atoms—their indivisibility, fullness, and smallness—does not imply or suggest any limitations to their number and shapes. So the

---

[54] L 142 = Aristotle. *De sensu* 441a18; πανσπερμίαν φησὶ τὸ πλῆθος τῶν σχημάτων, Philoponus. *In de an.* 67.30; L 143 = Aristotle. *Met.* 1009a26–28.
[55] L 207 = Aetius I 12.16; Eusebius. *Praep. Evang.* XIV 23.2.3.
[56] τὰς διὰ σμικρότητα καὶ ναστότητα ἀτόμους ἀπείρους οὔσας κατά τε τὸν ἀριθμὸν καὶ τὰ σχήματα, L 237 = Simplicius. *In de caelo* 609.18–19.
[57] Galileo Galilei. "Excerpts from The Assayer." In *Discoveries and Opinions of Galileo Galilei*. Trans. Stillman Drake. Garden City, NY: Doubleday, 1957, 237–38.

infinity of the atoms is primarily *negative*: there is no ground for them to be limited; hence, they are unlimited or infinite in number. Because there is no reason for the atoms to be finite in number, their infinity cannot be properly grasped by reason, which thinks in finite terms, and even less so by the senses. So how do we know their infinity? The only other way of conceiving the infinite is by imagination, and yet it represents the infinite negatively by not being finite. But is the infinity of the atoms, then, actually or potentially infinite? Is the number of atoms such that there can always be a greater number of them than any given one, and thus the number of atoms would be that of the natural numbers? There is no clear answer to these questions in the extant fragments, but one fragment that comes from Epicurus suggests that the number of differences in shapes of the atoms (ταῖς διαφοραῖς τῶν σχημάτων) is indeterminate or incomprehensible (ἀπερίληπτα) because the observed number of their varieties cannot be explained by a finite number of shapes. In other words, the number of letters in the world alphabet is not finite. But then the number of atoms of each form is absolutely, or simply, infinite (ἁπλῶς ἄπειροι), whereas the number of the differences among the forms is not infinite but only incomprehensible or indeterminate.[58]

That the followers of Epicurus revised the atomistic doctrine ascribed to Leucippus and Democritus by accepting the actual infinity of the number of atoms, while taking the number of their sizes to be inconceivably great but not infinite, is further supported by testimony from Alexander of Aphrodisias preserved by Philoponus.[59] The reason for this revision might be that if the number of atoms is infinite, and each comes in an infinite variety of forms, then there will be an infinity of infinites, which appears

---

[58] ταῖς δὲ διαφοραῖς οὐχ ἁπλῶς ἄπειροι ἀλλὰ μόνον ἀπερίληπτοι, L 234 = Epicurus. *Epist.* I 42.

[59] ἐκεῖνοι [the followers of Epicurus] μὲν γὰρ κατὰ μὲν τὸ πλῆθος ἀπείρους τὰς ἀτόμους ὑποτίθενται, κατὰ δὲ τὰ σχήματα ἀπεριλήπτους μέν, οὐκ ἀπείρους δέ, L 141 = Philoponus. *In de gen. et corr.* 12.7–9.

to be greater that the infinite. And yet, if the infinite is taken as countable or isomorphic with the set of natural numbers, as both Democritus and Epicurus seem to consider it, then the resulting infinity will be exactly the same in its cardinal number, or equal to the infinity of natural numbers. Yet, this argument was made and elaborated only much later by Georg Cantor with the development of set theory.

So Epicurus' answer to the question proposed by the ontology of his predecessors suggests that the number of forms or shapes of the atoms is potentially infinite, or is larger than any given number, whereas the number of all the atoms is infinitely infinite, which might be understood as either equally potentially infinite (similar to the infinity of natural numbers), or as actually infinite, complete, and such that one cannot take anything beyond and outside it. The number of the atoms may very well be actually infinite. Yet, there is neither textual evidence nor a reason in Democritus' understanding of being and non-being that provides a definite answer to the question of whether the number of atoms is potentially or actually infinite. It remains incomprehensible and infinite beyond (textual) reason.

Infinity of the void. Aristotle reports that for Democritus "the eternal and the infinite have no origin, and the cause is the origin but the eternal is infinite (τὸ δ' ἀεὶ ἄπειρον)."[60] This means that, since being and non-being have no origin and thus no cause that might make them be, they are equiprimordial, eternal, and infinite. Everything that is—being and non-being—is un-original: atoms have no origin (ἀγενήτους),[61] and such also is the void. Only that which comes to be is infinitely original.

Being and non-being are thus infinite, yet they are opposite in their relation to infinity. For while atoms are continuous, indivisible,

---

[60] τοῦ μὲν ἀεὶ καὶ ἀπείρου οὐκ ἔστιν ἀρχή, τὸ δὲ διὰ τί ἀρχή, τὸ δ' ἀεὶ ἄπειρον, L13 = Aristotle. *De gen. animal.* 742b20–22; cf. *Phys.* 251b15; L14–21.
[61] L 230 = Philoponus. *In Phys.* 398.11–15.

and infinite in number, the void is equally continuous and yet is one and infinite in its divisibility and extension. As Simplicius explains, "Democritus considers the nature of the eternal to be small entities infinite in number. Besides them, he accepts place as infinite in magnitude."[62] Void is the infinite (ἄπειρον) in which the infinity of the atoms moves.[63]

Aristotle himself argues against the void as infinite as do his followers, particularly Simplicius. For Aristotle, the infinity of the void implies an ontological impossibility: if there is an infinite void as infinite place (τόπος), then the body in it should also be infinite because in the eternal there is no difference between possibility (ἐνδέχεσθαι) and being (εἶναι).[64] So a body that can be in any place in the void will be in every place, which is impossible. Yet, this objection does not hold for Democritus, because for him non-being as the void *is* in actuality, and not potentiality, and is that *in* which being, not as one infinite body but as the infinity of smallest beings as atoms, is and moves.

Being and non-being thus establish two kinds of the infinite. One infinite is *in* the other: the infinite number of atoms always move in the infinite void.[65] And while the atoms are infinite "from above" (infinite in number) but indivisible "from below" (each atom is indivisible), the void, on the contrary, is infinite "from below" (infinitely divisible as extension in which atoms are) but indivisible "from above" (there is one void). This distinction matches exactly the already mentioned Aristotelian distinction between numbers and magnitudes, which behave exactly in the same way with respect to infinity and divisibility.

---

[62] τὴν τῶν ἀϊδίων φύσιν εἶναι μικρὰς οὐσίας πλῆθος ἀπείρους· ταύταις δὲ τόπον ἄλλον ὑποτίθησιν ἄπειρον τῷ μεγέθει, L 172 = Simplicius. *In de caelo* 295.2–3.
[63] L 295 = Simplicius. *In de caelo* 242.21–23.
[64] L 1, L 140 = Aristotle. *Phys.* 203b29–30.
[65] L 16 = Simplicius. *In de caelo* 583.20–22. Cf. ἀεὶ κινεῖσθαι τὰ πρῶτα σώματα ἐν τῷ κενῷ καὶ τῷ ἀπείρῳ, L 16 = Aristotle. *De caelo* 300b8; χωρίον κενὸν μέγεθος ἀπεριόριστον, L 265 = Dionysius apud Eusebius. *Praep. Evang.* XIV 23.2.3.

Infinity of the worlds. If the alphabet of the book of world is infinite, and the void in which it is being written is infinite, then the number of books is infinite too. In other (finite) words, worlds are infinite in number. Or, because the void is infinite and the atoms are infinite in number, there are an infinite number of worlds.

An atomistic argument preserved in Philoponus suggests that if a world exists in a part of the void, it should be in the entire void. The argument is based on the principle of *isonomia*, which suggests that there is no reason for a world to be here rather than there, which is why the world should be everywhere in what it is in, or in the void.[66] This principle has already been used above in response to the question of why atoms are infinite in their number and shapes—for there is no reason for them not to be. But because the void is infinite, the worlds in it are also multiplied to infinity.[67] The conclusion that the infinite number (τῷ πλήθει) of worlds came to be in the infinite void out of the infinite number of atoms is further supported by a substantial number of testimonies.[68]

But where are we in this unfathomable infinite? In its transcendence of any limit, infinity remains unknowable and thus threatening in its eternal indifference. So the question is how we can meaningfully inhabit an infinite world. A way out would be to place us in the middle of the infinite. Hence, as Simplicius mentions, most thinkers, including Democritus, say that the Earth is in the middle of the cosmos.[69] According to another not particularly reliable testimony, our world is a sphere (σφαιροειδῆ τὸν κόσμον),[70] which suggests that the infinite should have a center. Yet, if there is an infinity of worlds, then there will be an infinite number of

---

[66] L 2 = Simplicius. *In Phys.* 28.25–26.
[67] ἀπείρου οὖν ὄντος τοῦ κενοῦ, ἄπειροι ἔσονται καὶ οἱ κόσμοι, L 1 = Philoponus. *In Phys.* 405.25–27.
[68] L 343–60; L 329 = Aristotle. *Phys.* 205b22–24; L 355 = DL 9.31; ἀπείρους τε εἶναι κόσμους, L 289, 366 = DL 9.44; L 345 = Simplicius. *In de caelo* 202.16–18; L 44 = Simplicius. *In de caelo* 310.6–7; L 1 = Simplicius. *In Phys.* 467.15–16.
[69] οἱ μὲν πλεῖστοι ἐπὶ τοῦ μέσου κεῖσθαι λέγουσι τὴν γῆν, L 403 = Simplicius. *In Phys.* 511.22.
[70] L 385 = Aetius II.2.2.

centers to them, and thus no preferable position for our being in them and their cognition. So we should appreciate the radicality of Democritus' approach, who long before early modern science put us in the middle of the infinite, in which we are lost among the innumerable atomic combinations and the immensity of one extended void, and yet which we embrace in our comprehension of its most fundamental constituents, being and non-being.

Accident and necessity. So being, infinite in number, and non-being, infinite in its extent and divisibility, produce an infinite number of the worlds. Constituted by the two ontological principles, then, the existent is also infinite, consisting of many beings or atoms that exist and yet constantly change their location and arrangement in one non-being, or are in incessant motion in the void. Therefore, the infinite worlds come to be and pass away, coexisting synchronously and existing in succession.[71] At any given moment, some worlds come to be, and others pass away.[72] The infinite worlds follow each other, and thus infinite worlds come to replace each other. Worlds in Democritus turn into other worlds, which consist of the same atoms or beings.[73] When one world dissolves and disappears, since the number of worlds is infinite, and they constantly come to change into each other, there is no necessity that a new world will be exactly the same.[74] So when one world perishes, it does not necessarily have to produce again the same world. And because the worlds are infinite in number and are moving eternally, they arise and perish an infinite number of times.[75] Their motions and transformations are thus infinite and eternal. The immense entirety of being and non-being thus consists of a grand total of

---

[71] L 347 = Aristotle. *Phys.* 203b25–26; L300 = Aristotle. *Phys.* 250b18–19; L 382 = DL 9.44.
[72] τοὺς μὲν γίγνεσθαι τοὺς δὲ φθείρεσθαι, L 348 = Aristotle. *Phys.* 250b19–20; L 343 = Simplicius. *In de caelo* 294.26–27.
[73] εἰς ἑτέρους κόσμους μεταβάλλοντες, L 344 = Simplicius. *In de caelo* 310.5–17.
[74] L 44 = Simplicius. *In de caelo* 310.7–8.
[75] L 301 = Simplicius. *In Phys.* 1121.5–9.

infinite worlds, constantly being born and disappearing, turning into each other without end.

Aristotle, for whom the world is one, limited, and eternal, cannot accept this endless infinity of worlds, which, having no end to their transformations, can have no *telos* or purpose. He offers a solution to the Democritean puzzle by claiming that in the beginning everything (the world) was potentially and not actually.[76] However, according to the principle of isonomia, there is no reason for a world to appear now rather than then, just as there is no reason for a beginning or an end of a change. This means that in Democritus' world, even if due to their weight the atoms themselves move necessarily in straight lines,[77] there is literally *no reason* for the existence of being and non-being, for the infinite atoms and the void, as well as for the motions and changes of things.

Put otherwise, the worlds are driven by *chance* rather than by necessity: the motion of things and their transformations are spontaneous (τὸ αὐτόματον),[78] or have no identifiable cause except for a vortex (δίνη),[79] an irrational force among things that, as combination of atoms, comes to be by accident (ὡς ἔτυχε), and yet eventually puts the world in order (τάξις).[80] But for Aristotle and his followers, the entirety of the transformations of things and worlds without a reason is itself unthinkable, ἄλογον, because for him

---

[76] ἦν ὁμοῦ πάντα δυνάμει, ἐνεργείᾳ δ' οὔ, L 381 = Aristotle. *Met.* 1069b23. According to Themistius' testimony, for the Atomists, before the world came to be in the infinite void during an infinite time, there were infinite bodies, as if indivisible (*ante mundum in inanitate ac tempore infinito innumerabilia corpora velut insectilia extitisse asserunt*, L 381 = Themistius. *In de caelo* 162.24–26).

[77] Atoms are solid (ναστάς). This makes them heavy (βαρέα) and the cause of heaviness in composite bodies, while the void is the cause of lightness (Simplicius. *In de caelo* 269.4). Those bodies that have more void are light (air), and those that have less void are heavy (earth, L 377 = Philoponus. *In Phys.* 644.25). Epicurus later denied even the necessity of the straight downward motion of atoms by famously assigning the swerve (*declinatio*, παρέγκλισις) to the atoms in order to preserve the freedom of the will (L 38 = Cicero. *De nat. deorum* I 25.69).

[78] L 18 = Aristotle. *Phys.* 196a24.

[79] L 18 = Aristotle. *Phys.* 196a26; L 23 = DL 9.45.

[80] L 305 = Aristotle. *De caelo* 300b31; Simplicius. *In de caelo* 589.4; and L 288 = Aristotle. *Phys.* 196a27–28.

the order in and of the being of nature should be accounted for by logos. Yet, for Democritus such order is the result of chance that governs the infinite transformations of the infinite worlds, and not reason or logos, precisely because the worlds and motions are infinite, and reason or logos can only rule, think, and sing the finite and the limited. The fleeing and ever-transforming order of things in the atomistic worlds is thus the result of an accident.

The infinity of worlds is thus a rather stunning concept for those who, like Plato and Aristotle, understand the world as governed by being, which is defined by and as limit (*Tim.* 32c–33a; *De caelo* 276a18ff). This makes the world one finite and beautiful cosmos, driven by the necessity of reason as being, rather than accident. But for Democritus, we stand in awe in front of an utterly fascinating, abyssal, immeasurable, sublime, fleeing, and ever transforming world, one of the infinite worlds, which we cannot know in its entirety, yet which we inhabit and come to know in its most fundamental constituents, in being and non-being.

Void as extension and empty place. This unfathomable multitude of worlds is infinite, "infiniting" in the void as its "where" or place. As Simplicius tells us, the followers of Democritus consider the void to be an empty place, or a place devoid of bodies.[81] Plato, Aristotle, and Simplicius, being afraid of the nothing of the void, thus try to exclude it from being and from the orders of the existent.[82] Yet, for Democritus the void is the place of and for bodies, which is besides the bodies and atoms but allows being to be. Therefore, *to be is to be in place*, or to be in the void. But there is no place for the void itself.[83] There is no "itself" to the void, since it is nowhere and everywhere.

---

[81] τὸν τόπον τὸ κενόν, L 250 = Simplicius. *In Phys.* 394.25–395.1; τὸ κενὸν εἶναι τόπον ἐστερημένον σώματος, L 250 = Simplicius. *In Phys.* 397.4.

[82] Aristotle says that Plato denied the existence of the void (κενὸν γὰρ οὐκ εἶναί φησι, L 338 = Aristotle. *De gen. et corr.* 325b3), which would suggest that χώρα as the receptacle of being (Plato. *Tim.* 52a) is not the void.

[83] Contrary to Sedley's claim that the void (vacuum) is "a quasi-substance and place-occupier." See David Sedley. "Two Conceptions of Vacuum." *Phronesis* 27:2 (1982), 180. See also the critique by Andrea Reichenberger. "Zum Begriff des Leeren in der

DEMOCRITUS: NON-BEING AS THE VOID 65

The void is thus the condition of the possibility of being, of the existence of the atoms. If being is fullness, then being as the being of indivisible atoms is the pure, impenetrable *inside*. The void, then, is pure *outsideness*. There is nothing to the void except for being outside.

Void, then, is a disembodied, empty extension. Such an extension is the negativity of the bodily, and yet it can be on its own because the void can exist without a body. Void is the extension (διάστημα) between the surrounding extremities of the body,[84] sometimes filled with a body and sometimes remaining empty. It is an extension (ἐπέκτασις)[85] as a pure interval in which something—anything bodily—can extend, protend, be placed, and thus can be. Simplicius even claims that the Atomists accept the existence of the void not only in the world (ἐν τῷ κόσμῳ) but also outside the world (ἔξω τοῦ κόσμου).[86] Yet, this outside is nothing, since the void is extended and an extension, not because of being as body that is placed in it, but despite and besides it.

As non-being without being, void is rather an *imaginable* extension. Indeed, the void can neither be perceived nor properly thought—only negatively: it is seen as darkness and is thought as being concealed, always dimly and only indistinctly. Void is an extension of and in the imagination that places indivisible beings within the void and makes them move by the power of imagination.

Empty of anything and for anything, the void is nothing but being extended. As pure extension, it is three-dimensional and uniform in every direction (πάντῃ ἀδιάφορον),[87] which means that it is not differentiated and has no preference for a being to be

Philosophie der frühen Atomisten." *Göttinger Forum für Altertumswissenschaft* 5:1 (2002), 105–22.

[84] τὸ διάστημα τὸ μεταξὺ τῶν ἐσχάτων τοῦ περιέχοντος τὸν τόπον ἀνάγκη εἶναι, L 254 = Simplicius. *In Phys.* 571.22–27.
[85] L 259 = Simplicius. *In de caelo.* 634.5.
[86] L 270 = Simplicius. *In Phys.* 648.13–14.
[87] L 266 = Simplicius. *In Phys.* 601.20–22.

placed in it. Powerless and impotent (ἀδύνατον καὶ ἀδρανὲς),[88] the void is entirely indifferent toward anything. Hence, there are no preferences in the void, no natural orientation, no up and down.[89] Void is a total *disorientation*.

Separation. So the void is powerless and impotent, and yet it extends. Non-being, disembodied in and as void, has no power of its own, and yet bodies are separated and divided by the void (διωρισμένα τῷ κενῷ).[90] The void divides and separates beings without having the power to do so. Rather, being excludes another being from being in the place it has in and of the void.

Constituted by the atoms, bodies are separated from each other by an empty interval (διάστημα) between the bodies that prevents them from being continuous.[91] The void is a pure *between*, μεταξύ, that extends between beings, making them discrete and causing bodies to be non-continuous. Only non-being, as has been said, is continuous, abyssally divisible ever further.

Bodies are therefore separated from each other in and by the void's non-power of non-being. But the void is not only between the bodies but is also inside the bodies as assemblages of atoms, dissipated and diffused within the bodies.[92] For the Atomists, this yields proof of the existence of the void, namely, from the rarefied and dense (διὰ τοῦ μανοῦ καὶ πυκνοῦ), explained by the dispersion of many void intervals (τὸ πολλὰ κενά) inside the body.[93] Aristotle and, as we will see, Simplicius vigorously reject this argument by questioning its very assumption because contraction and extension of a rarefied body mean for them the exclusion and inclusion of

---

[88] L 251 = Simplicius. *In Phys.* 533.18–19.
[89] L 361 = Aristotle. *De caelo* 308a.17–18.
[90] L 261 = Aristotle. *De caelo* 275b29–30. Cf.: τῷ κενῷ διείργεσθαι, L 269 = Philoponus. *In de an.* 67.19–20; L 268 = Themistius. *In Phys.* 123.16; Simplicius. *In Phys.* 648.20. Cf. L 252 = [Aristotle]. *De Mel., Xenoph., Gorgia* 980a6 (ascribed to Leucippus).
[91] L 255 = Aristotle. *Phys.* 213a28–29; L 270 = Simplicius. *In Phys.* 648.11–12; L 26 = Cicero. *Acad. priora* II 38.121.
[92] τὸ παρεσπαρμένον κενόν, L 259 = Alexander apud Simplicius. *In de caelo.* 634.10; ἐγκατεσπαρμένον, L 270 = Philoponus. *In Phys.* 613.21.
[93] L 256 = Aristotle. *Phys.* 216b22–217a3.

some other bodily element, such as air or water. Contrary to the Atomists, Aristotle and Simplicius take body to be a continuous, and thus infinitely divisible, magnitude. From their perspective, a body is indivisible only as a logical subject but is always further (potentially) infinitely divisible as a magnitude. The two ontologies are at odds and are mutually exclusive of each other, since the Atomists and the Aristotelians cannot agree on their understanding of being and thus inevitably argue past each other. And yet, even if they realize their irreconcilable difference, they keep talking to each other in a desperate attempt to fathom the unfathomable, the non-being of the void.

Void and motion. Since void is the place for being as placed in the void, it is also the place for motion in which bodies come to be constituted out of atoms, transform, and move in place in ever-changing, infinite worlds. Void is that in which the atoms are and move, or, in the words of Epicurus, beings move in non-being (φέρεται τὰ ὄντα ἐν τῷ μὴ ὄντι).[94] The infinites are transformed in the infinite: the infinite number of atoms move in one infinite void (ἄπειρα ἐν ἀπείρῳ τὰ κινούμενα).[95]

Infinite in number, atoms are carried spontaneously through the world in a vortex or whirl (δίνη).[96] Since the void is an empty extension where motion is possible from one empty place to another, the Atomists accept only locomotion, while Aristotle recognizes several kinds of motion as change, including locomotion (κατὰ τόπον, φορά), change in quantity (κατὰ μέγεθος), and change in state (κατὰ πάθος).[97] The atomistic locomotion is eternal[98] and thus does not cease to be. Atoms never stop and they keep striking each

---

[94] L 490 = Plutarch. *Quaest. conviv.* VIII 3.2.
[95] L 305 = Aristotle. *De caelo* 300b31.
[96] φέρεσθαι δ' ἐν τῷ ὅλῳ δινουμένας, DL 9.44; L 288 = Aristotle. *Phys.* 196a26–28.
[97] L 304 = Aristotle. *Phys.* 260a26–28.
[98] Motion is *sempiternum* for Leucippus (L 309 = Themistius. *In Met.* 16.34–35) or is *ex aeterno tempore.* L 15 = Cicero. *De fin.* I 6.17.

other, regrouping and thus producing new atomic compounds (τὰ συγκρίματα) and composites (συστήματα).[99] But the void itself is motionless (τὸ κενὸν ἀκίνητόν ἐστιν) because it is one and empty, providing the place for motion.[100] Besides, as has been said, it has no place in which it could have moved. Void is the condition of the possibility of motion as locomotion (διὰ τὸ κενόν).[101]

Aristotle attempts to refute the existence of the void, which, on the contrary, for him, constitutes the condition of the impossibility of motion, because for him bodies cannot move in the void at all (ἀδύνατον κινηθῆναι), since there are no distinctions in the void, no up and down, and no resistance, which defines the speed of a body. In the void, a body both would not move at all and would move with the greatest speed or instantly.[102] For Aristotle, there is no reason why a body in the void would move here rather than there, so no body will ever move. In the void, everything is totally disoriented, displaced, and misplaced.

Yet, for Democritus bodies move precisely because there is no resistance, no differentiation, and no preference in the nothing of the void. Motion, then, becomes the testimony and proof of the existence of the non-existent or the void, because if there is no void, there can be no motion.[103] Physics as the science of motion, then, is natural history as an account of places that bodies occupy and leave, or topography, which, similar to the *Periplous*, describes sailings around the void from one inhabited place to another. Motion is a permanent and immanent state of the atoms and bodies caused by the indifference of the void, which cannot cause anything

[99] L 289 = DL 9.44. Atoms join together and intertwine, thereby giving rise to new compound bodies: συντιθέμενα δὲ καὶ περιπλεκόμενα γεννᾶν, L 146 = Aristotle. *De gen. et corr.* 325a34.; L 307 = Cicero. *De fato* 20.46.
[100] L 304 = Alexander apud Simplicius. *In Phys.* 1196.12–13.
[101] L 313 = Aristotle. *Phys.* 265b24; L 332 = Aristotle. *Phys.* 265b17; L 333 = Simplicius. *In Phys.* 1318.33–34, 1320.16–17.
[102] L 314 = Aristotle. *Phys.* 216a16–21; 217a3–10.
[103] L 5 = Aristotle. *Phys.* 214b28–29; L 257 = Aristotle. *Phys.* 216a23–24; L 260 = Aristotle. *Phys.* 214a22 = Philoponus. *In Phys.* 630.15–16.

but rather offers itself to being in its withdrawal from being. Being, then, is being in place, or being emplaced, which can always change or move precisely because non-being does not define being and allows it to be *in* non-being.

Void as non-being. Once again, Democritus' fundamental ontological claim is incisive and concise: there is the full (τὸ στερεόν or τὸ πλῆρες), which is being (ὄν)—and the void, which is non-being (οὐκ ὄν).[104] As non-being that has nothing of its own, void can be defined only negatively: it is not a body (τὸ γὰρ κενὸν οὐ σῶμα).[105] Positively, void is extension, which, however, is also defined negatively, as empty, and it is thus devoid of bodies or atoms as beings. In Aristotle's interpretation, which is his own understanding of non-being, void is the privation of being.[106]

And yet, as we have seen, the truth of being and non-being lies in the depths and is obscure. Indivisible, imperceptible, and unseen, being is hidden in plain sight, and the void deceptively reveals itself as that where nothing is, as emptiness and darkness. Being, which is meant to be clear, simple, and precise, sinks into the unfathomable non-being of the great void (μέγα κενόν).[107] Being is infinitely split into infinitely many discrete indivisibles in one infinite, continuous non-being.[108] Yet, as said, void has no power for dividing or multiplying being because it is non-being and has no being of its own. Rather, non-being *disrupts* being, making it plural and mutually impenetrable: in the infinite plurality of beings, one indivisible being is exclusive of another being. Hence, all beings are mutually other to each other and to their common other, to the void as non-being.

---

[104] L 238 = Aristotle. *Phys.* 188a22.
[105] L 263 = Alexander. *In Met.* 60.5.
[106] τὸ γὰρ κενὸν μὴ ὄν τι καὶ στέρησις δοκεῖ εἶναι, L 249 = Aristotle. *Phys.* 215a11; τό τε κενὸν μὴ ὂν καὶ τοῦ ὄντος οὐθὲν μεῖόν [Bekker, μὴ ὄν] φησιν εἶναι, L 146 = Aristotle. *De gen. et corr.* 325a27-28; cf. Themistius. *In Phys.* 129.8-9.
[107] L 289 = DL 9.44; L 291.
[108] L 295 = Simplicius. *In de caelo* 242.21-22.

So being and non-being in Democritus are not just opposites (ἐναντία)[109] but are unmediated opposites. Becoming is not a mediation between being and non-being because bodies that come to be and pass away are the combination and separation (σύγκρισις καὶ διάκρισις)[110] of beings as atoms in non-being as the void. Beings are being constantly shuffled in non-being, although not by non-being, which remains an indifferent, empty extension as a possibility of void, but spontaneously and without an ultimate end.

As not mediated, being and non-being should be contradictory,[111]—and yet they are not because being is, but such is also non-being. Non-being *is*. The void *is* (κενὸν γὰρ εἶναι).[112] Non-being is thus the condition of the existence of being as beings because being is *in* non-being: atoms are *in* the void.

Nothing. As non-being, void is nothing. Nothing is void and is forever voided. Nothing is empty because it is nothing, no thing. Nothing is nothing, yet because it is nothing, it is not nothing but the condition of possibility of being. Since nothing is nothing, it does not affect something, or being, which already *is* in nothing and cannot be otherwise. Therefore, nothing *is*.

This paradoxical conclusion follows from the atomistic ontology, according to which void *is*, ἔστι κενόν.[113] And since void is non-being, then nothing is. As an infinite and abyssal emptiness, void is the existing, extended nothing. And because the Atomists take being to be bodily in its substance, they have to assume the void to be that in which there is no body, or nothing at all.[114] Nothing is in nothing, and hence nothing is *in* the void and *is* void.

---

[109] L 188 = Philoponus. *In Phys.* 110.9–10.
[110] L 328 = Aristotle. *Phys.* 187a31.
[111] τὸ δὲ πλῆρες γὰρ καὶ τὸ κενὸν τὰ ἐναντία, L 8 = Aristotle. *Met.* 1009a22–25; Alexander. *In Met.* 304.2–5; L 188 = Philoponus. *In Phys.* 110.9–10.
[112] L 146 = Aristotle. *De gen. et corr.* 325a31.
[113] L 259 = Simplicius. *In de caelo.* 634.4–5.
[114] οἰόμενοι δὲ τὸ ὂν ἅπαν εἶναι σῶμα φασίν, ἐν ᾧ ὅλως μηδέν ἐστι τοῦτ᾽ εἶναι κενόν, L 255 = Aristotle. *Phys.* 213a29–31.

Nothing comes from nothing. Because nothing is nothing, it cannot affect anything, and thus it cannot affect nothing. Hence, Democritus has to argue against Xeniades, who taught that everything comes out of nothing and dissolves into nothing.[115] For Democritus, on the contrary, nothing comes from nothing. Nothing comes to be from nor is destroyed into non-being.[116] Because nothing is nothing, its coming to being from non-being is indifferent, or is not different, from not coming to be. The being of nothing is thus non-being that paradoxically *is*.

Everything already is, even if it be nothing. Nothing has no power to generate anything, being or non-being, and thus itself. Hence, nothing produced is in the atomistic world, neither void as non-being or being as indivisible beings. When a world perishes, it does not disappear into the nothing of the void, but rather ceases to be together with the nothing of non-being and the void. There is no generation from nothing, and from being(s) nothing comes to be.[117] Nothing is indifferent and can only contain or afford being to be in the extended, empty nothing.

Δέν *and* μηδέν. For the Atomists, "being exists no more than non-being (οὐθὲν μᾶλλον τὸ ὂν τοῦ μὴ ὄντος εἶναί φασιν, Aristotle. *Met.* 985b8)." Or non-being *is* no more than being, hence, non-being *is*. If non-being is nothing, then nothing is. Yet, because it is nothing, it is indifferent to being and being-something. As we have seen, Democritus' central principle that regulates the location and distribution of being in non-being, that of isonomia, is formulated negatively and suggests that there is no reason for a single atom or the entire world to be here and now rather than there and then. This also implies that things are exactly the same way in the small as they are in the large of the world(s), or that what

---

[115] ἐκ τοῦ μὴ ὄντος πᾶν τὸ γινόμενον γίνεσθαι, καὶ εἰς τὸ μὴ ὂν πᾶν τὸ φθειρόμενον φθείρεσθαι, L 75 = Sextus. *Adv. math.* VII 53.
[116] μηδέν τε ἐκ τοῦ μὴ ὄντος γίνεσθαι μηδὲ εἰς τὸ μὴ ὂν φθείρεσθαι, DL 9.44.
[117] ἐκ μὲν γὰρ τοῦ μὴ ὄντος οὐκ εἶναι γένεσιν, ἐκ δὲ τῶν ὄντων μηδὲν ἂν γενέσθαι, L 42 = Plutarch. *Adv. Colot.* 8.

and how something is and happens in the microcosm, so it is in the macrocosm.[118] The principle of isonomia, then, is itself grounded in nothing because "nothing is more such than such (τὸ μηδὲν μᾶλλον τοιοῦτον ἢ τοιοῦτον εἶναι)."[119] Put otherwise, there is no grounding of isonomia, which means that it can only be postulated.

Because nothing is nothing, it can be neither properly thought nor adequately expressed in logos, remaining obscure and yet absently present as the non-being of the void. Nothing can be said about nothing. So everything we say about nothing is beside the point. Hence, Democritus has to invent radically new ways of speaking negatively about nothing as the utter and ultimate negativity. He has to speak at the limit of language and think at the brink of thought. According to Plutarch, "thing [δέν, a neologism] is no more than nothing [μηδέν; literally, no-thing], where 'thing' stands for body [as being], and 'nothing'—for the void [as non-being], for, according to him, the void has its own proper nature and existence."[120] Δέν, then, is the other of nothing and thus is μη-μηδέν, not-nothing. Or being is not-non-being.

Thus, Democritus' apparently simple and transparent ontology of "there is being and non-being as the atoms and the void" is deeply paradoxical and ultimately elusive for thought and thus can only be imagined. For non-being allows being to be. There is no non-being *in* being. But being is *in* non-being.

---

[118] εἰ γὰρ ἐν μικρῷ κόσμῳ γίνεται, καὶ ἐν μεγάλῳ, L 10 = Aristotle. *Phys.* 252b26–27.
[119] L 2 = Simplicius. *In Phys.* 28.25–26.
[120] μὴ μᾶλλον τὸ δὲν ἢ τὸ μηδὲν εἶναι, δὲν μὲν ὀνομάζων τὸ σῶμα, μηδὲν δὲ τὸ κενόν, ὡς καὶ τούτου φύσιν τινὰ καὶ ὑπόστασιν ἰδίαν ἔχοντος, L 78 = Plutarch. *Adv. Colot.* 4, 1108f; L 185 = Galen. *De elem. sec. Hipp.* I 2.

3

Plato

Non-Being as the Other of Being

Ὁπόταν τὸ μὴ ὂν λέγωμεν, ὡς ἔοικεν, οὐκ ἐναντίον τι λέγομεν τοῦ ὄντος ἀλλ' ἕτερον μόνον.

Whenever we speak about non-being, as it seems, we speak not about something opposite to being but only about the other.[1]

Plato's discussion of being and non-being is an attempt to understand being as reflected in and against its other. In the *Sophist*, it takes place as a renewed conversation with and robust critique of his two main interlocutors: Parmenides, the "father" of thinking about being, and the Sophist Protagoras, the elusive likeness of the philosopher. And while the Eleatic thinker appears to be the same of the philosopher, he turns out to be his other, whereas while the Sophist seems to be the other, he turns out to be surreptitiously the same of the mirror image of the philosopher. In the debate, what appears to be transpires as the other to what is, or being, yet being too is other to its other. Plato's entire dialogue is thus about the other.

Dramatis personae. Every dialogue is a conversation between a number of interlocutors, at a minimum two speakers, who propel the dialogue through the exchange of rejoinders. In the *Sophist*,

---

[1] The Eleatic Stranger to Theaetetus (Plato. *Soph.* 257b3–4).

they are five speakers—Socrates, Theodorus, the Eleatic Stranger (or visitor, ξένος), Theaetetus, and a silent listener, the Younger Socrates.

The dialogue begins with a brief exchange between Theodorus, who opens the dialogue by introducing the guest, and Socrates, who introduces the topic—the discussion of the sophist as set against the politician and the philosopher—and then settles on the figure of the sophist as someone who is hard to grasp, yet who might help in understanding the not fake but true philosophers (οἱ μὴ πλαστῶς ἀλλ' ὄντως φιλόσοφοι) in their activities, intentions, and aspirations (*Soph.* 216c). After Socrates chooses the main speaker, who then chooses his interlocutor, he remains silent after uttering just six rejoinders, still speechlessly present to every turn of the thought.

Everyone is strangely doubled in the dialogue and then doubled once again: there are two silent Socrateses; two older interlocutors (Socrates and Theodorus) and two younger ones (the Stranger and Theaetetus); two philosophers (Socrates and the Stranger) and two mathematicians (Theodorus and Theaetetus); two speakers coming originally from Attica (Socrates from Athens and Theaetetus from Sounion) and two from far away (Theodorus from Cyrene and the Stranger from Elea). And everyone in one way or another is the other of Socrates. So the dialogue is full of hints and reflections by, in, and of the other.[2]

Theodorus is Socrates' other as a mathematician who uses a different method of studying being, visualizing the mathematical objects in drawings and studying the drawn in the imagination, and then discovering the properties of that which can only be thought as exempt from the grip of change. Yet, mathematics in Plato serves as a propaedeutic to philosophy, since both study

---

[2] As Alejandro Vigo has argued, Plato's ontology and his doctrine of the forms in particular is a metaphysical transposition of the Socratic dialogical practice. See Plato. *Fedon*. Trans. Alejandro G. Vigo. Buenos Aires: Colihue Clásica, 2009, xvi–xxi, 54–63.

the invariable properties of that which is and can only be thought (*Rep.* 522c ff.).[3] Elsewhere, Socrates ironically calls Theodorus "the measure of diagrams" (*Theaet.* 169a), in a clear reference to Theodorus' friend Protagoras, whose assertion that the "human is the measure of all things" has become programmatic for the sophists.[4] Socrates the Younger is the other of Socrates as his namesake, *homonymous* to him (ὁμώνυμος, *Soph.* 218b; *Theaet.* 147d), silently present in two of Plato's dialogues as Socrates' reflection and becoming a speaker, the interlocutor of the Stranger, in the *Politicus*, a continuation of the *Sophist* in developing the program of the study of the sophist, the politician, and the philosopher. Theaetetus is the other of Socrates as his "homoeidos" in that he looked very much like him: snub-nosed, bug-eyed, poor—and remarkably smart (*Theaet.* 168e).[5] Finally, the Stranger is the other of Socrates in that he assumes the Socratic role of the master dialectician, posing questions and leading the discussion: a friend of the followers of the Eleatic thinkers, he follows the Parmenidean path and yet is critical of Parmenides. The Stranger is indeed strange; he is without a name, misplaced among the turbulent life of the *polis*, a true philosopher whose name *is* the philosopher, who thus embodies Socrates as his real other in the philosophical investigation of being. Remaining silent, Socrates thus does act and speak through his *anonymous* other (*Soph.* 216a–c).

Thus, the other is reflected and present in dialogue in many ways—in the interlocutors, the method, and the main topic, which is the definition of the sophist and which is reached in many ways. The core of the dialogue is the discussion of being, which is being

---

[3] According to Diogenes Laertius, Plato followed Epicharmus the Comic in making a distinction between being as thinkable and becoming as sensible, which is ever fluid and is constituted by those things from which number is taken away and therefore can neither be equal nor determinate nor have quantity or quality to them (DL 3.9–10).
[4] Quoted in full, "Human is the measure of all things, of the existing as they are and non-existing as they are not (πάντων χρημάτων μέτρον ἄνθρωπον εἶναι, τῶν μὲν ὄντων ὡς ἔστι, τῶν δὲ μὴ ὄντων ὡς οὐκ ἔστιν)," Plato. *Theaet.* 152a.
[5] Debra Nails. *The People of Plato: A Prosopography of Plato and Other Socratics*. Indianapolis: Hackett, 2002, 275.

thought, unthought, and rethought against non-being. So in a sense, non-being is the main theme of the discussion, lurking, to the extent that it is non-being and is not, behind the clarifying speech and exacting thought, always silently and stealthily present at every turn of the debate.

Two main theses related to non-being discussed in the dialogue are Parmenides' claim that non-being does not exist (*Soph.* 241d ff.) and the sophist's contention that falsity or the lie does not exist in speech or reasoning precisely because there is no non-being (*Soph.* 259d ff.). The sophist does not assert or deny but produces a speech that does not pretend to be true and only imitates what is an attempt to persuade others (*Soph.* 233d, 265b). Hence, both Parmenides and the Sophists deny non-being in the order of the existent, the said and the thought. Yet, the two interlocutors—the Stranger and Theaetetus—intend to refute them.

The way of logos. Everything that can be said and argued for and against is inscribed into the structure and possibilities of the λόγος.

As the way of argument that relies on accepted premises, follows a number of steps of reasoning, and arrives at a conclusion, "rational" λόγος is opposed to "myth." Practiced as philosophical by Parmenides (fr. 2.1–2), the μῦθος is a word, speech, tale, narrative, inquiry, or investigation, which is speech that does not need any support besides and beyond the immediately said. The narrated is the truth that does not need justification, and in this sense, as the Eleatic Stranger now suggests in an explicit critique of Parmenides, it looks naive, as if told to children (*Soph.* 242c). Telling, then, is delegated to the authority of the teller—in Parmenides' case, to the goddess who by the invariance of her being makes sure that the told corresponds to being in being said. With λόγος, it is different: logical speech is an activity of thinking and talking with others who are humans, not gods, the truth of which is never immediate but can only be established—if at all—through a number of steps of a sustained reasoning that uses its own means and resources. The mythical story does not need justification within the myth, whereas

the logical narrative should be self-justificatory, following the implicit and explicit rules immanent in the λόγος.
Long speech, short speech. In the very beginning of the discussion of being, Socrates asks the Stranger how he wants to proceed—by long speech or by questioning (μακρῷ λόγῳ ... ἢ δι' ἐρωτήσεων, *Soph.* 217c, 225b). As Socrates says in his debate with Gorgias on a different occasion, the long speech (μακρολογία) is well laid out and is rhetorically beautiful, meant to seduce the listeners. The short speech (βραχυλογία, *Gorg.* 449b–c), on the contrary, is built by brief rejoinders that consist of perspicacious questions and simple "yes/no" answers that are implicit in the questions and thus imply a constant reference to being and non-being. This Socratic short speech is meant to demonstrate what a thing is, disclosing its essence through speech and reasoning. The long speech is attributed to a sophist, whereas the short speech is ascribed to a philosopher. As a brilliant example of the latter, we have Parmenides' speeches, which Socrates had a chance to attend when he was younger (*Soph.* 217c). Long speech is an uninterrupted monological enunciation meant to persuade the listener by any available means, including, in the case of the sophist, illicit means, that is, those not abiding by the rules of λόγος but furtively and inconspicuously going against them. Short speech, on the contrary, is the way to understanding what a thing is (τί ποτ' ἔστιν, *Soph.* 217b)—in this case, being. Such a speech is always accompanied by the intention to understand the very procedure of the justification, which, in the end, might also be the justification of itself. And yet, λόγος can also miss itself and thus go wrong, which happens all too often and which the Σωκρατικὸς λόγος (cf. Aristotle. *Poet.* 1447b11) is meant to avoid. In other words, λόγος follows its own immanent rules that it obtains through discursive self-study or self-reflection.

Ironically, however, the distinction between long and short speech is not as clear cut as it pretends it to be. Parmenides' poem is an example of a long speech that does not provide a logical justification of itself: as a "myth," for it does not need to do it. And the Platonic dialogue, as the way of questions and answers, is itself a long one, taking a few hours. Moreover, in the case of the *Sophist*, it is a speech that, according to Theodorus' testimony, has been heard before and memorized by the Stranger (*Soph.* 217b). An important implicit distinction here is between written and oral: whereas a long speech is delivered orally, it is carefully composed and written in advance, while a short speech comes out of a spontaneous and often haphazard oral exchange that is later sedimented in the written Platonic dialogue. Thus, it becomes a skillful imitation, a fine reproduction and an inevitable betrayal of the oral, because, once written, the oral becomes stiff and inflexible, thus being unable to defend itself (*Phdr.* 275c–277a). And while Parmenides' poem is a mythological written account of the seen and heard presented in the form of a monological address by the goddess, Plato's speech is a logical written dialogue that reproduces an oral dialogue, whose purpose is the self-reflection of the philosopher's thinking and activity as established and regulated by being itself.

When philosophy discovers λόγος, first in Parmenides' oral disputations, as opposed to his myth-oriented writing, then in Socrates' conversations or the λόγος Σωκρατικός, and then in the imitative written dialogues in Plato, λόγος always reflects on its structure and range of possibilities.

Weaving-together. The defining act of the λόγος is binding together or interweaving various terms (συμπλοκή; cf. *Polit.* 279b–281d), which brings, or ties together, parts of speech, not just one after another but in a syntactically meaningful way. The elementary case of such syntactic binding is connecting a name or noun, or that which acts and is then interpreted as subject, with a verb, or that which designates action or πρᾶξις (*Soph.* 262a–b), which then becomes a predicate. Λόγος thus weaves together the warp and woof of the said into a fabric, textile, or text in such a way that it produces a pattern that becomes displayed, seen, or heard along the way of speaking, with all its digressions, impasses, and achievements.

This is the most fundamental characteristic of λόγος: it always binds together something with something else or something different. There is always an implicit or explicit distinction in the λόγος of saying or acting—and that which is said about or acts. Λόγος cannot be about something that is one: "being" or "Socrates" or "is" or "speaks" is not a λόγος. It is thus never single and singular but is always about *something* (τινός, *Soph.* 262e). Λόγος brings, weaves together, and moves through by two: "being is" or "Socrates speaks." By being fundamentally dual or split-bound, λόγος allows for a contentious struggle, or disagreement, with itself. It can go against itself. All it needs is a negation, the "not."

The logical binding-together, then, amounts to assertion and negation, or saying and saying-away, φάσις and ἀπόφασις. This act of saying and saying-not (both of which are the acts of saying and are different from not saying) establishes ἀντιλογία, or controversy within the λόγος itself, translated into establishing the *opposites*. Since λόγος is an elementary dual, it excludes a third, which might mediate between the opposites, which in this case are contradictories.

Here lies the watershed between the philosopher and the sophist: for the philosopher, λόγος is speech and thought meant to disclose what a thing is and to provide its definition in such a way as to avoid the simultaneous unmediated saying and saying-not, or assertion and negation. Even in its formal structure of asking questions and answering them, the philosophical λόγος displays the opposites, by which it is propelled and the coincidence of which it wants to avoid. The sophist, on the contrary, ignores, often deliberately veils, and sometimes openly embraces the unmediated coincidence of saying and saying-away by saying whatever can be persuasive to the listeners. The sophist thus practices the ἀντιλογικόν, contentious debate about anything, disputation based on either disguised or conspicuous acceptance of contradictions present in speech (*Soph.* 232b–e). Protagoras was apparently the first proponent of the view that for everything there is an opposite claim[6] for which one should be able to argue with equal force. The philosopher aims at reaching the essence of a thing in speech and reasoning by using the devices that come from λόγος, whereas the sophist only imitates such reasoning. Aristotle defines sophistry as only an apparent and pretend wisdom.[7] And in the definition of his elusive opponent that the philosopher reaches at the very end of Plato's dialogue, the sophist is an illusionist who only imitates dialectical reasoning, deceiving and confusing the listener by alleged contradictions (*Soph.* 268c–d).

So the true philosopher is thus opposed to the sophist in the use and application of λόγος that tries to avoid contradictions along the way of reasoning. This is why, as the Eleatic Stranger stresses, while the philosopher constantly turns to the idea of being, which is not easy to discern because of the dazzling radiance of the realm to which it belongs, the sophist always escapes into the darkness of non-being (*Soph.* 253e–254b). However, neither the utter darkness nor the all-encompassing light allows for divisions and distinctions, and thus neither can be seen or thought on its own and properly discerned from its other. Therefore, the sophist happens to be in dangerous proximity of the philosopher as his other, whom the philosopher wants to repudiate and reject and yet desperately needs as his counterimage in order to better understand himself. The other appears to be the same, which is why the philosopher spends so much effort in trying to convince himself of the real distinction between himself and the sophist. Standing in complete darkness and light, the two figures are elusive, and the one appears

---

[6] δύο λόγους εἶναι περὶ παντὸς πράγματος ἀντικειμένους ἀλλήλοις, DL 9.51.
[7] ἡ γὰρ σοφιστικὴ φαινομένη μόνον σοφία ἐστί, Aristotle. *Met.* 1004b18–19. However, Aristotle distinguished between the philosophers (himself and his students), the dialecticians (Socrates, Plato, and their followers), and the sophists, claiming that whereas all three intend to understand being, τὸ ὄν, only the philosopher is able to do so, while the dialectician discusses anything while misplacing the application of the capacity of reasoning, and the sophist differs from the philosopher by his very way of life, that is, by using and abusing reasoning to promote his interests. *Met.* 1004b15–26.

to be diametrically opposite to the other—and yet turns out to be a mirror reflection of the other that makes the right the wrong and the right the left. Looking into a distorted reflection can be entertaining, and yet it is misleading. And if indeed the philosopher is the other of the sophist who appears treacherously to be the same, then there is no need to dedicate a whole separate dialogue to the philosopher, and so it remains forever unwritten by Plato.

The fundamental regulating principle of λόγος is then based on recognition of its basic duality in binding this and that, later called predicate structure, in a way that should avoid the simultaneous saying and saying-away about the said. This is the principle of noncontradiction, which Plato formulated even before the famous account in Aristotle. After its philosophical self-study, or self-practice in shared speeches, λόγος comes to recognize and establish itself as legitimate and eventually self-transparent only once it manages to avoid contradiction, or the unmediated binding-together of the opposites, the simultaneous assertion and denial of the same about the same, at the same time, in the same respect, and in one and the same way.[8]

Speech and reasoning. Being and λόγος. Because of its fundamental duality, λόγος can apply the weaving together of distinguishing and binding to itself and thus produce long chains of reasonings or reasoned conversations. As Plato suggests, besides the λόγος the soul is also equipped with expressive opinion or cognitive belief, δόξα, as well as with imagination or representation, φαντασία (*Soph.* 260e–261a, 264a). Belief and representation can be (and for the most part are) confused about how things are in being and becoming, but λόγος is supposed to rectify this confusion or make them right in expressing what and how a thing is. However, since the bind between two logical terms that are implied in such an expression is not always evident, the λόγος needs

---

[8] αὐτὰς αὑταῖς ἅμα περὶ τῶν αὐτῶν πρὸς τὰ αὐτὰ κατὰ ταὐτὰ ἐναντίας. Plato. *Soph.* 230b. Cf. Aristotle. *Met.* 1005b19–20, 1051a10–12.

to establish this connection through a number of consecutive links in a step-by-step progression, whose end cannot be jumped to but has to be reached by discursive silent reasoning, or διάνοια, which is the binding together of the thought in a certain order. Λόγος is therefore *discursive*—it goes through, runs, and builds a chain of deductions by following its own immanent rules in the search for the conclusion, where the *this* of that which is will be finally connected with the *that* of the how it is in a right way—or the predicate will be shown to properly inhere in the subject.

The discursivity of λόγος thus follows from its duality and is realized in and as speech, which proceeds in a syntactically permissible way to form a sentence, which then can be discursively and logically connected with another sentence. As such, λόγος realizes itself in an exchange of rejoinders between interlocutors, which Socrates and Plato refine into a dialogue of a particular kind—the dialectical dialogue, exemplified in the *Sophist*. Otherwise, λόγος presents itself in and as discursive thinking, or διάνοια, which can and should be straightened according to the rules and principles of λόγος. For this reason, Plato explicitly identifies διάνοια with λόγος, discursive thinking with reasoned speech (διάνοια . . . καὶ λόγος ταὐτόν, *Soph.* 263e). Discursive thinking is then the soul's silent conversation with itself (*Soph.* 263e): διάνοια is the silent λόγος, and λόγος is the voiced διάνοια.

The identification of διάνοια with λόγος, coming from the Eleatic Stranger, sounds like an implicit critique of Parmenides' identification of non-discursive thinking with being (τὸ γὰρ αὐτὸ νοεῖν ἐστίν τε καὶ εἶναι, fr. 3), of the thinking that is achieved non-discursively in an *act*. But for the thought that has to discursively justify what it establishes and comes to think, being can only be disclosed in a consistent, successive reasoning that is not an act but is always a *process*. As dual and constituted by binding or bringing two terms together in the right way, λόγος, in contradistinction to reason-νοῦς, cannot comprehend and think the simple.

The relation of λόγος to being is thus an uneasy one. Λόγος cannot grasp being in its simplicity and entirety at any step in its reasoning, but has to struggle with partial and always incomplete representations. In doing so, λόγος tries to stay away from non-being, which is unaccountable and dangerously contradictory for λόγος, which λόγος can only avoid by protecting itself with the carefully built and preserved logical barriers, ultimately relying on the principle of non-contradiction.

Truth and method. Therefore, the reasoned and conversational justification of what and how a thing is cannot be given or revealed in an act but needs to be established in a sequence of justified steps of reasoning, which might succeed, and then will be true, or fail, and then will be false. Λόγος is therefore potentially correct, or aims at establishing the right connection between that which is and how it is, or the truth of a thing. But being true is only possible and thinkable as opposite to being false.

Λόγος is always about *something,* τινός, which means that a discourse and thought about nothing as "not something," μὴ τινός (*Soph.* 262e), appear logically impossible. Logical saying and reasoning is thus negatively regulated by the other of something, of what is—by nothing, which cannot be logically expressed but "is" (or is) a precondition for saying and thinking something as not-nothing. This something, then, is always of a certain kind, or quality, ποῖος, which is inherent in what is told and thought about it, either explicitly or more often implicitly, and which needs to be brought out of concealment or oblivion in and by the process of speaking and reasoning. As such, the said and the thought can either be the case ("Theaetetus is sitting") or not ("Theaetetus is flying," *Soph.* 262e–263a): again, with reference to the other and non-being as the impossibility of being of a certain kind.

Truth, or the true (ὁ ἀληθής), then, transpires or becomes apparent[9] in the λόγος which speaks or reasons about the existent as existent (τὰ ὄντα ὡς ἔστιν), whereas the false (ὁ ψευδής), on the contrary, speaks about the other of the existent (ἕτερα τῶν ὄντων), taking the non-existent as existent (τὰ μὴ ὄντα ... ὡς ὄντα, *Soph.* 263b). Plato thus stands for the correspondence theory of truth (rather than for coherence or consensus), to the extent that the logically said should correspond to or "recollect" the what is and is always *already* there: perceptually, sedimented in belief, represented in the imagination, and finally conceptually achieved in thought as the form or idea of the thing (cf. *Phd.* 72e; *Men.* 81b–86b). The thought and the truth about it should respond, or co-respond, to each other.

The false or mistake, then, is a failure of the λόγος to establish a correct connection between the terms, a deviation of understanding in binding them together (παραφόρου συνέσεως, *Soph.* 228d). The λόγος that misses the proper order of things builds an incorrect association of the existent that is beside the point (ἕτερα τῶν ὄντων, *Soph.* 263b). It thus has no measure (ἀμετρία) with what is and what it intends to say, think, and express, which it then cannot comprehend or learn (ἀμαθία, *Soph.* 229c). Still, the λόγος can correct itself once it runs into a contradiction or is forced to say the contrary to what it has originally asserted: this is elenchic reasoning. Otherwise, the said and thought incorrectly can be refuted pragmatically, by deeds (ἐν ταῖς πράξεσιν ἔργων, *Soph.* 234e). Being mistaken or making mistakes, however, is possible only if there is a right way to the end of reasoning, or to a conclusion that is justified by the entire reasoning or speech that follows its immanent logical rules and procedures. So in the refutational or elenchic dialogue, which ends provisionally in an impasse, confusion, error,

---

[9] Literally, ἀληθής means "unconcealed," which becomes a major theme in Heidegger. Perhaps a better interpretation of truth in the *Sophist* is Klein's rendering of it as "unforgotten." Jacob Klein. *Plato's Trilogy: Theaetetus, the Sophist, and the Statesman.* Chicago: University of Chicago Press, 1977, 63.

mistake, or falsity, one has to resume walking the way in the hope of achieving its end.

The right λόγος, then, presupposes and is inextricably bound to a method, μέθοδος (*Soph*. 235c), a pursuit of establishing the correct binding of the terms by means that are worked out of, and recognized by, logical reasoning. Because of the fundamental duality of the λόγος, the method is based on the recognition and avoidance of contradictory, unmediated statements, which cannot be upheld, grasped, and accounted for. Because of the troubling and elusive absent presence of non-being to being as being-thought, contradiction is always imminent to logical discourse and reasoning, which, facing the impossible coincidence of the opposites, crumbles and stops. In order to be, to start anew and succeed, it needs method.

Making distinctions is fundamental to λόγος: every reasoning and every philosophical dialogue that attempts to arrive at a definition (also a λόγος) of something starts by making distinctions, which in principle can always be made differently. There are a few heuristic rules that one has to keep in (logical) mind, such as the need to begin with simple and easy before moving on to difficult and complex (*Soph*. 218d), with the evident (*Soph*. 242b), with the most important (*Soph*. 243d), or to be consistent in reasoning at its every step and turn (συνακολουθεῖν, *Soph*. 224e). But the preferred method practiced by Socrates, Plato, and their interlocutors is that of division, or διαίρεσις, which is the art of distinguishing (διακριτικὴ τέχνη, *Soph*. 226c), of artfully and skillfully choosing appropriate distinctions.[10] The method used in the *Sophist* and the related dialogue, the *Politicus*, to provide a definition of its main subject implies cutting into two or distinguishing between two terms (διαιρεῖν δίχα, *Soph*. 225a; διχῇ τέμνειν, *Soph*. 227d), one of which is then again distinguished into two, doing so recursively,

---

[10] See Paolo Crivelli. *Plato's Account of Falsehood: A Study of the Sophist*. Cambridge: Cambridge University Press, 2012, 7–9.

until the required definition is finally achieved (*Soph.* 235c)—in this case, of the Sophist. Diagrammatically and thus almost geometrically, by drawing lines, the method of division can be represented as distinguishing "in breadth and length" (κατὰ πλάτος and κατὰ μῆκος, *Soph.* 266a); graphically, as | and —.

A remarkable feature of the method is the clarity and simplicity of its outline and practice: make a simple distinction between this and that into two and keep repeating it. But even if the searched-for conclusion—the definition—can be arrived at as univocal, the same method itself can be applied in many different ways: the same end can be achieved in many different ways. Such a plurality of ways of reasoning is reflected in λόγος being always plurivocal, in its λέγεται πολλαχῶς, or the possibility of everything being said, thought, and attained in many ways. Thus, the Sophist alone gets four different, yet mutually consistent, definitions in the dialogue by application of the method of division (*Soph.* 221c–226a, 266a–268d). Plato eventually obtains the truth of a thing or a being in his skillfully directed dialogical speeches by means of dialectic, or dialectical knowledge, διαλεκτικὴ ἐπιστήμη. This is the ultimate method based in the duality of λόγος and its capacity of properly discerning what a thing is or its form or idea and how it is distinct from, and connected with, many other forms or beings (*Soph.* 253d).[11]

Aristotle's own way to the truth of being lies solely in the λόγος, which, on the one hand, must respect and follow its own intrinsic principle of non-contradiction, thus avoiding any contradictory statements or unmediated principles in the constitution of being. And, on the other hand, everything is said and thought by λόγος in many ways, as possibly another, and not the other, to the said and thought. It comes as no surprise, then, that Aristotle criticizes the Platonic method of διαίρεσις or the division into two (εἰς δύο,

---

[11] See Dmitri Nikulin. *Dialectic and Dialogue*. Stanford: Stanford University Press, 2010, 30–9.

De part. anim. 642b5 ff.): for him, everything is always divisible not into two terms that are the other to each other, but into a plurality of distinct terms that are other to each other, which, however, never comes with an explanation of why there are exactly so many of them.

The impossibility of logically pinpointing a concept but rather accepting its inevitable proliferation points at otherness that lurks behind this multiplication of the said and thought, which further points at an as yet obscure impact of non-being onto the existent.

The Sophistic impossibility of a lie. The discursive, logical work of dialectic is careful and long and can be revealing, but it also can be long-winded and tedious, even if the live dialogue always draws in others, who become silent interlocutors following the twists and turns of reasoning with implied silent objections and rejoinders, which in the end are delegated to the reader. Philosophical reasoning intends to achieve the truth as the definition of what a thing is that holds in the end and is thus sometimes achieved, even if it is never guaranteed and can be achieved otherwise, by a different path. So Socrates often prefers to wander off, leaving definitive conclusions to others, such as the Eleatic Stranger.

But does the philosopher achieve wisdom? Dialectic can only reveal partial truth, the one about a particular thing or concept, but when it comes to an integral vision of the being of beings, λόγος and therefore dialectic have to be abandoned for the non-discursive thinking, or vision, of reason-νοῦς. Yet, trained logical thinking does not accept non-discursive thinking and is suspicious of it, being afraid to abandon itself for something that it deems—literally—irrational.

So the possibility of truth depends on the possibility of non-truth, lie, mistake, error, or falsity. Only when one makes an effort to think straight can one get to the truth of a thing, of understanding the existent as existent, of attaining to being. Otherwise, careless, misguided logical thinking will be inevitably mistaken in taking non-being as being because of non-being that is always admixed to being (*Soph.* 260b–c, 263d).

But both together and against Parmenides, the sophist denies existence to non-being as not participating in being in any way and thus as incapable of being thought or said. Hence, an error or lie for the sophist is impossible.[12] The self-defeating sophistic argument that a false λόγος or argument is impossible is a veiled reference to Protagoras' (in)famous promise to teach his students to make or fabricate (ποιεῖν) the weakest argument the strongest one.[13] For the Sophists, *any* λόγος will do, especially the one that is more advantageous for the current rhetorical situation. But if the lie does not exist, then there is no truth either and anything goes. Therefore, producing artful appearances in speech as real (*Soph.* 265b), the sophistic λόγος is paradoxically always truly false.

Being by way of speaking. Being discursive, partial, and always a work in progress, the normal state of λόγος is confusion. Sophistically, it is deliberately perplexed, and philosophically it only rarely straightens itself up by getting to the truth of a thing. Λόγος is in a state of constant wandering. It is a way to truth that can wander off differently: it is plurivocal, and it always can be said or performed in many ways. In doing so, λόγος can either try a different genre or invent a whole new one, philosophy, sophistry, poetry, history, drama, epistle, diary, memoirs, gazette, and the like, or a new subgenre within each one. The sophistic λόγος intentionally builds itself as always confused and confusing, in this way avoiding the burden of the responsibility of proving itself right. But for Plato, it constructs itself as *the* method of reasoning—dialectic—as the preferable way to the searched end, at which point λόγος becomes the definition of the thing thought and told about.

So when Plato approaches being in the *Sophist*, he does so from the perspective of λόγος. The *what* of being transpires in the *how*

---

[12] Τὸ παράπαν μηδ᾽ εἶναι ψεῦδος· τὸ γὰρ μὴ ὂν οὔτε διανοεῖσθαί τινα οὔτε λέγειν· οὐσίας γὰρ οὐδὲν οὐδαμῇ τὸ μὴ ὂν μετέχειν, Plato. *Soph.* 260d.
[13] Aristotle. *Rhet.* 1402a24. Cf. Plato. *Apol.* 18b–c; *Soph.* 233d.

it can be told about and thought in discursive reasoning, staged as a philosophical dialogue. So how can it be that someone (the sophist) can produce only a semblance, which in reality is not and says something that is not true?[14] Being in the midst of things, immersed into becoming, we only anticipate being and we hope for understanding or at least a brief glimpse into it. But if the truth of being is at all achievable by the logical, dialectical means that Plato and his dialogical companions lay out, then the very possibility of such a truth lies in non-being as that which makes being potentially meaningful and intelligible for us. Such a possibility appears as an impossibility of the paradoxical being of non-being (τὸ μὴ ὂν εἶναι, Soph. 237a). Parmenides warns us not to walk this way (fr. 7), but Plato and the strange, anonymous Eleatic thinker go against their father in proving him wrong.

But if only being is properly thinkable, how can we even utter the utter non-being (Soph. 237b)? In the realm of unreliable reflections, fleeing images, engraved pictures, and petrified writings (τὰ γεγραμμένα, Soph. 232d), we are always already under the spell of non-being. Yet it is elusive. And if dialectic is meant to provide a reliable method for thinking and understanding being, at least in part, how can and should non-being be thought? We don't know—yet, but we begin with saying, λέγειν, which is the action and activity of λόγος.

As said, λόγος is always about something, and therefore everything that is said is said about something that exists, or is. Something, "τὸ τί" (Soph. 237d), is that which can be referred to by name or by definite description. And yet, we do not know how to describe non-being or even what its name should be. "Non-being" is not a name because a name names something, a τί, and non-being is not something—it is nothing. It is not a definite description either, since there is nothing definite about non-being. So "non-being" names

---

[14] τὸ γὰρ φαίνεσθαι τοῦτο καὶ τὸ δοκεῖν, εἶναι δὲ μή, καὶ τὸ λέγειν μὲν ἄττα, ἀληθῆ δὲ μή, Plato. Soph. 236e.

something that is not nameable and hence not thinkable, not sayable, unutterable and irrational, not referable, not graspable, and illogical.[15] But because non-being is not, it is not a logical subject, and thus it cannot have any predicates joined to it by the copula and thus, strictly speaking, it cannot even be unsayable and unthinkable.

One-many. Being and number. If everything that can be said, thought, or named is something, it is one. So if being is that which is, then it is something that is said and discursively thought as one.

But if λόγος is always about something, then saying something not about a thing, or about nothing, amounts to saying nothing. For nothing is not something, not a thing, and if every thing that is named, spoken about, or thought is one, then nothing is neither a something nor a this, whereas any thing is either something, an *a*, or a this one, a *the*, τὸ τί. It is λόγος again that suggests an important distinction according to its immanent rules that are sedimented as grammatical rules: it can only be meaningful if it expresses the category of *number*, which in Greek has singular, dual, and plural forms. One-something is τί, two—τινέ, and many are τινές (*Soph.* 237d–e). This category and its forms are applied to anything that is and can be said and thought, and so the category of number transgresses merely a linguistic usage and thus comes for Plato from the ontological structure of being. The dual number, which is missing in most contemporary languages, is crucial for Plato for saying and thinking because it represents the first concrete plurality as the *other* of one, while many is a representation of otherness as an indefinite *another* (other and other). Two is *not* one, whereas many is sheer many in which nothing (yet) can be distinguished. So the λόγος carefully preserves this distinction of the plural forms in saying and expression.[16]

---

[15] ἀδιανόητόν τε καὶ ἄρρητον καὶ ἄφθεγκτον καὶ ἄλογον, Plato. *Soph.* 238c, cf. *Soph.* 238e.

[16] Among various ways of speaking about plurality by using dual, triple, plural, collective plural, etc., there is a rare form, the paucal number or paucialis, which designates *few* (*paucus*) things, amounting to two to four. This means that speaking about and giving an account of two, three, and four things is different from speaking about either one or

Therefore, every act of saying that presupposes a discerning act of discursive thinking always implies a distinction of, and in, number, which becomes a fundamental ontological category for Plato. As is common with Plato, a fundamental concept—in this case, number—is often mentioned in a dialogue rather in passing, so that both the reader and the listener are invited to think through the implicit premises and implied consequences. Hence, we never find a systematic theory of number in the Platonic dialogues, but rather we have a few significant references to it. In the *Sophist*, Plato makes a brief, yet significant, mention of number (ἀριθμός), which belongs to the sphere of being, or beings, of everything that is (τῶν ὄντων), including the cosmos (*Soph.* 238a–c). The cosmos itself is structured and regulated according to number, which becomes apparent in the course of time as the image of eternity and being, which makes us turn to studying the nature of the cosmos and eventually to philosophy (*Tim.* 35a–b, 37c–38a, 47a).

As Plato argues in the *Politeia*, when we refer to something as the "same," it is seen as both one, ἕν, and an infinite plurality, ἄπειρα τὸ πλῆθος (*Rep.* 525a). According to Aristotle's testimony, number in Plato is constituted by one and two, or the "indefinite dyad," ἀόριστος δυάς, which themselves are not numbers but the indivisible intelligible principles of the unity and plurality in number (*Met.* 1081a14, 1088a6–8; cf. *Parm.* 143d–144a; Simplicius, *In Phys.* 453.22 ff.). It is in this sense that we need to consider Plato's claim that one is indivisible in and for discursive logical reasoning (τῷ λόγῳ) and appears only in numbers, which are never applicable to the perceptible and thus are present only to being (*Rep.* 525d–e). Because of these two principles of one and plurality, there are different numbers with distinct properties, which are applicable to being. In this way, being is number.

many, which begins with five. Perhaps it is not by chance that there are four interlocutors in the *Sophist*. Four seems to represent the special case of *few* as *not too many*, as twice two, two multiplied by itself, with which one can still have a meaningful communication and an overseeable number of relations (six, for four interlocutors).

Being is spoken of and thought as one. But if it is just one without and apart from many, it cannot be thought or even named because any act of thinking and naming refers to the plurality of other entities implied in saying and thinking, without which neither the act of thought nor the thing thought is possible or meaningful. This is why there is a *plurality* of ideas or forms of being, which constitute the intelligible cosmos (*Tim.* 30c). As Plato argues in the *Parmenides*, being is one, and yet being is also many (πολλά) because one-being (ἕν-ὄν) already establishes an elementary plurality as duality, where one is the other of being and being is the other of one. If being is only one without and apart from many, it cannot even be, be thought, or said in any way (*Parm.* 127e, 137c–157b).[17] Being and one, then, should be distinct not only ontologically and numerically but also nominally, in their name, because if being is only one or identical with one, then there will be two different names for one and the same, and hence there will be not one but many (two), at least in and for logical thinking and speaking. And if the name is different from the named, then again there will be two beings and not one, or being will be nothing apart from the name (*Soph.* 244b–d).

Therefore, being is also not-one or many, which means that being is a synthetic unity of one and many, or one-many. This also means, contrary to Parmenides' contention (fr. 8), that being is *not* a whole, τὸ ὅλον, because the whole is a one in which many parts can be distinguished, whereas being cannot have parts if it is the only one (*Soph.* 244d–245e). The whole is one (*Parm.* 145e), but if being is one and many, it is not the whole. Being, τὸ ὄν, is thus one but also many, or is *beings*, τὰ ὄντα. Being one, being is always many—but *not* infinitely many (ἀπέραντα, *Soph.* 257a), because an indefinite plurality is not thinkable but stands outside being.

---

[17] See: Raúl Gutiérrez. *El arte de la conversión. Un estudio sobre la República de Platón*. Lima: Fondo Editorial PUC, 2017, 304–7.

Hence, contrary to Parmenides, both one and many are logically and linguistically invoked when number is applied to being because only being is what it is as one and is in this way distinct from another being within the many discernible and only thinkable forms of being.

Number regulates the entire sphere of being and everything that can be known through opposition and distinction, such as odd and even, "is" and "is not" (cf. *Theaet.* 85c–d). But one and many are not applicable to non-being because when we say and (attempt to) think non-existing things (μὴ ὄντα), we refer to many, and when we say non-being (μὴ ὄν), we refer to one. And yet, being is not applicable to non-being, and thus neither is it applicable to the categories of one and many. Non-being is not connected to, nor participates in, one and many in any way (*Soph.* 238a–c). This means, again, that non-being is not graspable, not thinkable on its own, and cannot be adequately expressed. It is only the act of *saying* that refers to non-being as one (*Soph.* 238e)—but a wrong and misguided one. Every act of saying is an act of λόγος, but in the case of non-being it attempts to connect the forms of the logical expression of being, one and many, with that which cannot be properly expressed and logically ordered.

Nothing. Nothing is not. Nothing is nothing, but because it is nothing, it is not nothing. Neither is non-being something. And yet, when speaking and thinking discursively, when we are logically binding together the terms of the thought and we say that they somehow refer to that which either is or appears as existent, we somehow have to name nothing as non-being, μὴ ὄν. But this is a desperate act of naming that which cannot be named or pointed at, because it is not an "it" or "that" and it is not—and never—(is) there. So "non-being" is *not* a name but an inevitable (for the philosopher) and deliberate (for the sophist) misnaming of the not nameable.

It is for this reason—or, rather, unreason—that we have to call (καλεῖν) non-being "itself" (αὐτό, *Soph.* 239a), even if there is no "self" to non-being, which is only nominated as such. Non-being is not and thus cannot be named.

In its unnamed elusiveness and unnumbered unaccountability, non-being is always hiding behind being. In his "plausible myth" (*Tim.* 29d) about the origin and life of the world, along with being and that which comes to be, Plato introduces a third kind or "form" that allows bodily things to appear. It is, however, altogether devoid of any form but provides a kind of unfilled "receptacle" (ὑποδοχή) or an empty "place" devoid of anything (χώρα). But these are metaphorical nominations of that which is utterly obscure and not nominable. It is not even a "that which." It is a strange unformed form that remains ever deformed, obscure, untransparent to the light of being and reason, difficult for understanding, withdrawn from reason and inaccessible to λόγος, defying any attempt to define and express it (*Tim.* 49a, 52a–b). So it is not really a form at all because, unlike the forms that are perfectly thinkable, this one—rather, not-one—is difficult and obscure (χαλεπὸν καὶ ἀμυδρὸν εἶδος, *Tim.* 49a).

Plato and the "friends of forms or ideas" (*Soph.* 248a) famously set being apart from becoming: being, οὐσία, is grasped in the soul by thinking as a plurality of intelligible forms and is always identical to itself (νοητά, διὰ λογισμοῦ ... ψυχῇ, ἀεὶ κατὰ ταὐτὰ ὡσαύτως), whereas becoming, γένεσις, is perceived in the body by the senses and is always other and another (σώματι, δι' αἰσθήσεως, ἄλλοτε ἄλλως, *Soph.* 246b–c, 248a; cf. *Tim.* 27d–28b). Non-being, however, cannot be understood on its own: it is neither sensible nor thinkable—but it appears as if in a dream in a not properly accountable "illegitimate reasoning" (λογισμὸς νόθος, *Tim.* 52b).

Nothing is thus "neither–nor": neither being nor becoming, neither same nor another, neither sensible nor thinkable nor logically unaccountable, but an indefinite "third" that does not connect or mediate between the two but provides a contrasting, obscure background for being against fluent becoming—a riverbed where the flux of the never-stopping change can keep flowing.

Negation. So λόγος always inevitably misnames non-being but inevitably always has to run into a logically unsolvable aporia. That which is not cannot be thought and said, and yet has to be. This means that non-being is illogical: it cannot be thought or reached by way of λόγος because it is neither one nor many and thus is not properly sayable or expressible. This is why whenever non-being is involved, even in its absence, it makes λόγος stunned and perplexed, claiming the opposite to what has been logically justified before (*Soph.* 238e). Facing non-being, logical, discursive saying and thinking panics, risking the possibility of crumbling and running into a contradiction. Therefore, λόγος is always tempted to abandon logical means and to try a different way of approaching non-being by suspending or canceling itself.

And yet, philosophical dialogue *is* a genre of λόγος and thus has to respect and take into account the immanent principles and rules of λόγος, attempting to straighten its reasoning and make it distinct from the all-permissive λόγος of the sophists. Λόγος lives off the fear of non-being, which it tries to avoid, turning non-being into a logically accountable negation, which transpires in the possibility of opposition, of claiming or saying the opposite to what has been said or established before. Only by respecting opposition and avoiding contradiction does λόγος follow its self-imposed fundamental principle of non-contradiction and progress in its motion toward a conclusion, which, if reached, makes a λόγος justified by its own means.

But opposition still needs to be established. In order to recognize an opposite, ἐναντίον, with respect to which the logical reasoning can run its way, λόγος needs negation, ἀπόφασις. Negation is introduced by, and as, a simple unitary particle, *not*, even if, as we already know, it is present in Greek in a double form (τὸ μὴ καὶ τὸ οὔ, *Soph.* 257b–c). But what is the extent of the negation—not, ~, μή, οὐ?

In the realm of becoming, of coming to be and passing away, everything, every thing, always negates itself without attaining itself or anything else that is definitive. So here, A is neither A nor ~A. And A is not properly because it never is. In the case of a logical proposition, "A is B," any of its three constituents—subject, copula, predicate—can be negated, which gives rise to eight different kinds of negative statements, considered in more detail in the discussion of Parmenides' forms of being in "being is being." Some of these negative statements can be true and some false, depending on the correspondence or non-correspondence, proper or improper call and response of and by the λόγος, to the thought act or the named deed ("Theaetetus is sitting"/ "Theaetetus is flying").

And in the realm of the intelligible forms, a form A allows everything to be and to be what it is and such as it is. If A stands for justice, then everything that is just is such because it has a particular causal relation to, or "participation" in, this form. But what then does ~A, non-justice, mean? If that which is just is determined ontologically by its form and then is logically distilled into a definition ("justice is X") that can be the basis to legal provisions and moral prescriptions, then the non-just is (just) everything else that is not just. Throughout the dialogues, Plato does not specify how many constituents or forms there are in the noetic sphere as a system of forms or the intelligible cosmos. But if being is indeed constituted according to number, then the forms should be finite in number—perhaps only ten (Aristotle. *Met.* 1073a20, 1084a15; *Phys.* 206b32–33), or even four (cf. *Tim.* 17a), because an infinite number is not intelligible. So the essential negation, ~A, as not what A is, refers to any other form without an indication of which one it is: not this one but *another* one. The essential negation, then, can work as a constitutive operation in the entire finite system of beings that have to be in touch with each other in order to be what each one is.

But if a form is negated existentially, then A *is not* (justice is not), or does not exist. The existential negation of a form, ~A meaning that A is not, destroys the form, annihilating and removing it from the cosmos of beings-νοητά. But every form, ὄν, within the multiplicity of forms or beings, ὄντα, *is* being. Therefore, the existential negation of a form is *non-being*, which *is not* and thus is neither one nor many. The negation of being, *not*, is therefore the negation of the *is*, and as such it is not the opposite but *the other* of being.

Opposites. Negation thus introduces opposition, ἐναντίον: this against that, where "that" can be either one of two or one of many. Translated into λόγος, negation, ἀπόφασις, suggests reference to either *another* or *the other*.

For Aristotle, everything cannot but be said in many ways, which includes even the one (πολλαχῶς τὸ ἓν λέγεται, *Met.* 1004a22). Since λόγος is plurivocal, it always allows and invites the inquirer to make distinctions. But since one cannot logically account or predict what and how many distinctions can be made, the number of such distinctions always remains indeterminate in advance. A concept can be discerned, or said, in three, four, five, six, or more ways (cf. *Met.* Δ), but one can always increase or reduce the number of such distinctions. In other words, no a priori system of distinctions can be analytically deduced from within λόγος. But there is an exception; opposition for Aristotle is the perfect, or greatest, distinction that we can possibly make (ἡ ἐναντιότης ἐστὶ διαφορὰ τέλειος, *Met.* 1055a16; μεγίστη διαφορά, *Met.* 1055a4). Why? Because it is a distinction into two, in which one of the two terms is established as the other of the one, so the derivation of the two terms is always logically univocally defined.

But for Plato, *one* is said in *one way* or univocally: it is one, although it becomes such and is thought as one only when thought together with and against many. But *many* for Plato is already said in *many ways*: in two ways, to be precise, as the other and another.

Returning to the understanding of being based on number, we have found two different accounts of plurality and opposition in the *Sophist* by the way of λόγος, as *two* and as *many*, which transpire in the distinction of one—two—many (ἕν—δύο—πολλά), which corresponds to the singular—dual—plural forms of speech (τί—τινέ—τινές, *Soph.* 237d). The first form of plurality, two (δυάς), which comes with and in the negation of being one, is mentioned by Aristotle in his account of Plato's ontology (*Met.* 1081a14). The second form, one–many (πλῆθος or πολλά) is discussed by Plato in the *Politeia* (*Rep.* 525a). Hence, we have two different models of plurality based on the kind of negation implied, which establishes two kinds of opposition. The other of one can be considered either through duality (two, δύο), as *the other*, ἕτερος, as not not-one (*Parm.* 157c)—or through an indefinite plurality (many, πολλά, πλῆθος), in which case the other is *another*, ἄλλος, one of many.

Being, then, can be understood along the same lines: as was argued, being is not just one because in the absence of the other or another one cannot be thought and does not exist. In order to be and be thought, being also has to be many beings. Being is therefore always one and many. Being-one is also being-many, so being is thereby being–other (ἕτερον) and other–one (*Parm.* 143b–c). This means that without the other as the other of two or "both" (ἀμφοτέρω), being is neither one nor many, and thus is not, or is not being. Therefore, being has to have the other, and this other is non-being.

The two different forms of otherness suggest two different kinds of the constitution of number, which is the constitution of being. If one, ἕν, stands for unity in numbers, then plurality, πλῆθος, makes numbers all of which are different from each other, without, however, establishing a definitive order or sequence in them. These are Plato's "ideal" numbers, all of which are different and mutually "incommensurable" and can be interpreted as cardinal numbers in contemporary terms. But when the plurality of numbers is taken as two or a dyad, δυάς, then numbers are arithmetical: two suggesting an order or sequence between them, so that each number is commensurable with every other one in the number of its units, differing by a unit from both the preceding and following one. These numbers can be considered ordinal. According to Aristotle, both kinds of number can be found in Plato (*Met.* 1080a24–1083a35).

In terms of logical opposites, speaking about Plato and his followers, Aristotle explicitly suggests that the two principles of all opposites are one and many (ἀρχαὶ δὲ τῶν ἐναντίων τὸ ἓν καὶ πλῆθος, Met. 1005a4–5). The two different forms of many can be taken, then, to stand for two different forms of opposition: two-δύο—for the contradictory opposition, when the two terms cannot be true together at the same time; and many-πολλά—for the contrary opposition, when two out of many can be true at the same time but in different respects, thus without violating the principle of non-contradiction.

And in terms of ontology, the two different forms of plurality refer to many, and they establish two forms of opposition: of *another* of being, which is another being, one of the intelligible plurality of beings; and of *the other* of being, which is non-being.

Mediation. Therefore, contrary to Parmenides, for whom being is one, for Plato being is one-many in a bound plurality of forms, where each form is one and yet each is not, and cannot be, without others (*Parm.* 142b–157b). Being is one only as a unique form, and it is conceptually distinct in its "what." Being is also one as being distinct from other concepts, such as motion and rest (*Soph.* 257a). In addition, being is many in the ordered noetic cosmos of forms in which each form is not isolated but is connected with other forms. Hence, being is always beings, and beings are being. This means that in their multiplicity, beings-ὄντα are regulated by one and many, ἕν and πολλά, where many designates the forms that are other to each other but not mutually exclusive. (Here, even the terms for "many," πολλά, πλῆθος, δυάς, are many and not mutually exclusive.) So as being, being-ὄν is constituted by the two opposing principles, one and many, or by one and two as the other of the one.

This means that in the constitution of being there is nothing else besides the two opposing constituent principles, or nothing between them, μεταξύ. Being is constituted by the duality of the "one-many," where many is exclusive and is the other of one.

(In this sense, various dichotomies that modern philosophy practices and tries to get rid of are inherited from Plato.)[18]

In this way, beings are mediated by each other because the forms are not mutually exclusive in the noetic realm and are only thought one at a time and only partially by λόγος. But when it comes to the constitution of being, its opposite constituents are *not* mediated because many is the other of one. This becomes the ground for the famous Aristotelian critique: the absence of mediation in the constitution of being in Plato should mean that one and many as the constituents of being are contradictory opposites that are meant to actually coexist, be inseparably together (συναμφότερα), and thus coincide, which amounts to a violation of the principle of non-contradiction, the most basic principle of being and thought.

Yet, because of his λόγος-centered approach, Aristotle misses the notion that being is the contradictory one *and* many only to λόγος or λογισμός as logical reasoning, which considers each form differently and in a particular aspect. But the νοῦς or νόησις as noetic reasoning (*Rep.* 524b–c), which is central in the consideration of being in Plato, thinks being simultaneously in its unity and multiplicity, both as one being and many beings—as the entire noetic cosmos, where forms mutually reflect each other. From this point of view, there is no violation of the principle of non-contradiction in the ontological constitution of being as one-many.

No opposite of being. So even if Plato believes that being is constituted by the opposites of one and many, being is not an isolated singular being but one of many beings, forms, or ideas. Together these beings, forms, or ideas constitute the thinkable that is thought in its entirety by the intellect-νοῦς and partially—one form at a time but never in full—by the λόγος. Therefore, being does not have an opposite. Hence, non-being is neither contradictory nor contrary to being. Non-being is not an opposite of being.

---

[18] See Lee Franklin. "Dichotomy and Platonic Diairesis." *History of Philosophy Quarterly* 28 (2011), 1–20.

Koinōnia. Being-ὄν is thus always beings-ὄντα, which, however, are not a collection of beings that exist side by side and become meaningful for each other only when they are bound together by λόγος as a result of a logical reasoning that shows that, translated into a logical concept, this form is implied by that one. The forms are already bound together in their mutual connection or they are "mixed" together. This "mixture" (σύμμειξις, *Soph*. 252b, 252e; μεικτόν, *Soph*. 254d) is not random but similar to speech-λόγος, which can only be meaningful when it recognizes that it can mix only some letters and not others (*Soph*. 252e–253a). Plato calls this association of forms or ideas participation (μεταλαμβάνειν), mutual association, or membership, which is a reciprocal *communication*, κοινωνία. This means that forms are connected in such a way that if we think one, we think it on its own, because it *is*, and not only represents, being.

Everything that *is*, or *is* being (εἶναι), is by participation in being as one-many (πρὸς τὴν τῆς οὐσίας κοινωνίαν, *Soph*. 250b). In this partaking, every being is what it is, and yet all beings are different and other to each other. It is in this sense that one should understand Aristotle's claim that Plato accepts three elements, where the mediating one—being—is a mixture of the other two (τὸ γὰρ μέσον μῖγμα ποιεῖ, *De gen. et corr*. 330b13–17), namely, of the one and many.

Every form as being does always actually, and not potentially, reflect in itself another form as that other form that is fully present in this form. In this sense, if we are capable of thinking a form, or being, on its own in a noetic act, we thereby think every other form in that same act, because all the forms are actually, and not potentially, connected and form a system of forms. But λόγος is incapable of doing that, as it thinks every form always partially— in what it is at every step of discursive reasoning—and as separate from each of the other forms. Logical thought and expression already deal with one *and* many (*Soph*. 251b; *Parm*. 157b–159b), where the "and" can never be dropped. The mutual connection of the concepts can only be logically established as a complex system of propositions, similar to Euclid's *Elements*, where a proposition is logically justified by reference to an accepted axiom or postulate or is deduced from a previously justified proposition or a number of them. Λόγος has to connect a concept that it clarifies in one of its aspects in a conclusion through an ordered arrangement of multiple steps of deduction from a number of accepted premises. The bare minimum of such a logical connection is the syllogism (Aristotle. *Top.* 100a25–27; *An. priora* 24b18–20). In the syllogism, two premises yield a conclusion with a necessity that amounts to the force of destiny. Plato explicitly or implicitly uses syllogisms in his dialogues to demonstrate that the forms are capable of connection and mutual communication (δυνατὰ ἐπικοινωνεῖν ἀλλήλοις, *Soph.* 251d). Κοινωνία is thus the way in which being is connected into and organized as beings in the noetic sphere of the one-many, where each form or being participates in and communicates with another one in its entirety and without interruption.

Every being therefore communicates with every being, whereas nothing has no power of communicating with nothing in any way (μηδενὶ μηδὲν μηδεμίαν δύναμιν ἔχειν κοινωνίας εἰς μηδέν, *Soph.* 251e). In this sense, non-being as nothing can be considered as a negative precondition for otherness or for othering among beings, whereby all beings are different and other to each other. Being what it is, *a* being is not *the other* but *another* to a being. This means that being is not opposite to being, or, again, being does not have an opposite. Non-being is therefore not the opposite of and to being.

The way of power and the deduction of categories. Now we need to take a step further and see how non-being is always admixed to being. Speaking through the Eleatic Stranger, Plato now makes a famous attempt to deduce the categories or, in Plato's terms, the "greatest genera" (μέγιστα . . . τῶν γενῶν, *Soph.* 254d; cf. *Soph.* 256d). These genera are the forms without which no act of thinking is possible and which allow one to understand being as one-many or as beings in their shared communicative plurality. In other words, categories are constitutive of being *qua* being.

So far, we have established that being is (1) thinkable and unchanging, in contradistinction to becoming, or *being is*. And (2) being is unique and yet plural, constituted by one and many, or being is *one* but also *many* as the other of one. But *what* is being in its being (εἶναι τὸ ὄν, *Soph.* 247d)?

In order to understand what something is, one needs to provide its definition, which has to be achieved by way of λόγος, through twists and turns of the argument. In the Socratic refutational dialogues, the definition is rarely achieved: the interlocutors come to agree on what a thing *is not*, thus referring to its non-being rather than to what it is, which remains to be found (cf. *Lach.* 199e).

Yet, a definition is possible, though not guaranteed: once in a while, dialectical reasoning can achieve the end of its logical journey, establishing the truth of a thing by following logical procedures at every step of the deduction, as a correspondence between the is of the thing and the how of its being thought and said. The possibility of failure comes from our inability to be non-discursive beings and see and keep all the ramifications of reasoning all at once. This means that we need to move on, using a reasoned and ordered step-by-step process. The possibility of success, of reaching the desired conclusion, is grounded in being itself. Yet, because everything is said and thought in many ways, the ways of achieving the logical end are always multiple, which is brilliantly demonstrated by the Eleatic Stranger, who reaches the definition of the sophist in several ways. Strictly speaking, each ending or conclusion is a different one, or each definition of the same thing differs from another such definition. Since λόγος, as has been said, cannot univocally grasp being that is thought non-discursively at its source (*Rep.* 511d), proving the mutual compatibility or coherence of different definitions is itself a different logical task. Plato does not undertake this task, leaving it to the unrushed, in-depth postgame analysis of the interlocutors.

The Eleatic Stranger defines being as *a* being of beings that are beings (τὰ ὄντα ὡς ἔστιν). Although trained in providing definitions, in this case, however, he proceeds not dialectically but establishes the truth of being through consensus, to the extent that this definition is agreed upon (συνομολογηθέν, *Soph.* 248a). So we cannot but agree that being is a power or *capacity*, δύναμις, of acting upon or producing something other (τὸ ποιεῖν ἕτερον ὁτιοῦν) or to be affected (τὸ παθεῖν), even by something minor and only once (*Soph.* 247d–e). Apparently, this agreement comes from the power of being itself.

Constituted as one-many within the noetic cosmos of mutually communicating beings, being is the paradigmatic cause for many things that are such as they are by participation in being. In this sense, being can be said to exercise its power over another or to affect it. Plato uses the substantivized verb ποιεῖν, which seems to suggest the production or creation of something that is not yet there—of imitations or images (*Soph.* 265b). Yet, ποιεῖν can also mean to "establish," "cause," "do something to another" (good or bad), or "act." This is why when the Stranger reiterates his definition of being, he uses δρᾶν, "to do" or "act" (*Soph.* 248c). Being—*a* being—exercises its capacity to act upon the other by being what it is, or being such "by its own nature" (πεφυκός, *Soph.* 247e). In this sense, being is thus a capacity that is never potential but is already fully actualized within the cosmos of other noetic beings.

But what does it mean that being is affected or acted upon (παθεῖν, *Soph.* 247e; πάσχειν, *Soph.* 248c)? If affection makes something reach a particular state because of something else, how can we say then that being is affected, if being is what it is only due to itself or its own "nature"? Being always is and is what it is—but not for us who are in the midst of things and are on the way to being, except for rare and mostly unexpected moments of a sudden stop at the understanding of or glimpse into being on the way to being, which for Plato and the entire philosophical tradition means coming to know being. Being is thus not yet for us until we come to it, often after or even when being entirely lost. In this sense, being is admixed with non-being, which for us is the not-yet-being. From Parmenides on, philosophy is defined as the enterprise of cognition of being by λόγος, of what is, against sophistic manipulations of being. Ontology embeds epistemology. Being can never be for us until and unless it is and becomes known. Knowledge is the action provoked by being itself. To know (τὸ γιγνώσκειν) is therefore to act somehow (ποιεῖν τι), or to bring the known to being by and through knowledge (cf. *Symp.* 205b-c). And to be known (τὸ γιγνωσκόμενον) is to be affected (πάσχειν, *Soph.* 248d-e). So, contrary to the understanding of knowledge as production, when the known is taken as constructed and produced as a result of the act of cognition, rather than existing on its own, ποιεῖν stands for the activation, or actualization, of knowledge, making explicit what is already implicitly known all along and is thus true, while the known is then expressed by "being acted upon," or πάσχειν.

As Plato keeps repeating and enacting in his dialogues, cognition is a deeply erotic enterprise, being a striving toward the good (*Symp.* 206e-207a), for the not yet known is an object of desire that knowledge attempts to attain in a process or act of thought. For this reason, the Eleatic Stranger explains being acted upon and acting, πάθημα and ποίημα, as exuded by those that stay in a shared communion or mutual communication.[19] Taken literally, this claim, πρὸς ἄλληλα συνιόντων, refers to those who are in a tight bind, attending to each other, living together, or having intercourse with each other, thus exhibiting distinct erotic overtones (cf. *Symp.* 195b, with an explicit reference to Eros). Accordingly, the communication, τὸ κοινωνεῖν, which characterizes the mutual involvement of the primary forms or categories and forms in general, has the same erotic connotation of beings bound to each other in a state of co-being that can be thought of as an intercourse, where each

---

[19] Πάθημα ἢ ποίημα ἐκ δυνάμεώς τινος ἀπὸ τῶν πρὸς ἄλληλα συνιόντων γιγνόμενον, Plato. *Soph.* 248b.

being or form both acts and is acted upon, and in this way is tied with the other while being what it is in and through this uninterrupted communion. In this sense, being is always being-together, being one in community and communication with others. To use a different metaphor, being is a dialogue of mutually communicating equal participants in which each one is and is what one is while communicating with others.

So to the extent that being is known or comes to be known, it is in motion or is being moved according to being acted upon in knowledge (κινεῖσθαι διὰ τὸ πάσχειν)—from unknown to us to the known and actualized (*Soph.* 248e). This means that motion or, broadly speaking, change, κίνησις, as not-yet achievement of the goal—in this case, the knowledge of being—is the expression of being as not-yet disclosed to us. To know being, we need to be there, arriving there by λόγος, which is always partial and incomplete at any step of the discursive saying and reasoning. The only hope is to come to the realization of being at the very end, in the λόγος or definition of being that still remains logically complex in distinguishing between the subject and the predicate, the defined and the defining. The full attainment of being is only possible in the non-discursive act of reason as νοῦς. The thinking of λόγος is motion that comes to rest at its end. The thinking of νοῦς is rest that it is also motion, to the extent that it constantly attains to itself without ever having left itself.

This is what being is: being *is* by being there on its own and yet in uninterrupted, constant communication with other beings. Plato expresses this notion by saying that being cannot stay unmoved (ἀκίνητον ἑστὸς εἶναι, *Soph.* 249a). Being, therefore, has life, which is the life of a perfect living being (ζῷον, *Tim.* 30b). It is that of the noetic cosmos, which is οὐσία that lives off and by communicating with beings. Being is alive, sharing life among beings. But since being is the power of self-actualization in knowing and known, it is also being-thought, or is intellection and intelligible. With Parmenides, Plato accepts being as thought—as thinking and thinkable, as already and always having been thought and thinking itself that allows to be thought by us. Therefore, being has life (ζωή) and thinking (νοῦς, Soph. 249a), neither of which has an origin or an end because being has no origin but only constitution. Thus, being moved and motion exist in beings. For Plato, against Parmenides, this means that if being is only and always unmoved and unmovable, then nothing can be and can be thought (Soph. 249a). The unmoved is literally nothing. But if that which is only and ever is in motion, as Democritus takes his indivisible beings or atoms to be, then again nothing can be thought and known, because it is always other and another, at which thought can never stop. If the same (ταὐτόν) is excluded from being, being cannot be. In order to be, being also has to be the same, which then can be distinguished from others in the community of beings with which it communicates and stays in communion. This implies that besides and together with motion there should be rest, στάσις, without which the same, equal to itself and always being in the same state (τὸ κατὰ ταὐτὰ καὶ ὡσαύτως καὶ περὶ τὸ αὐτό, Soph. 249b), cannot be. Hence, reason-νοῦς can only be if it is in motion that is also simultaneously at rest, as the thinking thinking itself, being both in motion and at rest, thus moving without ever having left itself.[20] But if such thinking is not different from or is identical with being, such is also being. Hence, the task of the philosopher is to think and say being as both moving and at rest.[21]

And yet, motion and rest are utterly opposite to each other (ἐναντιώτατα, Soph. 250a), which means that by themselves they are incompatible and unmediated: motion does not rest, and rest does not stand still. Motion and rest do exist on their own, in so

---

[20] That reason-νοῦς thinks in a "standing motion," or the motion of thought that is always at rest, was systematically developed by Proclus. See Stephen Gersh. Κίνησις ἀκίνητος: *A Study of Spiritual Motion in the Philosophy of Proclus*. Leiden: Brill, 1973, esp. 103–6.
[21] ὅσα ἀκίνητα καὶ κεκινημένα, τὸ ὄν τε καὶ τὸ πᾶν συναμφότερα λέγειν. Plato. *Soph.* 249d.

far as each is a category and thus a form—yet at the same time, each one is, or exists, only through participation in being (τὴν τῆς οὐσίας κοινωνίαν, Soph. 250b). This means that motion and rest are mutually unmixed (ἀμείκτω πρὸς ἀλλήλω), incompatible or contradictory,[22] whereas being is a mixture of the two (τὸ ... ὂν μεικτὸν ἀμφοῖν, Soph. 254d), or it is compatible with motion and rest. So while the opposites are thus mutually incompatible, being is compatible with everything because everything that exists participates in being. As unchanging, being can be said to be stable, and as known, it moves. By itself, being neither moves nor stands still but rather "embraces" motion and rest. This means, again, that being is not opposite to anything, including motion or rest but, in a sense, it mediates the contradictory opposites, allowing either one to participate in it.

Other. Priority of the negative. At this point, we need to observe that motion as the negative category in the pair of the opposite categories takes priority, if not in the being of the categories—either one equally exists by participating in being—then at least in the order of their deduction and understanding. Even more important is that, not having an opposite and not being opposite to anything, being is different from anything else or is something *other* (ἕτερον ... τι) to the two main categories of motion and rest (*Soph.* 250c).

By way of deduction, Plato first introduces motion as the other of rest and rest as the same to itself. Within the pair of the opposite categories of motion and rest and being as the third, each one is *other* to another and *same* with relation to itself (*Soph.* 254d ff.). This means that, in addition to the two categories introduced so far, one has to accept another pair of the opposite categories of *other* and *same*.

---

[22] While motion is resting (as a category), it is not rest (as a different category). See C. D. C. Reeve. "Motion, Rest, and Dialectic in the *Sophist*." *Archiv für Geschichte der Philosophie* 67 (1985), 47–64, esp. 59–61.

With the introduction of other and same, ἕτερον and ταὐτόν, the number of the fundamental categories comes to five. Everything that is participates in a particular way in being, motion and rest, same and other (*Soph.* 254e ff.). Besides, all the categories are mutually connected through communication: each one is the same, and yet each one is different from the other one. Hence, being is not just the same (to itself), or is not the same to the same, because otherwise motion and rest will be the same, to the extent that they both participate in being (*Soph.* 255a–c). Yet, being is not just the other (to itself and another), because then nothing can participate in being and therefore nothing is—but nothing is not. Hence, being should be considered both by itself and for the other (τῶν ὄντων τὰ μὲν αὐτὰ καθ' αὑτά, τὰ δὲ πρὸς ἄλλα, *Soph.* 255c). In the *Sophist*, Plato mentions three main pairs of opposites: motion–rest, other–same, and one–many (*Soph.* 252c). Yet, only the first two pairs are categories, whereas one and many, ἕν and πλῆθος, are *not* considered categories, even though they are important in the constitution of being. The reason is that one and many are the constituents of being, and so they cannot be opposite categories, because being itself has no opposite.

In the two paired categories, every opposite participates in every other opposite (μετασχὸν τοῦ ἐναντίου, *Soph.* 255b). Thus, motion and rest participate *both* in same and other. Not being the same, they cannot be just other to each other either because otherwise motion will stop and rest will move, and so they will not be opposites to each other (*Soph.* 255a–b). So in a sense, there are only two opposite categories in Plato: those of the primary unmediated opposites, of the mutually deducible other or motion, and the same or rest.

In this way, in the constitution of categories, the negative category of the other takes priority—not ontologically but logically by way of deduction—over the positive one of the same. Without other, everything would be the same and therefore unmoving and unthinkable.

Without other, one cannot make any distinctions.[23] If other or otherness is negativity in being and the categories, then negativity underlies the categories as forms and so is the key to understanding being-something.[24] Other regulates the being of everything by participation: everything is the same by being the other to the other. Yet other is *not* other by being the same to the same. This is why the most absurd and ridiculous philosophical position for Plato is the one that does not accept that something be considered other by participating in, or sharing, a property of the other (κοινωνίᾳ παθήματος ἑτέρου θάτερον προσαγορεύειν, *Soph*. 252b). So now the understanding of being hinges on the understanding of the other.

Other of the other. All the categories are by participating in each other. They are all "mixed" others or bound together, woven together into a fabric of beings. Within the categories, each one is what it is and thus is the same by participating in the same, ταὐτόν. But each one is also other to each other, not because of itself or its own nature, but by participating in the other as the form of the other, ἕτερον.[25] Hence, everything that is, is both same and other. Every category is the same to itself but is not the same to the same. The form of the same itself gets its sameness in the opposition to other. And every category is other to the other, including the form of the other, to the extent that it is other (τὸ δέ γ' ἕτερον ἀεὶ πρὸς ἕτερον, *Soph*. 255d), which it too obtains in opposition, and being other to, the same. This means that while the same is not same to the same, the other is other to the other.

Once again, we see that other is not entirely symmetrical to the same within the system of categories. In the opposition of

---

[23] Aristotle writes διαφορὰ ... καὶ ἑτερότης ἄλλο, which is very much in line with Plato's argument. Aristotle. *Met*. 1054b23.

[24] The primacy of the negative in the understanding of categories can be further seen in that, apart from "rest," στάσις also means "discord" or "sedition," a civil war as the war with itself. Interested in the project of a political arrangement that would avoid and exclude civil discord, Plato cannot miss this other meaning of στάσις, ironically hiding behind the stability of the shared being.

[25] ἓν ἕκαστον γὰρ ἕτερον εἶναι τῶν ἄλλων οὐ διὰ τὴν αὑτοῦ φύσιν, ἀλλὰ διὰ τὸ μετέχειν τῆς ἰδέας τῆς θατέρου. Plato. *Soph*. 255e.

motion—rest, other is paralleled by motion, which Plato introduced into the discussion as the first category (*Soph.* 248e ff.). Therefore, other is fundamental for the interaction, participation, and plurality of being *qua* beings.

But is the other of the other a double negative that is the same? The other of the other is the same only for the other as category: ἕτερον is the other of all the other categories and so is the same to itself as the other or the form of otherness. And yet, other as category is constituted in the opposition to same, and in this sense it is also not same but the other to itself. In all the other categories, the other of the other, ἕτερον τοῦ ἑτέρου, is *another*, ἄλλο, one out of many. As Plato argues, the other of the same can be either motion or rest. Hence, the other of the other of motion is another to the same or rest, and in this sense, it is both other and not other (*Soph.* 256a–d). Motion participates in being, and through this participation is the other of the same, and thus not same or other. But motion is also the same as a category. Therefore, motion is same and other, although in a different respect. In this way, as every other category, motion *is* (as existent and participating is being) and *is not* (as the other of being).[26]

Non-being is a murky dead-end of discursive reasoning, which takes non-being as nothing—hence, nothing to think (*Soph.* 250c–251a). And yet, as this reasoning shows or rather hints at, non-being, which is not, is not a form and not an opposite of being, which does not have an opposite and is surreptitiously lurking in every category and every form. Why? Because of the primacy of the other, of its being the other to others, making everything other to the other and different from the other and one another. Other others itself. Other makes all other paired categories other to being, thus turning each one into *non-being* (ἕκαστον οὐκ ὄν ποιεῖ, *Soph.* 256e). Therefore, as Plato somewhat hesitantly acknowledges, there is an infinite, or undefined and ungraspable, amount of non-being

---

[26] ἡ κίνησις ὄντως οὐκ ὄν ἐστι καὶ ὄν, ἐπείπερ τοῦ ὄντος μετέχει, Plato. *Soph.* 256d.

in *any* category of being (ἄπειρον δὲ πλήθει τὸ μὴ ὄν, *Soph.* 256e; cf. *Rep.* 525a). Never being there, non-being is always stealthily present in its absence to being in an indeterminable, unspeakable, and logically unthinkable yet necessary way.

Non-being as the other of being. In the set of categories, the existence of which is determined, scripted, and directed by being, the other is given the role of protagonist, acting with and against its own other, the same. For this reason, Plato begins the deduction of categories with motion in the motion–rest opposition and dedicates more attention to other in the other–same duo. The primacy of the negative suggests that each category should have its negative reflection, or unmediated, contradictory opposite. The only exception is being, which does not have an opposite but is "mixed" with, or is partaken of by, the two pairs of the opposites, which exist because and to the extent that each one participates in being (*Soph.* 254d). In this sense, being is the *other* of everything that is, the *other* of others.[27] As one, being remains indistinct and non-distinguishable until it defines itself through many in the multiplicity of beings. Strictly speaking, only being *is*, and everything else is because of being, but, as different from or other to being, everything else is also not being. Therefore, wherever there is another or others (τὰ ἄλλα), being is not (οὐκ ὄν), or there is *non-being* (*Soph.* 257a).

If non-being is the primary negative, and a "nulliplicity" does not stand in opposition to being, then non-being is neither a category nor a form, and is thus elusive and not properly thinkable, similarly to matter or the "receptacle" of the world described by Plato in the *Timaeus*. The understanding of non-being in relation to being, then, is the fundamental problem that the philosopher has to address (*Soph.* 250d, 254c–d). Because non-being is not, reasoning about it always faces a possibility of a paradox or aporia. So, on the one hand, Plato has now established the existence of non-being

---

[27] τὸ ὂν αὐτὸ τῶν ἄλλων ἕτερον εἶναι λεκτέον, Plato. *Soph.* 257a.

(εἶναι τὸ μὴ ὄν), which is characterized as an oxymoronic "really existing non-being" (ὄντως μὴ ὄν, *Soph.* 254d). On the other hand, since being itself is the other to all other categories, being is neither of them and thus does not properly exist in them.

As we have seen, the other plays a fundamental role in Plato's ontology, where it is "mixed" with all the categories and is the other of the other except for the other itself, so that its being "itself" presupposes the opposite of the other, but still the other itself as the other to itself. The other is distributed through being and beings, which means that the other others itself in others and thus has "parts," τὰ μόρια, or various ways in which it is reflected in other beings.

If Plato has argued against the sophists that non-being is, or exists, to the extent that the other exists by participating in being, non-being still is not considered as the opposite, ἐναντίον, of being as its opposite category (*Soph.* 257b), which being does not have. Rather, non-being is a "contrary," ἀντίθεσις, to being as the other of being. Such a "contrary" differentiates various kinds of beings as contraposed to each other, similarly to the way other differentiates the kinds or branches of knowledge-ἐπιστήμη (*Soph.* 257c). The other is distributed and clastated differently in different beings.

A "part of the nature of the other," then, is the *other-of* particular beings (τῶν ὄντων, *Soph.* 258a), or kinds of beings, which makes them other to each other.[28] It is in this sense that the other of the beautiful and the just exist (*Soph.* 257c–e), as well as that the not big and big do equally exist (τὸ μὴ μέγα καὶ τὸ μέγα αὐτὸ εἶναι, *Soph.* 258a; cf. *Soph.* 257c–e). This is why, as Aristotle reports, Plato and his followers consider non-being as "big and small," taken either

---

[28] See Edward N. Lee. "Plato on Negation and Non-Being in the *Sophist.*" *The Philosophical Review* 81 (1972), 267–404. Lee argues that each part of the other "defines a non-being which is *not* also something in and of itself: a non-being that has no proper nature 'all its own,' but whose being consists precisely and exclusively in its *not* being something else" (287).

together or separately, if "small" is the other of "big."[29] However, since being is determined by the one and many (or "big and small") that constitute number as being, one and many are not applicable to non-being (*Soph.* 238a–b), which means that it cannot be numbered. So Aristotle misses the point here when he says that for Plato all the opposites can be reduced to the opposition between being and non-being as well as to one and many, so that rest is reducible to one and motion to many.[30] For non-being is not the opposite of being but its other.

Besides, because being has no opposite, its other or "contrary" is the other of the other as a "part" that is not the "whole" of the other, which, as category, does not have parts. In this way, non-being as the other of being is also the other of the other as the form of otherness.[31] Such otherness is expressed, again, by the negation of μή, as μὴ ὄν (*Soph.* 257b). Therefore, even if non-being is and has its own nature (*Soph.* 258b), which is the other of being, non-being equally is not because as non-being it is not being.

An important paradoxical conclusion follows from here. As Plato briefly mentions, the good is "beyond" being (ἐπέκεινα τῆς οὐσίας, *Rep.* 509b), or " ", and, by not being being, it is the other of being. In this sense, being is one (*Soph.* 257a), but only as the other of non-being. But since non-being is the other of being, then non-being is *the good*. This is certainly an unexpected conclusion, especially since in the later tradition, grounded in the Anselmian ontological proof, being is considered to be the best that can be possibly

---

[29] τὸ μὴ ὂν τὸ μέγα καὶ τὸ μικρὸν ὁμοίως, ἢ τὸ συναμφότερον ἢ τὸ χωρὶς ἑκάτερον, Aristotle. *Phys.* 192a7. Cf. Plato. *Rep.* 524c.
[30] πάντα ἀνάγεται εἰς τὸ ὂν καὶ τὸ μὴ ὄν, καὶ εἰς ἓν καὶ πλῆθος, οἷον στάσις τοῦ ἑνὸς κίνησις δὲ τοῦ πλήθους. Aristotle. *Met.* 1004b27–29.
[31] Non-being can also be understood as "being different from something." Job Van Eck. "Non-being and difference: On Plato's *Sophist*," 256d5–258e3. *Oxford Studies in Ancient Philosophy* 23 (2002), 63–84. See also: Francesco Fronterotta. "Il non essere e la strategia dello straniero di Elea: deduzione o rimozione?" *Rivista di storia della filosofia* 70:1 (2015), 143–62, esp. 158–61. This interpretation, however, does not account for the radical difference of non-being to being as its other, not just a being as being-something, either specific or in general.

thought and thus the universal good. But for Plato, non-being is not evil but a necessary component in the constitution of everything that is, including the cosmos, which, despite its limitations and inability to be always the same in its every part, is still beautiful and is the best possible imitation of the noetic realm and the unadulterated thinking of the νοῦς that thinks itself through these forms. It will be Plotinus who will explicitly argue for the identity of the good and non-being.

Hence, a logical study of being and non-being in the existent runs into contradictory statements (ἐναντιώσεσιν), which, however, can be reconciled by pointing out that being, as well as non-being, is in many different ways (πολλαχῇ, *Soph.* 259a–b). So rather than being stated in many ways, being *is* in many ways for logical reasoning and discursive expression. And as its other, non-being too is—and is not—in many ways.

This is where the way of λόγος has led Plato's others, the Eleatic Stranger and Theaetetus, who in the end have to recognize not the failure but a certain dissatisfaction with their inability to ultimately grasp and pinpoint non-being in its elusive otherness. Non-being "is" or is non-being. Non-being does not participate in the categories; rather, it is a "part," a non-visible yet central aspect of one of it, of other, which stands for negativity and multiplicity and without which being as beings cannot be. As such, non-being is neither identical to itself nor distinct from itself. Therefore, non-being is also not non-being. Being other to everything that is, non-being is the other of being.

4

Diogenes

Non-Being as Convention

ζῆν ὀρθῶς οὐ δυνήσῃ μὴ ἐπιστάμενος

You will not be able to live properly if you do not know how.[1]

A live and living response to Plato's ponderings on being and non-being is found in Diogenes of Sinope. For Diogenes, sophisticated attempts at thinking being lead to the inculcation of (un)justified beliefs that draw us away from being, which only transpires in life according to nature.

For Diogenes, being is not to be thought but lived, or enlived. In polemics with Plato, which go beyond the exchange of arguments between school, Diogenes invents his own method of enacting being, thereby doing away with non-being, with everything unnecessary that stands in the way of being as being enlived or living well. The good life for Diogenes is not a moral life based on moral principles, since these principles themselves are either the sediments of habit (and as such are artfully conventional and thus only obscure being) or they are products of theoretical reflection, which shields us from being by being thought in fixed forms that do not allow for well-being.

The nothing of non-being figured prominently in Diogenes' life, since his philosophical stance vis-à-vis being and non-being was

---

[1] Dio Chrysostom. *Discourses 1–11*. Trans. J. W. Cohoon. Cambridge, MA: Harvard University Press, 200, X 28.

inscribed into his way of life. An exile to a foreign city, he faced insecurity most of his life, during which he converted the uncertainty of the nothing of the chase for perceived socially approved goods into the confidence of being as the being-well of life.

Nothing is certain about the writings of Diogenes: we only have the titles of dialogues and tragedies ascribed to him; a later writer even contested that Diogenes ever left anything in writing at all (DL 6.80). Writing is futile, because, as already Plato recognized (*Phdr.* 274b ff.), it cannot grasp the life of thought but has to put it into plastered layers of fixed arguments and established concepts that always tell the same thing. Dialogue, then, might be a minimal compromise between live action in speech and thought—and its systematic theoretical account. But all later testimonies have an anecdotal character based on hearsay and a live tradition of its transmission, interpretation, and reinvention that point at Diogenes as still present and alive in his spirit, if not in body.

Diogenes is mentioned only once by a contemporary philosopher in his writings—by Aristotle in the *Rhetoric* and by the nickname "the Dog" (ὁ Κύων, *Rhet.* 1411a24). Diogenes continues to live and flourish in collective recollection generations and centuries later, where his contours transpire through the sedimented layers of transmission, reinterpretation, distortion, and mixture with other doctrinal, anecdotal, and apocryphal components borrowed from different traditions.[2]

---

[2] The fragments of Diogenes are collected in *Socratis et Socraticorum Reliquiae*. Vol. 2. Ed. Gabriele Giannantoni. Naples, Italy: Bibliopolis, 1990, 227–509 (referred to as G, followed by the fragment number). See also Diogenes the Cynic. *Sayings and Anecdotes, with other Popular Moralists.* Trans. and ed. Robin Hard. Oxford: Oxford University Press, 2012; Georg Luck, Ed. *Die Weisheit der Hunde: Texte der antiken Kyniker in deutscher Übersetzung mit Erläuterungen.* Stuttgart: Kröner, 1997; I. M. Nakhov, Ed. *Anthology of Cynicism.* Moscow: Nauka, 1984. Most of the sources are much later: Diogenes Laertius, who has preserved the most extensive collection of testimonies on his namesake, lives some five hundred years later. See Diogenes Laertius. *Lives of Eminent Philosophers.* Vol. 2. Trans. R. D. Hicks. Cambridge, MA: Harvard University Press, 2000 (henceforth, the references are to Book VI as DL 6, followed by the section number). Desmond argues for a robust consistency of the Cynic tradition from Diogenes to Sallustius: William Desmond. *Cynics.* Berkeley: University of California Press, 2008, 6–8.

The way Diogenes lives by being outside, literally and figuratively, and opposes or thematizes non-being is inscribed into his life. Because Diogenes was exiled from his hometown of Sinope for counterfeiting money (παραχαράξαντος τὸ νόμισμα, DL 6.20),[3] he belongs to neither his home *polis* or to a new one. Diogenes is homeless and a refugee, which makes him not only find home in a tub but also forces him to constantly wander within the city and migrate between Athens and Corinth, living in the open and spending nights at temples (DL 6.23; *Ep*. 16; Dio. *Disc*. 6.2–3).[4] Since Diogenes does not have a house and a home, he does not have a private life, which in antiquity was the life within the household. His life is all out in public, without anything to hide or intentionally left private. Nothing can be hidden in public, which is the space of the *polis* and the being of Diogenes' life. Yet this being remains concealed in plain sight because of the commonly accepted ways of improper living. Every place, then, is his home, and his house is the whole world ([Lucian], *Cynicus* 15). Diogenes belongs to the world, κόσμος, which is the place for every living being, in which the firmly established ontological and political distinction between *polis* and *physis* no longer holds. This is why, when asked where he came from, he is the first to reply: "I am a cosmopolitan" (κοσμοπολίτης, DL 6.63). By belonging to the entire world, Diogenes belongs to being.

For and against nature. As the Stranger suggests in Plato's *Sophist*, it is not easier to tell what is being than it is to tell what is non-being.[5]

---

[3] See Dio, *Disc*. VI 1, VIII 1. Diocles suggested that it was Diogenes' father who counterfeited money (DL 6.20). Judged by the number of test cuts on the drachms (five out of twenty-seven of those minted during Diogenes' lifetime and practically all the drachms of the fifth-century BCE issue), which were meant to verify the authenticity of a coin, defacing the currency was very common in Sinope. See Richard Ashton and Stanley Ireland, Eds. *Bosporus-Aeolis*. Pt. 9 of *Ashhmolean Museum, Oxford*. Vol. 5 of *Sylloge Nummorum Graecorum*. Oxford: Oxford University Press, 2007, 227–93.

[4] See "The Epistles of Diogenes." Trans. Benjamin Fiore. In *The Cynic Epistles: A Study Edition*. Ed. Abraham J. Malherbe. Missoula, MT: Scholars Press, 1977; henceforth *Ep*., followed by epistle number.

[5] τὸ ὂν τοῦ μὴ ὄντος οὐδὲν εὐπορώτερον εἰπεῖν ὅτι ποτ' ἔστιν, Plato. *Soph*. 246a.

So those who discuss being are engaged in a gigantomachy about being (γιγαντομαχία... περὶ τῆς οὐσίας, *Soph.* 246a). This is what Diogenes does, whose lived life turns into a "battle for being." This battle begins with an insurrection against the corruption of public life and results in a radical turn against both existing philosophical practices and established public morals. Since the theoretical and practical approaches to being are inscribed into the established ways of the *polis*, the turn is away from it—to nature.

Everything that is comes from nature (*Ep.* 21).[6] Nature is being, and being is nature and in nature. Being is already there for us. Being is us until we choose to turn away from it. By studying nature, we can again be what we already are but have prevented ourselves from being.[7] Enliving being or living according to nature depends on us because nature, as Diogenes proves by his entire life, allows us to revert to that being that we have abandoned and that allows us to live well (τοῦ καλῶς ζῆν, DL 6.65).

According to tradition, the "epiphany" of how to live according to nature occurred when Diogenes saw a mouse that did not need a bed, was not afraid of darkness, and was not seeking unnecessary pleasures (DL 6.22). This made him realize that the corruption of being, which in the city becomes moral and political, comes from the overzealous cultivation of unnecessary needs within the *polis*, which eventually results in illness, unhappiness, and misery. In the state of being-away from being, we are worse off than both gods and animals (Dio. *Disc.* 6.22). Socrates, who exemplifies the Cynic ideal of living well according to nature while still residing amidst the *polis* that eventually kills him, is a kind of a Silenus, or half-god and half-animal (Plato. *Symp.* 221d–e). But unlike Socrates,

---

[6] See *Ep.* 21. See also *Diogenis Sinopensis quae feruntur epistulae*, in Vol. 2 of *Die Kynikerbriefe*. Ed. Eike Müsele. Paderborn: Schöningh, 1994. The Cynic Epistles were written by different Cynic authors sometime between the second century BCE and the second century CE (see G 423–64). See also Giannantoni, op cit., 423–64; Abraham J. Malherbe "The Epistles of Diogenes," in *The Cynic Epistles*, 6–19; Eike Müseler. *Die Kynikerbriefe*. 2 vols. Paderborn: Schöningh, 1994.

[7] Cynicism is the study of nature: ὁ γὰρ κυνισμός... φύσεώς ἐστιν ἀναζήτησις, *Ep.* 42.

Diogenes strives to go back to the divine by living out the being of nature.

Non-being. Non-being, then, is life against nature. Nothing as non-being is therefore not death, which is simply a cessation of existence and a return to the original elementary state of nature. This is why we should not be afraid of death, much like the mouse is not afraid of death. Nothing is not total darkness because in darkness is life and a good life at that, as the mouse knows. Nothing lurks in the excess of the necessary that is sufficient for life. Nothing transpires in the life of convention, which gets refined into many strands of the theoretical, practical, and productive. Since we still are living beings, we cannot abandon being, or rather being does not altogether abandon us, manifesting itself in everyday bodily and mental moves and needs. Yet, the socially mediated refinement of these needs yields a life that shoves being off, even if it is always there near at hand and within reach.

Non-being shows itself (off) in an indefinite variety in societal life by hiding and eclipsing being. Hence, non-being is not generative of being in any way, but it prevents being from being enlived by us. Yet, the nothing of non-being is not a "nothing-in-itself," if one is to use Hannah Arendt's term. Diogenes refrains from any attempt to think nothing because such thinking follows convention and thus remains within non-being, or to enact non-being because it would only lead away from the good life. Non-being as nothing-in-itself remains unsayable and inexpressible for Diogenes. And if non-being is unsayable, then one should live the life that demonstrates its impossibility by enacting it rather than by arguing against it. Diogenes speaks not apophatically but erotetically in an act by asking questions that alone can be the answers to the question about non-being and being. Can one say what cannot be said? In a sense, this sentence is not a question but itself *is* a way of saying the unsayable. So the question "Can one say the unsayable?" is in fact a response to the question "*How* can one say the unsayable?"

Against theory. As exposed by Diogenes, nothing is contravened by the being of the good life, which, however, is not immediately evident but remains hidden in plain sight and is marked by double negation, οὐ – μή: you will not be able to live properly if you do not know how (Dio. *Disc.* 10.28). Yet, this knowledge is *not theoretical* because the *how* of the being of the good life has to be enacted by living being out, without haste or fear, staying prepared for every fortune.[8] Hence, for Diogenes being cannot be reached by a dialectically refined argument because such an argument does not lead to the understanding of what is good for us but only to what appears to be such (DL 6.42). Under the guise of philosophy, then, theoretical disputations contaminate and renounce the good that we already have (Stobaeus 33.14). Theoretical life is a form of corruption of being by the convention of how to think about it, which misses being and thus, instead of clearing the way to being, leads us toward non-being.

By living according to nature or enacting being in nature, we can become reflectively aware of our being—but only to be able to leave this awareness behind in the good life. For the reflective awareness or account of being belongs to the theoretical exercise of logos developed in the confinement of the *polis*, which has corruptive power and thus should be abandoned for the *cosmopolis*. Living well and enliving being should thus fully revert to being that is not immediately reflective.

For this reason, Diogenes develops an "antitheoretical" position, rejecting not only dialectic but also mathematics, including music and astronomy as mathematical disciplines of the quadrivium, as well as the Academic triad of ethics, physics, and logic (DL 6.28, 73; Stobaeus 30.6).[9] In doing so, he follows Socrates, who in his youth

---

[8] τὸ γοῦν πρὸς πᾶσαν τύχην παρεσκευάσθαι, DL 6.63.

[9] In the list of Diogenes' works, we do not find a single title that would suggest an interest in mathematics, science, or logic. See Richard Heinze, Ed. *Xenocrates: Darstellung der Lehre und Sammlung der Fragmente.* Hildesheim: G. Olms, 1965, fr. 1. Later, Cynic-inclined Bion also speaks explicitly against mathematics as useless. Jan Frederik

became interested in the study of nature but later turned to ethics (Plato. *Phd.* 96a–99d). Yet, Socrates still dialectically reasons about ethics, whereas Diogenes demonstrates it by enacting being in (the good) life.

Against Plato. In his antitheoretical stance, Diogenes turns against Plato, the thinker of being. In their "battle for being," Diogenes and Plato are engaged in a gigantomachy in which Plato stands for a god who thinks being and Diogenes represents a giant who lives being through. Diogenes forcefully criticizes Plato for both his method, which is dialectic, and for his philosophical approach, which is the search for definitions. Plato called Diogenes "dog" (κύνα), to which Diogenes replied that this was true because he keeps coming back to those who have sold him (DL 6.40): Diogenes continuously attacks the philosophers and "dialecticians" who try to get rid of him.

From Diogenes's perspective, Plato's lectures or school discourses are just a waste of time.[10] Based on logical subdivisions, the dialectic is worthless because such knowledge cannot be translated into knowing the being of the good life. If, as said, knowing being means knowing how to live well, then any logical distinctions are nothing but impediments because being is not to be achieved as and at the end of a dialectical argument by way of logos but is enlived at any moment on the way of one's life according to being or nature.

The account of the dialectical way to being should be abandoned, because knowing being is knowing how to live well, which, without a ready at hand account, justification, or logos of such being, appears publicly as a foolish wisdom, the mockery of serious philosophizing, as Socratic not-knowing, or even as an oblivion

---

Kindstrand, Ed. *Bion of Borysthenes: A Collection of the Fragments with Introduction and Commentary.* Uppsala: Acta Universitatis Upsaliensis, 1976, fr. F5–F10.

[10] τὴν δὲ Πλάτωνος διατριβὴν κατατριβήν, DL 6.24. The pun here is the opposition of διατριβή, discourse, to κατατριβή, which is Diogenes' neologism and a hapax legomenon, suggesting a wasteful and worn-out, and thus useless, discussion.

of being and obliteration of its reflective awareness. That is why, when reproached for philosophizing without knowing, Diogenes replied: "Even if I only pretend to have wisdom, it is philosophy."[11]

Diogenes therefore rejects Plato's attempt to give definitions, including the definition of being. For if being has anything to do with number, then it is pointless because of the uselessness of mathematics. If being is form, then it is meaningless because it is to be established dialectically. When Plato was talking about forms, Diogenes once observed: "I see a table and a cup but do not see tablehood and cuphood," to which Plato responded: "You have eyes to see (θεωρεῖται) a table and a cup but no reason (νοῦν) to see (βλέπεται) the tablehood and cuphood" (DL 6.53). But Diogenes refuses to recognize reason-νοῦς that might allow an unmediated access to being because such reason does not enact being in living well. Therefore, Diogenes rejects Plato's political project, which was meant to educate philosophers who have "seen" and understood being to go back "down" to the *polis* in order to provide a rationally justified constitution to political life that would enact justice (*Rep.* 472b ff.). For, again, living well means living according to nature and not according to an artificially constructed legal and rational convention of the *polis*, which exemplifies non-being and only draws us away from being.

One can then but mock the self-contained, utterly serious activity of dialecticians, refuting them not by logical means but by comic jeering. According to the famous anecdote, when Plato and his disciples defined "human" as a biped and featherless animal, Diogenes plucked a rooster and brought it to Plato's school, saying, "This is Plato's human." Of course, a smart dialectician should always be ready to start anew or modify the definition, so, in order to counter this counterexample, it was added: "and with broad nails" (DL 6.40). Yet, no theoretical or dialectical ruse can refute

---

[11] εἰ καὶ προσποιοῦμαι σοφίαν, καὶ τοῦτο φιλοσοφεῖν ἐστι, DL 6.64.

Diogenes' enacted demonstration of the human as the being that can live well according to being, which is being in and of nature.

Against the Sophists. Diogenes' stance against the sophists is similar, to the extent that they are engaged in the same enterprise of (re)defining being, even if negatively, doing so by confusing the dialecticians and disproving their conclusions by imitating theoretical argument. But the parody of logos still belongs to the realm of logos. No matter whether one gets a thing logically right or wrong, it will not lead to being because being can only be enacted.

Hence, the dialecticians, or the followers of Plato, and the sophists are similar: for Diogenes, they are ignorant and yet believe themselves to be wise.[12] Knowledge of oneself, then, is knowledge of one's ignorance of being as enacted in the good life. But the ignorance that thinks to know something by logos or its rhetorical transformation is indeed ignorance.

While dialecticians are determined to get right the logos of being, the sophists only imitate it by playing rhetorical tricks. However, Diogenes, who rejected rhetoric (DL 6.47), finds a way to counter sophistic tricks by mocking the imitation of the dialectical reasoning—a way that rejects both the dialectical argument and its sophistic suspension. Diogenes does so by exposing the implicit pragmatic contradiction and thus the untenability of the sophisms.

Thus, Diogenes was reportedly provoked by a "dialectician of the Platonic school," who for the later tradition is indistinguishable from a sophist. When the sophist asked Diogenes to confirm that Diogenes was not what the sophist was, the sophist concluded that, since he himself was human, then Diogenes was not. Rather than logically exposing the ambiguity of being what one is in contradistinction to another concretely exemplified being, Diogenes refutes the sophism pragmatically: the conclusion is untenable, and if you

---

[12] ἀμαθεῖς ὄντες πεισθῶσι σοφοὶ εἶναι, Dio. *Disc.* 10.32.

want it to hold, begin with me.[13] In other words, if you begin with me, you will refute yourself by showing that you are not human and therefore are not even in a position to utter and submit the sophism. If you are a sophist, you will have to be silent and keep refuting yourself because you are shielding yourself from being by submitting to the non-being of a sophistic convention that cuts you off from the being of life according to nature. So against those who offer sophisms and riddles (σοφίσματα ... καὶ γρίφους), Diogenes practices a life of being that is in plain view, stripped (γυμνόν) of the unnecessary and is open for everyone to follow (*Ep.* 50).

Ergon. Diogenes' way of addressing another famous sophistic syllogism is exemplary. The syllogism suggests that what you have not lost you have; you did not lose horns; therefore, you have horns (DL 6.38; Aulus Gellius 18.2.9). Touching his forehead, Diogenes responded: "I do not see any."[14] The refutation of the sophism thus comes neither as a logical rejection of a seemingly incorrect argument built on the ambiguous use of "to have" nor as an appeal to empirical evidence—but by *touch*, by an action that repudiates the sophistic conclusion.

In a later epistle ascribed to Diogenes, its Cynic author retorts to those who live according to artificial conventions that cover up arrogance and impropriety: I can respond to you with a word or an argument, λόγος, but nature or being itself will reprove you with a *deed* or ἔργον.[15]

This is the action that Diogenes enacts when refuting Plato, the dialecticians, and the sophists. It is *ergon*, which is neither an act

---

[13] "*Hoc quidem ... falsum est, et si verum fieri vis, a me incipe* (That is a lie, but if you want it to be true, begin your proposition with me)," Aulus Gellius. *Noctes Atticae* 18.13. 7–8. See also ibid., 18.2.9: "*quod ego sum, id tu non es; homo ego sum: homo igitur tu non es* (What I am, that you are not. I am a man; therefore, you are not a man)." In *The Attic Nights of Aulus Gellius.* Trans. John C. Rolfe. 3 vols. Cambridge, MA: Harvard University Press, 1927.

[14] "ἐγὼ μέν," ἔφη, "οὐχ ὁρῶ," DL 6.38.

[15] κἀγὼ μὲν ὁ κύων τῷ λόγῳ, ἡ δὲ φύσις τῷ ἔργῳ ὁμοίως πάντας ὑμᾶς τιμωρεῖται, *Ep.* 28.5.

of theoretical reasoning nor a practical moral action.[16] Nor is it an activity of poietic production that creates something outside of and beyond the action itself. It is an act that demonstrates the untenability of a claim by exposing it as pragmatically self-contradictory by a simple move or gesture that at the same time points in the direction of being that remains missed in a definitive argument, a model moral action, or an archetypal work of art.

Ergon is thus an action that does not fall under θεωρία, πρᾶξις, or ποίησις. It does not produce a theoretical logos or argument that would disprove the opponent's logos because it would then be engaged in the refutational ἀντιλογία or controversy about being, which for Diogenes still remains within the realm of dialectical thinking that lives off the discussion of being but never reaches it. Nor is *ergon* a practical moral action whose purpose lies within itself, nor a productive act whose purpose is outside and external to the act of making (Aristotle. *Polit.* 1254a5).

Ergon is situated within the often dramatic and public enactment of the being of the good life and is a deed that also suggests the work of accomplishment: Diogenes acts to achieve and live the good life and show others how to do the same. Therefore, *ergon* is not an ethical act that follows a set of principles, nor is it a product of the understanding of such principles. It is a deed to be achieved and enlived in the battle for being.

Ergon refers to what *is* by showing *what* is in its enactment as *how* it is, in the life worth living. This means that to accomplish the being of the good life, one has to know (ἐπίστασθαι, Dio. *Disc.* 10.17) *how* to enlive it, as opposed to either theoretical knowing of the what and the practical following of the patterns or norms of action. It is only through the life of *ergon*, then, that one can accomplish the task of knowing oneself (γνῶθι σαυτόν, Dio.

---

[16] ἔργον or ϝέργον is apparently of the same root as "work," embracing, for instance, tillage, as is also understood by Hesiod, or weaving. In the *Iliad*, it stands for the deeds of war, which do not produce anything but do allow a hero to obtain κλέος, fame or glory, which might enable him to overcome mortality in the perpetuity of poetic lore.

Disc. 10.22), which is the knowledge of *how* to enact being and which for Diogenes is neither theoretical nor practical moral action but that of an *ergon*. The being of being human in nature, then, cannot be logically deduced, ascertained in practice, or produced by making but is demonstrated in and by a deed. In this sense, life according to nature or the enlived being is the life of *ergon*, of constant striving and attainment. As such, it is different from the understanding of life as πρᾶξις and is not in Aristotle.[17] The life of *ergon* is difficult and requires the toil of accomplishment.[18] In *ergon*, one should be capable of enacting the good life, which is not guaranteed but is a task to be achieved that requires determined acting out of all of one's might, which then can become exemplary and worth remembering and passing on, as are many *erga* of Diogenes.

Against Zeno. Returning to the refutation of dialectical and sophistic arguments, Diogenes' rebuttal of Zeno is exemplary, since it is performed in and as an *ergon*. Zeno rejected the possibility of motion, thus making the same claim as Parmenides, for whom being is and is one, only negatively: non-being, which transpires primarily through motion, is many and therefore is not.

According to Aristotle's account, also mentioned by Sextus and Simplicius, Zeno argued that if everything is at rest when it is equal to itself, then such always is the moving in the moment of "now," so that the flying arrow is motionless.[19] This claim appears to be paradoxical, since it is established by an argument that appears to contradict everyday experience. And yet, Aristotle refutes the paradox not by reference to ordinary experience but logically, which is why

---

[17] ὁ δὲ βίος πρᾶξις, οὐ ποίησίς ἐστιν, Aristotle. *Polit.* 1254a7. For Aristotle, ἔργον can also mean work required to produce something. See *Polit.* 1254a27–28, 1256a9.

[18] ἔργον ἐστί means "it is difficult."

[19] εἰ γὰρ ἀεί, φησίν, ἠρεμεῖ πᾶν ὅταν ᾖ κατὰ τὸ ἴσον, ἔστι δ' ἀεὶ τὸ φερόμενον ἐν τῷ νῦν, ἀκίνητον τὴν φερομένην εἶναι ὀϊστόν, Aristotle. *Phys.* 239b5–7. ὥστε καὶ Διογένη τὸν κύνα τῶν ἀποριῶν ποτε τούτων ἀκούσαντα μηδὲν μὲν εἰπεῖν πρὸς αὐτάς, ἀναστάντα δὲ βαδίσαι καὶ διὰ τῆς ἐναργείας αὐτῆς λῦσαι τὰ ἐν τοῖς λόγοις σοφίσματα, Simplicius. *In Phys.* 1012.24–26. See also Sextus. *Adv. Phys.* II 68–69.

in Aristotle's account it is a paralogism. He points out that time does not consist of indivisible "nows," just as a continuous magnitude does not consist of indivisibles (*Phys*. 239b8–9) because the indivisible is the *limit* of the continuous: "now"—of time, point—of a line.

Yet, for Diogenes such a refutation still falls within dialectical and thus theoretical activity, which misses the point entirely, since an argument can be countered by another argument, none of which leads to being as enacted and enlived. Instead, he responds to Zeno with silence, saying the unsayable by the action of walking: Diogenes stood up and walked about (ἀναστὰς περιεπάτει, DL 6.39). The impossibility of motion is thereby disproved by the "self-evidence" or "clarity" (διὰ τῆς ἐναργείας, Simplicius, *In Phys*. 1012.25–26) of motion as enacted in action that is the deed or *ergon* of the living body.

In this way, Diogenes reorients the entire philosophical debate by refusing to answer the dialectical question "What is X?," reserving only the possibility of answering the question "Is this X?," which he does by and in a non-dialectical and non-theoretical *ergon*. This response means enacting the recognition of the untenability of the proposed argument without reflection, or thinking being as an enlived unreflective act of being, which is life accomplished according to nature.

Life ascetics. One thus has to achieve being in the good life by *ergon*, which is neither a theoretical reasoning or rational justification nor an action according to an accepted or implied set of norms and prescriptions. Yet, one needs to resume the *ergon* every day, as life gets renewed every day. Being cannot be thought or realized once and for all but needs to be enlived again and again, always anew. Therefore, the *ergon* of the good life means constant and strenuous *exercise* or ἄσκησις of both the body and the soul (DL 70–71). In this sense, the good life is "ascetic," because it implies a persistent, restrained enactment of being. Such was Socrates' lifelong *ergon* (Xenophon. *Mem*. I.5).[20] To achieve the good life, the

---

[20] Xenophon. *Memorabilia*. In *Memorabilia, Oeconomicus, Symposium, Apology*. Trans. E. C. Marchant and O. J. Todd. Rev. Jeffrey Henderson. Cambridge, MA: Harvard University Press, 2013.

Cynic has to wage a struggle (πόνος) against the non-being of the conventional. One has to train oneself for such a life and practice it as an ἀγών, a competition or contest in public before the eyes of other people who might then learn from this lifelong competition and join it. Diogenes was wondering why people compete in wrestling and running but never in goodness (καλοκἀγαθία) that would allow them to live the good life.[21] This is why when asked for his writings, Diogenes replied that one should prefer real, honest, and true (ἀληθινή) training to any written instructions (DL 6.48; cf. *Ep.* 27). The goal of such an agonistic ascetic exercise, ἄσκησις, then, is the renewed and continuing lifelong battle for being against non-being. Living well requires self-discipline and thus ascetics.

Contra praxis. Diogenes' living the rigorous "ascetic" life, which consists of exemplary and spectacular *erga*, is thus a critique of *theōria*, of the exercise of pure theoretical reason. But it is equally a critique of πρᾶξις, of the exercise of practical reason that still follows theoretically and dialectically established norms, which Diogenes takes to be entirely conventional, hypocritical, and thus belonging to the realm of non-being. Moreover, his enliving of being is also a critique of *tekhnē*, of art as the production of unnecessary and unnatural devices that create artificial needs that corrupt people by artfully distracting them from the life according to nature and thus from being. Since animals do not use artificial devices, in a sense they are better off than humans (Dio. *Disc.* 10.16), and so we need to imitate and follow animals in artlessness by cutting off everything that is unnecessary and conventional to the extent we can. Therefore, the way to "ascetic" living is to use what nature has already equipped us with: for instance, a hand rather than a cup (DL 6.37). The only art Diogenes recognizes is the moral art (τέχνη ἠθική, which is the title of one of his lost works, DL 6.80); it is precisely the art of exercise-ἄσκησις in the achievement of *erga*.

---

[21] ἀγωνίζεσθαι... περὶ δὲ καλοκἀγαθίας μηδένα, DL 6.27. See also Stobaeus 4.112.

Liberation and freedom. Polis as the seat of non-being. Such an exercise opens a way to being in the good life, to which Diogenes' own *erga* are a testimony. Although it is life according to nature, there is nothing natural to it, since cognitively, sensuously, socially, and politically we already are in an unnatural situation of living the life of the *polis*, as political animals whose animality is subdued, transformed, and eventually almost canceled by an artificially established set of norms and rules. For Diogenes, the city as the seat of political power is based on law, νόμος, which is a customary convention, κατὰ νόμον, and as such it is contrary to that which exists by nature, κατὰ φύσιν (DL 6.71–72; cf. *Ep*. 39).[22] Since the city stands against, suspends, and rejects nature through unnecessary artificial devices and habits detrimental to the good life, the way to live well is to return to nature by turning against convention and thus suspending the suspension of nature. Those who live against nature—and this is the predicament of civilization and its political expressions—will be inevitably punished by nature, as was Icarus (Dio., *Disc*. 4.120). Conventional norms are meant to direct us toward collectively reaching freedom, but in fact, for Diogenes, it only subjugates us into living against nature and thus living poorly rather than living well even when being poor. So the task of the ascetic Cynic exercise is to break away from these artificial forms of self-enslavement.

Therefore, one should begin with the liberation from the established, corrupt existing form of life, which is that of the *polis*. If the city corrupts while nature liberates, one can—and for Diogenes, should—try to turn the world-κόσμος into the city-πόλις and

---

[22] Diogenes apparently inherited the opposition between convention and nature (ἀντιτιθέναι... νόμῳ δὲ φύσιν, DL 6.38) from the sophists. Yet, unlike the sophists, Diogenes stresses the sufficiency of the means nature provides us, which are sufficient for living without oppressing other people. See A. A. Long. "The Socratic Tradition: Diogenes, Crates, and Hellenistic Ethics." In *The Cynics: The Cynic Movement in Antiquity and Its Legacy*. Ed. R. Bracht Branman and Marie-Odile Goulet-Cazé. Berkeley: University of California Press, 1996, 34–35.

return the city to the world. The only true polity, then, is the world and is in the world.[23]

But to be its citizen, a cosmopolitan, is a difficult task because it requires a radical reestablishment and reenactment of our life in its entirety. *Cosmopolis* is itself a paradoxical concept, since the city-*polis* is complementary to the world-*cosmos*. The two are differently structured and governed: the city-*polis* is a human product based on the *nomos* of custom, whereas the world-*cosmos* exists of and by itself and is governed by the universal logos. *Polis* is the seat of non-being as convention that hides and distorts being, while *cosmos* is the seat of being, where we can liberate ourselves from non-being. Therefore, to claim that one is a cosmopolitan, as Diogenes does for the first time in history, is to recognize and enact one's simultaneous existence in both the political and natural worlds, in the two domains that are not identical and yet can no longer be separate, to the extent that the citizens of the world cohabit the two realms by suspending the unnecessary in the conventional and enliving a commonly shared good life.

Against convention: negative freedom as liberation. One should therefore begin first by liberating oneself from the *polis*. Such a liberation is negative freedom as freedom-from. This is the freedom from fear as fear-of in its different forms: the fear of poverty, illness, shame, infamy, lower social position, exile (πενία, ἀδοξία, δυσγένεια, φυγαδεία, *Ep.* 31), and death. Ultimately, this is the liberation from the fear of non-being.

The liberation that Diogenes seeks to attend through the *erga* of his life is thus freedom from non-being that politically and socially shows itself in oppressive moral, social, political, and religious habits or in the law-*nomos* as arbitrary and repressive conventions of the city. But custom is not in the order of things but is something of the city, bourgeois, fancy, and improperly refined (ἀστεῖον, DL 6.71), and is therefore unnecessary and superfluous. Liberation

---

[23] μόνην τε ὀρθὴν πολιτείαν εἶναι τὴν ἐν κόσμῳ, DL 6.72.

from the grasp of the non-being of the conventional, then, can only be achieved through strenuous exercise, the ascetics of the mind and body, by practicing indifference (ἀδιαφορία) and limiting one's needs to the basic "natural" ones,[24] by rejecting everything that is superfluous, unnecessary, and enthralling—whether it be luxury, property, proper appearance and attire, wealth, power, and fame. And if fear, epitomized in the fear of death, is removed, there is nothing else left to fear or be distressed by (δυσχερές, Dio. *Disc.* 6.42). For nature knows no death, but, as an embodied being, it always comes back in one form or another.

Asocial behavior as provocation. Negative freedom, therefore, is to be achieved by a constant suspension and interruption of the conventional by calling it into question in and by *erga*, which are exemplary of being as embodied and enlived. Being is thereby liberated from the non-being of the habitual by intentional provocation.

Negative freedom as liberation from the conventional is accomplished not so much by questioning others with the intention of showing them the misery of their current state (Dio. *Disc.* 9.2, 10.1), for even when ironic, such inquiry falls within the theoretical activity meant to establish customary, even if correct, ways of behavior. Liberation comes as a shock, resulting from Diogenes' provocative *erga* in his expressly *asocial behavior.* Staged for the others, such *erga* are performed in public as theatrical pieces, directed and performed by Diogenes himself. His performance is public and yet asocial in that it is critical, diagnostic, and therapeutic and is meant to help citizens of the *polis* recognize the possibility and necessity of becoming cosmopolitans.

These theatrical acts are intentionally provocative and as such are memorable. Diogenes is well remembered in the popular tradition for his fearless breaking of social prohibitions, which is commonly perceived as "shamelessness" (ἀναίδεια). Provocation is a

---

[24] See Léonce Paquet, Ed. *Les Cyniques grecs: Fragments et témoignages.* Ottawa: Les presses de l'Université d'Ottawa, 1988, 8–9.

radical protest against the ubiquitous hypocritical moral, social, and political norms. One can make a provocation only against the conventional and not against the natural, because only the conventional can be examined, suspended, and changed.

Diogenes' provocative behavior is often so asocial that he has earned the reputation not only of being reproachful and having a sharp and reviling tongue (λοιδορῆσαι, Dio. *Disc.* 9.6), of pouring scorn and treating people haughtily (κατασοβαρεύσασθαι τῶν ἄλλων, DL 6.24) but also of being mad. Even Plato famously calls him "Socrates gone mad" (Σωκράτης μαινόμενος, DL 6.54). Yet, Diogenes opposes the folly (ἄνοια) of others (Dio. *Disc.* 9.1) in order to help them recognize the oppressive character of unquestioned norms, which many do, praising Diogenes as not mad but as the wisest of all people (Dio. *Disc.* 9.8). So Diogenes' being wise does not differ from his being mad because both states defy established conventions.

There are numerous preserved examples of Diogenes' asocial behavior, told, retold, and cherished in the memory of his stunned but eventually grateful spectators and listeners. Thus, we see him wandering around in plain daylight with a lamp in search of a real human (DL 6.41), whistling like a bird (DL 6.27), spitting into his host's face (not finding a worse place to do it) (DL 6.32), throwing the already mentioned plucked rooster into Plato's school (DL 6.40), coming half shaven to a banquet (DL 6.33), standing naked under the rain (DL 6.41), walking barefoot on snow (DL 6.34)...[25]

Diogenes' *erga* intentionally challenge commonly accepted practices, questioning and negating them. We hear about Diogenes walking in the Stoa in the direction opposite to the

---

[25] In walking on snow, Diogenes is perhaps imitating Socrates, who was known for doing the same thing. See Plato. *Symp.* 220b; Xenophon. *Mem.* 1.6.2. See also Aristophanes' *Clouds*, in which Socrates is described as walking barefoot (*Nub.* 103–104; *Clouds*. In *Clouds, Wasps, Peace*. Trans. and ed. Jeffrey Henderson. Cambridge, MA: Harvard University Press, 1998, 363.

habitual one and, when being laughed at, retorting that those who are used to walking opposite to nature for their entire lives should not blame him for choosing the course of his leisurely walk (Stobaeus 4.84). Dressing and looking like a beggar (Dio. *Disc.* 8.1) and living in a tub (DL 6.23), Diogenes publicly challenges seemingly unshakeable norms and institutions. He recognizes no limits in his fight against the customary, performatively putting into question unquestionable taboos, such as trying to eat raw meat (DL 6.34), the privacy of sex (DL 6.46, 69), and the prohibition of cannibalism (DL 6.73). Diogenes' insulting gestures also target the false and detrimental pretense of rhetoric and sophistry. Thus, he points at Demosthenes and a sophist with his middle finger (DL 6.34; Epictetus. *Discourses* III 2.11), saying that only a finger separates people from madness: if you show them the middle finger, they will think you are mad, but if the little finger, they will not think so (DL 6.35). Perhaps the decisive act of Diogenes in the refutation of the sophists at the end of his speech about living well consists in squatting on the ground and performing an indecent and disreputable act (ἐποίει τι τῶν ἀδόξων), which confused the sophists and made them shout in outrage (Dio. *Disc.* 8.36).

Choosing to appear mad, Diogenes is a sane guide and companion on the way of being toward the good life. His performative negative *erga* are neither dialectical arguments nor practical advice but publicly visible acts questioning oppressive customary habits that liberate himself and others from such norms that only exemplify a commonly distributed non-being.

Against arrogance. Targeting customs and prejudices that distract us from living well, Diogenes acts much like Socrates who constantly questioned Athenians about their ways of living and knowing how to live. And yet, there is a difference between the two: while Socrates addresses his fellow citizens, Diogenes addresses everyone as citizens of the world, and while Socrates never turns away from the *polis*, Diogenes suggests going to nature.

Most importantly, as Foucault observes, while Socrates targets *ignorance*, Diogenes targets *pride*.[26]

It is pride and vanity that embody the aberration of being by convention. This is why when Diogenes saw in Olympia beautifully dressed young men from Rhodes, he laughed at them and said (or likely should have said): "This is vanity (τῦφος)," but when he saw young people from Sparta dressed shabbily, he said "This is vanity too, but of a different kind" (Aelian. *Varia hist.* IX 34).

Those who are engaged in theoretical investigations of being, then, do it out of vanity in an attempt to gain social prestige and establish themselves as worthy of *kleos*, the perennial glory bestowed by the tradition on heroes for their deeds.[27] Plato's political project of giving the philosophers all the political power in the dialectically justified project of the commonly distributed good (*Rep.* 473c–474c passim), then, appears suspicious as an attempt not only to usurp power but even more to bring the *polis* ever farther from the life according to nature. From this perspective, Plato's effort to improve tyrannical regimes by rational and dialectically verified political constitutions is self-defeating and only leads away from being and nature, which becomes ultimately excluded and conquered by the *polis*'s strict hierarchical arrangement based on *nomos*. This is why Diogenes reproaches Plato for forfeiting his freedom by serving and flattering Dionysius (DL 6.58) and sharing meals with tyrants, whereas Diogenes' own practice of poverty is the life of liberation from the unnecessary.

Philosophy's yearning for recognition by political power is thus a sign of corruption in which striving for truth masks vanity. This is why Diogenes keeps attacking Plato's vainglory (κενοσπουδία),

---

[26] Michel Foucault. *Fearless Speech*. Ed. by Joseph Pearson. Los Angeles: Semiotext[e]), 2001, 127.

[27] Diogenes' critique of prestige as the driving force within society prefigures Rousseau's attack on *amour propre* as the spring of social and political evils. See Jean-Jacques Rousseau. *Discourse on the Origin and Foundations of Inequality among Men, or Second Discourse*. In *The Discourses and Other Early Political Writings*. Trans. and ed. Victor Gourevitch. Cambridge, MA: Cambridge University Press, 2002, 152, 218.

pride, and arrogance (τῦφος). Yet, Plato in turn accuses Diogenes of vanity and arrogance under the guise of humility (DL 6.26). So when Diogenes is standing naked under the rain, Plato sees nothing in this *ergon* but the love of fame (φιλοδοξία, DL 6.41).

Vanity thus might appear under the appearance of not being vain. If vanity is the expression of the conventional that, as non-being, can never be something definitive but keeps presenting and proliferating itself under different semblances, then vanity can appear as not vanity, and not vanity as vanity, in different ways, which Plato distinguishes dialectically, while Diogenes distinguishes by his *erga*.

So Plato and Diogenes genuinely miss each other's ways of living and attaining to being against non-being. Thus, Diogenes once asked Plato for wine and dried figs, and Plato sent a whole jar. To this act of generosity, which again can be interpreted as making a show out of it, Diogenes replied: "If someone asks you how many are two and two, will you answer " 'Twenty?'," thus scoffing at Plato's philosophy as talking without end (ἀπεραντολόγον, DL 6.26). And yet, one cannot banish the impression that, while constantly attacking each other, the two thinkers-actors dearly love each other, even if they each hesitate to recognize it. They keep talking past each other—and yet they keep talking.

The seemingly contradictory nature of Diogenes' ergon. And yet, Diogenes' attitude to being as nature and to non-being as convention is marked by a peculiar seeming contradiction, which he does not notice or perhaps prefers not to. Indeed, his suggestion of living according to nature, which should help us get rid of everything that is unnecessary and detrimental, does not really mean returning to the wild, to the life in woods and caves, nor even going back to pastoral life in the country. While striving toward the good life according to nature, Diogenes lives off and remains in the *polis*, never leaving the city but scavenging on its margins looking for food, abiding at the political outskirts, and cleansing the *polis* through his incessant critique. Being free to wander, he never leaves the *polis*: when leaving one city (Athens), he never ends in the mountains or on a beach but always in another city (Corinth). His repeated migration from one city to another appears to be a failed attempt to ultimately liberate himself from the political in favor of the natural and to fuse the natural with the political. He neither uses the products of nature nor produces his own subsistence within the *polis*. Therefore, returning to nature means returning to the good life as it was originally meant and provided for us by nature while still staying within the *polis*. In fact, the *polis* has to be transformed into a place that is inhabited and enlived in accord with nature, with being that does not detract from us and does not distract us from living well. This means a complete transformation of our commonly shared lives in and into a *cosmopolis* that does not break into mutually self-hostile enclosures under the weight of habitual non-being. Only the cosmopolitan life, then, can be the life of freedom and well-being in being.

Therefore, striving for liberation from the unnecessary and becoming a citizen of the anticipated *cosmopolis* by means of strenuous exercise, the Cynic is still not autonomous, still using the city's moral and physical decay for the attainment of nature. In this respect, Diogenes' nature is *domesticated*. It is an artfully and unnaturally cultivated nature. Being, searched for and asserted by Diogenes, is deeply immersed and intimately tied to non-being. For this reason, he is a dog, and not a wolf.[28] Because he has neither a house nor a master, he is a stray dog. Yet, among the dogs, he is a celestial one (DL 6.77): Sirius, the brightest star in the night of human delusion.

---

[28] Aristotle simply calls Diogenes "the Dog," ὁ Κύων (*Rhet.* 1411a24). See also DL 6.26; Dio. *Disc.* 4.3, 8.11, 17; *Ep.* 40, 44; and G 143–51. For Plato, dogs are the perfect guardians of the state (*Rep.* 375e), gentle with those whom they know and ferocious with strangers. But Diogenes, seemingly ferocious with everyone, does *not* protect the existing state but attacks it all the time, guarding his own ideal polity, about which he wrote his own *State* (DL 6.80), which, however, we do not have. Cf. *Ep.* 41: only the dog (Cynic) can succeed in acting in accordance with virtue. See also: Giannantoni, Ed. "Diogene: l'epiteto 'cane'." In *Socratis et Socraticorum Reliquiae*. Vol. 4. Naples, Italy: Bibliopolis, 1990, 491–97.

Scandal. Those who understand the "as-ifness" of Diogenes' provocative *erga*—gestures, words, actions—learn from them. Those who don't are scandalized.

Scandal is the public reaction to the violation of moral, legal, social, and political customs and practices, exacerbated when such breaching is perceived as intentional and deliberately provocative. Because scandal confronts and suspends the existing habitual ways of thinking and acting, it is indispensable for questioning and suspending the underlying norms, which are often implicit and taken for granted—until their boundaries get transgressed. Scandal is therefore an *ergon*.

Apparently, the oracle urged Diogenes to counterfeit *political currency* (τὸ πολιτικὸν νόμισμα), which even he himself did not understand at first and so he took the advice literally (DL 6.20). The oracle, however, meant the "reevaluation of all values," which does not imply reverting to certain originary, upright but now lost political and moral laws (those of the *polis*). Rather, it implies recognition of the fact that the *polis* should return to living well and thus become a *cosmopolis*, which alone can reconcile *nomos* with *physis*. Recoining political currency, we always remain political beings in the search for nature.

Diogenes clearly intends to cause scandal by his actions and to outrage the public when he asks to be buried face down or goes to a theater when everyone is leaving, explaining that this is what he was doing all of his life—going against the grain (DL 6.32, 64). Scandal always is—and has to be—*public*. In antiquity, the private is the space within the household. But for Diogenes, who does not have a home and whose home is the whole city, there is no distinction between public and private, so private is public and public is private. Hence, his *erga* that are meant to be public are scandalously put on public display and are played out during assemblies, communal celebrations, and games—in the streets, squares, theaters, and stadiums (Dio. Disc. 8.6), suspending the up to now unquestioned and seemingly unquestionable stereotypical rules of thinking and behavior.

The public space of Diogenes' scandalous *ergon*, then, turns into the space of *spectacle* and thus becomes *theater*. For this reason, scandal has the structure of a theatrical act in which everyone wants to be a spectator, but no one wants to be an actor: one likes to see how people, thoughts, and institutions get publicly ridiculed, but no one wants to be ridiculed. And yet, scandal is a spectacle that engages and involves everyone present in its performance. Thus, the spectators inevitably become actors on the public stage because the scandalous *ergon* highlights what they have been taking for granted as the meaning of public and private life (its semantics) and its rules and norms (its syntax). However, it is ultimately Diogenes who is the protagonist, director, and playwright of the drama of the public scandal.

Positive freedom as self-containment and as simplicity of life. But the negative freedom of liberation from the non-being of the conventional and unnecessary should pave the way toward the positive freedom of the good life in and of being according to nature. Negative freedom comes with public and theatrical scandal, which should allow for the positive freedom that needs to be achieved, exercised, and enlived through "ascetic" exercise.

Against the corruption of the *polis* that abounds in wealth and luxury, Diogenes accepts, embraces, and stresses his own poverty (G 220–246; *Ep.* 32, 33),[29] using it as a powerful critical device meant to expose the hypocrisy and moral failure of the powerful and the rich, thus turning his poverty into a public theatrical scandal. Poverty for Diogenes is a way to philosophy, and what philosophy puts in words or *logoi* (τοῖς λόγοις), poverty does in deeds or *erga* (ἐν ἔργοις, Stobaeus 4.32, 11 = G 223). Voluntary poverty differs from the poverty caused and enforced unto others by the abundance of wealth, which signifies inequality and thus has to be

---

[29] See William Desmond. *The Greek Poverty: Origins of Ancient Cynicism*. Notre Dame, IN: University of Notre Dame, 2006, 31–103. Cf. [Plato]. *Eryxias* 401d–e.

abolished. Voluntary poverty means the simplicity of life. Striving toward simplicity or shabbiness (εὐτέλεια, *Ep*. 34) means putting aside everything unnecessary that prevents us from living well according to being. This, again, means exercise (ἀσκεῖν) in everyday actions that would allow for the simplicity of life (βίου λιτότης, *Ep*. 27). Otherwise, the imitation of a simple and unpretentious life might itself be pretentious and vain, concealing pride, as Diogenes observes in the poorly dressed youth from Sparta, and which Plato suspects in his harshly criticized yet deeply loved opponent.

The ultimate purpose of such a life, then, is the positive freedom of self-reliance or self-sufficiency (αὐτάρκεια). When asked who is really rich, Diogenes reportedly replied, "The self-sufficient" (ὁ αὐτάρκης).[30] Self-reliance, however, differs from contemporary autonomy, which means self-legislation: unlike Plato, Diogenes does not provide the law either for himself or for the city. The positive freedom he intends for us to achieve is the freedom of self-containment and voluntary poverty (against wealth), of simplicity and health (against excess), of moderation and virtue (against pleasure).[31] By liberating ourselves from the conventional, from the dictates of fashion and shame, we can enlive being as life according to nature, which is the good life of simplicity, moderation, and self-sufficiency.

Positive freedom as the freedom of speech. The other way in which positive freedom is expressed within the *polis* on the margins of the *polis* against the *polis* is the freedom of speech (παρρησία). It points toward the possibility of *cosmopolis* as the place of freedom for all that is not outside and not separate from nature.

Free speech translates the personal freedom of daring to speak openly and freely into public freedom because the logos always needs the other with whom it shares itself. As an *ergon*, logos can

---

[30] *Texte und Kommentare*. Vol. 2 of *Gnomologium Vaticanum*. Ed. Leo Sternbach. Berlin: De Gruyter, 1963, apothegm 743n180 = G 241.

[31] DL 6.31; *Ep*. 9, 16, 25, 27; Dio. *Disc*. 10.16. "Diogenes said that true pleasure lies in having one's soul in a calm and cheerful state" (*Gnomologium Vaticanum* 181 = G 300).

only be enacted with others and openly to others—only then is it free. This means that logos is public, needs a public, and is (to be) performed in public. In the *ergon* of free speech, being appears as liberated from non-being and free in logos, which is thought put to speech.

Free speech is the speech that questions, challenges, and suspends commonly accepted norms, conventions, and institutions. In his ἄσκησις, Diogenes performs his provocative and often scandalous *erga* of free speech in public, unashamedly trespassing the limits between the private and the public, which becomes an integral part of public life, both irritating and cherished.

However, free speech is not a given but has to be fought for and constantly reasserted. Freedom of speech,[32] then, is a major—if not the most important—freedom in the hoped-for *cosmopolis*. No wonder, then, that Diogenes claims that παρρησία is the best in us (κάλλιστον, DL 6.69; ἥδιστον, Dio. *Disc.* 4.15). Through free speech, public spaces become liberated from the non-being of the dominant conventional social and political norms and free for being with and together with others.

As the exercise of positive freedom, παρρησία is always a critique of existing corrupt morals, habits, and conventions. Such a critique, which is neither theoretical nor practical, aims at truth that is not established dialectically but is demonstrated and publicly disclosed as being acted out in an *ergon* (Dio. *Disc.* 8.3).

Because the positive freedom-for (being of the good life and self-reliance) begins with the negative liberation or freedom-from (non-being of convention and authority), free speech is *dangerous*. Speaking truth in public, which is going against the grain, requires courage. And if courage is indeed the primary and originary virtue (both as the "archaic" virtue of the heroic age and the model for other virtues), then free speech is primarily virtuous because it is

---

[32] In Cicero, *libertas loquendi* (with reference to the Stoics) means calling a thing plainly by its name.

courageous.[33] This is why being a philosopher means living according to virtue and nature.[34] Yet the fear of saying, hearing, and knowing the truth of being eclipsed by the non-being of the conventional is mutual in both the one who acts and speaks and the one who attends and listens, because a person might never be the same after saying and hearing an uncomfortable truth. This is why free speech makes a tyrant afraid (Dio. *Disc.* 6.57), which includes not only a usurper of power but also oppressive conventional customs and habits. The courage to speak and the implied courage to listen and hear, then, are indispensable for the "ascetic" exercise of positive freedom.

The free speaker is the free thinker who in his *ergon* is not bound by the constraints imposed by an authority, either of the law-*nomos* (because it is a convention) or of social standing (equally a convention) or of the ruler (whose imposition of power is fortuitous and willful) or of excessive and constantly sought-for pleasure (because it is contrary to the order of things). Diogenes refuses to pay tribute to the conventional and simply cancels all the debts, both his own and everyone else's, in a radical and audacious *ergon* by the gesture of their abatement and rejection, since "by nature" one only owes to oneself the effort of living well. Diogenes is in no one's debt, because, paradoxically, he both owns nothing (he has no property) and everything (he has the whole world, as its citizen, shared with others).

Comedy and theater. Free speech is logos that stands together with nature as being and as such is opposed to law-*nomos*, on the one hand, and to passion-*pathos*, on the other, which stands for non-being.[35] Logos is not only reason that can liberate us from non-being and lead to being, even if not so much by an ordered and

---

[33] For Aristotle, magnanimous is the one who speaks freely (παρρησιαστής), because to care for opinion more than for truth and hide one's thought is cowardly. *NE* 1124b26–31.
[34] τὸ κατ' ἀρετὴν καὶ φύσιν ζῆσαι, *Ep.* 25.
[35] ἀντιτιθέναι... νόμῳ δὲ φύσιν, πάθει δὲ λόγον, DL 6.38.

orderly reasoning—but it is also speech that allows us to be theatrical in the public space and to share liberation and freedom with others.

As was said, scandal is a theatrical act in which everyone becomes involved in the course of its action. Since free speech *is* a scandal, always unpredictable and always unforeseen, it too needs to be performed theatrically in public, on the stage of the city's squares and arenas, invariably attracting interlocutors by the free speaker's provocative *erga* (Dio. *Disc.* 8.10).

Since Diogenes' theatrical public performance is an improvisation and thus has no script, he is free to experiment with genres, such as sententiae, aphorisms, apophthegms, chreiai or short pointed anecdotes, and iambic derision. But free public speech exposes the wrong and the conventional by ridicule, hyperbolic metaphor, and farce, accompanied by jest and joke (Dio. *Disc.* 9.7). As such, free speech is performatively closest to *comedy*, which, in Aristotle's account, comes out of iambic poetry that uses agonistic public verbal battles, scoffs, sarcasm, pungent gestures, improvisation, sententiae, provocative language, and acrimonious acts.[36] All of these are abundant in Diogenes' *erga*.

Comedy begins with a complication and moves by a mutually shared action in which, however, one of the characters stands out as the mastermind or thinker on stage who stirs the plot toward resolution of the conflict. Diogenes is exactly such a comic hero on the public stage of the *polis*. He chooses to comically impersonate a mythological hero in an intentional parodistic allusion to Heracles, who is *the* hero of the Cynic ἄσκησις that requires commitment

---

[36] Aristotle. *Poet.* 1448b31–1449a6. See also "Archilochus." In *Iambi et elegi Graeci ante Alexandrum cantati*. Vol. 1. Ed. M. L. West. 2nd ed. Oxford: Oxford University Press, 1989, fr. 41–44, 46; 18–20. See also M. L. West. "Iambus." Chap. 2 of *Studies in Greek Elegy and Iambus*. Berlin: De Gruyter, 1974, 22–39. Another closely related dramatic genre is mime (of Sophron; later, mimiambs by Herodas), which presents short comic scenes from everyday life in the form of a monologue or dialogue. See Herodas. *Mimiambs*. Trans. and ed. Graham Zanker. Liverpool: Liverpool University Press, 2009. Plato is said to have imitated Sophron's mimes in his dialogues (*Anon. Proleg.* 1.3; Aristotle. *Poet.* 1447b10–11).

and labors comparable to those of Heracles (Dio. *Disc.* 6.28–35; Ep. 36). Yet in comedy, in order to be taken seriously, the hero has to become a fool. In the search for simplicity and self-reliance, which suspends the conventional norms of behavior and thinking, Diogenes intentionally appears under the guise of a trickster, alazon, or buffoon. The fool is the one who fools around, who acts strangely and out of place, who seems to be mistaken but in fact dares to tell the truth of being.

While Socrates is explicitly present in Aristophanes' Old Comedy in the *Clouds*, Diogenes appears implicitly in Menander's New Comedy, becoming the prototype for the cherished comic figure of the smart slave or servant who appears to be a simpleton and yet outsmarts everyone else.[37] In one of his comedies *The Groom*, Menander explicitly mentions Diogenes' pupil Monimus, who was once a slave (DL 6.82–83). And in a satirical play *Sale of Diogenes*, ascribed to Menippus, when asked what he can do, Diogenes replies: "I can rule over people" (DL 6.29), thus becoming a comic mastermind on the stage of public theater.[38]

In comedy, it is the fool who is wise, which he demonstrates by enacting his "foolish wisdom," which shocks others but from which they can also learn about (socially and politically embodied) being and non-being, the good life, and the ways of its achieving. This wisdom allows one to recognize and know one's ignorance and enables others to learn and do the same (Dio. *Disc.* 10.32). The slave is thus the mastermind behind development of the argument and comic plot, who plans and stages a whole new dramatic frame in order to trick the seemingly wise and steer the action toward the being of the good life.

---

[37] See T. G. A. Nelson. *Comedy: An Introduction to Comedy in Literature, Drama, and Cinema*. Oxford: Oxford University Press, 1990, 89–102; and Diego Lanza. *Lo stolto: Di Socrate, Eulenspiegel, Pinocchio e altri trasgressori del senso comune*. Turin: Einaudi, 1997.

[38] Heinrich Niehuis-Pröbsting. *Der Kynismus des Diogenes und der Begriff des Zynismus*. 2nd ed. Frankfurt: Suhrkamp, 1988, 206–21.

The comic slave stands out by being "the other" of everyone else. He looks differently, speaks differently, dresses differently, and acts differently. As Plato argued in the *Laws* (*Legg.* 816e), comedy depicts base and ridiculous things and therefore should be left to slaves and foreigners. And Diogenes is precisely this kind of character, since he is not only a foreigner but also reportedly was once enslaved (DL 6.29-30, as was also Plato when he spoke truth to Dionysius, calling him a tyrant, DL 3.19). However, a foreigner or slave is never a bore, exactly because he can see—and tell—things differently. In this sense, a philosopher is a comic figure and a foreigner to his own country[39] because he despises and ridicules the convention of common sense and is ready and capable of thinking beyond the accepted political divides and cultural prejudices, of transgressing social differences, and driving action toward equality and freedom. Being excluded from the social ranks of the *polis*, the stranger is the one who allows for liberation and freedom for everyone, through his personal example and publicly enlived free speech.

Political implications of freedom. Freedom and power. Steering and directing the comedy, the slave becomes the master of comedy, the architect of its plot. The master turns out to be the slave in comedy insofar as he has to follow the twists and turns, the traps and clearings along the way of the action. In comedy, the master is the slave of the slave, and the slave is the master of the master. The master's power enacts non-being as convention. And if the figure of the comic slave as the mastermind of action stands for the poor and dispossessed, then Diogenes enlives the life of being in public that provides both liberation and freedom for all against the oppressive conventionality of *nomos*, the rule of wealth, and the power that does not provide well-being for anyone. Diogenes' famous response "Move away from the Sun" (ἀποσκότησόν μου,

---

[39] Hans Blumenberg. *Das Lachen der Thrakerin: Eine Urgeschichte der Theorie.* Frankfurt: Suhrkamp, 1987, 33-41.

DL 6.38)[40] to Alexander, who wants to display his unlimited power by showing off his imputed capacity to fulfill any desire and grant any wish, demonstrates that Diogenes' free speech puts him beyond the bounds of customary political limitations. Diogenes exemplifies the power of freedom as the freedom of speech that even the most powerful ruler cannot match because the ruler is enmeshed in convention and thus is incapable of being liberated from non-being. Once Alexander realizes the futility of this power, which cannot even prevent him from obscuring the light of the Sun, he can only recognize that he would have liked to become Diogenes (DL 6.32; Ep. 33.4). Only the poor and dispossessed one, personified in Diogenes, is free, insofar as he is the master of pleasure, property, and fame (ἡδονή, χρήματα, and δόξα), whereas the ruler is a slave of them (cf. Ep. 4 [to Antipater], 5 [to Perdiccas]). So for Diogenes, the poor and the oppressed rule over the powerful and the rich who cannot even rule themselves, possessed by their possession and the desire to have the whole world at their disposal. But the world is the world of being in nature that cannot be conquered or ruled by the non-being of convention.

For Diogenes, anyone who does not rule oneself is a tyrant who disregards nature and acts against it and who is ruled by pleasure, wealth, and fame. Power and wealth can be recognized as legal, and yet they are tyrannical if they do not limit or suspend—cancel and deny—themselves. No wonder that for Diogenes nobody becomes a tyrant because of poverty but only because of wealth. The tyrant is at war with others but primarily with himself. Every form of power is thus tyrannical if it does not acknowledge and follow self-discipline and a self-restricting life according to nature. The Cynic ἄσκησις is therefore tyrannicide, which kills and overthrows the tyrant of pleasure and pride in oneself.

---

[40] Cf. Cicero. *Tusc. disp.* V 32, 92 = G 33; Dio. *Disc.* 4.15; Plutarch. *De exilio* 15, 605d–c = G 32; *Ep.* 33.

Diogenes is beyond the power of the ruler and of the city because he has moved from the conventional to, if not nature, then at least the very margins of the political, where he becomes unreachable to power as the embodiment of law. Diogenes speaks freely in the face of a ruler and the majority of people, but not because he is not afraid: he is not afraid because he dares to speak freely. Free speech is the palpable testimony to his freedom. It is thus the poor and dispossessed who rule over the rich and powerful in the comedy staged by Diogenes on the public scene of the city, because the dispossessed are free from the oppression of the unnecessary—of social prestige, power, and wealth.

Thus, through his *erga*, his acts, actions, and speeches, Diogenes demonstrates the possibility of liberation and freedom for all by publicly enliving the being of the good life according to nature and criticizing the non-being of the conventional in his intentionally scandalous acts of body and speech.

5

Aristotle

Non-Being as Thought in Many Ways

τὸ δὲ μὴ ὂν μηδέν ἐστιν.

Non-being is nothing.[1]

τὸ μὴ ὂν λέγεται πλεοναχῶς.

Non-being is said in many ways.[2]

The famous opening sentence of Aristotle's *Metaphysics* runs like this: "All people by nature strive to knowledge."[3] In doing so, we begin with what is more evident to us before we move on to what is evident by nature (τῇ φύσει, *Phys.* 184a16–18). This should also be the case, then, with non-being. Yet, if non-being is utter negativity and is not, how can it be evident on its own?

In another famous opening section in Book B of the *Posterior Analytics*, Aristotle distinguishes between four kinds of what we search for (τὰ ζητούμενα), which correspond to the four kinds of knowledge: the "that" (τὸ ὅτι), the "why" (τὸ διότι), the "if" (εἰ ἔστι), and the "what" (τί ἐστιν, *An. post.* 89b23–35). And if about some things we ask "why" (the Sun is eclipsed), once we already know "that" (it gets eclipsed), we ask a different question about others: "if something is or is not simply" (a centaur or a god). So if

---

[1] Aristotle. *De gen. et corr.* 318a15.
[2] Aristotle. *Phys.* 225a20.
[3] Πάντες ἄνθρωποι τοῦ εἰδέναι ὀρέγονται φύσει, Aristotle. *Met.* 980a21. All the references in this chapter are to Aristotle's works, except when noted otherwise.

Non-Being in Ancient Thought. Dmitri Nikulin, Oxford University Press.
© Oxford University Press 2025. DOI: 10.1093/oso/9780197781616.003.0005

something can be understood in its *what*, we need first to find out *if* it at all *is*, or exists. And if we know *that* it is, then we can then ask *what* it is. But if non-being *is not*, how can it have an understandable *what*?

Being and non-being. Aristotle's understanding of non-being is inscribed into his ontology. That the striving to know comes naturally (πέφυκε), and is such by nature (φύσει), suggests that ontology is itself rooted in nature, which is thus also the source of our knowledge and understanding of being and non-being. Aristotle's cosmos is the world of natural things that exist, that are what they are due to nature as being the cause of their being as a life of temporal existence and motion. Their being is not a being in motion but the being of beings that are moving and moved, and thus are in constant change, which has to be understood not just in the form of an opinion but of a justifiable rational account, ἐπιστήμη, or knowledge based in logos as reasoning.

Knowledge, then, is of that which is primary, on which everything else depends in its being and which accompanies being.[4] This is being, οὐσία, or being *qua* being, ὂν ᾗ ὄν, and the principles and first causes (*Met.* 1003a21–32, 1003b16–19; *Phys.* 184a11 ff.). Yet, if Aristotle is right in that the first for us is not the first in the order of being ontologically and epistemologically, then we are in a precarious and strange situation, since we are always facing the not-first, the other of being, or non-being.

That which is on its own (τὸ αὐτὸ καθ' αὐτὸ ὄν) is always primary to that which exists due to the other (*Phys.* 257a30–31). This is being, τὸ ὄν, the existing, οὐσία, or substance, that which exists on its own and thus does not need any other to support it in its being. It is the first in the order of being and cognition (*Met.* 1003b17–18). Substance is the cause of being of each thing:[5] that

---

[4] πανταχοῦ δὲ κυρίως τοῦ πρώτου ἡ ἐπιστήμη, Aristotle, *Met.* 1003a21–32, 1003b16–17.
[5] τὸ γὰρ αἴτιον τοῦ εἶναι πᾶσιν ἡ οὐσία, Aristotle. *De an.* 415b12–13.

is, of its *is* and its *what*. That being is on and of its own means that it is "separable" (χωριστός, *Met*. 1029a27-28) in its being and in thought and is thus independent of other beings. Hence, being is always the being of *a* being existing either by nature or through art (*Phys*. 192b8 ff.). It is a concrete thing, which is thus one, the one at which we can point with a gesture and turn toward in perception and thought, and identify it as *this one*, τόδε τι (*Met*. 1029a28).[6] So Aristotle's answer to the question of "if" being is (εἰ ἔστι) is affirmative: it is, or does exist. Its "that" (τὸ ὅτι) is such that it exists within the ever-transforming world as one of many beings. Its "why" (τὸ διότι) comes from within itself as a natural being or from the other if it is an artificial one. It can be one of many causes but predominantly is the purpose or "for the sake of," which means that being is the end in itself. And the "what" (τί ἐστιν) of being is its essence, the τὸ τί ἦν εἶναι (*Phys*. 185b9), which is expressible in a definition in and by logos.

One of the most important aspects of being is that it is a *substrate*, ὑποκείμενον, the "underlying," that which "lies under" all changes without being transformed itself. Substrate bears all the properties and is the ontological and logical subject described by its predicates. However, as subject, it can never be in a position of a predicate, or is not "said" or predicated of another subject—it cannot be an accidental property of any other subject or substance (*Phys*. 186b34, 190a36-b1; *Cat*. 2a12-13). Subject does not speak about another subject—only about itself and only when being asked by logos.

As being that underlies, substrate never lies—one only needs to inquire and investigate it properly by means of logos (for Aristotle, by syllogism), which should reveal the truth about being. Since the substrate lies under itself, and not against another substrate,

---

[6] Christopher Shields argues that the science of being *qua* being studies both being as such and all beings (or existent things). See "Being *qua* Being." In *The Oxford Handbook of Aristotle*. Ed. Christopher Shields. Oxford: Oxford University Press, 2012, 343-71.

nothing is opposite or contrary to substrate as substance,[7] which can be taken as the definition of substance.

But that which has no opposite *remains* (τὸ μὲν μὴ ἀντικείμενον ὑπομένει, *Phys.* 190a18–19) because without opposites there can be no change. Therefore, the substrate *remains* since it is not opposed to anything. That which lies *under* (all predicates and properties), ὑπο-κείμενον, is *not* that which lies *against*, ἀντι-κείμενον (the other) (*Phys.* 190b13). Being is that which always is, underlying all change, but does not change in its being and concept and as such is not opposed to another. In this way, being is *a* being—this one—or one being among many: being for Aristotle comes in the plural, as being*s*, ὄντα.[8]

So when there is a change, transformation, or motion in a being, being itself as a substrate remains the same as substrate but acquires different properties referred to it as a subject. When a human (ἄνθρωπος) learns something (playing the lyre), she changes from uneducated to educated (μουσικός), but the human *remains* and *is* (ὑπομένει ... καὶ ἔστι) what she is in her "what," or essence (being human). But the human is now different in her accidental property (educated), which does not belong to her "what," or essence, because both an educated and a not educated human is human. Therefore, having changed, the human as substrate remains, although having become educated—while the state of being uneducated (τὸ δὲ μὴ μουσικὸν καὶ τὸ ἄμουσον) does not remain (*Phys.* 190a10–13).

So that which was not there before—the uneducated—is opposed to the educated, which now becomes a predicate that characterizes the substrate, although not in an essential way and is thus accidental to it. This means that the *not* of the other that now

---

[7] οὐθὲν οὐσίᾳ ἐναντίον, Aristotle. *Met.* 1087b2; cf. *Cat.* 3b24–25; *Phys.* 189a32–33.
[8] On Aristotle's critique of the Parmenidean monism: Timothy Clarke. *Aristotle and the Eleatic One*. Oxford: Oxford University Press, 2019, 76ff.

is said of the substrate refers not to the substrate but to its predicate: uneducated as the opposite to the educated.

This means that non-being, the uneducated state of μὴ μουσικὸν καὶ ἄμουσον, does not exist by itself and is not anything on its own, but only that which can be detected and understood when it is opposed to that which is in the substrate. This non-being is *privation*.

The ontological trinity. That which is or a being that has an *is* and a *what* thus comes to be from that which underlies any change, which is substrate, and from that which makes a being what it is and be the thing that it is, which is form, μορφή or εἶδος.[9] Form, then, characterizes a thing or substance in its "what" and is that which the underlying substrate accepts in order to be and to be what it is. When a human (the substrate) receives the form (educated), she becomes an educated human, which now can be expressed by logos. The form becomes logically transparent in the definition—a logos—of what a thing or substance is, which is the defining description of that without which a thing can no longer be what it is. This is the essence of the substance. Thus, a human is still human if not educated, but is not such without logos or as not being political (πολιτικὸν ζῷον, *Polit.* 1253a7-8), which for Aristotle belongs to the essence of being human and thus transpires in the definition. Substrate and form are thus the beginnings, or principles, ἀρχαί, of everything that is, since everything comes to be from substrate and form.[10]

So in a sense, as Aristotle says, one may recognize just two beginnings of that which allows things to be and be what they are. But in a different sense, one may accept three of such beginnings or principles (*Phys.* 190b29-30). Why? Because that which lies under all the transformations and changes, the substrate, does not have anything lying against or opposite to it. But that which

---

[9] γίγνεται πᾶν ἔκ τε τοῦ ὑποκειμένου καὶ τῆς μορφῆς, Aristotle. *Phys.* 190b20.
[10] As Aristotle observes, form is one (ἓν δὲ τὸ εἶδος, *Phys.* 190b28), whereas substrate is one in number but two in form (*Phys.* 190b23-29), namely, as a concrete formed substrate, this one (τόδε τι)—and as an indefinite possibility of receiving a form.

characterizes the underlying, which is the form, is not or does not exist on its own, but only in that which is capable of receiving it. As such, form is opposite to that which is not the form or is a non-form. This non-form is privation or lack of form, στέρησις. In the absence of form, strangely enough, privation is also somehow a form[11] because without privation as non-being (of the form) no change is possible, from the non-educated (privation) into educated (form).

Substrate is being potentially, capable of accepting a form, and as such it does not have an opposite. So the substrate is a yet-to-be being. When the substrate accepts form, it becomes substance, οὐσία, a definite *this* one, τὸ τόδε τι, and being, τὸ ὄν. So form is being, but it is not separable: it is what it is only in logos as thinking and definition and is embodied in a substrate. As this kind of being, form does not exist on its own and is opposite to non-being, which is privation. Hence, we have to recognize three beginnings for the understanding of that which is: the substrate, τὸ ὑποκείμενον; the definition, ὁ λόγος; and privation, ἡ στέρησις, as the opposite of the definition (*Phys.* 191a10–14). Notably, the three principles or starting points for understanding what is grammatically are of three different genders: neuter (substrate), masculine (definition), and feminine (privation).

In this way, the trinity of the principles that for Aristotle are to be recognized in order to understand and explain everything that is, moves, and changes are substrate, logos, and privation. Otherwise, they can be also rethought as *matter* as the underlying substrate, which underlies all changes and as such has no opposite but potentially allows for a definite being but itself is not yet a being; *form* as being that is not separable and thus does not exist on its own and as such is an opposite but can only be recognized as concretely embodied in the substrate; and *privation* that is non-being as the lack of being and as such is the opposite of being.

---

[11] ἡ στέρησις εἶδός πώς ἐστιν, Aristotle. *Phys.* 193b19–20.

Logos. What is being? In no way can we answer this question univocally and unambiguously for Aristotle because being is said in many ways, λέγεται πολλαχῶς, and such is everything that is said or thought.[12] Logos itself is perhaps the most plurivocal of all: it can hardly be translated, because it stands for being, thinking, reason, definition, relation—it is all logos, and it can be even more. Logos translates everything but does not translate itself and is thus better left untranslated. Logos is reasoning and thus reasons about itself. In this way, it can become reflective and speculative through human beings, who in their very definition or logos are animals having logos (*Polit.* 1253a9–10; cf. *NE* 1098a3–5) or beings taken over by logos, which enables us to think, speak, make distinctions but unable to see being in its original undivided simplicity. Logos itself is not a continuous thinking but moves in leaps, or steps, of reasoning.

Logos orders and arranges everything. Every order for Aristotle is logos.[13] Logos grinds everything simple and turns it into a multiplicity behind which lurks a unity that can only be said or represented by a plurality and considered inevitably under many different aspects. This means that that which is said univocally or in one way only, τὰ μοναχῶς λεγόμενα, cannot be (*Met.* 1012a29–30). So not only being but also becoming is said in many ways (*Phys.* 190a31; *De caelo* 280b14–20). One is said in many ways, nature is said in many ways, opposite is said in many ways, and potentiality is said in many ways (*Met.* 1012b34ff.; *Phys.* 255a30–31). Motion or

---

[12] Aristotle. *Met.* 1003a33. πολλαχῶς λέγεται τὸ ὄν, *Phys.* 185a21,185b6; cf. *Met.* 1017b10–26. Berti argues that, although being is plurivocal and is said in many ways, being in Aristotle has a "focal" or main meaning, that of substance that is primary both logically and ontologically (*Met.* 1030a29–30), but that, against Patzig and Frede, is not the prime mover that has only ontological primacy, since its essence is pure activity (*Met.* 1070a1, 1071b19–20, 1072b11, 1073a30). Enrico Berti. "Multiplicity and Unity of Being in Aristotle." *Proceedings of the Aristotelian Society* 101 (2001), 185–207. See also Pierre Aubenque. *Le problème de l être chez Aristote. Essai sur la problématique aristotelicienne.* Paris: Presses Universitaires de France, 2013, 134–44.
[13] τάξις δὲ πᾶσα λόγος, Aristotle. *Phys.* 252a13–14.

change is said in many ways (*Phys.* 227b3). Even distinctions can be said in many ways!

In its discerning power, logos makes distinctions not only within that which is and thus can be thought and said, but also within non-being, where seemingly nothing can be differentiated and distinguished in the said and the thought. Anxious to protect itself from non-being, logos thus attempts to overthink and over-say that which cannot be properly said and thought, yet can be—but only negatively and in a radically non-logical way. And even the non-existing non-being can be said in many ways (*Phys.* 225a20), of which, however, as Aristotle explains in the *Physics*, the main two are the ways of matter and privation. But privation too is said in many ways: in general, or when something is capable of having something by nature, or when something is capable of having something by nature but does not have it (*Met.* 1019b16–19, 1046a31).

By saying everything in many ways, logos attempts to think everything distinctly and precisely. So said in many ways means thought in many ways. Every concept can and has to be thought in many ways in order to avoid confusion and indistinctness that non-being brings into being and thinking. Therefore, non-being too is said and is to be thought in many ways—as matter and privation, each of which in turn is said and thought in many ways.

Through multiple careful logical distinctions, logos establishes itself as all-pervasive and even takes on the role of being. Logos *is* being in the ontological trinity of being–substrate–privation. In this sense, the logical distinction between multiple ways of saying and thinking about something is a self-referential and reflective study of the logos by logos, the self-directed investigation of the extent of the logical power of logos by and in logos.

As being, logos provides the meaning of the existing in the thought and said. Hence, logos is knowledge. Knowledge, ἐπιστήμη, is the power and capacity of logos (*Met.* 1046b7–8, 16–17). Logos is capable of knowledge, always striving to make it explicit, to bring it out of itself by itself, that is, logically. In language, it orders being grammatically: as substantivized infinitive (τὸ εἶναι) and its derivatives (οὐσία, ὄν), which all point toward a verb, activity, or act, defined in and by the act and as such fixed by logos. Being is simply *to be*—but then, under the restless discerning power of logos, this simplicity of the infinitive begins breaking down into distinctions for us logical beings, which begins with simply being and being-something.

So all knowledge to which we are made to strive for by nature as part of nature has to be arranged and divided according to logically defensible categories and rubrics. Being appears under various guises and names, which, in the then current absence of special terminology, Aristotle has to invent himself, much to the envy of us moderns, who have to either use the traditional, effaced, and historically loaded concepts that have long lost their meaning or acquired a plethora of different ones or to invent new concepts that are hardly understood and are not recognized by those who act and think within different contexts and traditions.

Being and non-being as opposites. Being has been characterized as being on its own, as substance that exists independently of anything other, underlying itself as substrate, as a *this* which is a subject that has an essence discernible and establishable by logos. When a being is, it has predicates and properties, some of which are essential and thus transpire in its definition or logos, established by the toils of logos, and some that can be safely omitted from the definition, which thus are not essential but accidental. In its *is*, being is substance defined according to logos (οὐσία ... κατὰ τὸν λόγον). In its *what* (τί ἐστιν), being is essence (τὸ τί ἦν εἶναι, *De an.* 412b10–11). But then again—being is said and thought logically in (so) many ways.

When Aristotle turns to being as plural beings, ὄντα, things existing yet transforming and capable of transformation, he argues that it is nature, φύσις, that is the beginning and cause of transformation and change. Nature is the cause of order in all things (*Phys.*

252a12). Nature is thus also said and thought in many ways—nothing can evade the ordering grasp of logos. So in one sense nature is the first underlying material substrate, because it already potentially is that which can be. But in another sense nature is form, ἡ μορφὴ καὶ τὸ εἶδος, that presents itself according to logos, τὸ κατὰ τὸν λόγον, or in the way logos chooses and is able to grasp and define what an existing thing is in its "what" (*Phys.* 193a28–31). The form is thus essential for a thing to be and to be what it is as actualized and activated, and yet the form is not independent or does not exist on its own, is not "separable" (*Phys.* 193b4–5), and thus is not substance. Form makes a thing what it is but remains at the mercy of logos, since form is ultimately thought and defined in and according to logos. Form forms but is not on its own.

Yet, the more one can find and establish distinctions in a definite thing, a concrete this, τόδε τι, the more it is substance and being, οὐσία, and the more it needs non-being, μὴ ὄν, as the other of the form, which is indefiniteness and the lack of a definite being, which is privation, στέρησις.[14] Thus, hot is form, εἶδος, and cold is its privation (*De gen. et corr.* 318b15–17). Therefore, again, form that defines a being in its being is the opposite of privation, or non-being.

Opposites and privation. Privation is thus said and thought to be an opposite of being from the perspective of the logos.[15] Hence, Aristotle concludes, in all the opposites one constituent is privation, so that privation is the *other* of the other opposite. Therefore, all opposites are reduced to being and non-being (in Aristotle) or one and many (apparently, in Plato).[16]

---

[14] Plotinus, who develops his own understanding of negativity, speaks of privation in the Aristotelian sense as a "removal," a "taking away" (ἄρσις) of being, a lack of quality (ἐρημία ποιότητος, *Enn.* II.4 [12].13.21–23), of a form that ought to be present (*Enn.* I.8 [51].11.10). As with Aristotle, privation for him is opposed to form and does not have an independent existence in itself but is always in something else (στέρησις δὲ ἀεὶ ἐν ἄλλῳ καὶ ἐπ' αὐτῆς οὐχ ὑπόστασις). Plotinus. *Enn.* I.8 [51].11.1–3.
[15] ἡ στέρησις ἐναντία λέγεται, Aristotle. *Phys.* 229b26.
[16] τῶν ἐναντίων ἡ ἑτέρα συστοιχία στέρησις, καὶ πάντα ἀνάγεται εἰς τὸ ὂν καὶ τὸ μὴ ὄν, καὶ εἰς ἓν καὶ πλῆθος, Aristotle. *Met.* 1004b27–28; cf. *Met.* 1061a19–20.

Opposites are fundamental for Aristotelian ontology because they are the beginnings, the principles of the existing, of beings in their being.[17] Yet, as such, opposites cannot directly affect each other (*Phys.* 190b33) and do not exist on their own, separately, and are thus not substances but always reside in a substrate (*Met.* 1087b1-2). In this sense, the substrate is other, τὸ ἄλλο, to opposites (*Phys.* 190b34-35), which confirms Aristotle's tripartite ontological scheme of being–substrate–non-being, where being and non-being are considered opposites. Without opposites, no distinction between things can be established (*Met.* 1055a4, 1054b31-32).[18] And without distinction, nothing can be thought. Distinction is fundamental to logos, which rules supreme through its discerning power in being and reasoning.

For Aristotle, an opposite (ἀντικείμενον, ἀντίθεσις, *oppositum*) is understood either as contrariety (ἐναντίον, *contrarium*) or as contradiction (ἀντίφασις, *contradictio*). The difference between the two is that contradiction does not allow for mediation between the opposites, between which nothing is, whereas contrariety does allow for mediation, or degrees, between the opposites.[19] So every change is a change into the unmediated or mediated opposite.[20] Examples of contradiction are odd and even and health and sickness, and of contrariety— hot and cold, high and low pitch, good and evil, just and unjust (*Met.* 1023a5-7).

So privation is one of the opposites. But what kind of opposite is it? In the *Categories*, Aristotle distinguishes the opposite (ἀντικεῖσθαι) into four different kinds: relation (τὰ πρός τι);

---

[17] τἀναντία ἀρχαὶ τῶν ὄντων, Aristotle. *Met.* 986b3.
[18] ἔστι δ' ἡ διαφορὰ ἐν τῇ ὕλῃ τὸ εἶδος, Aristotle. *De part. anim.* 643a24.
[19] See Aristotle. *Cat.* 12a11-2; *An. post.* 72a11-14; *Phys.* 227a23; μηδέν ἐστι μεταξύ, *Met.* 1055b1-2; ἀντιφάσεως δ' οὐδὲν ἀνὰ μέσον, φανερὸν ὅτι ἐν τοῖς ἐναντίοις ἔσται τὸ μεταξύ, *Phys.* 227a23-26.
[20] ἡ δὲ μεταβολὴ πᾶσιν εἰς τὸ ἀντικείμενον ἢ τὸ μεταξύ, Aristotle. *De an.* 416a33-34.

contrarieties (τὰ ἐναντία); privation and having (or disposition) (στέρησις καὶ ἕξις); and assertion and negation (κατάφασις καὶ ἀπόφασις).[21] The examples of these four kinds of opposites are the double and the half as a relation; good and evil as contrarieties; blindness and sight as privation and possession; and "sitting"-"not sitting" as assertion and negation.[22] Privation is the opposite of that which does not exist there where it should exist by nature (*Cat.* 12a29–31). When one defines privation, one should say of *what* it is the privation and *what* is the deprived (*Top.* 147b35–148a2). Privation, then, is prominent when negation is used in defining what is: thus, to be blind is not to have sight when one should have it by nature (*Top.* 143b33–35). This means that privation as negative, as a lack of being, cannot be a subject but only *of* the subject and that privation does not establish the difference distinctive of a being.[23]

A further distinction that can be made here is that privation transpires when a being does not have something without qualification or does not have what it should have by nature or does not have something when it is removed by force (*Met.* 1046a31–35). In all these cases, privation is the opposite of non-being as non-having. What is important is that in opposition (ἐναντίωσις), privation is one of the opposites, or one of the opposites is always thought and said as a privation of the

---

[21] Aristotle. *Cat.* 11b16–23; cf. *Met.* 1055a38ff. Cf. a similar distinction but of two terms: within one and the same genus, the opposite is either contradiction or privation, ἔστι γὰρ τὸ ἐναντίον ἢ στέρησις ἢ ἀντίφασις ἐν τῷ αὐτῷ γένει. *An. post.* 73b21–22. Another way of distinguishing the opposites is into contradiction, relation, privation, and contrariety. *Met.* 1057a34–37.

[22] In contradistinction to Aristotle, Proclus distinguishes between the privation of being and the privation of the good, arguing that it is better not to exist than to have evil existence: *melius autem non esse quam male esse: hoc quidem enim est entis, hoc autem boni privatio/* κρεῖττον δὲ τὸ μὴ εἶναι τοῦ κακῶς εἶναι· <τὸ μὲν γάρ ἐστι> τοῦ ὄντος, <τὸ δὲ> τοῦ ἀγαθοῦ στέρησις, Proclus. *De malorum subsistentia.* In *Tria opuscula: De providentia, libertate, malo.* Ed. Helmut Boese. Berlin: De Gruyter, 1960, 39.41–42; 228–29.

[23] οὐκ ἔστι δὲ διαφορὰ στερήσεως ἢ στέρησις, Aristotle. *De part. anim.* 642b22.

other.[24] Thus, rest is the opposite of motion and is the privation of motion.[25]

However, a difficulty here is with privation as the opposite of something that admits of mediation or a middle, μέσον—for example, the privation of just as unjust, if there can be something that is neither just nor unjust. What might be privation in this case? The solution that Aristotle offers is to recognize privation only in the ultimate genus in its definition or logos. In this case, if the just is defined by the disposition or possession, ἕξις, that makes one obey the law, then the unjust will not be the one who does not have this disposition altogether but the one who disobeys the laws while having the just disposition (*Met.* 1061a22–27). In this sense, in opposition to form, privation is *somehow* a form (ἡ στέρησις εἶδός πώς ἐστιν, *Phys.* 193b19–20). Yet, privation is not really the form but rather is the non-form that negatively or privatively defines the genus.

So it seems that privation is a kind of unmediated contradiction (ἀντίφασίς τίς ἐστιν, *Met.* 1055b3–4). However, one might still argue, as Aristotle does in the *Categories*, that privation and possession are not unmediated opposites either and thus are contrarieties because that which by nature should possess something (e.g., sight) at a different time might or might not have it—but it will have it as it will happen to be, or accidentally (*Cat.* 13a3 ff.). The accidental, τὸ συμβεβηκός, is found in every thing but does not belong to its essence and thus does not transpire in its definition or logos, which is why it is difficult to grasp accidental being. Thus, the mole is blind because of the privation of sight in the genus, whereas a person is blind because of the accidental privation of sight in the individual (*Cat.* 12a26–27; *Met.* 1011b19–20). Therefore, strictly speaking,

---

[24] Aristotle. *Met.* 1055b18. ἀεὶ θάτερον τῶν ἐναντίων λέγεται κατὰ στέρησιν, *Met.* 1055b26–27. The opposite (ἐναντίον) designated by privation is determined through the other (διὰ θατέρου). *Top.* 147b10–11. Opposite is the primary privation, which is the removal of one of the opposites, ἡ γὰρ στέρησις ἡ πρώτη τὸ ἐναντίον, αὕτη δὲ ἀποφορὰ θατέρου, *Met.* 1046b13–16.

[25] ἐναντίον γὰρ ἠρεμία κινήσει, Aristotle. *Phys.* 226b15, 229b25. ἡ γὰρ ἠρέμησις στέρησις κινήσεως, *Phys.* 251a26–27.

privation and possession belong neither to those opposites that have a middle or allow for mediation nor to those that do not admit of it. Privation, then, is the *de*privation that robs substance of its being and essence (οὐσίας δὲ στέρησις, *Met.* 1011b19). Therefore, privation is non-being as the opposite of being *qua* being (*Met.* 1005a13). Privation deprives a being of its meaning, and, hence, privation is *alogical*. For this reason, privation avoids being understood univocally as either a contradiction or contrariety.

The principle of non-contradiction. Everything that can be understood is understood and accounted for by logos and thus becomes justified and fit for knowledge. The thus understood and known is being. Hence, logos protects itself and its offshoots, us as logical beings, from non-being by establishing logical barriers around itself and reducing non-being to logical categories and especially to privation. And if privation is a principle that stands for non-being in beings as things of nature, then contradiction stands for non-being in logos as the guiding principle of its activity and functioning. This is why Aristotle also finds another way of distinguishing the opposition, ἀντικείμενον, into contradiction, contrariety, relation, and privation (*Met.* 1057a34–37). In this way, the nothing of privation in things is protected from alogical confusion by distinguishing it from contradiction in and by logos.

Aristotle tries to think the unthinkable—nothing—by regularizing it by logos, splitting nothing according to its many-voiced meanings that are said in many ways and even making it into a principle—that of privation. Yet, in its absence, the negative is full of surprises, eluding the logos in its ultimate meaning, which is the lack of being and meaning.

The way to protect ourselves from nothing through logos is by establishing and carefully guarding our thinking and being, which can become well-being by maintaining one main principle of being and thinking. This is the principle of non-contradiction, which defends us from the potentially destructive power of non-being and which cannot be justified any further with reference to another principle. Apparently, it is the most "evident" statement (*Met.* 1063b15) that clarifies itself and makes possible everything else that is correctly said, discursively thought, and propositionally arranged according to the logos. Non-being threatens to destroy logos by contradiction, by the unmediated confluence of contradictory opposites, which cannot be and cannot be thought. By trying to think contradiction, logos cancels and destroys itself. Why? Because contradiction is the impossible made possible by thinking that brings non-being into being.

Contradiction, ἀντίφασις, is saying-against as setting-against, ἀντίθεσις, of that which cannot be said and thus established and thought, because it is placed against an indefinite something in the negative that cancels out the posited. What can be said and thought by and in logos is either-or, is or is not, but not both being and non-being (*De int.* 21a37–22b2) because the opposite, unmediated sayings or thoughts annihilate each other if both are asserted at the same time.

This is why Aristotle defines contradiction as the setting-against that does not have anything in the middle, no in-between.[26] This means in particular that privation is to be distinguished from contradiction, also because privation cannot be univocally considered as either mediated or non-mediated.

Therefore, logos has to shield itself against the power of *nihil*. Since without logos nothing can be properly thought, done, or produced, the main logical principle has to be protected in every possible way, and its violators and trespassers are to be persecuted, excluded from the sayable, and denied access to well-being in being and thought.

Nothing intrudes into our being and thought, wreaking havoc by making everything confused, indiscernible, not clearly seen, doing so eventually through contradiction. To counter and fend off

---

[26] ἀντίφασις δὲ ἀντίθεσις ἧς οὐκ ἔστι μεταξὺ καθ' αὑτήν, Aristotle. *An. post.* 72a12–13.

nothing, Aristotle holds on to the apparently most firm principle of being and thought (*Met.* 1005b11–12) that requires avoiding contradiction in thinking and speech by all means. This is the way in which logos tames and conquers non-being, escaping non-being in the ordered and ordering saying and thinking.

There are several formulations of the principle of non-contradiction in Aristotle. Notably, these are as follows: (1) it is impossible for the same both to be and not to be in the same and in the same respect;[27] (2) the opposites cannot simultaneously exist in or belong to the same;[28] (3) the most certain and firm opinion that stands on its own is that the opposite statements cannot be simultaneously true;[29] (4) the opposite statements cannot be true about the same at one and the same time.[30] In all these cases, the principle of non-contradiction is applicable to statements, propositions, or expressions, all of which are *sayings*, φάσεις, of and by the logos. In all these cases, be and not be, is and not is, said and not said, thought and not thought, are *impossible* (οὐκ ἐνδέχεται) when considered, said, or thought together at once, simultaneously, and at the same time (ἅμα). As was said, a substrate is capable of receiving and mediating opposites, but the opposites cannot exist at once (ἅμα) and at one and the same time, for otherwise it would amount to violation of the principle of non-contradiction (*Met.* 1051a10–12). Perhaps the impossibility of such coexistence comes initially from recognition of the impossibility of a thing to both be and not be, which itself could be deduced from the impossibility of two things being in the same place at the same time.

Declaring the ontological and logical impossibility of the unmediated coincidence of opposites excludes non-being from being

---

[27] τὸ γὰρ αὐτὸ ἅμα ὑπάρχειν τε καὶ μὴ ὑπάρχειν ἀδύνατον τῷ αὐτῷ καὶ κατὰ τὸ αὐτό, Aristotle. *Met.* 1005b19–20.
[28] ἅμα δὲ οὐκ ἐνδέχεται τὰ ἐναντία ὑπάρχειν τῷ αὐτῷ, Aristotle. *De int.* 24b9.
[29] βεβαιοτάτη δόξα πασῶν το μὴ εἶναι ἀληθεῖς ἅμα τὰς ἀντικειμένας φάσεις, Aristotle. *Met.* 1011b13–14; cf. *Met.* 1011b16–18.
[30] οὐκ ἐνδέχεται τὰς ἀντικειμένας φάσεις περὶ τοῦ αὐτοῦ καθ᾽ ἕνα χρόνον ἀληθεύειν, Aristotle. *Met.* 1063b15–16.

as being thought. Being and non-being, assertion and negation, cannot *be* without mediation, because the opposites then mutually destroy and cancel out each other (as happens, for Aristotle, in Plato, *Phys.* 192a21–22), reducing the existent to sheer *nihil*, about which nothing can be said and thought. In order to save things and itself, logos has to carefully avoid contradiction.

True and false. However, the first two formulations of the principle of non-contradiction can be understood as referring not only to the *said* but also to the *is* of things, to the being of an actual substance. In order to avoid confusion, the thinking and saying of logos has to be precise in its multiple distinctions and careful in binding the subject with its predicates. But where is the truth of things, then? Is it in the things themselves or in saying and thinking of and about them? Is being true and non-being false? A thing is and is what it is, originating in nature and guarded by its three principles of form, matter, and privation. Being simply is, and then it is what it is.

The true and false for Aristotle is *in thought but not in things* (ἐν διανοίᾳ ἀλλ' οὐκ ἐν τοῖς πράγμασι, Met. 1027b30–31). This means that being *qua* being is not true, and non-being is not false: they are such only for the thought and the corresponding speech, for the logos of them. When a substance as substrate is, it is but is not true or false. It simply underlies, and as such neither signifies a truth nor lies. What is, being, lies against logos as substrate that should not lie to logos about what it is as underlying being. The *is* of a substance is not rationally deducible from anything else and can be first assured by sense-perception but as such presents a challenge to logos that has then moved to the disclosure of the *what* and *how* of that which is. Logos thus takes it as its task to expose, denounce, clarify, order, and explain that which is inherent in being, in the subject as substrate.

The true is thus *not* being but is the *thought* about being. This is the thought to which the entire tradition of philosophy is accustomed and is the assumption on which it operates. This is already the case in Parmenides and Plato: being is, but the true is *that* being is, and not being on its own. Why is this the case? Because, as Aristotle argues—says and thinks—being as true and non-being as false (τὸ δὲ ὡς ἀληθὲς ὄν, καὶ <τὸ> μὴ ὂν ὡς ψεῦδος) only transpire when there is a connection (σύνθεσις) or disconnection (διαίρεσις), agreement and disagreement, combination and division, binding and loosing, in speech and thought. Therefore, true is the assertion of that which is connected and the negation of that which is disconnected, and false is that which *contradicts* such connection and disconnection or is the unmediated opposite of it (*Met*. 1027b18–23). Only then the *saying* and *thinking* (τὸ λέγειν) that *being is not* is false and *non-being is* is false; and *being is* is true and *non-being is not* is true.[31]

So quite surprisingly, it is not the case that true and false define contradiction. On the contrary, it is contradiction as negativity, as the impossibility of the (unmediated) being of non-being and the non-being of being, that defines the true and the false. The whole truth depends on, and is defined by, contradiction, its recognition, correct division, assignment, setting up, and breaking down of all of its constituents.[32] Without contradiction there is no refutation (*Soph. el*. 177a16), and thus no argument—logos—that establishes itself as true once its contradictory has been rejected. Contradiction is thus fundamental for the functioning of logos, for without the recognition and self-protection against contradiction, logos breaks down, and the orderly constructed cosmos of thought and speech is annihilated by being exposed to an alogical, originary chaos, which may be productive of the whole of being and beings, but which is utterly unthinkable (cf. Hesiod. *Theog*. 117–25).

Discursive and non-discursive thought. The truth of being thus consists in the binding and separation of the constituents of the

---

[31] τὸ μὲν γὰρ λέγειν τὸ ὂν μὴ εἶναι ἢ τὸ μὴ ὂν εἶναι ψεῦδος, τὸ δὲ τὸ ὂν εἶναι καὶ τὸ μὴ ὂν μὴ εἶναι ἀληθές, Aristotle. *Met*. 1011b26–27.
[32] τὸ δὲ σύνολον περὶ μερισμὸν ἀντιφάσεως, Aristotle. *Met*. 1027b19–20.

said and thought by logos in such a way that they do not constitute a contradiction. That which is thought and said or predicated as inherent in the subject, P in S of S is P, has to be thought out and said as properly distinguished and thus bound in truth. But the terms of a true statement about being that are kept both together (τὸ ἅμα) and separately (τὸ χωρίς) occur in thought (νοεῖν) differently or as a *different* logos (ἄλλος λόγος) because they are not thought in succession (μὴ τὸ ἐφεξῆς) but as one (ἕν τι).[33] Yet, thinking in succession, ἐν διανοίᾳ, is how logos works, reasons, and thinks, whereas a non-successive or non-discursive thought is that of the reasoning-νοεῖν, which for Aristotle is the *other* of discursive thinking-λέγειν.

So truth for Aristotle is formed by the discursive thinking of logos that binds and separates its terms without contradiction but connects S and P correctly, the way P is inherent in S. But S–P or S is P is a complex saying and thought, since it consists of a subject and a predicate and a copula. But what about being as such, mere being or simple being? How can being be true if it is taken on its own and is not connected to anything (a predicate) by logos and thus is not part of a proposition? According to the definition of true and false, being cannot be true or false on its own, and as such cannot be thought by logos. This is why Aristotle has to recognize that the truth of and about the simple and its "what" or essence, which is not given in the form S is P, cannot be thought logically, because it is *not even in discursive thinking*.[34] But where? The thought of being should then be in non-discursive thought, in νοεῖν, as the *other logos* or the *other of logos*.

It is non-discursive thought, νοῦς, that is capable of grasping being as simple, as being *qua* being, as a subject that encompasses all its inherent predicates that are not yet extracted, said, or thought by the logos in an orderly and systematic way through an argument

---

[33] πῶς δὲ τὸ ἅμα ἢ τὸ χωρὶς νοεῖν συμβαίνει, ἄλλος λόγος, λέγω δὲ τὸ ἅμα καὶ τὸ χωρὶς ὥστε μὴ τὸ ἐφεξῆς ἀλλ' ἕν τι γίγνεσθαι, Aristotle. *Met.* 1027b23–25.
[34] περὶ δὲ τὰ ἁπλᾶ καὶ τὰ τί ἐστιν οὐδ' ἐν διανοίᾳ, Aristotle. *Met.* 1027b27–28.

that will arrange the right connections and disconnections as true and false while avoiding contradiction. Only such thinking-νόησις is activity and actuality,[35] in which being is present in full and in its simplicity, undivided by predicative logical expression. Only νοῦς exists on its own, as separable, unmixed, non-discursive, and thus atemporal or eternal (*De an.* 413b24–26, 430a14–25). This is what such thinking is in its essence: pure activity of thought that thinks nothing except for itself as not distinguished from itself and thus not in the subject-predicate form and non-discursively. Only such thinking can be of being as simple. This is why Aristotle is always laconic in his discussion of νοῦς, since it escapes logos as its other. For everything that can and should be thought properly has to be supported by an argument, or the extended logical thinking that runs from premises in a number of calculated steps, which connects the subject with the predicate in the justified and true conclusion.

This means that being-ὄν as being true in and for logos is different (ἕτερον) from mere being, or being simply, primarily, and properly (τῶν κυρίως, *Met.* 1027b31). Logical being, or being as it is dissected and bound together in and by the dianoetic, discursive logos in an orderly succession, is *different* from the simple being of non-discursive thought. Simple noetic being is the being of simple, non-composite things (τὰ ἀσύνθετα, *Met.* 1051b4–17), of which non-discursive thinking does not bind S and P into S is P, but rather establishes S as S, or as "*S is.*" The truth of the simple being is a kind of a "touch" (τὸ θιγεῖν) that perceives in simultaneity and a non-discursive "say" (φάναι) that does not assert (*Met.* 1051b24). This non-assertive "say" is merely an expression of a non-composite as simple, of being that is both said (φημί) and clarified (φανάω) non-discursively, without explanation, by shining on its own.

But being on its own is not a thing. It is said or expressed by a verb (an infinitive) that stands and is said on its own, and is thus substantivized, becomes a noun, which, however, does not yet

---

[35] ἡ νόησις ἐνέργεια, Aristotle. *Met.* 1051a30–31.

specify whether this substantive is or is not. A verb thus becomes itself a subject without predicates—simply, "to be." Yet, for Aristotle "to be" (τὸ εἶναι) and "not to be" (μὴ εἶναι) do not indicate a thing or an act (πρᾶγμα). Hence, mere "being" on its own is *nothing* (οὐδέν ἐστι)! It is empty and only suggests a connection (σύνθεσις) that cannot be thought (non-discursively, νοῆσαι) without compounds (*De int.* 16b19–25). Being, then, is first logically meaningful and discursively thinkable only when it becomes either a subject in S–P or a copula in "S is P," but not on its own as a subject S that does not relate to a P or as a copula "is" that does not connect or bind anything.[36]

Being-simply or simple being is thus *inaccessible* and unthinkable to discursive thought, which is the thought of logos. Rather, such being is thought at once and non-successively by the *other* thought, which is not logos, and in this sense it is alogical, and yet capable of grasping the simple being by as if touching it. For logos, being as simple remains unreachable and is thus not a being or non-being; it is not a being that can be dissected into the subject and predicate, which will then be brought together as true in full compliance with the principle of non-contradiction. The attempts of logos to think non-being results in contradiction, since logos cannot think either being or non-being on their own or being and non-being together—but only in strict separation and opposition as unmediated. However, for the thought as νοῦς, contradiction

---

[36] On the distinction and continuity between the complete and incomplete uses of the existential and predicative use as the copula in the *Sophist*, see: Lesley Brown. "Being in the *Sophist*: A Syntactical Enquiry." In *Plato 1: Metaphysics and Epistemology*. Ed. Gail Fine. Oxford: Oxford University Press, 1999, 455–78. Ackrill argues for a clear distinction between the two (where the role of the copula is played by the verb μετέχειν, to participate); see J. L. Ackrill. "Plato and the Copula: *Sophist* 251–259." In *Essays on Plato and Aristotle*. Oxford: Oxford University Press, 1997, 80–92. Owen, on the contrary, suggests that this distinction cannot be univocally traced in Plato. G. E. L. Owen. "Plato on Non-being." *Plato 1: Metaphysics and Epistemology*, 416–54. The whole debate, however, rests on the assumption that the *Sophist* is primarily concerned with predication and reference rather than with the ontology of being and non-being. On the distinction of being standing for existence and copula as distinctly formulated only in the medieval logic, see Charles Kahn. *Essays on Being*. Oxford: Oxford University Press, 2009, 41–61.

does not exist or is not meaningful because it neither applies to nor regulates simple being or being-simply, ὄν ᾗ ὄν, being as it is.

Negation. If privation is non-being in beings as a principle, then contradiction is non-being in and for logos as the guiding principle of its activity. Contradiction arises from the unmediated coincidence of being and non-being (κατὰ τὸ εἶναι καὶ μὴ εἶναι, *De int.* 21a39): the same cannot both be and not be at the same time and in the same respect, or opposites cannot simultaneously belong to the same. Contradiction is thus based on negation. This is why in the *Categories* Aristotle distinguishes privation from negation.

Yet, the true and false belong to logos and not to being. Hence, being and to be only *means* (σημαίνει) to be true, whereas non-being is not true but false both in affirmation and negation.[37] So negativity in the form of negation is essential for logos and its proper functioning, for without negation there is no opposition, no contradiction, and no principle of non-contradiction, which depends on recognition of the impossibility of the unmediated opposition of being and non-being (*An. priora* 63b34–35; *An. post.* 72a13–14, 77a30). And contradiction is central for establishing the truth in and through logos, which always implies negation. In particular, it is the performative contradiction of discursive thought that allows one to ascertain the true because if nothing is true— there is nothing about which one can say that it is true—then this very claim would be false, and therefore there would be no single true logical statement (*Met.* 1062b7–9).

Negation is itself opposite to assertion, so the two are the elementary acts of logos, which are the acts of saying and thinking about being, expressing the "is" and "what is" in speech (φάσις, *De int.* 17a8–9). Assertion (κατάφασις) is the saying or predicative statement (ἀπόφανσις) that puts something down (κατά) about something, and negation (ἀπόφασις) is a saying that takes away

---

[37] τὸ εἶναι σημαίνει καὶ τὸ ἔστιν ὅτι ἀληθές, τὸ δὲ μὴ εἶναι ὅτι οὐκ ἀληθὲς ἀλλὰ ψεῦδος, ὁμοίως ἐπὶ καταφάσεως καὶ ἀποφάσεως, Aristotle. *Met.* 1017a31–33.

something from (ἀπό) something else (*De int.* 17a26–27), without which there is no refutation. Yet, there is no mediation between affirmation and negation, which means that they stand in contradictory opposition to each other, to the extent that the two primarily refer to *is* as opposed to *not is* (*is not*) without mediation.

(1) When *is* is used existentially, then each statement consists of two terms, S *is*, where *is* stands in the position of the predicate ("human is"). This statement is *existential*, or refers to *if* (εἰ) something, S, *is* or exists. The negation (~) of S *is* produces four cases, which make up two pairs of opposite (—) statements, different from each other depending on whether the subject (noun) or the predicate (verb) is negated: S is — S ~is; and ~S is — ~S ~is. Here, non-being as *is not* (οὐκ ἔστι) is a contradictory opposite to being as *is* (ἔστι).

(2) When, however, an attribute is joined to the subject by *is* as a copula, then there are three terms in the statement: S is P ("human is just"), grammatically expressed by a noun, verb, and adjective. In this case, one also has four (not eight) cases. Here, one does not negate the subject, because, first, nothing is opposite to a subject as substance, and, second, the statement in this case is *essential*, or refers to *what* (τί) something is. The four cases, then, are: S is P — S ~is P; and S is ~P — S ~is ~P. In the first cases, when negation is applied to the attribute, it produces *privation* ("not just," οὐ δίκαιος), while in the other two it does not, because it refers to the verb as copula, which, when negated, does *not* have a privative meaning (*De int.* 19b14–30).[38]

---

[38] "That which is always capable of being" is opposite to "that which is not always capable of being," and "that which is always capable of not being" is opposite to "that which is not always capable of not being." Aristotle. *De caelo* 282a4–9.

When Aristotle speaks about privation as an opposite of the form that determines the change in the substrate from privation to form, or from non-being-something to being-something, he mentions the example of someone who becomes educated from being uneducated. The "uneducated" is μὴ μουσικόν or ἄμουσον (*Phys.* 190a12) and is expressed by μή negativum and ἀ privativum. Grammatically, the negation of the predicate can be denoted by the particle μή or οὐ, "not," whereas the privative negation of an attribute can be signified by a privative prefix ἀ-, "un-" or "in-" (unequal, invisible, ἄνισον, ἀόρατον, *Met.* 1022b323–34). Correspondingly, one can discern two different forms of negation, predicative with "not" and attributive with "in-/ un-," which can be further interpreted as the existential (μή/οὐ) and essential (ἀ-) negatives.

Most importantly, when combined together, the two uses of *is*, the existential (which starts with εἰ) and the essential (which originates in τί), establish the logical (material) *conditional*: if—then, τί εἰ ("what—if?," τὶ δέ, εἰ). Negation of a proposition, then, establishes its reversal (ἀνάπαλιν) in the conditional (if A is B, then ~B is ~A, *Top.* 124b7). And if the conditional (→) and negation (~) are defined and established, then the other logical operators, *and* (&) and *or* (V), can also be expressed through them, on which the entire edifice of logic can then be built (which is itself a proposition in the form of a conditional).

Double negation. Is negation self-referential, or can it negate itself? Negation is always *of* something. Yet, this something can be nothing. What then is the negation of nothing? If nothing is non-being and as such is contradictorily opposite to being, then its negation should be being. Correspondingly, the negation of being should be non-being or nothing. Hence, double negation works in and for contradictory opposites, or those opposites that do not allow for mediation. Such for Aristotle are being and non-being, which stand in contradictory opposition. So when something changes from non-being to being, or comes to be, then non-being has been abandoned.[39] Double negation, then, is valid for logical statements that respect the principle of non-contradiction. In this case, A= ~ ~A. Being is not non-being, and non-being is not not non-being. However, if an opposition is that of a contrariety that allows for mediation, such as quantitative change, for instance, becoming cold from being hot, then the double negation is not applicable, since not hot might amount to being warm rather than cold. In this case, A≠ ~ ~A.

But when it comes to being and non-being, the situation is even more complex because Aristotle distinguished between two kinds of non-being, absolute (privation) and relative (matter), both distinguished from being (form). Contradictory logical opposition is binary, but the ontological opposition in this case is ternary, even if each of the three ontological principles is opposed to the other as contradictory. So double negation does not work when applied to the very principles of the existent because, depending on the situation, the negation of being may amount either to absolute non-being or relative non-being; the negation of absolute non-being may mean either being or relative non-being; and the negation of relative non-being may signify either being or absolute non-being. In this case, the negation functions like the one in the rock-paper-scissors game, where, depending on a particular constellation, the outcome can be different, since rock negates scissors but is in turn negated by paper, whereas scissors negates paper. This means that, despite a common perception that double negation is indispensable in his logic based on the contradictory opposition and the exclusion of the third, it is not universally applicable in Aristotle when it comes to ontology.

Non-being and nothing. The negation of being results in non-being. When substance already is, it changes or moves toward non-being, and thus is not (*Phys.* 226a6–10 passim). But in order for a being to perish, it already should be.[40] So being is primary,

---

[39] ἐκ τοῦ μὴ ὄντος εἰς τὸ ὄν, ἀπολέλοιπεν τὸ μὴ ὄν, Aristotle. *Phys.* 235b13–15.
[40] εἶναι γὰρ δεῖ τὸ φθειρόμενον, Aristotle. *Phys.* 226a9–10.

and non-being as its negation is derivative. However, the negation (ἀπόφασις) of something is simply its absence (ἀπουσία), whereas the negation of a being as substance is privation, which is that of the underlying substrate as deprived of something (*Met.* 1004a14–16). In other words, negation as privation is always of a substrate, which is deprived of something and ultimately of being, while negation as absence is not necessarily so, because one can negate also that which does not exist. In a different sense, however, absence can mean privation as cause, for one and the same can be the cause of opposites by its absence (ἀπουσία) or presence (παρουσία). Thus, the presence and absence of a captain can be the cause of the survival or perishing of a ship (*Met.* 1013b12–16). In this sense, absence as privation is the opposite to presence as being (*Phys.* 191a7).

But non-being is *nothing* (τὸ δὲ μὴ ὂν μηδέν ἐστιν). Non-being is not a this, τί, or a particular thing, nor a category, such as quality, quantity, or place (*De gen. et corr.* 318a15–16). This statement is rather paradoxical because non-being is not and such is also nothing, so non-being and nothing cannot be identical. However, if non-being is not being, then it cannot be but nothing. Yet, since nothing is nothing, nothing can be said or thought of and about it. Still, Aristotle finds a way to include nothing into the system of distinctions generated by logos in its struggle against the nothing of non-being by making it, if not thinkable, then at least having a proper place within the system of principles that regulate being *qua* being and all beings.

Nothing, μηδέν, has no relation to (πρός) anything. In particular, nothing has no relation to number (*Phys.* 215b13): nothing can be counted or calculated in nothing. In nothing there are no distinctions, not a single one.[41] Strictly speaking, even this distinction about nothing cannot be made. Distinctions are brought about primarily by form in that which is determined in its being by form. But opposition is a distinction, and distinction is otherness.[42]

---

[41] τοῦ μηδενὸς οὐδεμία ἔστι διαφορά, Aristotle. *Phys.* 215a10.
[42] διαφορὰ γάρ τις ἡ ἐναντιότης, ἡ δὲ διαφορὰ ἑτερότης, Aristotle. *Met.* 1004a21–22.

Therefore, if one can establish a logical opposition, then the nothing of non-being as the unmediated other of being can be included in the system of thinkable and mutually deducible logical propositions. So Aristotle's way out of the impasse of the unthinkability of nothing is to elevate it to non-being as a *principle*, ἀρχή, of everything that is—in fact, to *two* main principles of non-being: of privation and matter. Each one of the two principles of non-being is opposite to the other as absolute and relative non-being, and privation as non-being is also opposite to form as being.

Non-being thus becomes primary and is not deducible from anything else, but rather it is a principle or beginning of all things, independent and opposite to non-being. Logos thus carefully plasters over and hides the initial dependence of being on non-being, which is hardly thinkable to systematic, propositional logical thought. As the principles or beginnings of everything that is and changes in the world, being and non-being are to be considered equiprimordial, opposite to each other and not deducible from each other or from anything (*Phys.* 188a27–30).

A further expression of the subjugation of non-being to being by logos is its insistence on distinguishing as many meanings of a concept as possible. And if being is said in many ways, then non-being as the privative negation of being is also said in many ways.[43] In its constructive power, logos keeps making fine-grained distinctions even where they seemingly cannot be made—in non-being, which is now split in many ways and appears as conceptually and categorically divided within ordered and ordering logical thought. And yet, non-being eludes the exacting power of reasoning. For if non-being is nothing, then nothing is said in many ways—literally. The multiple distinctions of being generate subtle logical distinctions, and yet they say and think *nothing* about being, which remains

---

[43] πολλαχῶς γὰρ καὶ τὸ μὴ ὄν, ἐπειδὴ καὶ τὸ ὄν, Aristotle. *Met.* 1089a16, cf. *Met.* 1046a31. τὸ μὴ ὂν λέγεται πλεοναχῶς, *Phys.* 225a20. This is why negation, expressed by the *alpha privativum*, is said negatively (ἀποφάσεις λέγονται) in as many ways as ἀ- is used in logos as speech (*Met.* 1022b32–33).

ultimately inaccessible to logos in the form of multiple properly arranged and systematically derived logical propositions.

Aristotle mentions that previous philosophers, apparently Plato and his followers, supported Parmenides' claim of the possibility of unconditional, direct, and simple generation of the existent from non-being,[44] or from nothing as preexisting (ἐκ μηδενός, *De gen. et corr.* 317b28–31). Aristotle himself considers it impossible (*Phys.* 187a34) because it is much more reasonable (εὐλογώτερον: the opposite cannot be said and thought) to say that being is the cause of the generation of non-being than the other way around.[45] However, *accidental* generation or coming-to-be from non-being into being (ἐκ τοῦ μὴ ὄντος εἰς τὸ ὄν) is possible.[46] Thus, something can change from privation, which is non-being, into something else in which privation is not, for example, by becoming hot or hotter from being cold (*Phys.* 191b13–15). The privative non-being as a principle regulates the becoming of the existent but is not part of the existent.

As opposites, being and non-being are the limits (ὅροι) of generation, of everything that exists in coming to be and passing away (*Phys.* 261a34). But none of the existent—of beings-ὄντα—is being or non-being on its own because that which is keeps its being as existence in change that is regulated by the opposite principles of becoming. And yet, being for Aristotle is *better* than non-being.[47] Therefore, the only way for the whole world to be is by constantly coming to be, or gaining being as at least a temporary existence, without ever being able to keep it that way because of the presence of non-being. Only in this way can being be perpetuated in the coming-to-be without ever becoming pure and eternal being (*De*

---

[44] ἁπλῶς γίγνεσθαί τι ἐκ μὴ ὄντος, Aristotle. *Phys.* 191b36–192a.
[45] τὸ ὂν τῷ μὴ ὄντι γενέσεως αἴτιον εἶναι, Aristotle. *De gen. et corr.* 336a20–22.
[46] See Keimpe Algra. "On Generation and Corruption I. 3: Substantial Change and the Problem of Not Being." In *Aristotle on Generation and Corruption, Book 1: Symposium Aristotelicum*. Ed. Frans A. J. de Haas and Jaap Mansfeld. Oxford: Oxford University Press, 2004, 91–121, esp. 104–10.
[47] βέλτιον δὲ τὸ εἶναι ἢ τὸ μὴ εἶναι, Aristotle. *De gen. et corr.* 336b28.

gen. et corr. 336b28–34). So coming-to-be, or incessant generation, is good and necessary, and Aristotle's entire philosophical project becomes an explanation of the necessity of becoming from and around being and the possibility of its rational, logical explanation. Why does Aristotle have a strong preference for being over non-being, when at the same time claiming that two out of three principles of the existent are those of non-being, and only one is being? Non-being for him is closer to an accidental (*Met.* 1026b21). And accidental is that which can both be and not be (ὑπάρχειν καὶ μὴ ὑπάρχειν, *Phys.* 186b18–20), or an accidental is not necessary and thus may not be (*Phys.* 256b9–10), does not characterize what a thing is and does not refer to the thing's being as *is* and *what*, which is defined by being as form. On its own, non-being is impossible, as, for example, the commensurability of the side of the square with its diagonal (*Phys.* 221b24–25). But *when* being is, it necessarily is, and when non-being is not, it necessarily is not, although not everything that is necessarily is, and not everything that is not necessarily is not.[48] Only the prime mover of everything that constantly moves and changes or comes to be is necessary in its being as the first and is itself unmoved,[49] because without it any change would need to go into an infinity of causes, in which case nothing will move or change, and so nothing will be the way it is. Only the necessary, non-accidental cause of becoming makes becoming as causally regulated in its transformations: this will be if that other happens, and if not, then not (εἰ δὲ μή, οὔ, *Met.* 1027a33). The necessity of becoming caused by being is thus obtained and logically expressed by two negations (μή, οὐ) and one conditional (εἰ), which, as was said, can be obtained solely from the combination of existential and essential meanings of being and negation.

---

[48] τὸ μὲν οὖν εἶναι τὸ ὂν ὅταν ᾖ, καὶ τὸ μὴ ὂν μὴ εἶναι ὅταν μὴ ᾖ, ἀνάγκη, Aristotle. *De int.* 19a23–24. See also *Phys.* 242a53–54; 242b71–72, 256a13–29, 257a6–7, 258b4–9.
[49] οὐσία ἀκίνητος, αὕτη προτέρα, Aristotle. *Met.* 1026a29–30.

Void. A further expression of Aristotle's attempt to subdue the *nihil* to the discerning and ordering power of logos is the *horror vacui*, or the rejection of the possibility of void, which is an inevitable, yet alogical, misrepresentation of the unrepresentable—of nothing among beings. Unless nothing is elevated to the principle of the existent, nothing cannot be and is not comprehensible, for nothing is nothing, and there is nothing to be known in nothing "as such," which does not even have an "as such."

Aristotle's main opponents in his discussion of the void are the Atomists who, in turn, argue against the Eleatic thinkers. For Parmenides and Zeno, being *is* and is *one*, whereas non-being *is not* and is *many*. Yet for the Atomists, on the contrary, being *is* but is *many* because being is, or are, atoms, whereas non-being—void—is *one* and somehow also *is* or exists as an empty extension that makes being possible as plural and as moving through the non-being of the void (*De gen. et corr.* 325a23–32). But for Aristotle, void as bodiless extension is physically and ontologically impossible and logically is a non-concept, which thus cannot be properly expressed or thought. As non-existing and thus as non-being, void is not even privative but simply impossible.

If nothing is not considered a principle of the existent, which void for Aristotle is not, then nothing is the subject only of opinion (δοξαστόν), which is precisely the opinion that nothing is nothing or that it *is not* (*De int.* 21a32–33). Therefore, void, κενόν, is also the subject of a (wrong) opinion. Void seems (δοκεῖ) to be a non-being or something non-existent and a privation.[50] Void only *seems to be* but is not and is not even non-being as a principle.

However, privation *is not* either, since it "is" absolute non-being or non-being as such—and yet at the same time it *is* a principle of beings, of the existent that constantly comes to be before passing away, always struggling for being. But, as Aristotle argues at length in *Physics* Δ 6–9, void does not exist, and as such it is a non-concept

---

[50] τὸ γὰρ κενὸν μὴ ὄν τι καὶ στέρησις δοκεῖ εἶναι, Aristotle. *Phys.* 215a11.

and not a principle or a beginning because it does not stand for anything and is not a beginning of change of any kind. Void *seems* to be a place in which nothing (οὐδέν) is and appears to be there where there is no body (*Phys.* 213b33–34).[51] Void *seems* to be that in which a body is not but can be.[52] Yet, in the void there are *no* distinctions (οὐκ ἔχει διαφοράν, *Phys.* 214b33–215a1), and it is nothing (μηδέν) that does not allow for making distinctions. There is no differentiation in void, which is why it cannot be the cause of motion of bodies.[53] Void thus has *no* relation (λόγος) in which a body could exceed it, similarly to the way nothing has no relation to number (*Phys.* 215b12–16). Nothing is not and hence cannot be anywhere. But in place there are distinctions, such as up and down (*Phys.* 211a3–4). For Aristotle, place is the immediate external limit of a body that embraces, or contains, a body and can be abandoned by the body (*Phys.* 210b34–211a3, 212a20–21). Therefore, void cannot be place. Place is not nothing and is thus not void.

Besides, void *seems* to be *extension* (διάστημα) of the body (*Phys.* 214a20). Yet, it does not exist on its own, as separate, so it is the body that extends. If void could exist as separate, then it would be a substance—but then within the limits of a body there would be two substances, the body itself and the void. Therefore, body cannot be the void. Finally, void *seems* to be *matter*. But this cannot be the case because matter is not separable from the body, while void should be, according to those who accept it (*Phys.* 214a13–16).

Therefore, as an embodied nothing, void does not exist. It has no relation to anything and thus cannot be thought but is only subject to opinion for Aristotle. It is Simplicius who will complete the discussion of the nothing of the void with detailed responses and objections to its imputed existence.

---

[51] δοκεῖ δὴ τὸ κενὸν τόπος εἶναι ἐν ᾧ μηδέν ἐστι, Aristotle. *Phys.* 213b31.

[52] ἐν ᾧ μὴ ἐνυπάρχει σῶμα, δυνατὸν δ' ἐστὶ γενέσθαι, Aristotle. *De caelo* 279a13–14.

[53] See Sylvia Berryman. "Democritus and the Explanatory Power of the Void." In *Presocratic Philosophy: Essays in Honour of Alexander Mourelatos*. Ed. Victor Caston and Daniel W. Graham. New York: Routledge, 2016, 183–91.

Infinite. Non-being does not provide limits (ὅροι) to the existent, which is in constant change and flux and as such it is neither being nor non-being but is always moving between these two opposite poles. Yet, everything that is, even for a brief time, is defined in its being and essence, the *is* and the *what*, by a cause, the main one of which is "for the sake of," or the purpose of and for a being. The purpose is the end, τέλος, which sets the limit for a being's temporal existence, the limit of change. For anything to be and to be what it is, then, means to be defined by its purpose and thus to be limited. The purpose as the end is the beginning not only of nature but also of production, since it always transpires in the natural and in the artificial (*EE* 1227b28–30; *Phys.* 192b8–32). Hence, the end *is* the limit, τὸ δὲ τέλος πέρας (*Phys.* 207a14–15).

That which has no limit is limitless or infinite, ἄπειρον, which can only be understood negatively, by negating the limit, as ἄ-πειρον, non-finite or a-finite. Infinite is not-finite, which means that the infinite has no end, no completion, and no purpose. Infinite, or the lack of limit and purpose, is the condition of every being in the world, in which everything attempts to reach its end, completion, and rest, and yet, due to the presence of otherness, of nothing as matter and privation, abandons it at the same time.

In the infinite itself, there is no beginning because it would then be its end—whereas the infinite is unlimited and thus has no end (*Phys.* 203b7). The infinite in beings transpires in the coming to be or becoming, and hence it is always *another and another* (τῷ ἀεὶ ἄλλο καὶ ἄλλο γίγνεσθαι, *Phys.* 206a22). This means that the infinite has no positive concept but is defined negatively: it is that in which one can take another step or part in either addition or division but never come to a completion. As applies to everything else in Aristotle, infinite is said in many ways, appearing differently in magnitudes through *division* and in numbers through *addition* (*Phys.* 204a2–7, 206a21–22, 207b1–5). Defined negatively, the infinite is that outside of which there is always something (οὗ ἀεί τι ἔξω ἐστί, *Phys.* 207a1–2) and not, as in modernity, that outside of which there is nothing.

The infinite therefore is not actual, because otherwise any of its parts would be an actually infinite quantity, which is impossible, for an actually infinite body or number cannot be, both logically or conceptually—since it is unthinkable, and physically—since it cannot be either simple or composite (*Phys.* 204a28–29, 204b4–22). So the infinite exists only potentially (δυνάμει), as another and another in a process of addition or division that can never be exhausted and thus has no end. As excess and defect, "more or less," the infinite exists only in thinking and not in reality.[54] The infinite is only potential but never actual, lacking in end or purpose. In this sense, the infinite as cause is akin to that of matter (ὡς ὕλη), and its being (τὸ εἶναι) is privation.[55] So we finally turn to matter.

Matter and privation: relative and absolute non-being. We have to return to the question with which we began: how does non-being as privation differ from non-being as matter as ontological *principles* of everything existent.

Matter in Aristotle is defined in its four aspects: as substrate, possibility, negativity, and indefiniteness.[56]

(1) *Matter as the first substrate. One matter for the opposites.* Whenever something is and is understood as such, it is defined by a form (εἶδός τι, *Met.* 1049a35; ὁ λόγος καὶ ἡ μορφή, *Met.* 1042a28–29). Yet, a being is a concrete substance, a *this one* (τόδε τι), which only exists in and as a substrate, which, in order to exist, requires ultimate matter and material substance.[57]

Matter is that into which everything changes, a non-being defined by the being of form. So all things have matter. All sensible

---

[54] οὐ γὰρ ἐπὶ τοῦ πράγματος... ἀλλ᾽ ἐπὶ τῆς νοήσεως, Aristotle. *Phys.* 208a15–16.
[55] ὡς ὕλη τὸ ἄπειρον αἴτιόν ἐστι, καὶ ὅτι τὸ μὲν εἶναι αὐτῷ στέρησις, τὸ δὲ καθ᾽ αὑτὸ ὑποκείμενον τὸ συνεχὲς καὶ αἰσθητόν, Aristotle. *Phys.* 207b35–208a2.
[56] See Heinz Happ. *Hyle: Studien zum Aristotelischen Materie-Begriff.* Berlin: De Gruyter, 1971, 296–7.
[57] τὸ ἔσχατον ὕλη καὶ οὐσία ὑλική, Aristotle. *Met.* 1049a35–36.

things or substances have matter, which is one of the meanings of nature (*Met.* 1042a25-26) and, as Aristotle mentions twice in passing, even non-sensible or mathematical things have their own "intelligible" matter (ὕλη νοητή, *Met.* 1036a9-12, 1037a4-5).[58] Therefore, matter is the *first substrate* of everything.[59]

So matter is an inalienable principle of nature, along with form and privation. Aristotle takes nature, which too is said and thought in many ways, to be either matter or form. He adds that nature is form rather than matter (ἡ μορφὴ φύσις, *Phys.* 193b18) because, although everything that moves and changes needs a substrate, it is form that actualizes a thing as this one in matter as its ultimate substrate.[60]

As substrate, matter is the substrate of and for the opposites, which, as said, cannot coexist or coincide in actuality, which would amount to the violation of the principle of non-contradiction. Yet, substrate has nothing opposite to it. Therefore, nothing is opposite (ἐναντίον) to matter (*Met.* 1075a34), which is the middle between the opposites.[61]

As a principle of nature, matter is one and the same for all things (*Met.* 1044a15-20; μία τῷ ἀριθμῷ, *Phys.* 217a25), big and small. However, every thing has its own matter (wood or bronze), and so there is a kind of "ladder of matters," when one matter is the matter for another (*Met.* 1044a20-21). And yet, ultimately there is one and the same matter for all things, their ultimate substrate.

(2) *Matter as possibility.* As the substrate of and for the opposites, matter allows for one of the opposites (e.g., hot and cold) to become actual from its other, privative opposite. This means that matter *is*

---

[58] Cf. Plotinus. *Enn.* II.4 (12); Proclus. *In Eucl.* 93.18-19. See Dmitri Nikulin. *Matter, Imagination and Geometry: Ontology, Natural Philosophy and Mathematics in Plotinus, Proclus, and Descartes.* Aldershot: Ashgate, 2002, 132-44.
[59] τὸ πρῶτον ὑποκείμενον ἑκάστῳ, Aristotle. *Phys.* 192a31-32. ἡ πρώτη ἑκάστῳ ὑποκειμένη ὕλη, *Phys.* 193a29.
[60] Aristotle. *Phys.* 193a28-31, 193b6-8. ἀρχὴ γὰρ ἡ φύσις μᾶλλον τῆς ὕλης, *De part. anim.* 643a17.
[61] ἔστιν ὕλη μία τῶν ἐναντίων, Aristotle. *Phys.* 217a22; *De gen. et corr.* 329a30-31. Cf. ἡ γὰρ ὕλη τὸ μέσον ἀναίσθητος οὖσα καὶ ἀχώριστος, *De gen. et corr.* 332a36-332b1.

both these opposites—but only potentially.[62] A general principle in Aristotle is that the actual being comes from that which exists potentially, or everything changes from being potential to being actual.[63] Yet, even if potentiality might precede actuality in the order of becoming, actuality (ἐνέργεια) is primary in form and substance.[64] And while not being anything definite (οὐκ ἔστι τόδε τι), matter always becomes something as definitive and thus harbors the possibility of a definite substance. In other words, matter is potentiality or *possibility* (δύναμις, *De an.* 412a7-9). As such, matter is not yet being but the substrate that harbors the possibilities for a particular substance that are realized, or become actual, when defined by the being of form.

But even as the first and ultimate substrate for the opposites, matter does not exist on its own or is not separable, but in its being it is the other to being as a set of possibilities.[65] Since potentially might not be actualized (μὴ ἐνεργεῖν, *Met.* 1071b13-14), matter is the potentiality that is not-yet being. Matter is non-being as being-possible.

In other words, matter contains all the possibilities for a thing to be and become actual as *this one* (τόδε τι).[66] As the first substrate, matter is the possibility for the actualization of being as a substance, the possibility of a form to be concretely and temporarily embodied in the world. For this reason, different forms realize their possibilities differently in matter or relate differently to matter.[67]

If and when matter is considered the matter of a thing that comes to be (when wood rots and iron rusts), the matter of this particular thing is perishable. In this case, it is privation that is perishable

---

[62] ἡ δυνάμει οὖσα ὕλη γίγνεται ἄμφω, Aristotle. *Phys.* 217a32-33; *Met.* 1069b8-9, 14-15; 1075a22-23.
[63] ἐκ δυνάμει ὄντος ἐνεργείᾳ ὂν γίγνεται, Aristotle. *Phys.* 217a23-24; *Met.* 1069b15-16.
[64] Aristotle. *Met.* 1050a2-5; ἡ ... ἐνέργεια βελτίων, *Met.* 1051a15.
[65] οὐ χωριστὴ μὲν ἡ ὕλη, τὸ δ᾽ εἶναι ἕτερον, Aristotle. *Phys.* 217a24-25; see also *Phys.* 212a1; ἀχώριστον, *De gen. et corr.* 329a30.
[66] ἡ μὴ τόδε τι οὖσα ἐνεργείᾳ δυνάμει ἐστὶ τόδε τι, Aristotle. *Met.* 1042a27-28.
[67] τῶν πρός τι ἡ ὕλη, Aristotle. *Phys.* 194b9.

or that makes a thing change into the opposite. However, when considered as a possibility (κατὰ δύναμιν) of the activation or actualization of a form or being-something, matter is not perishable but *is*, or exists, ἔστι.[68] So as potentiality and possibility for a thing to be and be what it is and can become, as a principle of and in nature, matter does *not come to be*.

But how does matter as possibility of a being relate to privation as non-being? If matter is a universal possibility of a concretely expressed being when the being of a form becomes actualized, then privation is the *impossibility* of being, its incapacity to be and to act. As privation of capacity or possibility, privation is *adynamia*,[69] a never-yet being.

(3) *Matter as negativity. Absolute and relative non-being.* As a pure possibility of and for being, matter is a non-being that can be actualized in a particular being of and as this one. As concrete matter, it is a possibility that has already been shaped and actualized in a particular way as a substrate—as wood or bronze, but as the ultimate matter in the "ladder," it can be shaped in any way and thus can become anything. Matter is always a not-yet being. This is a "relative" non-being for Aristotle. So matter is non-being, but only accidentally,[70] because it is either the first substrate of each thing (and hence, although not being determinate, is not nothing)—or it can be a formed matter (bronze or wood) as the cause of accidental being, which can be enmattered or become realized otherwise, differently from what and how it currently is (*Met.* 1027a13–15).

Privation, on the contrary, is not a possibility for anything to be, but rather it is an opposite that makes a thing change. Privation is thus a never-being or never-yet. It is an "absolute" non-being, or non-being "as such," "by itself" (καθ' αὑτήν, *Phys.* 192a5), where

---

[68] Matter is ἄφθαρτον καὶ ἀγένητον, Aristotle. *Phys.* 192a25–29; τὸ ἀγένητος εἶναι, *Met.* 999b12–14; οὐ γίγνεται, *Met.* 1069b35.
[69] ἀδυναμία δὲ ἐστὶ στέρησις δυνάμεως, Aristotle, *Met.* 1019b15–16; στέρησις γὰρ ἀδυναμία διωρισμένη, *Met.* 1058b27–28; cf. *Met.* 1021a25.
[70] τὸ ... οὐκ ὂν εἶναι κατὰ συμβεβηκός, Aristotle. *Phys.* 192a3–5.

there is never even a "such" or "itself" that could not be because absolute non-being does not have anything of its own, either as actuality or as possibility.

The difference between matter as non-being and privation as non-being, then, is that privation is non-being by itself (ὅ ἐστι καθ' αὑτὸ μὴ ὄν), from which comes something (γίγνεταί τι) in which privation is not anymore (*Phys.* 191b15–16). Matter, on the contrary, is still there—and is always there—when something comes to be or gets actualized in matter. This is why matter is close to substance and somehow is substance (as substrate), but privation is not a substance or being any way (οὐδαμῶς, *Phys.* 192a5–6).[71]

So the relentless logos still finds a way to establish a distinction in non-being, where a distinction can hardly be made. This distinction can be expressed in many ways by two different negative particles μή and οὐ or by a negative particle and a privative prefix ἀ- or by not and non-, so that matter can be considered not-being and privation non-being, or even a-being.

(4) *Matter as indefiniteness.* In its negativity and the never yet fully disclosed range of possibilities, matter by itself is a sheer indefiniteness. Matter is thus defined negatively, as not-yet (as possibility) or not this (particular thing). Matter cannot define being (τὸ ὄν) as either this one or a quantity or anything other (ἄλλο). Matter is expressed or said and thought by logos (λέγεται) through negation: it is neither this nor that nor anything else definite (μήτε... μήτε... μήτε..., *Met.* 1029a20–21). Hence, matter is not a definite something (*De an.* 412a7–8).

For this reason, matter does not differentiate, or, technically speaking, it does not speciate or produce the specific difference (οὐ ποιεῖ... διαφοράν, *Met.* 1058b6) that defines a species and is brought in by the form. And while the matter of a particular

---

[71] ἡμεῖς μὲν γὰρ ὕλην καὶ στέρησιν ἕτερόν φαμεν εἶναι, καὶ τούτων τὸ μὲν οὐκ ὂν εἶναι κατὰ συμβεβηκός, τὴν ὕλην, τὴν δὲ στέρησιν καθ' αὑτήν, καὶ τὴν μὲν ἐγγὺς καὶ οὐσίαν πως, τὴν ὕλην, τὴν δὲ οὐδαμῶς, Aristotle. *Phys.* 192a3–5; cf. *De gen. et corr.* 319a1 ff.

thing—wood or bronze—is a definite something and thus is a substrate, matter as prime matter, ὕλη πρώτη, as the ultimate substrate, is already not said, or predicated, of anything else. So ultimately matter is not a definite *this* (οὐ τόδε τι οὖσα), and as such it is utterly *indefinite* (ἀόριστα, *Met.* 1049a24–1049b2). Matter can become anything. For, as Philoponus explains, matter potentially is all physical forms but nothing in actuality.[72] In this way, matter is defined negatively, being elusive to exacting thought (as non-being) and yet necessary for anything to exist at all (as a principle).

As indefinite, matter is potentially infinite in its inextinguishable potentiality, which is only actualized in a partial and specific way by the being of the form. But the infinite is the matter for completion of a magnitude only potentially and never actually, because matter does not have form (εἶδος): matter is that which is embraced or encompassed (περιέχεται), whereas form is that which embraces (*Phys.* 207a21–22, 207a35–207b1). On its own, matter has no form.[73] Infinity is thus only potential and never actual. As such, the infinite is unknowable (ἄγνωστον, *Phys.* 207a25–26). Having no limit, matter therefore has no end of itself.

Knowledge of non-being. So what and how do we know about non-being at the limit of thought and speech, when logos gasps? That it is a necessary principle in the constitution of nature, from which the logos protects itself by splitting it into two—absolute and relative non-being, privation and matter, non-being and not-being—none of which can be properly thought or known to the extent that it is non-being.

As non-being and indefiniteness, matter by itself is unknowable.[74] But as underlying nature, matter can be understood and known *analogically* (ἐπιστητὴ κατ' ἀναλογίαν, *Phys.* 191a8): as bronze relates to statuary, wood to bed, the formless to the formed—so

---

[72] δυνάμει γάρ ἐστιν ἡ ὕλη πάντα τὰ φυσικὰ εἴδη, ἐνεργείᾳ δ' οὐδέν, Philoponus. *In Phys.* 173.4–5.
[73] εἶδος γὰρ οὐκ ἔχει ἡ ὕλη, Aristotle. *Phys.* 207a26.
[74] ἡ δ' ὕλη ἄγνωστος καθ' αὑτήν, Aristotle. *Met.* 1036a8–9.

matter relates to substance, a definite something, and being (*Phys.* 191a7-12). And while a substrate is expressed or made known by an affirmative statement,[75] matter as the first substrate—the underlying substrate for anything material and thus changing—is understood only by analogy with the material of which a concrete thing as substance consists or is made.

Still, matter on its own can be known and understood only *negatively*, or apophatically: it is made known or revealed (δηλοῦται) by negation (ἀποφάσει, *Met.* 1058a23-24). This is how we understand matter as a set of yet to be realized possibilities—by negating a particular form and thus coming to that which originally should have it potentially. Therefore, we know potentiality by negating the form. In the last instance, as indefiniteness and negativity, matter is understood in purely negative terms, as *not this*, as that which is not and is never-yet.

With regard to privation as absolute non-being or utter negativity, it cannot be a subject, and thus one cannot speak about it affirmatively. This means that privation is not properly accountable, is non-definable on its own, or is defined in a rather paradoxical way: its definition as an absolute or radical non-being is a non-definition that points toward the never definable in finite terms in a definitive understanding of it.

Thus, for Aristotle non-being cannot be known. And yet, logos manages to make something known even about that which is not, or at least makes it expressible within the system of distinctions that it establishes—but only analogically and negatively.

---

[75] ὑποκείμενον τὸ καταφάσει δηλούμενον, Aristotle. *Phys.* 225a6-7.

6
Plotinus
Non-Being as the One

καὶ γὰρ λέγομεν ὃ μὴ ἔστιν· ὃ δέ ἐστιν, οὐ λέγομεν

For we say what [the one] is not, but what it is, we do not say[1]

Aphormae: the starting-points. Only being is. Only being can be thought. In thinking being, thought becomes identical with being.

These are the fundamental insights of the ontology formulated and developed by Parmenides. Yet, the undercurrent of the other ontology transpires already in Parmenides and is more distinctly spelled out by Plato, even if Aristotle opposed and criticized it. It is the ontology that accepts being as constituted by something that is not being, by the other of being, which *is not*, and therefore is not straightforwardly thinkable. But it is Plotinus, who lacks the poetic gift of Parmenides, the stylistic brilliance of Plato, and the scholarly precision of Aristotle, who becomes *the* thinker of non-being as the constitutive power to being.

Being is, but it is not primary. Nothing is primary—for us, anyway, who are always late to think that which is and has already happened. But nothing is nothing and so is not. Hence, nothing is not nothing. It is elusive. It cannot be. Nothing is not and thus "is" non-being. If being is, it has to be from elsewhere and because of the other than being that is not being. But what is this not being that makes being possible?

---

[1] Plotinus. *Enn.* V.3.14.6–7.

Being is, and, as already Parmenides asserts, it is thinkable *qua* being. As thinkable, it is unique and thus is this one as different from an other and another. Therefore, as Plotinus states, being cannot be unless it is one (*Enn.* VI.9.1.1–3). But it cannot be just one because it is in contradistinction to another being. Hence, being cannot be just one but is also many. But it cannot be just many but is also one because it is always this one being. The non-being of being is the other of being as one-many and therefore is one.

So, the sheer one without any other is outside any multiplicity that might allow us to think it in distinction to everything else— and so to be, because being comes as distinct and thinkable in what it is and as it is. But the other of being is not. It is non-being and nothing that, however, is responsible for the being of being. This is Plotinus' main philosophical insight that constitutes the *other* ontology, which to a great extent is lost to philosophy throughout much of its later history.

The one beyond being. So, for Plotinus, the non-being responsible for being is one. It is the one. The one is the one only (ἓν μόνον, *Enn.* V.4.1.15), one alone (μόνον γὰρ ἓν ἐκεῖνο, *Enn.* V.1.7.20), entirely and purely one (τὸ καθαρῶς ἕν), unrelated to anything other (οὐ κατ' ἄλλο, *Enn.* V.5.4.6–7, VI.8.8.12), to which nothing other is present or can be added (τὸ πάντως ἕν, ἐν ᾧ μηδὲν ἄλλο πρόσεστι, *Enn.* VI.2.9.6).

Since the one is not and is not anything, it is not that the one *is* not but rather that it is *not*. The one is nothing—of the existent— and yet it allows for being to be. Therefore, the copula "is" cannot be attached to the one. And yet, since we are situated in our being and thinking by oscillating between being and its fluent reproduction and representation, everything we think and say of necessity refers, mostly negatively, to the one as that which makes being possible. So Plotinus speaks about the one that "is" beside many as *beyond* being. The one transcends all things (ὑπερβεβηκὼς δὲ τὰ πάντα) and is above them (αὐτὸς ὑπὲρ αὐτῶν ὤν, *Enn.* V.5.12.47– 50). Only the one is one, but, because it is above being, the one is not, and so it cannot be thought on its own. The one has no existence. But as such, it has no essence or a definite "what" either because essence is only of that which is. So the one is only "it" without a "what," because the "it" is before the "what."[2] Hence, we can have only an oblique, peripheral, or mirrored glimpse of the one as implied or reflected in and by the many, among which we ourselves are always situated.

Therefore, if there is many, there should be one *before* many (δεῖ πρὸ τῶν πολλῶν ἓν εἶναι, *Enn.* V.6.3.21–22). But because everything that is is one and many, there is always a trace (ἴχνος) of the one in every being (*Enn.* V.5.5.14, V.5.10.2). Explicitly referring to Plato's *Parmenides* (142a, 144e), Plotinus assumes that the one is the first one that is properly (κυριώτερον ἕν) one, whereas everything else, including being and thought, comes second (*Enn.* V.1.8.23–27). This second, which is one-many (ἓν πολλά), is being (*Enn.* V.3.15.21–22) and, in Parmenides' sense, is the intellect, which always brings multiplicity to unity and thinks unity as and in multiplicity (πολλὰ ἐν ἑνί, *Enn.* VI.5.6.2). And the third is one and many (ἓν καὶ πολλά), which is the soul, although sometimes Plotinus also calls the intellect one and many (*Enn.* VI.2.21.7).

The whole of Plotinus' thought about being, which he develops systematically throughout his writings, is rooted in the wonder of the one that is before being (*Enn.* VI.8.8.13) and is non-being (τὸ δὴ πρὸ τούτου θαῦμα τοῦ ἕν, ὃ μὴ ὄν ἐστιν, *Enn.* VI.9.5.29–30). This is the crucial insight into being and the nothing of non-being as the other of being. This *before* comes before any ontological or logical distinctions and thus can hardly be adequately grasped by us who can only approach it indirectly.

The famous passage that Plotinus and the entire Neoplatonic tradition keep referring to is Socrates' occasional remark in the *Republic* that everything that is and is known in what it is is such because of something else—the good—that is *beyond being* (ἐπέκεινα

---

[2] τὸ δέ ἐστιν ἄνευ τοῦ "τὶ" ἕν... τὸ γὰρ "αὐτὸ" πρὸ τοῦ "τὶ," Plotinus. *Enn.* V.3.12.50–52.

τῆς οὐσίας, *Rep* 509b) in its dignity and power. And while Plato leaves this claim without further development, Plotinus builds his understanding of ontology and epistemology on this statement, asserting and arguing throughout the *Enneads* that since the one is non-being, it is *beyond* being.[3] Or, rather, the one is being. The one radically transcends being and the thought of it and of everything that is or strives to be in some way.

So the non-being of the beyond-being is productive of being but itself cannot be thought, and its reflection in being and thought is only oblique in and as that which it is not. And yet, the one as beyond being is necessary and inevitable because being cannot be without it.

Hence, for Plotinus "there is nothing above" (μηδέν ἐστι τὸ ὑπερκείμενον, *Enn.* VI.7.22.20–21), which means both that *there is* nothing above and there is *nothing* above. The one is a ὑπερκείμενον for and of being that precedes being. This "superstrate" comes in contradistinction—but not in opposition, since nothing opposes that which is before and beyond being—to being as the Aristotelian ὑποκείμενον as the underlying substrate of all things.

As not being, the one is not substance but beyond substance (πρὸ οὐσίας, *Enn.* VI.2.17.7), because substance is something defined and limited (ὡρισμένον, *Enn.* V.5.6.5–7) and thus is not only one but also many, whereas the one is neither limited nor defined but rather is the source of any definition and limitation as mere one.

Transcendent to being, the one also transcends thought. It cannot be properly thought, remembered (*Enn.* V.5.12.13), imagined, or represented in any way.[4] In its beyond-being, the one excuses itself from being and any form of presence, even in its absence. The one is thereby everywhere, since that which is not

---

[3] Plotinus. *Enn.* V.1.8.8, V.1.3.11, V.3.14.16–17, V.4.1.10, V.4.2.38–42, V.5.6.1, V.6.6.30, VI.2.3.7, VI.2.17.22–23, VI.7.39.34, VI.7.40.26, VI.8.9.28, VI.8.19.13, VI.9.11.42.

[4] See John Bussanich. "Plotinus' Metaphysics of the One." In *The Cambridge Companion to Plotinus.* Ed. Lloyd P. Gerson. Cambridge: Cambridge University Press, 1996, 38–65.

somewhere is not there where it is not (ὅσα δὲ μὴ ποῦ, οὐκ ἔστιν ὅπου μή, *Enn.* V.5.9.19)—and thus nowhere. The one remains and stays in nothing (μένει ... ἐν οὐδενί, *Enn.* V.5.8.16–18), since it does not have anything or anywhere else to be in (*Enn.* V.5.9.8). In its beyond-being or non-being, the one is *nothing*—of being and among being.

Other than being. In its radical transcendence, the one is *other* than and to anything else (ἕτερον ἁπάντων, *Enn.* V.3.11.18, V.4.1.5–6). However, the one itself has no otherness (*Enn.* VI.9.8.33–34). The one is other and different to and from everything else precisely because it is before everything (πρὸ πάντων, *Enn.* V.3.11.19). But before there is anything, the one is nothing—to and of being. So there is nothing before being. But there is also *nothing*, μηδέν, before the one. Therefore, the one is the first at its own disposal (αὐτεξουσίως, *Enn.* VI.8.20.31, 34). As absolutely different from everything, the one remains itself by itself (τὸ τοίνυν διάφορον πάντῃ αὐτὸ πρὸς αὐτὸ μένει, *Enn.* V.3.10.50–51) and thus has nothing other but itself alone (ὃ μηδὲν ἔχει ἄλλο, ἀλλ' ἔστιν αὐτὸ μόνον, *Enn.* VI.8.15.25–26). Hence, there is only one one or one principle (μόνον, *Enn.* V.1.7.20), for otherwise the one will not be one but many and thus will determine itself as the other and thus not as itself.

This "itself" is itself from itself (αὐτὸς παρ' αὐτοῦ αὐτός, *Enn.* VI.8.20.19). Yet, this "itself" is one beyond any multiplicity and thus is utterly *simple* (ἁπλοῦν) before all things and as such other than everything that comes after it (*Enn.* V.4.1.12, VI.7.37.18–19, VI.9.5.24). Everything else is complex, including being, and therefore is not one but one-many (τὸ μὴ ἕν. . . ἓν ἄρα πολλά, *Enn.* V.3.15.10–11; cf. *Enn.* V.3.17.8–9). Being, then, is other (ἄλλο) to the one after the one (*Enn.* VI.5.4.17).

Complexity can therefore be understood as an oppositional enhancement of simplicity: the complex is itself *and* something else in relation to itself. But the simplicity of the one is not oppositional because the one is not opposite to anything else before anything is. The one is thus not simple but rather is before and beyond the simple that is defined in contradistinction to the complex. So the one is the other to anything other before there is any other: it is "other than all the things which come after it" (πάντων ἕτερον τῶν μετ' αὐτό, *Enn.* V.4.1.6). In this sense, the one is not not-other.

Ἀρχή: *beginning, principle, origin, and source.* If nothing is, there is no beginning. And yet being is, and not just is but is to be known in what it is, how it is, and why it is. In other words, being is to be reflective. Being is to be thought *qua* being by thought as being. Being has to think itself and the reason of its being. Yet, the reason of being's being is not being itself. It is the other of being that makes being be.

That being *is* is already included in the very concept of being. But *why* being is does not follow from its concept. If the one is other than being, the other of anything that is or might exist in any way, then being is also other than the one and yet not opposite to the one because the one transcends being and thus any opposition or distinction. Being is the other to the other of being. Because being is one but also many, it cannot be without one, which is the one beyond many. As one-many, being can only be because there is the one beyond being.

Because the beyond being is always inextricably already there by not being, being has to have a reason for its being and not just be there. One should recognize, then, that being should have a principle that makes it be and be what it is. Being cannot be without its beyond or the other.

This means that there is a principle of being beyond and before being, which is *the* principle of being or the one principle. Indeed, the principle cannot originate itself, for otherwise it is not the beginning. As the origin of being, the one cannot have an origin and is thus unoriginal. And there cannot be two or more beginnings because either one will be the beginning of the other, or they will be generating each other and thus neither will be the principle. Hence, there is no principle of the universal principle or the principle of all things (*Enn.* VI.8.11.8–9).

The beginning is the beginning of that which begins but itself is without beginning. Therefore, again, the beginning is not, or there is no beginning *in* being but there is the beginning *for* being. There is *nothing* before the principle (μηδὲν ἔχουσα πρὸ αὐτῆς, *Enn.* V.5.9.7–8) or before the beyond-being.

Plotinus speaks about the beginning, source, or root (ἀρχή, πηγή, ῥίζα) of being (ἀρχὴ τοῦ εἶναι) and of everything that is.[5] This is the principle of all things (ἀρχὴ γὰρ πάντων) that is not among them (*Enn.* V.2.1.1–2). Since the principle and beginning of being is prior to being, the principle of being is not a genus of being (*Enn.* VI.2.9.36–37). So the beginning cannot be thought formally or in generic terms. It is not properly thinkable in its uniqueness but is singular beyond distinction.

The one as productive of being. If there is a beginning of being, then being is being by being brought to being or constituted *qua* being. In other words, being is generated or produced by its principle. This is the conclusion we must arrive at if we accept that being is not the first to the extent that it is not only one but also many.

In what follows, I will be using the term *produce* and its cognates. *Production* has acquired a rather bad reputation within recent use by philosophers, who have argued that being is not a thing and thus cannot be produced or fabricated because production objectifies being and makes it into an object constructed by thought rather than the source of the very thought about being. And yet, I take it that *producing* can still be justified in the context in which Plotinus talks about being because being is drawn or "led" to be by its source and origin without thereby being objectified.

Paradoxically, then, that which does not come to be—being— has to come to be, although not temporally and not even logically

---

[5] Plotinus. *Enn.* V.5.10.14, V.5.11.10–11, VI.6.9.38–39, VI.8.19.16–17, VI.9.5.24, VI.9.9.1–2.

because logical distinctions and the concept of following and ordering themselves follow after being. Therefore, if being comes along with thought and is thinking in some sense, the production of being, ποίησις, is not properly thinkable or accountable for. Rather, it can be narrated only after and from the point of view of being, or perhaps it may be hinted at poetically.

In the account of being, Plotinus thus has to adopt the language of production, τὸ ποιεῖν. This might be misleading because such production is neither creation *ex nihilo* by something that already is nor a fabrication based on a preconceived model nor a natural reproduction of that which has already been perennially passing on its form while losing its temporal physical constitution. However, for Plotinus, the production or generation of being means making being be by and on account of that which is not, never is, and never will be, but that is indispensable for anything to be at all. The source and origin of being remain forever turned toward itself (ἐπιστραφέντος ἀεὶ ... πρὸς αὐτό, *Enn.* V.1.6.17–19), keeping altogether "quiet" (ἡσυχία, *Enn.* V.3.12.35–36), never belonging to being. In general, where there is prior and posterior—and such is the order of the existent—the posterior takes its being (τὸ εἶναι) from the prior (*Enn.* VI.1.25.17–18). But the origin of being does not need to be in order to produce being. Moreover, if the principle of being existed, it would not have been able to produce being because the produced is to be radically other to its principle. Hence, the source of being produces being without being itself, and its production is free and unconditional (ἀπόλυτον, *Enn.* VI.8.20.6).

Potentiality, possibility, and the power to produce. Such production can be considered or posited as the primary activity of the one, the first without being (ἐνέργειαν τὴν πρώτην τίθεσθαι ἄνευ οὐσίας, *Enn.* VI.8.20.9–10; cf. *Enn.* VI.1.15.9–10). Yet, this is a unique kind of act because it is not grounded in, or does not come from, a substance. Because the one is the other of everything that is in some way, what comes from the one must be different from the one (ἄλλο δεῖ παρ' αὐτό, *Enn.* V.3.15.38). And if the other of the one is being, that which produces it cannot be being or substance. Therefore, the one produces not by and on account of its being, which it does not have and does not even need (οὐδὲν τοῦ εἶναι δεόμενος, *Enn.* VI.8.19.16–19). The principle of being is not being as the activity and actuality of a substance—but the *power* of and for the production of all being (πάντων δύναμις, *Enn.* V.4.1.36; cf. *Enn.* III.8.10.1, V.3.15.32–33, VI.7.32.31), which primarily produces being as the other of the beyond being. And although the one is simple (*Enn.* V.3.15.2–3), it has all the things already in itself (τῷ πρότερον ἔχειν αὐτά, *Enn.* V.3.15.29–30), but only potentially, without having any one as definite.

Since such power surpasses being, it cannot be extinguished in and by a finite act. Therefore, this power is utterly negative because it defines being and makes it definite without being defined itself and thus is indefinite or infinite (ἄπειρον, *Enn.* V.5.10.19–23). But this infinity is not privative, since the one is beyond being, and thus there is nothing of which it can be deprived. Because it is infinite, it cannot be extinguished. Many things have a power to produce, but this one is the power of powers, an enormous and inconceivable power (ἀμήχανος δύναμις, *Enn.* V.3.16.2–3).[6] The productive power of the one is defining without being defined. It is differential to the extent that it is other to everything that is and comes to be as different and differentiated in its being as being produced as not one but one-many. The productive power of the one is thus the inextinguishable capacity for being to be as the other of the one beyond being.

Necessary production and the cause of itself. Since the one is not being but beyond being, it acts without acting, without being moved or changed (*Enn.* V.1.6.22–23). As absolutely simple, the one needs nothing (*Enn.* V.3.13.16–17). And yet, in producing being, it is activity without substance. It is beyond substance, that is, hyperessential. It acts out of itself without having an itself, since

---

[6] This term is often used by Plato (e.g., in *Phaedo* 95c8).

nothing is established before such an act, and hence nothing can be discerned before being is there by the act of the beyond-being. This means that the activity of the one as an act without being does not differ from its potentiality as the inextinguishable potency to produce the other of the beyond-being.

As such, the one is the cause before causation, the cause of the cause (*Enn.* VI.8.18.38; cf. *Enn.* VI.9.6.27), or the cause of itself, *causa sui* (αἴτιον ἑαυτοῦ), the hyperessential act of itself from itself through itself (*Enn.* VI.8.14.41). However, this is not a self that can be defined except for its retrospective recognition from the point of view of being that attempts to think its origin. The cause of the cause is the cause as the productive power (αἴτιος δύναμις), the single source of being (*Enn.* V.5.10.12–13, VI.8.14.31, VI.9.9.2), of thinking (τοῦ δὲ νοεῖν αἴτιον, *Enn.* V.1.4.29), the cause of all things, which, however, is none of them (τὸ δὲ πάντων αἴτιον οὐδέν ἐστιν ἐκείνων, *Enn.* VI.9.6.55).

So when the one produces being that it does not have, it does so not by chance (ὡς ἔτυχε, *Enn.* V.3.15.36) and not by choice or planning but produces all the same (ὅμως, *Enn.* V.3.15.32–37). Since it produces in an act beyond being and substance, it produces eternally, before any temporal distinctions can be made and thus before any "before" and "after," which exist only *after* being is there, now thinkable as *caused* but not on account of itself.

So the productive act of the inextinguishable power of the one can only be understood as *necessary* (*Enn.* V.4.1.39), although only from the point of view of thinking constituted by such an act, which then recognizes it as necessary. In this sense, the necessity of producing being is a post-necessity, recognized by being in its thinking only *when* being already is.

The gift of being. But why does the one produce being? Because the cause of all causes is itself exempt from being, it cannot be thought. As utterly simple and surpassing being, the one has no thought of itself and does not think itself (*Enn.* V.3.13.34–36, V.6.2.2–3). Therefore, the one itself does not think or reflect on what it will produce (μηδ' ἐνθυμηθεὶς ὃ ποιήσει, *Enn.* V.3.15.36) because thinking is not there yet but itself has to be constituted. As the cause of being, the one does not need anything, including being, thinking, and reflection. So the question can only be answered from the perspective of being as thought and thinkable, which is the only standpoint that we can have on the one as the productive cause of being.

From the viewpoint of the produced, that which is and cannot be otherwise is perfect to the extent that it realizes its completion and fulfillment, τέλος, as its end or purpose. In its infinite producing power, the one cannot but produce, although it does not impose such a necessity on itself by itself, which is rather an inevitable expression of the perfection of the producing cause. But this is a different kind of perfection: it is the perfection that makes the perfection of being possible. The one is thus perfect before and above being and thinking (*Enn.* V.6.2.14–16). It is the most self-sufficient (αὐταρκέστατον, *Enn.* V.4.1.12, VI.9.6.17–18) and thus has to produce without needing what it produces.

Without the necessity of producing being, the one would not be perfect but would withhold something to itself, namely, the most precious of all that is—being. But this would make the cause of all things *envious* (φθονῆσαν, *Enn.* V.4.1.35) and thus *not* the most perfect. So Plotinus has to assume that everything that is perfect produces (πάντα δὲ ὅσα ἤδη τέλεια γεννᾷ, *Enn.* V.1.6.38). But the one is forever perfect beyond being and thus produces in an eternal act of producing (τὸ δὲ ἀεὶ τέλειον ἀεὶ καὶ ἀίδιον γεννᾷ, *Enn.* V.1.6.38–39; cf. *Enn.* V.4.1.27–28, V.4.2.36–37).

The one is perfect beyond the teleological perfection of being because it seeks nothing and needs nothing. But here we come to the limit of thought about the productive power of the beyond-being and can only describe it poetically or metaphorically as overflowing (ὑπερερρύη) in its superabundance (τὸ ὑπερπλῆρες, *Enn.* V.2.1.7–9), as a radiation (περίλαμψις) from the one remaining unchanged

(*Enn.* V.1.6.28–29, V.3.15.6). And if being is light emitted by the one, its source is a darkness that can never be seen or conceived.

So producing being is an act of generosity. Being is a gift. And yet, the one bestows the gift of being without having it. It produces or gives what it *does not have* (ποιεῖ ἃ μὴ ἔχει, *Enn.* V.3.15.35–36; διδόντος ἐκείνου ἃ μὴ εἶχεν αὐτός, *Enn.* VI.7.15.19–20). It gives that which it does not own. For the one as the source and origin of being gives or produces another as the other to itself (ἕτερον ποιοῦν, *Enn.* V.4.1.28; ἄλλο, *Enn.* V.3.15.38) different from the one. The act of producing being is thus an act of goodness that points toward the good that itself is not but is the source of everything good or perfect in its being.

The one as the good. The main philosophical principle accepted by Plotinus is that the origin or source of the existent is better than that which comes after the origin (*Enn.* VI.8.9.9–10; cf. *Enn.* V.8.1.30–31). This guiding principle has to be postulated because it is itself not deductible, since it refers to that which is before any possible deduction, justification, and thought. Hence, since the one is the first before anything else, the one is the best (τὸ ἄριστον, *Enn.* VI.8.10.26). So the best is non-distinguishable from the first or the one apart from many and beyond being. Therefore, the one is the good (τἀγαθόν, *Enn.* V.5.10.11, V.5.11.1–2). The good is therefore the first (*Enn.* VI.2.17.2–3), or the good is one beyond many or partless (ἀμερές, *Enn.* VI.7.18.39–40) and as such does not belong to the realm of being, which alone harbors distinctions and multiplicity. As the one, the good is the other to everything that is, but not other to itself (οὐ γάρ ἐστιν ἄλλο αὐτοῦ τὸ ἀγαθόν, *Enn.* V.6.5.11–12). It is radically other to being and thought, which are (is) generated by the one-good and as such bear(s) a reflection of the good, which is reflected in thinking.

Plato in his dialogues never explicitly identifies the good with the one, even if Aristotle ascribes this position to him (αὐτὸ τὸ ἓν τὸ ἀγαθὸν αὐτὸ εἶναι, *Met.* 1091b14). But Plotinus is unambiguous about their consilience, precisely because the beginning is always better and simpler than that which begins. Therefore, the one as the beginning and the productive source of being is better than being and as such is the good of and for being. As the beginning of being, the good itself is not being but rather is the highest (ὑπέρτατος, *Enn.* VI.8.16.9), thereby surpassing being. That the good is beyond being is also Plato's verdict in *Republic* 509b, which becomes foundational for Plotinus and subsequent Neoplatonic thought.

This means that the good of being is being one (*Enn.* VI.5.1.14–20). As such, the one is also the good of thinking or the intellect (*Enn.* VI.8.4.33–34), since, for Plotinus, as for Parmenides, being and thinking is (or are) the same. Being one-many, the intellect cannot grasp the good in its simplicity and oneness but it can only accept the good through the forms by and in which the intellect thinks and contemplates (ἐν τῷ θεωρεῖν, *Enn.* VI.7.15.9–11). This means that the good as the one, and the one as the good, is not properly graspable for thinking or, again, it is beyond being and thus cannot be thought.

The good beyond being. The one is not the "is" in any sense, since it is beyond being and thus not in and of being. So, paradoxically, the one is not even the good because "is good" is not applied to it (*Enn.* VI.7.38.1–3). The one has no predicates because it is one without many. "One is one" is beyond tautology and identity, before they become meaningful. "Is" as a copula is beside the point, if the point is the one. Predication or "is" is not applicable to the one, so the one is not a subject. Therefore, *nothing* can be properly said or thought of it.

The good does not need to think itself (*Enn.* VI.7.38.24–25), since every act of thinking adds something to the thought, while the good is the one. The good is altogether simple and is unrelated to anything, or it is related to nothing (ὅλως πρὸς οὐδέν) because it is beyond and before all things (ἔστι γὰρ ὅπερ ἐστὶ καὶ πρὸ αὐτῶν). Rather, we have to take away or abstract the "is" (τὸ "ἔστιν" ἀφαιροῦμεν) from the one (*Enn.* VI.8.8.14).

The one "is" the "supergood" (ὑπεράγαθον), since it is the good not for itself—for it is utterly self-sufficient and does not need anything (*Enn.* VI.7.23.7–8, VI.7.37.29–31)—but for others (*Enn.* VI.9.6.40–41, 57). The one is *the* good (τἀγαθόν) but not *a* good (μὴ ἀγαθόν) because it has nothing in itself, not even goodness (*Enn.* V.5.13.1–2). This means that the one is the good differently, elusively, in another way, beyond all goods (ἄλλως τἀγαθὸν ὑπὲρ τὰ ἄλλα ἀγαθά, *Enn.* VI.9.6.55–57). It is the good by having nothing (τῷ μηδὲν ἔχειν ἐστὶ τὸ ἀγαθόν, *Enn.* V.5.13.8–9). So strictly speaking, the good is nothing (οὐδέν) of the existent, for it is the first and thus has not come to be (μηδὲ γέγονε, *Enn.* VI.8.7.35–36): the good brings nothing to itself and thus needs nothing. Thereby, the good is beyond intellect, life, and beauty (*Enn.* V.3.16.38, V.5.11.18–19, VI.7.42.17). On its own, the good is *nothing*.

Yet, the good is not a privative nothing that would hold to itself because it is the source of being, goodness, thinking, and beauty. For this reason, Plotinus describes the good in terms of self-directed activity (ἐνέργεια), which, however, is beyond the intellect (ὑπὲρ νοῦν, *Enn.* VI.8.16.35) and thus beyond being and as such cannot be grasped or thought. The good is the act without being, activity without substance.

The good as the object of desire. The one-good is the good of all things (ἀγαθὸν τῶν πάντων) because all things are by depending on it, each in a different way (*Enn.* V.5.9.36–37). Since all things originate from the one and strive (σπεύδει) toward the one, they therefore strive toward the good (*Enn.* VI.2.11.26–27) because the one is the good and the good is the one.

But how is the one good the good of other things, which are many? Here Plotinus follows Aristotle's understanding of the good as the object of desire toward which all things strive (οὗ πάντ' ἐφίεται, *EN* 1094a3; cf. *De an.* 433a27–29). Thus, for Plotinus, all things desire the good (*Enn.* VI.7.20.18; cf. *Enn.* VI.7.35.24). Desiring the good, they strive toward the good. The good of being, then, is its activity (ἐνέργεια) toward the good (*Enn.* VI.2.17.28–29). For every thing, being is a good, although not just being but a good being or being with the good (εἶναι γὰρ θέλει ἕκαστον οὐχ ἁπλῶς, ἀλλὰ μετὰ τοῦ ἀγαθοῦ, *Enn.* VI.2.11.19–20).

But since the good is beyond being and thought, and in this way is nothing for and among being, the good cannot be attained and is thus the unreachable object of desire (*Enn.* VI.8.7.3–4, VI.8.15.1–2). The desire, however, does not constitute the good because the good is not good by being desirable or desired but is desirable (ἐφετόν) by being good (*Enn.* VI.7.25.16–18). The desire of the good therefore objectivizes *the* good by making it *a* good that can be multiplied and that appears different for different things in different situations—but may be also misplaced and thereby become a false good.

Via negativa. Knowledge comes with the distinction of the subject properly connected to a predicate and appropriately expressed in speech or logos. Hence, knowledge means the correct binding of multiplicity into unity, and it distinctly refers to what is, or being. But the one transcends and precedes any multiplicity and "is" beyond being and thus is beyond speech and thought (κρείττων λόγου καὶ νοῦ, *Enn.* V.3.14.18). Therefore, the one cannot be known or expressed in any way.

A thing may have many names; for example, a thing can be misnamed; and there can be a name without a thing or a reference. But the one is different because it is absent in its presence. The one is. The one is not. So the one is unnamable. "The one" is a name that is assigned from the perspective of the many by discriminative thinking and distinctive speech to that which has no name and can have no name.

Unnamable. The one thus has no proper name (*Enn.* VI.9.5.31). "The one," then, is a purely negative naming, which inevitably is a misnaming because it stands for the not-being as never-being. The negation of "one-many" is "the one." With Plato, Plotinus says that the one surpasses everything in power and is thus the greatest of all things (μέγιστον . . . ἁπάντων, *Enn.* VI.9.6.7). Yet, this too is a negative description because "the greatest" in this case means surpassing everything in productive capacity to such an extent that this capacity can have no measure in comparison with any finite productive capacity but is infinite, which, in turn, means not-finite but beyond any determination.

For Aristotle (in Heidegger's interpretation),[7] the essence of logos as discerning speech and thinking is the assertion of the disjunction ("or") and the exclusion of the conjunction ("and") in assuming truth and falsity. Logos can either assert or deny, and thus it can be true or false about, one and the same thing in one and the same respect and at one and the same time—but not both. However, in the one there is no identity of the object, no distinction in reference to the other, and no sequence of temporality—and hence neither "or" nor "and." So properly speaking, nothing we can say about the one can be true or false—only about that which it makes be.

The one is therefore unsayable, unspeakable, and ineffable (ἄρρητον) because everything that is spoken about has a "what," τί (*Enn.* V.3.13.1–2), which the one does not have. Yet, "ineffable" itself is a name that names something that cannot be named and is thus unavoidably misplaced as a name. The one is therefore unnamable: it can be named, and therefore it can be called anything. Plotinus chooses to use "the one," which, strictly speaking, is a non-name for that which cannot be said or thought but is only named postfactum—*after* the inevitably failed yet necessarily renewed attempt of saying the unsayable and thinking the unthinkable.

---

[7] Martin Heidegger. *The Fundamental Concepts of Metaphysics: World, Finitude, Solitude.* Trans. William McNeil and Nicholas Walker. Bloomington: Indiana University Press, 1995, 304–33; *Die Grundbegriffe der Metaphysik: Welt–Endlichkeit–Einsamkeit.* Vols. 29–30 of *Gesamtausgabe.* Ed. Friedrich-Wilhelm von Herrmann. Frankfurt am Main: Vittorio Klostermann, 1983, 441–83.

Therefore, the one "has no name" (οὔτε ὄνομα αὐτοῦ, *Enn.* V.3.13.4), so we only make signs and significations about it (*Enn.* V.3.13.5-6). Not having an "is," the one does not have a "what," so we can only speak around and *about* (περί) the one, always trying to approach, yet always missing it—but we cannot speak or say the one (*Enn.* V.3.14.1-2).

Speaking negatively. So how can one speak about the one? On the one hand, we cannot speak about it (οὐ λελογισμένης, *Enn.* VI.8.14.30) because the one is above being, thinking, and speech. On the other hand, we should because the one is the beginning and the source of everything and the good for all things. So we are unable not to speak about the one. We should use a special way of referring to the non-referable. We should speak negatively, through the negation of anything that might be asserted positively about the existent. Hence, as Plotinus says, the one must be primarily said in *what it is not* (δεῖ πρότερον λέγειν ἃ μὴ ἔστιν, *Enn.* V.3.10.33-34). About the one we cannot say either that it is "in this way" or "not in this way" (οὐδὲ τὸ "οὕτως" εἰπεῖν δύνασθαι οὐδ᾽ αὖ τὸ "μὴ οὕτως"), but it is something besides (παρά) these. The one is not this and not that. Hence, it is indefinite or without definition (ἀόριστον), and thus it should be said as nothing of these (οὐδὲν ἐκείνων εἶναι, *Enn.* VI.8.9.41-44). We can only say what the one is not, but we cannot and do not say what it is, always speaking from the perspective of what comes next (*Enn.* V.3.14.6-8) or from that of being. Now, Plotinus asks: is the one not what it is (οὐκ ἔστιν ὃ ἐστι; *Enn.* VI.8.12.1)? No, because it is not and has no "what." Therefore, the one is *not* what it is, οὐκ ἔστιν ὃ ἐστι. One just needs to remove the question mark in the original question.

So we can make opposite claims about the one without violating the principle of non-contradiction because double negation is not applicable to it. Thus, the one is beyond active actuality (ἐπέκεινα ἐνεργείας, *Enn.* VI.7.17.10; cf. *Enn.* VI.8.20.14)—but also it is the primary actuality (ἐνέργεια πρώτη, *Enn.* VI.8.18.51, VI.8.20.9-10).

This means that the one should be understood *negatively*. The one is not this and not that. It is not being, not intelligible, and it does not have quality, shape, or relation to anything because it is before everything else, before any other (πρὶν ἄλλο). So everything about the one can only be said by negating or removing anything that can be said or thought (ἐν ἀφαιρέσει, *Enn.* VI.8.11.30–35). If we want to speak about the one, we should *not* say "that" or "is" (*Enn.* VI.9.3.51–52) at all. Not having a name, the "one" is a removal or negation (ἄρσις) of multiplicity (*Enn.* V.5.6.26). If the existent is one-many or one and many, then the one is not-many.

Plotinus mentions four ways of knowing the good as the one: analogically (by analogies, ἀναλογίαι), negatively (by negations, ἀφαιρέσεις), by knowledge of those things that come from it, and by degrees of ascent to the one (ἀναβασμοί, *Enn.* VI.7.36.6–8; cf. Plato, *Symp.* 213c3). Yet negatively is the preferred way because we cannot even say "not this" (μὴ τοῦτο) about the one, since it is without conception (ἀνεννόητον) of "this" (*Enn.* VI.7.29.20–21). We can negate the negation, but even the double negation will not lead us to the one because it does not have a "what." So the one is the negation itself that cannot be negated. It is radical negativity, the un-, the *not*.

Therefore, if there is an imperative of speaking about the one by not speaking about it in the way in which we refer to the existent, then it is: remove, exclude, separate, cancel everything, let everything else go (τὰ ἄλλα πάντα ἄφες, *Enn.* VI.8.21.26–30; cf. *Enn.* VI.7.36.15), "take away everything" (ἄφελε πάντα, *Enn.* V.3.17.38)!

Hence, in order to have some kind of an understanding (σύνεσις)—always inadequate—of the one, we should go beyond, depart from (ἀποστῆναι), and abandon knowledge and its expression in reasoned, discursive speech, or logos (*Enn.* VI.9.4.1–9). All knowledge, that is. But it is difficult even to express and explain this (δύσφραστον, *Enn.* VI.9.10.7–20). No interpretation and understanding of the one is ever definite and final because no thought, no logical thinking, ever goes beyond being. The one will be always, inevitably missed—but missed necessarily. The one is—is *not*—what is left in and as a residue of the negation of any concrete representation or knowledge, hard won by the process of ordered, assertive, and exclusive logical reasoning.

The one is nothing of and for thought, of what can be possibly thought. Anything that we might conclude about the one—including this very reasoning—is inevitably negative and beside the point. Nothing is and can be said and thought about the one—but only negatively—by suspending speech and thought. What is left unsaid and unthought is the one as the other of being and thought.

The one itself is beyond thought, and thus, as Plotinus says, the one does not know itself and does not need to know itself, which means that there is no ignorance about the one, or the knowledge of the one is not different from the ignorance of the one (*Enn.* VI.9.6.46–48). This does not imply a skeptical stance, however, because such negative speech and thought do not suggest that nothing can be said or thought about the one. Rather, they suggest that any knowledge, including that which Plotinus tries to express at length in his works, or *erga*, is not knowledge of the kind I can have about the existing. It is a *docta ignorantia* that can only be expressed in negative terms.

Being. One and many. So being is originated or produced by that which is not being but is beyond being, which is the one. Being, then, is not the one but the other to the one. Therefore, being is *not* one (οὐχ ἕν, *Enn.* VI.2.1.13, 31, VI.2.2.1) but is *one-many* (ἓν πολλά, *Enn.* VI.2.17.25). Being cannot be one without many because it would then not be being but beyond being. And being cannot be many without one because, lacking any unity, it would then be scattered and thus would not be and be thought. This means that many does not come from many, but the many of being as one-many comes from not-many.[8]

---

[8] οὐ γὰρ ἐκ πολλοῦ πολύ, ἀλλὰ τὸ πολὺ τοῦτο ἐξ οὐ πολλοῦ, Plotinus. *Enn.* V.3.16.12–13.

Here, Plotinus follows Plato's *Parmenides*, which is central to his understanding of being and the one. In the *Parmenides*' first hypothesis, Plato demonstrates that the one without many cannot be thought, perceived, or expressed in any way because it cannot have any distinctions or predicates, which would make it already not one but also many. Therefore, the one beyond and apart from the many cannot be and does not even exist (*Parm.* 137c–42b). But without the one, ἕν, the pure many or multiplicity, πολλά, cannot exist either and cannot be thought in any way and is thus "beneath" being (*Parm.* 165e–66b). But once in the second hypothesis, the one considered along with the many becomes thinkable and begins to exist: it is being that can be thought in its distinction to non-being and becoming and is also plural to the extent that it can be thought in many distinct forms (*Parm.* 144b–57b).

Being is therefore *one-many*, unity in plurality, the being in and of beings or forms. In being, the one is pluralized and multiplied and as such it is the cosmos of beings of intelligible forms that are and cannot be otherwise. Being is a *synthesis* of one and many. Being for Plotinus is thus *one-being* (ἓν ὄν, *Enn.* VI.2.11.36; τὸ ὂν ἕν, *Enn.* VI.4.11.16–17; ἕν ... τὸ ὄν, *Enn.* VI.6.18.42–43) in which the one and being are not identical but being depends in its being on the one. As both united to and distinguished from the one, one-being is one-many.

Being as the other of the one. The many bound by the one in being as one-many, then, is constituted as one-being, where being and one in being-*and*-one, or being-one, are not identical but are other to each other. As we have seen, the one is other than being, and hence being is other than one as being's productive power beyond being (*Enn.* VI.5.4.17). In this way being is, again, one-many or one-being.

This means that *to be is to be different*. To be is to be the other of the one or to be one-being as one-many, where one is multiplied into beings, and many is bound by the one into the unity of being.

Therefore, being is *complex*. For only the one is simple before and beyond all things or, rather, beyond simplicity, if being simple means being distinct from being simple, which, in turn, refers to being as not simple, or complex. Since being for Plotinus is produced or generated, it has to be multiple because that which produces is always simpler (*Enn.* V.3.16.7–8).

So in the consideration of being, we should begin with the other as the other to and of the one, the other that is not just one but also many. This otherness is constituted by one-being as the same being and yet in which one-being are other to each other. This first otherness cannot be nothing because it presupposes and is bound to the same in being's unity of one-many that constitutes same-other, as Plato has argued in the *Sophist* (254d ff.). Together, the sameness (ταὐτόν) and the otherness (θάτερον) are two constitutive principles of being and the intellect (*Enn.* III.7.3.8–11) as one—many or one—being.

Being is produced by the one-good, where the one and the good are not other to each other, unlike one and many in one—many and one and being in one—being. As such, being is the other of the good and thus is not the good. Yet, in its reflected goodness, being is good, which it derives from the good. Being is a gift of that which in its goodness gives what it itself does not have. Therefore, everything receives its being as good from being the multiplicity of one-many. So for Plotinus, being-good is posterior to being and being something, or to the "is" and the "what," even if it always accompanies them.[9]

Although the one itself is not, because it is beyond being, for being as the other of the one it is impossible not to be (οὐκ ἔστι μὴ εἶναι, *Enn.* VI.7.12.18) because, as has been said, the one produces being with necessity. So our inability not to speak and think about that which cannot be said or thought—about the one in its utter

---

[9] ὕστερον γὰρ τῆς οὐσίας καὶ τοῦ τί ἐστι τὸ εἶναι αὐτὸ ἀγαθόν, κἂν ἀεὶ συνῇ, Plotinus. *Enn.* VI.2.17.20–21.

negativity and surpassing of being—can be taken as the rendering of the structure of the double negation in the form of "not possible not to," which in modal logic amounts to "necessary." And yet as said, the double negation does not pertain to the one itself, which is beyond being and above non-being. Therefore, the *negatio negationis* as the structure of ontological and logical necessity can only refer to and represent the one as bound by the many in being. So, contrary to non-being, being cannot not be (*Enn*. VI.5.1.23–24), and thus it always is.

As such, being cannot but be because it is the necessary other of the one that produces one-many with necessity and yet as a gift. This means that being is on its own (ἐφ' ἑαυτοῦ) but also not on its own (*Enn*. VI.5.3.12) because it is self-sufficient *qua* being but in turn depends as being in its being-is, being-what, and being-good on the one-good. As such, being is perennial and hence does not come to be and yet it is produced (non-temporally and before time comes to be) by the one beyond being in its overwhelming goodness. Being is and cannot be otherwise.

Being and thought. But being not just is—being is thought. Being *is* thought. Plotinus borrows this fundamental insight from Parmenides (fr. 6), whom he explicitly quotes several times: "thinking and being is the same" (τὸ γὰρ αὐτὸ νοεῖν ἐστί τε καὶ εἶναι, *Enn*. V.1.8.14–18, V.9.5.29–30; νοῦς δὴ καὶ ὂν ταὐτόν, *Enn*. V.4.2.43–44; cf. *Enn*. VI.7.41.18).

Why are—is—being and thinking the same? Because both are (is) constituted exactly in the same way: as that which is first necessarily produced by the one, besides and after the one, as the first one-many, as the first *other* to and of the one. Therefore, both have (has) the same structure and thus are (is) the primarily other to the one as not-one but one-many.

The thinking that thinks primarily after the one has to think itself because no other multiplicity is posited at this point. So thinking that is being can only think itself as being, which is the intellect or νοῦς. Since such thinking-thought is being, everything that has been said about being applies to it too: the intellect is one-many (ἓν πολλά, *Enn.* VI.7.14.12) and can only be one-many because it is after the one, for otherwise it would have been the one. Yet the one is beyond being and thus beyond thinking: the one is not thinkable and does not think, for it does not need anything, neither being nor thinking (*Enn.* V.3.12.48–49), and thus is neither thinking nor intellect (*Enn.* V.4.2.3–5, V.6.2.17–20, VI.7.8.17–18). The one is before, above, and beyond thinking and the intellect (πρὸ νοῦ, *Enn.* V.3.11.20, VI.8.18.28–29, VI.9.3.36; ἐπέκεινα νοῦ, *Enn.* V.3.12.47–48; τὸ ὑπὲρ τὸ νοεῖν, *Enn.* VI.8.15.20–21; ὑπὲρ νοῦν, *Enn.* VI.9.8.25). In a sense, paradoxically, it is not even thinkable that the one is not thinkable because the very concept of "not being thinkable" is thinkable. So strictly speaking, it is not even thinkable that the one is not thinkable. It is not thinkable only in the thinking that primarily thinks itself but cannot think its own radical other or the one.

Thinking the one. But how does the intellect as being, as one-many, think the one? Since the one is beyond being, it cannot be thought. Hence, the intellect in its attempt to think the one-good inevitably misses it each time, although, as has been said, the very attempt at thinking the unthinkable is itself inevitable and necessary.

The thinking of the intellect, then, can be described as a renewed motion toward the one-good, driven by the desire for the good (τοῦτό ἐστι νοεῖν, κίνησις πρὸς ἀγαθὸν ἐφιέμενον ἐκείνου, *Enn.* V.6.5.8–9). The desire to embrace the good in and by thought keeps the intellect trying to think the one-good, which, however, cannot be achieved because it is absolutely simple and one and thus cannot be thought.

As being, the intellect is good because there is a trace (ἴχνος) of the one in every being (*Enn.* V.5.5.14, V.5.10.2), and the one is the good in its singularity. The goodness of being as thought and thought as being transpires as definiteness, as many defined by the one. In the case of the intellect, it is the definiteness of the form and number (*Enn.* VI.6), which always is, is what it is, and can be thought as such. The form as thought by the intellect is being, and thus being is thought.

As we have seen, being is the (good) gift of the one-good. Therefore, the one, which is shapeless and formless (ἄμορφος καὶ ἀνείδεος, *Enn.* VI.7.17.40, VI.7.32.9–10) and has no limit (ὅρον οὐκ ἔχοντος, *Enn.* VI.7.17.15–16), gives the gift of the form to the intellect without having it. Form, then, is a *trace* of the formless (τὸ γὰρ ἴχνος ἀμόρφου μορφή, *Enn.* VI.7.33.30). Correspondingly, being as reflected in the thinking of the intellect is a trace of the good (*Enn.* VI.7.18.2–3). The intellect, then, has the form of the good by thinking the good (*Enn.* V.6. 4.5) or, rather, by trying to think that which is beyond its grasp.

Being and thinking, or being-thinking, is produced out of necessity by the one, originating from non-being as the beyond-being of the one. Yet, being is not just one but is also multiple and such also is thinking. As one-many, being-thinking not only is but always inevitably tries to return to and think the one, which it inevitably misses because the one cannot be thought, whereas thinking establishes distinctions within the multiplicity of the thought. Therefore, such thinking is not yet defined thinking and thinks unintellectually (ἀνοήτως, *Enn.* VI.7.16.14).

As Plotinus concludes in a late treatise that brings together his lifelong thinking about the one and many, when the intellect attempts to think that which is beyond being, "wishing to attain the simple, [the intellect] always comes out to apprehend it as something other multiplied in itself" (ἄλλο ἀεὶ λαμβάνων ἐν αὐτῷ πληθυνόμενον, *Enn.* V.3.11.1–5). By striving toward the one as the sole source and origin of being, the intellect tries to see or grasp the one but cannot achieve it because the one is utterly simple and thus is apart from many and beyond being. So the intellect is the sight not yet seeing, and, while trying to think the one, it instead apprehends something else rendered as many or multiplied in itself and thus produces the many (πολὺ ποιήσασα, *Enn.* V.3.11.1–8).

The indefinite defined as being. Being is thus originated by the one but comes to be defined as one thinking that thinks itself as many when turning to the one. Therefore, the one as non-being or as beyond-being that is never-being comes to be multiplied in being as one-many. The indefinite in the intellect thus becomes one in the fully defined one-many (καὶ τὸ ἄπειρον οὕτως ἐν νῷ, ὅτι ἓν ὡς ἓν πολλά, *Enn.* VI.7.14.11-12).

In this sense, the intellect is a kind of circle, always striving toward the one but turning around the one in an unrealizable yet productive attempt to know the one. The one, then, is a kind of center that spreads out without spreading out (*Enn.* VI.8.18.7 ff.). And while turning around the one in the attempt to return to the one, the intellect returns to itself by thinking what it has produced as noetic representations of the not representable. The intellect comes back to itself and sees or thinks, and this seeing or thinking is the intellect (τῇ ἐπιστροφῇ πρὸς αὐτὸ ἑώρα· ἡ δὲ ὅρασις αὕτη νοῦς, *Enn.* V.1.7.5-6). But that which the intellect comes to think is something other after the one itself (ἄλλο μετ' αὐτὸ τὸ ἕν, *Enn.* VI.5.4.17). So the first movement of the intellect constitutes the utter otherness (ἑτερότης) that separates (κεχωρίσθαι) the intellect from the one (*Enn.* V.1.6.53). The intellect is thus the first other after the one, so the one is the first and unachievable other for the intellect, remaining absolutely different beyond any difference and distinction.

In the ever-renewed attempts at thinking the unthinkable, the intellect produces many objects in the thinkable (πολλῶν γὰρ ὄντων τῶν ἐν τῷ νοητῷ, *Enn.* VI.5.4.20-21) bound by the unity of thinking. These noetic objects are thus the inevitable multiple misrepresentations of the one, which the intellect comes to understand as the objects of thought. In this way, the multiple forms of thought are produced by thinking—attempting to think—the one. These are the forms in which and through which the intellect comes to think itself. Unlike the modern Cartesian mind, the intellect does not realize itself immediately but is mediated by its forms, which, however, are of its own making.

The indefinite dyad. This means that the thinking of the intellect is at first indefinite in its striving to grasp the one. Not yet a defined being, thinking becomes such only when it turns toward the good, which it does not have, does not know, and cannot reach. Only by looking at the one (πρὸς αὐτὸ βλέπον) but not seeing it does the intellect become intellect or the definite thinking that thinks itself as defined by its objects or the forms (*Enn.* V.2.1.1–11). Before becoming one thinking that thinks itself as multiple intelligible objects, or one-many, the intellect is a not yet defined thinking but becomes such only when it thinks distinct and distinguished forms which it itself produces. In this self-constitutive act, the "when," "before," and "after" do not constitute a temporal sequence or succession, but they become such only when the intellect comes to analyze itself in logical terms.

Following a long-established Platonic tradition originating with the Pythagoreans and transmitted by Aristotle, Plotinus calls this original, not yet defined, intellection or thinking the *indefinite dyad*. So he concludes: "Thinking that sees the intelligible and turns toward it and as if perfected and limited [or defined] by it, is itself indefinite like seeing but is defined by the intelligible. This is why it is said: "from the indefinite dyad and the one come the forms and the numbers, and this is the intellect."[10] This indefinite

---

[10] νόησις δὲ τὸ νοητὸν ὁρῶσα καὶ πρὸς τοῦτο ἐπιστραφεῖσα καὶ ἀπ' ἐκείνου οἷον ἀποτελειουμένη [καὶ πελειουμένη], ἀόριστος μὲν αὐτὴ ὥσπερ ὄψις, ὁριζομένη δὲ ὑπὸ τοῦ νοητοῦ. διὸ καὶ εἴρηται· ἐκ τῆς ἀορίστου δυάδος καὶ τοῦ ἑνὸς τὰ εἴδη καὶ οἱ ἀριθμοί· τοῦτο γὰρ ὁ νοῦς, Plotinus. *Enn.* V.4.2.4–9. As Proclus relates, according to Speusippus the "ancients" (the Pythagoreans) believed that if the one is considered on its own, separate and single, without anything else and with no other element added to it, nothing else will come to exist, and so they introduced the indefinite dyad as the principle of beings (τὴν ἀόριστον δυάδα τῶν ὄντων ἀρχὴν εἰσήγαγον [*In Parm.* VII 501.3–11 = Leonardo Tarán, Ed. *Speusippus of Athens: A Critical Study with a Collection of the Related Texts and Commentary.* Leiden: Brill, 1981, fr. 48]). The indefinite dyad is mentioned in Aristotle. *Met.* 1091a3–5; cf. *Met.* 987b33, 988a13; and Anatoly apud [Iamblichus]. *Theologumena arithmeticae.* Ed. V. De Falco and U. Klein. Stuttgart: Teubner, 1975, 7–14. See also Willy Theiler. "Einheit und unbegrenzte Zweiheit von Plato bis Plotin." In *Isonomia: Studien zur Gleichheitsvorstellung im griechischen Denken.* Ed. Jürgen Mau and Ernst Günther

"seeing" (ὅρασις) is the intellect itself (*Enn.* V.1.7.5–6). Apparently, in the constitution of numbers as the forms of being, the one (ἕν) is the principle of sameness (ταὐτόν), and the indefinite dyad (ἀόριστος δυάς) is the principle of otherness (θάτερον) that bring together one-many into a uniquely defined unity within a particular number. The initial act of seeing is as yet unlimited and indefinite, as if thinking "unintelligently" (ἀνοήτως, *Enn.* VI.7.16.13–14). Before thinking is defined by what it thinks, it is indefinite and thus it is infinite or not finite. It becomes definite only when it thinks itself in and as the forms. Another way of referring to the infinite is as "big and small" (μέγα καὶ σμικρόν, *Enn.* VI.6.3.29), which stands for otherness in the Platonic tradition.[11] The indefinite dyad is thus an appropriate metaphor for the thinking that turns toward the one, at which point it is as yet indefinite and then, producing its own objects of thought, becomes thinking that thinks itself as definite and defined in and by thought.

Νοῦς, νόησις, νοητά. The intellect thinks. The intellect is by thinking. And every act of thinking is thinking of something. The original act of thought is the attempt to think its origin, or the one, which, however, cannot be thought because it is beyond being and is not thinkable. Yet, this necessarily failed attempt of thinking-νόησις establishes a thought-νοητόν. Repeated, it produces a multiplicity of thoughts-νοητά. Therefore, the originally indefinite thinking becomes definite and is defined by what it thinks and is thus the being of one-many as thinking-thought(s).

This is why Plotinus says that the intellect-νοῦς has one power to think the forms and another to look at that which transcends it by "not thinking" (τὸ μὴ νοεῖν) "differently" and "in another way"

Schmidt. Berlin: Akademie, 1964, 106–7; John M. Rist. "The Problem of 'Otherness' in the *Enneads*." In *Le Néoplatonisme*. Ed. Pierre Maxime Schuhl and Pierre Hadot. Paris: Éditions du Centre national de la recherche scientifique, 1971, 77–87.

[11] τὸ μέγα καὶ τὸ μικρόν, Aristotle. *Met.* 987b20; 988a13–14; cf. *Met.* 987b26, 1089a35–36; *Phys.* 203a15–16.

(ἄλλως), by a kind of logically unaccountable direct apprehension and reception (ἐπιβολῇ τινι καὶ παραδοχῇ, *Enn.* VI.7.35.19–23, 29–30).

In being what it thinks, the intellect as thinking and thought (τὸ νοοῦν καὶ τὸ νοούμενον) is thus double (διπλοῦς), whereas only the one is simple (ἁπλοῦς, *Enn.* VI.9.2.36–37). The intellect is both the activity of thinking and the actuality of thought. Yet, the intellect is not a composition of two complementary opposing parts, but a complex unity, the first real synthesis (σύνθεσις) of an inseparable duality of oneness and otherness, a unity in diversity (*Enn.* V.4.2.9–12; VI.6.7, VI.9.2.29 ff.).[12]

So the intellect is being by being produced by the one, first as the indefinite thinking that defines itself as one thinking that thinks many intelligible objects, or forms, and thus thinks itself as the thinking that thinks what it has produced. The intellect thereby establishes the thought by thinking it and thus makes it actual.[13]

However, thought is not unique and is monolithically one but many because in its thinking (νόησις or νοοῦν) the intellect establishes the thinkable (νοητόν, νοητά or νοούμενον) as the plurality of the noetic forms by thinking them, which makes them actual or beings (ἔστιν ἄρα ὄντα, *Enn.* V.9.5.11–13). In this way, the intellect is what it thinks (αὐτός ἐστιν ἃ νοεῖ, *Enn.* V.9.5.7). Every thought or form (ἰδέα), then, is the limit (πέρας) of the intellect at rest, when it stops at a thought, while the thinking of the intellect is the movement of the form (*Enn.* VI.2.8.23–24).

Yet, the plurality of the thus established intelligible forms are not disconnected objects of thinking because they all *are* being as one-many, which is thinking that thinks them without interruption. In this way, the thinkables-νοητά are not mutually isolated but form a unique *intelligible cosmos*, κόσμος νοητός, a self-contained system

---

[12] See Eyjólfur Kjalar Emilsson. *Plotinus on Intellect.* Oxford: Oxford University Press, 2007, 141–44.
[13] Dominic O'Meara. *Plotinus: An Introduction to the Enneads.* Oxford: Oxford University Press, 1993, 62–65.

of forms.[14] In this intelligible, living, and beautiful cosmos, everything is the whole and does not have "more" (*Enn*. VI.3.20.42). All of its constituents are distinct and unique, and yet they are mutually connected without separation and reflect and are reflected in each other. Theythus form an uninterrupted communication of forms or κοινωνία (cf. Plato. *Soph*. 254b–c; *Rep*. 476a). In the intelligible cosmos, each noetic form is in actual communication with every other one in a unified multiplicity as archetypes and the substance of the intellect's thinking (*Enn*. VI.9.5.22–23).

The intellect is thus both one and multiple, simultaneously divisible and indivisible (ἀδιάκριτον καὶ αὖ διακεκριμένον, *Enn*. VI.9.5.16). It is a complete system of distinct forms, one ordered unity (ἓν συντεταγμένος, *Enn*. VI.8.17.14), a living multi-colored sphere. All parts of this sphere are mutually transparent and reflect each other (*Enn*. VI.7.15.25), a chorus (*Enn*. VI.9.1.5), in which the whole is constituted by each of its elements but yet is not reducible to any of them.

In this way, the objects of thought are not different from the thinking of the intellect and are not given to it as an already existing world of forms, as portrayed in Plato's *Timaeus* (*Tim*. 29a), where the demiurge-νοῦς looks at and follows in its production the ever-existing independent set of forms. But for Plotinus, thinking and thought are one,[15] to the extent that intellect produces what it thinks, the entire noetic cosmos—which is a synthetic unity of plurality. Only the one is one and thus utterly simple, but the intellect is a unity of the duality of thinking and thought. So the intellect is not simple (οὔτε νοῦς ἁπλοῦν, *Enn*. VI.7.13.1) but is one-many.[16] In the intellect, thinking is always the thinking of thought, and

---

[14] Plotinus. *Enn*. II.4.4.8, III.3.5.17, III.8.11.36, IV.7.10.35, IV.8.3.8, V.8.1.1, V.9.9.7, VI.9.5.14.
[15] ἡ νόησις καὶ τὸ νοητὸν ἕν, Plotinus. *Enn*. V.3.5.28–29; ἡ νόησις καὶ τὸ νοητὸν ταὐτόν (V.3.5.32); ἐν ἅμα πάντα ἔσται, νοῦς, νόησις, τὸ νοητόν, V.3.5.43–44; νοῦς γὰρ καὶ νόησις ἕν, V.3.6.7).
[16] See John Bussanich. *The One and Its Relation to Intellect in Plotinus*. Leiden: Brill, 1988, 10–14.

thought is always the thought of thinking. Or, again, thinking and being is (are) the same.

Therefore, the Parmenidean thesis of the congruence of being and thinking in Plotinus' interpretation means the following: the intellect is unity in multiplicity or one in many, the intellect has everything (all forms as thoughts) at once, the intellect *is* and cannot be otherwise, the intelligibles are always the same by being thought by the intellect, the intellect constitutes being by thinking it, and being gives the intellect thinking and being by being thought (*Enn.* V.1.4.22–28).

Reflexivity. So the intellect, thinking, and thought are (is) the same (ταὐτὸν νοῦς, νόησις, νοητόν, *Enn.* VI.7.41.12). In other words, the intellect thinks and knows itself in its thinking that thinks the thinkable that it itself produces. This self-thinking constitutes self-knowledge in which the knower, the known, and the knowledge coincide (ὁμοῦ ὁ ἐπιστήμων, τὸ ἐπιστητόν, ἡ ἐπιστήμη, *Enn.* VI.6.15.19–20). In the fullness of its being, the intellect returns to itself in knowledge as self-movement. which is the sight of being and actuality.[17] In this way, the being of the intellect is self-directed, or reflective, activity (*Enn.* V.3.7.18–19).

The intellect's thinking of itself or self-thinking is thinking itself through the other, and thereby as the same, because thinking comes to coincide with what it thinks (*Enn.* VI.7.39.11–13). In this way, the intellect thinks itself in and through the mediated immediacy in thinking that thinks what it itself has produced as its other as thought. In this way, by establishing what it thinks, the intellect thinks itself as the same (intellect) and yet as other (thought) (*Enn.* VI.7.39.5–6; cf. *Enn.* V.1.4.34–37, with reference to Plato's *Sophist* 254d ff.), doing so without full coincidence and yet without separation. Moved originally toward the one as its origin and the one as the good, the intellect keeps moving within itself by thinking itself

---

[17] ἡ ἐπιστήμη αὐτοκίνησις ὄψις οὖσα τοῦ ὄντος καὶ ἐνέργεια, Plotinus. *Enn.* VI.2.18.8–9; cf. *Enn.* V.3.5.32–33.

as thinking its thought(s). In doing so, it has already moved and reached itself without having left itself. This is being as the thinking thought.

Non-discursivity of the intellect. Thinking itself as thought, the intellect has always already thought itself. This is what the intellect is: it is "already and always already" (ἤδη καὶ ἀεὶ ἤδη, *Enn.* VI.2.8.10). This is what being is: it always already is. Being is already-being. This means that the intellect does not seek what it thinks but has it (νοεῖ δὲ οὐ ζητῶν, ἀλλ' ἔχων, *Enn.* V.1.4.16; οὐ ζητεῖ, ἀλλ' ἔχει, *Enn.* V.3.4.18). So the intellect thinks the noetic in an atemporal and non-discursive act, at once and all together (*Enn.* VI.4.4.24), eternally, before time comes to be after the intellect (*Enn.* III.7.3). The intellect attends to itself in the already completed movement of thinking that thinks itself in and as the intelligibles. Therefore, it does not need the justification of the motion from one object of thought after another in a reasoned process because it attends to the noetic cosmos all at once in one act of thought that does not need a succession or sequence of acts. Hence, the intellect needs no logical discursive reasoning (νοῦς δὲ αὐτὸς αὐτὸν οὐ συλλογιζόμενος περὶ αὐτοῦ, *Enn.* V.3.9.21–22), and thus requires no proofs (οὐδ' ἀποδείξεως, *Enn.* V.5.2.14).

In thinking without going through a number of steps, the intellect is quiet and at peace (ἡσυχία, *Enn.* III.9.1.15–18, V.3.7.13–14). Yet, unlike the quietness of the one (*Enn.* V.3.12.35), the non-discursive stillness of the intellect is the attending to being in the non-discursive act of thinking itself as the thought that has already been achieved.

And then, by the unconditional rejection of the discursive and suspension even of the non-discursive, the intellect can return in un-thinking to that which cannot be thought, to the one, in not-knowledge and abandoning any attempt at thought.

Logos. Thinking thus constitutes itself by trying to think the unthinkable—the one, non-being. However, *qua* being, it cannot think non-being because it is nothing, but it comes to think itself as being that coincides with itself in thinking and thought. This is the one-many of the intellect that thinks non-discursively or in a single act. What it thinks is a form as a simple concept, in which all its properties are latent and yet apparent to the intellect, which thinks it in its communication and community with other concepts or forms. And if the beyond-being cannot be said or expressed, the concept can be—but with a simple name ("number" or "beauty") that does yet tell us what it is and how it is. In order to think a concept in all or at least some of its properties, it has to be thought out and said discursively, when a predicate inherent in a subject is arrived at in a number of ordered steps of reasoning.

This is λόγος. Logos is one and many (λόγος γὰρ εἷς καὶ πολύς, *Enn.* VI.4.11.16, V.3.10.29). And just as the logos in its utterance or expression is an image of the logos in the soul, the soul is itself the logos of the intellect as its offspring and sedimented being or "hypostasis" (νοῦ δὲ γέννημα λόγος τις καὶ ὑπόστασις, *Enn.* V.1.7.42). However, it is an obscure logos because, even if the soul for Plotinus does not descend altogether into multiplicity, and there is always something of the soul in the intelligible (*Enn.* IV.8.8.2–3), in its being soul belongs to the plurality of one and many.[18] This means that the soul has to bring itself together and clarify itself as logos in and through logos. So in its being logos is soul and soul is logos.

Belonging to a multiplied and fractured reality, the soul has to reason logically and discursively (λογιζομένη, *Enn.* V.1.11.1; τὸ διανοούμενον, *Enn.* V.1.7.42–43). As discursive thinking, διάνοια, logos expresses and brings together into the unity of a conclusion the multiplicity of the steps of reasoning, making one after another (ἄλλο καὶ ἄλλο, *Enn.* V.3.17.23–24), thinking another after another (ἀλλ' ἄλλο ἄλλο, *Enn.* V.3.1.12).

---

[18] εἰκών τίς ἐστι νοῦ· οἷον λόγος ὁ ἐν προφορᾷ λόγου τοῦ ἐν ψυχῇ, οὕτω τοι καὶ αὐτὴ λόγος νοῦ, Plotinus. *Enn.* V.1.3.7–8; ἡ ψυχὴ λόγος νοῦ... ἀλλὰ ψυχῆς μὲν ἀμυδρὸς ὁ λόγος., *Enn.* V.1.6.45–46. Cf. Plato. *Parm.* 157b–159b; Chrysippus. SVF II 135. See also Michel Fattal. *Platon et Plotin: Relation, Logos, Intuition.* Paris: L'Harmattan, 2013, 43–81.

Out of many, logos makes one. We are logos and therefore can think and say only through it. So everything that was said up to now is a desperate attempt to grasp non-being in logos. Νόησις is an act; λόγος is a process. Νοητά stay in communication-κοινωνία in the noetic sphere, where each thought is thought non-discursively by the intellect in an act as one, which, however, reflects every other form. But λόγοι, which are all contained in the soul (*Enn.* V.7.1.9–10), are plural and disjunctive with each other. For this reason, they need to be arranged by logical thinking or λογισμός into a system in which each one is achieved as a conclusion of discursive reasoning. The relation between the logical constituents within a system is not immediately evident but yet can be established deductively from other logical claims that are either starting points (definitions, postulates, and axioms) or themselves have been established on the basis of other propositions (theorems and lemmas). In this way, all systematic claims are logically mediated and thus connected to each other. Euclid's *Elements* is exemplary of such a system.

The intellect embraces all its thoughts in thinking them all at once, brought together non-discursively (οὐ τῇ ἐν διεξόδῳ) and having always already gone through them (ἀεὶ ἐπεξελθών, *Enn.* VI.2.21.27–32). So the intellect needs no logoi, no proofs or arguments, because it already binds all the logoi as if into one great, complete, all-embracing logos (εἷς οἷον λόγος, μέγας, τέλειος, πάντας περιέχων, *Enn.* VI.2.21.29–30), which represents the noetic cosmos. But the discursive, fractured thinking in the soul already needs proofs.

So when Plotinus says that the intellect is logos (ὁ νοῦς λόγος, *Enn.* II.4.5.8), he means that the intellect is a fully developed system in which all the deductions have already been made and all the conclusions have been reached. It is one logos that unites all partial discursive logoi and is grasped non-discursively by the intellect, which *is* this complete and completed non-discursive system of thoughts.

Hence, the non-discursive thought of the intellect never errs. But logos has to straighten itself out, investigate itself, and establish the ways for itself to follow in order to build a proper connection between one and many in what it thinks and says. And it does so by establishing multiple means, rules, styles, and directions, as Prodicus and Aristotle know. Plotinus follows them in this: everything is said and thought logically in many ways (λέγεται πολλαχῶς), and one thought can be reached by numerous paths.

... And then, unconditionally rejecting the logical and discursive and suspending even the non-discursive, the intellect returns in un-thinking to that which cannot be thought, to the one, in not-knowledge and eventually abandons any attempt at thought.

Non-being: matter and the one. Yet, a problem with non-being is that, although not being a substance and not having a proper concept, it is said, λέγεται, in many ways, or rather *appears* in many ways to and through logos. Whenever we might think we have grasped non-being, it turns out differently precisely because it is non-being. So non-being also makes its appearance as an indefinite other of being, always different, other and another, among beings. As the other of the one, it is the other of the other of being. This is matter.

Hence, Plotinus also has to recognize that which is not and never will be being, which he associates with matter as non-being as the "below being." Non-being, then, determines being from the "above" (as the one) and "below" (as matter) in a paradoxical and logically barely graspable evasion of being, which Plato labels paradoxically as "real non-being" (ὄντως τὸ μὴ ὄν, *Soph.* 258e).

Plotinus refers to both the one and matter as non-being (one: μὴ ὄν ἐστιν, *Enn.* VI.9.5.30; οὐκ ὄν, *Enn.* V.2.1.6; οὐδὲ τὸ ὄν, *Enn.* VI.9.2.46–47; matter: οὐκ ὄν, *Enn.* II.4.16.26; μὴ ὄν, *Enn.* II.5.4.11, III.6.7.11–12). Matter is nothing, μηδέν, or literally "not one," but the one as the superabundant good is equally nothing (*Enn.* VI.9.7.1).

So for Plotinus matter is nothing on its own, unlimited, infinite, indefinite (τὸ ἀόριστον, *Enn.* II.4.14.26; τὸ ἄπειρον καὶ τὸ ἀόριστον, *Enn.* II.4.15.1-2, 10, 17; ἀπειρία, *Enn.* III.6.7.8), "runs away from the idea of limit" (τὸ ἄπειρον φεύγει... αὐτὸ τὴν τοῦ πέρατος ἰδέαν, *Enn.* VI.6.3.15-16), a never determined potentiality, absence of any determination, need (πενία, *Enn.* I.8.3.16, II.4.16.20, III.6.14.8), the most deficient of all (πάντων ἐνδεέστατον, *Enn.* VI.7.27.11). Matter remains forever unaffected and is inalterable because nothing in it can be subject to change (*Enn.* III.6.10.21-22). Matter is "a kind of unmeasuredness (ἀμετρία) in relation to measure, and unboundedness (ἄπειρον) in relation to limit, and formlessness (ἀνείδεον) in relation to creating form, and perpetual neediness (ἀεὶ ἐνδεές) in relation to what is self-sufficient; always undefined, nowhere stable, subject to every sort of influence, insatiate, complete need" (*Enn.* I.8.3.12-16).

This is a kind of "definition" of matter. And yet, matter has no logos or definition because on its own it is altogether irrational or alogical (ἄλογος), a shadow of logos and a falling away from logos (*Enn.* VI.3.7.8-9). Logos is inevitably led astray by the infinite (*Enn.* II.4.15.13), is always distorted, suffers, and only gets worse in matter (ἐν ὕλῃ γὰρ ὁ λόγος χείρων, *Enn.* VI.3.9.33-34; cf. *Enn.* II.4.15.13).

Plotinus returns to the problem of matter again and again throughout his work in an attempt to grasp the ungraspable. In *Enn.* II.4 (12) and III.6 (26), he uses both Plato's terminology, describing matter as receptacle and nurse (ὑποδοχὴ καὶ τιθήνη, *Enn.* III.6.13.12; cf. *Enn.* II.4.6.1; *Tim.* 47e), and Aristotle's substrate of all things (ὑποκείμενον, *Enn.* III.6.7.1-3, III.6.10.8; *Phys.* 192a31). As a receptacle of form, matter is "not yet stable by itself, and is carried about here and there into every form, and since it is altogether adaptable, becomes many by being brought into everything and becoming everything" (*Enn.* II.4.11.40-42). And yet, matter is an empty receptacle. It is sheer many in the absence of the one. It is nothing, and thus it cannot be known. Plotinus here turns to Plato's language from the *Timaeus* (*Tim.* 52b), which describes matter as always seen in its opaqueness and obscurity by non-seeing, by non-thought, and thus by a kind of "illegitimate reasoning" (λογισμὸς νόθος, *Enn.* II.4.10.8, 11, II.4.12.33–34; cf. *Enn.* II.4.10.5), which, however, does not lead to any clarification of the reasoned.

Just as is true of the knowledge and expression of the one, knowledge of matter is necessary and yet impossible. It is either utterly negative or apophatic—or analogic, where matter (dis)appears as "darkness" (τὸ σκότος, σκοτεινή, *Enn.* I.8.4.32, I.8.8.40, I.8.9.20, II.4.5.7) or unfathomable "depth" (τὸ βάθος, *Enn.* II.4.5.6–7), inaccessible to the gaze of the intellect and never illuminated by the light of its being. Seeing the non-visible in the darkness with the eyes wide shut amounts to seeing nothing. Nothing is seen without seeing and nothing is thought without thinking. So thinking nothing means not thinking a thing that might have a concept, but a strange, non-conceptual, spurious thinking by a "non-intellect" (οὐ νοῦς, *Enn.* I.8.9.18) that does not think because that which is thought has no concept and is not.

Impossible distinctions: the non-being of the one and matter. But if matter is not a thing, is nothing, how can it be told apart from the one, which, strictly speaking, is nothing too? Because neither is thinkable nor permeable for and by logos, a very difficult question remains for Plotinus. Without logos no distinctions are possible, for logos is about making distinctions. The difference between the one and matter is thus a no-difference and no-distinction that can only be established from the point of view of an already existing, complete system of distinctions of the intellect and logos, that is, in and from the position of being. Because logos cannot but multiply what it says and thinks, doing so always differently, the non-distinctive distinction between the one and matter becomes plural. Even non-being is said and thought in many ways.

Hence, Plotinus proposes several different ways of characterizing the indistinguishable distinction between the non-being of the one and of matter.

Matter as privation. As we have seen, matter for Aristotle is a principle of nature, along with form and privation. Matter is the first substrate and a seat of possibility for all things yet to be realized. As such, matter is relative non-being but not non-being as such or absolute non-being, which for Aristotle is privation. Therefore, on his account matter is not privation.

However, as Plotinus argues in the conclusion of his treatise *On Matter*, although matter is other to everything and nothing but other (μόνον ἄλλο; ἄλλα, *Enn.* II.4.13.30–31), it is *not* otherness as such (ἑτερότης) because only the one is radically other in its beyond-being and abounding power to everything that is in some way. Rather, matter is to be considered "part of otherness" (μορίῳ ἑτερότητος), as other in opposition to proper beings, or logoi (ἀντιταττομένῳ πρὸς τὰ ὄντα κυρίως, ἃ δὴ λόγοι, *Enn.* II.4.16.1–3), which are fully determined in their existence by distinctions and oppositions to each other. Therefore, contra Aristotle, as non-being matter for Plotinus is privation because privation is opposite to being, to that which exists in, and is expressed by logos.[19] Matter is formless, and such is privation as that which is opposite to form and does not have an independent existence of itself but is always in something else.[20]

As privation of being, in its utter negativity, matter can be best expressed through negation. Grammatically, it is referred to negatively and privatively by ἀ-, *alpha privativum*. Even the beginning of the alphabet is a reference to negativity. Thus, matter is infinite, indefinite, formless, shapeless, measureless, without quality, without quantity, impassible, insatiate, bodiless, without

---

[19] διὸ καὶ μὴ ὂν οὕτω τι ὂν καὶ στερήσει ταὐτόν, εἰ ἡ στέρησις ἀντίθεσις πρὸς τὰ ἐν λόγῳ ὄντα, Plotinus. *Enn.* II.4.16.3–4.
[20] στέρησις δὲ ἀεὶ ἐν ἄλλῳ καὶ ἐπ᾿ αὐτῆς οὐχ ὑπόστασις, Plotinus. *Enn.* I.8.11.1–2.

magnitude, unthinkable: ἄπειρος, ἀόριστον, ἀνείδεον, ἄμορφον, ἄμετρον, ἄποιος, ἄποσον, ἀπαθής, ἀκόρητον, ἀμέγεθες, ἄνοια, and so on.[21]

In this way, matter is absolute non-being that is unconditionally distinct from being without having being itself. Thereby, matter is also distinct from the one because the one is beyond being, before any distinctions and oppositions can be established, and thus beyond logos. So matter is the "other being" (ἕτερον ὄν, Enn. II.4.16.26) and, if being is always already-being, matter is never-yet being, forever deprived of being and as such "is" below and after being.

Production of matter? Another possible point of differentiation between the one and matter is implicit in the question of whether for Plotinus matter has been produced. On the one hand, as nothing and utter indefiniteness, how can matter be produced? The one is equally indefinite and "is" non-being and nothing—of and among being(s). But on the other hand, the only non-generated matter is that which generates, which is the one, so matter has to be produced. So the one and matter have to be the same but also not the same. Yet this claim cannot be properly attested and asserted by logos because the one is the source of the same and other as established by logos and of the logos itself.

The question of whether matter has been produced has provoked a rather heated debate in recent years. Indeed, on the one hand, some passages in Plotinus suggest that the lower soul produces something worse than itself, an image of itself that is non-being (ποιεῖ εἴδωλον αὐτῆς, τὸ μὴ ὄν, Enn. III.9.3.11) or indefiniteness (ἀοριστία, Enn. III.4.1.5–12; cf. Enn. II.4.15.19–20).[22] These texts, however, are fragmentary and come from Plotinus' early treatises

---

[21] Plotinus. Enn. I.8.3.13–16, I.8.4.27, I.8.6.42, I.8.8.38, I.8.10.1, II.4.3.1–2, II.4.8.1, II.4.9.4, II.4.10.1, II.4.12.34–38, II.4.15.17, 33–34, II.4.16.9–10, III.6.18.30, VI.9.7.12.

[22] Denis O'Brien. *Plotinus on the Origin of Matter: An Exercise in the Interpretation of the Enneads.* Naples, FL: Bibliopolis, 1991, 24–25.

that are not specifically dedicated to discussion of matter and never explicitly mention matter as produced by the soul or provide an argument for identifying the soul's own image with matter. Besides, these passages do not refer to the one as producing everything that is—and that which is not. Others have argued that non-being is already present at the very beginning of the sequence of production of the existent beginning with the one.[23] Besides, if matter is privation, how can privation be generated? Privation deprives that which is and is generated by the one, but privation itself—which for Plotinus, unlike for Aristotle, is not a principle of being but is a complete lack—comes after the deprived. The indefiniteness and nothingness of matter make it very difficult, if not impossible, to provide a clear, unambiguous answer to the question of the generation of nothing by nothing, of non-being as privation and never-yet-being by non-being as ever-before-being.

Matter vs. the one. Plotinus establishes a number of other distinctions between the one and matter within his systematic account, but he does so from the position of being, because in its indefiniteness nothing can be distinguished from nothing nor non-being from non-being.

Speaking apophatically, matter is neither soul nor intellect nor life nor form nor logos nor limit (οὔτε δὲ ψυχὴ οὖσα οὔτε νοῦς οὔτε ζωὴ οὔτε εἶδος οὔτε λόγος οὔτε πέρας, *Enn.* III.6.7.7–8) nor power. But such is also the one. So all the distinctions are again differentiated by logos, which does not penetrate either the one, which is pre-logical, nor matter, which is alogical.

Thus, the one is the first, whereas matter is the last (εἶδός τι ἔσχατον, *Enn.* V.8.7.22–23; cf. *Enn.* I.8.7.19, 22). If the one is

---

[23] Jean-Marc Narbonne. "Le non-être chez Plotin et dans la tradition grecque." *Revue de la philosophie ancienne* 10 (1992), 115–33; "La controverse à propos de la génération de la matière chez Plotin: l'énigme résolue?" *Questio* 7 (2007), 123–63. See also the discussion in Kevin Corrigan, "Is There More than One Generation of Matter in the 'Enneads?'" *Phronesis* 31 (1986), 167–81; John Phillips. "Plotinus on the Generation of Matter." *International Journal of the Platonic Tradition* 3 (2009), 103–37.

beyond being, matter is "below being." But, again, this can only be ascertained from the systematic point of view of being and logos.

Besides, the one is the "unspeakably great" power that produces being and all things (δύναμις πάντων, *Enn.* V.3.15.32-33), whereas matter is powerless and is not power in any sense (οὔτε δύναμις, *Enn.* III.6.7.9). Matter can never be actualized (*Enn.* II.5.4.3-18), cannot produce anything on its own, and is thus opposite to producing (ἀντιτεταγμένως τῷ ποιεῖν, *Enn.* V.3.15.36). Being potentially (δυνάμει) all things, matter is always only an "announcement" (ἐπαγγελλόμενον, *Enn.* II.5.5.1-4), an empty "promise" that can never be fulfilled.

Moreover, the one is shapeless and formless but generates form, whereas matter is shapeless and formless but receives form and is farthest from form (*Enn.* VI.7.33.30-33). The one generates being, whereas matter is powerless and incapable of generating anything. The one gives without having, whereas matter receives without possessing. The one is always absent in its presence, whereas matter is present in its absence.

Intelligible matter. But matter is also different from itself: present in its absence to everything, it even appears in the thinkable—as intelligible matter among the forms. In the *Ennead* II.4, entitled *On the Two Kinds of Matter* in Porphyry's *Vita Plotini* (4.45; 24.46), Plotinus provides an account of intelligible matter. As we have seen, the notion of intelligible matter comes up without any elaboration in Aristotle as the matter of non-sensible things—for instance, of mathematical objects. Plotinus mentions that some philosophers accept a different kind of matter in the intelligible (ἐν τοῖς νοητοῖς) that underlies the forms and incorporeal substances (*Enn.* II.4.1.17-18), discussing it at length in the early *Enn.* II.4 (12). The treatises of the middle period, *Enn.* II.5 (25) and *Enn.* III.6 (26), make a few occasional mentions of ὕλη νοητή, whereas the important late *Enn.* I.8 (51) does not refer to intelligible matter at all. However, in the immediately preceding *Enn.* III.5 (50), intelligible matter resurfaces as characterizing the distinction of δαίμονες, or spiritual beings that are intermediate between gods and humans (*Enn.* III.5.6.44).[24]

Why should Plotinus accept the rather unusual concept of matter in the intelligible? Except for exegetical purposes, the main reason is that the unlimited and indefinite is ubiquitous and hence is also present in being among beings in the form of plurality or the many in and of the one-many. Plotinus says: "The unlimited is present both in the intelligible and in the sensible, where the former is a kind of form or the archetype (ἀρχέτυπον) for the latter as the image (εἴδωλον, *Enn.* II.4.15.21–22)." Yet, the unlimitedness as darkness and opacity in the intelligible is different from that in the sensible and so differs the matter(s).[25] Therefore, intelligible matter exists as the archetype of the other matter, which is absently present to physical things in the world. Besides, if physical things form a cosmos, then it has to be an imitation (μίμημα) of the intelligible cosmos (κόσμος νοητός), and if there is matter here, there should be matter there (*Enn.* II.4.4.7–11). And if matter is the substrate of bodily things, then there should be corresponding matter as the substrate of intelligible things, of the forms-εἴδη (*Enn.* II.4.4.2–7). The intelligible matter is still indefinite, yet it is relatively less indefinite than bodily matter and thus can be considered the form of the utterly formless. So, broadly speaking, anything that comes in the order of being as more ordered and less multiple can be taken as the form to that which is more dispersed or has a great presence of the many. In this way, in the order of the existent, the ontologically "higher" is the form of the "lower," which establishes a whole "ladder" of matters. This structure is commonly present in Plotinus: that which is more potential is matter or recipient to what is more actual or form, as the soul is matter to the intellect (*Enn.* II.4.3.1–5, V.1.3.22–23, V.9.4.10–12).[26]

---

[24] See Dmitri Nikulin. *Neoplatonism in Late Antiquity*, 90–115.
[25] διάφορόν γε μὴν τὸ σκοτεινὸν τό τε ἐν τοῖς νοητοῖς τό τε ἐν τοῖς αἰσθητοῖς ὑπάρχει διάφορός τε ἡ ὕλη, Plotinus, *Enn.* II.4.5.12–14.
[26] Cf. Paul Kalligas. *The Enneads of Plotinus: A Commentary*. Vol. 1. Princeton: Princeton University Press, 2014, 310–11.

But what is intelligible matter? Because matter is a possibility for being, intelligible matter is the indefinite potentiality for being. Intelligible matter, then, can be considered the *indefinite dyad*, ἀόριστος δυάς. And, as was argued, the indefinite dyad stands for the not yet definite and not defined thinking, for the original indefinite intellection or vision of the intellect that searches for and attempts to think its source and origin, the one. However, since the one is beyond being, it is not thinkable or representable in any way. So inevitably missing its origin, such thinking is indefinite. The intellect becomes definite and self-defined only when thinking the forms or intelligible objects that it itself has generated in attempting to go back to the one. Before that, it is an indefinite being or indefinite thinking, which is the indefinite dyad. And this is intelligible matter for Plotinus.

So paradoxically, matter is the first and closest to the one—as the intelligible matter of the noetic cosmos, as sheer multiplicity, as the many without one, as the indefinite thinking attempting to think its origin. And yet, matter is also the last and farthest from the one—as bodily matter, a total lack of being, and only a potentiality for the embodiment of bodily things in the physical cosmos. Matter is thus both before the definite being and after it.

Evil. But perhaps the ultimate (dis)appearance of negativity in and as non-being in its lack of definiteness is evil. In both the early *Enn.* II.4 (12) but especially throughout the late *Enn.* I.8 (51), Plotinus portrays matter as evil: κακὸν ἡ ὕλη (*Enn.* II.4.16.16, VI.7.28.12).[27]

Being much more immersed in the world, the soul in its partiality, discursivity, and greater affinity with multiplicity inevitably encounters evil, which transpires as the soul's restlessness, itself

---

[27] See Kevin Corrigan. *Plotinus' Theory of Matter-Evil and the Question of Substance in Plato, Aristotle, and Alexander of Aphrodisias*. Leuven: Peeters, 1996; Jean-Marc Narbonne. "Matter and Evil in the Neoplatonic Tradition." In *The Routledge Handbook of Neoplatonism*. Ed. Pauliina Remes and Svetla Slaveva-Griffin. London: Routledge, 2014, 231–44.

rooted in the soul's audacity (τόλμα) and the desire to be on its own, independent of the order of being (*Enn.* V.1.1.4–6). The soul thus always faces non-being that escapes form, definition, and organization. However, this is not the absolute non-being (τὸ παντελὲς μὴ ὄν, *Enn.* VI.9.11.35–38), which remains ungraspable. The ultimate many without the one on the way of descent into multiplicity is matter. Because matter is the last (τὸ ἔσχατον), it is sheer otherness, and thus nothing is the one. The last is that after which nothing whatsoever can be or come to be. And this is evil (*Enn.* I.8.7.19–20). As the last and ultimate, matter is evil. However, evil is necessary for Plotinus because it is necessary that after the first, which is the good, there be a next and then the last (*Enn.* I.8.7.16–23). Only the good as the one and the first escapes evil and matter or rather has never approached it (*Enn.* VI.7.28.26–28).[28]

Moreover, because the one is the good, matter "has nothing at all of the good" (*Enn.* I.8.7.21–23). Therefore, matter is not good but evil. Everything desires the good, but nothing desires matter. So matter as evil has to be distinguished from the one because there is no evil either in the one as the source of being or in being or the intellect. Therefore, evil is only among the non-existent or matter.

No wonder, then, that Plotinus describes both matter and evil in the same terms: as non-being (οὐδὲ γὰρ τὸ εἶναι ἔχει ἡ ὕλη, *Enn.* I.8.5.9–10), darkness (*Enn.* II.4.5.7), need (πενία), deficiency (ἔλλειψις), infinite and indefinite (ἄπειρον), and lacking the good (*Enn.* II.4.16.17). And yet, since neither matter nor evil is, and thus neither one is a subject, no predicates or properties can be assigned to them, and so the two cannot be properly identical or distinct. Matter remains a not properly thinkable or graspable "kind of form

---

[28] Proclus criticizes Plotinus' understanding of matter: for Proclus, matter is necessary but not evil. See Proclus. *De Malorum Subsistentia; On the Existence of Evils*. Trans. Jan Opsomer and Carlos Steel. Ithaca, NY: Cornell University Press, 2003. See also Christian Schäfer. *Unde malum: Die Frage nach dem Woher des Bösen bei Plotin, Augustinus und Dionysius*. Würzburg: Königshausen & Neumann, 2002, 105–66.

of non-existence" (εἶδός τι τοῦ μὴ ὄντος, *Enn.* I.8.3.4–5)—not a real form but an ever-elusive non-form of the non-existent.

Finally, as we have seen, Plotinus characterizes matter as privation. But such is also evil as indefiniteness and absolute deficiency (ἄκρατος ἔλλειψις, *Enn.* I.8.4.23–24, I.8.5.5). This is the privation that is opposite to all form and being and thus has no existence on its own (*Enn.* I.8.11.1–3). Hence, evil can be considered *privatio boni*, the privation of the good (παντελῆ στέρησιν ... ἀγαθοῦ), although not of *a* good (τινα ... ἀγαθοῦ, *Enn.* I.8.12.1–5). Therefore, again, matter is evil as non-being—as privation both of form and of the good.

In this way, paradoxically, matter cannot be properly distinguished from the one because non-being is indistinguishable from non-being. And yet, there is an absolute difference between the one and matter that is hardly graspable by thought—the non-distinguishable distinction between the first and the last, the good and the evil, the not yet being and its utter privation, the above being and the below being.

7
Simplicius
Non-Being Voided

οὐκ ἔστι κενόν.

Void is not.[1]

Simplicius is one of the last great thinkers of ancient philosophy, separated from Plotinus by almost three hundred years, longer than the time that separates Aristotle from Parmenides. With Simplicius, a tradition of a thousand years finds its completion: what could be said and thought about being has been accomplished, so the logos turns scholarly, leaving extensive footnotes on the margins of its own previously produced texts that testify to its inventive and adventurous philosophical wanderings. From Simplicius we have voluminous commentaries on Aristotle, including one on Epictetus' *Enchiridion*, but no original writings. One of his main concerns is smoothing out perceptible distinctions between Plato and Aristotle in order to finally bring the edifice of philosophy to its completion on an indisputable and uncontroversial foundation. However, in these mostly exegetical texts, we discover a treasure trove of minute yet valuable arguments and extensive excerpts from ancient thinkers, which allow us to rethink and restore the aporetic and often difficult way of thought without seeking its finalization within a system of the kind we find in Proclus' *Platonic Theology*.

---

[1] Simplicius. *In Phys.* 667.34.

The concept of void is central to Simplicius' interpretation of non-being, which comes with an inherited Aristotelian conceptual apparatus in its logical approach to being. As we have seen, for Aristotle, void is a logical misrepresentation of the unrepresentable, a disembodied embodiment of nothing. In that which is and lives on its own—in nature as φύσις—nothing manifests itself through the void.

But is there any void, and what is it? In cosmology, void stands for either an extended interval that can be occupied by a body or for a paradoxical unitary non-being as the other of being in its multiplicity and atomic dispersion.[2] In either case, the void can be taken as the condition of the possibility of motion of a body. Aristotle dedicates the central chapters of Book 4 of the *Physics* to the discussion of void, right after the consideration of place and preceding that of time. In his massive commentary on the *Physics*, Simplicius dedicates an ample amount of space to the void, which results in some fifty pages of a close reading and an explanation of Aristotle's argument that abounds in subtle observations on the void, at times convoluted or terse, and the impossible consequences of its acceptance.[3]

Aristotle lays out the program of the study of the void (περὶ κενοῦ), closely followed by Simplicius, by suggesting that we need to find out *if* the void is or not (εἰ ἔστιν ἢ μή), *how* it is (πῶς ἔστι), and *what* it is (τί ἐστιν, *Phys.* 213a13; cf. *Phys.* 208a28–29; *In Phys.* 646.3, 693.5–7). In the already mentioned opening section of Book 2 of the *Posterior Analytics*, Aristotle asserts that in order to know a thing, we should look for its "that" (τὸ ὅτι), "why" (τὸ διότι), "if"

---

[2] On Simplicius' reading of Plato's *Sophist* and the interpretation of non-being as the other of being, as the "eidetic alterity," see Marc-Antoine Gavray. *Simplicius lecteur du Sophiste. Contribution à l'étude de l'exégèse néoplatonicienne tardive.* Paris: Klincksieck, 2007, 77–88.

[3] Aristotle. *Phys.* Δ 6–9, 213a12–218b28; Simplicius. *In Phys.* 1–4, 642.32–694.29. Translations of the latter text follow, with some modifications, Simplicius. *On Aristotle on the Void.* Trans. J. O. Urmson. Ed. Peter Lautner. In *Philoponus: On Aristotle Physics 5–8 with Simplicius: On Aristotle on the Void.* Trans. Paul Lettinck and J. O. Urmson. London: Bloomsbury, 2014.

(εἰ ἔστι), and "what" (τί ἐστιν, *An. Post.* 89b23-35). In order to know *what* a thing is (τί ἐστιν), one should first find out *if* a thing is (εἰ ἔστι). So knowing "how" a thing is means its "that" (τὸ ὅτι) and "why" (τὸ διότι). According to Simplicius, Aspasius interprets the "how" as the "what" (*In Phys.* 656.4-5), that is, how a thing is according to its properties, which Simplicius himself accepts, though reducing the "how" to accidental attributes (τὰ ὑπάρχοντα, *In Phys.* 520.27-521.2).[4] Therefore, the central question in the discussion of the void is the connection between its "if" and "what," or finding out whether or not the void exists and what it is.

If we follow the *if/what* distinction, we might ask: what if we are searching for the *what* of something that does not exist in the proper sense? As we have seen, Plotinus' one is beyond being and properly is not, yet in its absence it is the source of being beyond logical thinking and distinctions. What can one say about void, then?

Opinion and common conception of the void. As we have seen, for Aristotle non-being is the subject of opinion (δόξα)—namely, that it is *not*, unless it is a principle of nature (*De int.* 21a32-33). But since void does not exist for Aristotle, it only appears or seems (δοκεῖ) to be a non-being and privation, which is a "common opinion" (κοινὴ δόξα) of the void (*Phys.* 213a21-22). But an opinion-δόξα can still be authoritative if it comes with a pedigree shared by many "ancients," or if it is held by a few "distinguished people" (τὰ μὲν πολλοὶ καὶ παλαιοὶ ... τὰ δὲ ὀλίγοι καὶ ἔνδοξοι ἄνδρες," Aristotle. *NE* 1098b27-28). Following this line, Simplicius takes the Pythagorean doctrine of the void as "distinguished" (ἔνδοξον, *In Phys.* 651.25), in that it is both ancient and is upheld by illustrious thinkers and thus has to be taken seriously, even if critically.

Plato famously distinguishes between the intellect (νοῦς) and true opinion (δόξα ἀληθής): while the former comes with true

---

[4] See Peter Lautner. In Simplicius. *On Aristotle on the Void*, 223-234n4.

reasoning (μετ' ἀληθοῦς λόγου), the latter is without reason or is irrational (ἄλογον) and yet can still be true (*Tim.* 51d–e). For Aristotle, an example of such a δόξα is Plato's own teaching of the principles (ἀρχαί), which Aristotle does not share (*NE* 1095a28–33). But the opinion about non-being cannot be true for Aristotle because it does not have a foundation in being and thus it does not belong to logically justifiable knowledge, which is about that which cannot be otherwise.

For Simplicius, however, rather than void, one has a "common conception" (κοινὴ ἔννοια) because "we cannot investigate whether something exists of which we have not already formed a conception (ἔννοια), just as we cannot investigate what it is unless we are already convinced that it exists" (*In Phys.* 653.11–12).[5] So if we are not convinced that something is or exists, we need to start with a "conception" of what it is considered to be as commonly conceived. In the case of the void, we begin with an ἔννοια that might become a concept if only we can find a definition that would express its essence. Yet, for Aristotle and Simplicius, void has no essence because, as both laboriously demonstrate, void does not exist. And without an *if*, εἰ, there is no *what*, τί. So in the case of void, we can only invoke its "common conception" or common opinion.

Plato, Aristotle, Epicurus, and the Stoics use ἔννοια as standing for a general idea with which we start questioning and investigation.[6] In Euclid's *Elements*, it becomes the "common notion" (κοινὴ ἔννοια) or "axiom," which is a proposition that we accept without further proof as a self-evident and indemonstrable truth.[7] Plotinus widely uses ἔννοια as a general conception of something that might not even be properly definable, such as matter or evil (*Enn.*

---

[5] Cf. Simplicius. *In Phys.* 18.1, 649.5, 656.28.

[6] Cf. Plato. *Tim.* 47a; Plutarch. *De comm. not.* 1075e–f.

[7] An example of an axiom is: "Things that are equal to the same thing are also equal to each other." Euclid. *The Thirteen Books of Euclid's Elements.* Vol. 1. Trans. and ed. Thomas L. Heath. New York: Dover, 1956, common notion 1; 222. See also Thomas L. Heath. "Notes on the Common Notions." In ibid., 221–22.

II.4.1.3), the ἔννοια of which is that of unmeasuredness, unboundedness, and formlessness (*Enn.* I.8.3.12–16).

When speaking about the Atomists' understanding of the void, Simplicius also calls it a "mere notion" (μόνη ἐπίνοια), which refers to something that does not actually exist (τὸ οὔτε ἐνεργείᾳ ὄν, *In Phys.* 648.10). Ἐπίνοια is also often used by Plotinus, particularly when speaking about matter as indefinite and shapeless, and thus having only a (vague) notion, or when talking about motion in the intellect, which cannot be found in (ἐπί) being but only with (μετά) being as intellect. Thus, it is not inherent in the subject but only in our notion of it (*Enn.* II.4.3.2, VI.2.7.19).

So the ἔννοια or ἐπίνοια of the void is a vague and not properly formed thought that refers to what seems to be non-being, which thought inevitably misses because of its nonexistence.

Interval and place. In the case of void, we thus need to begin with a common opinion or a general conception of what it is considered to be and then examine it critically. If void does not exist, then it does not have a proper notion or concept, and hence it is referred to only vaguely or non-conceptually. The ἔννοια of the void, or what the void is commonly conceived to be, is an interval (διάστημα) or a place devoid of body (τόπος ἐστερημένος σώματος, Aristotle. *Phys.* 214b18; *In Phys.* 657.7, 658.22–23). However, Aristotle develops a very specific understanding of place, which is discussed in the *Physics* right before the void and which was not only commonly known throughout antiquity but also into modernity, when the rethinking of the Aristotelian concepts of place and motion led to the creation of physics as we know it today. For Aristotle, place is the border or limit of the surrounding body (τὸ πέρας τοῦ περιέχοντος σώματος, *Phys.* 212a6, 20–21),[8] and is a kind of unmoving vessel (ἀγγεῖον ἀμετακίνητον, *Phys.* 212a15–16).[9] Such a concept of place is already criticized

---

[8] Cf. Aristotle. *Phys.* 211a2–4.
[9] Cf. Aristotle. *Phys.* 209a28–29.

and rejected by Aristotle's closest disciple, Theophrastus, who takes place to be an order (τάξις) and arrangement (θέσις) of parts into the whole in a body, similar to the constituents of an organism (*In Phys.* 639.13–22).[10]

But if place is considered the Aristotelian way, which Simplicius accepts, taking place as "the limit of the container, and not an interval as such" (πέρας τοῦ περιέχοντος ἔστιν ... διάστημά τι καθ' αὐτὸ οὐκ ἔστι, *In Phys.* 657.15–16), then the common conception of void as an empty place or interval devoid of body becomes meaningless. For place is understood as a function of the body, as the external limit *of* a body, and thus it cannot even be thought in the absence of or without a body. The void then will be a non-void, a nothing without a concept.

Following Aristotle, Simplicius distinguished *two kinds* of void in the extant accounts. The first kind of void is that between and outside the bodies, also including the void outside the cosmos (*In Phys.* 648.1). If, as Alexander suggests, body is that which has three dimensions (τρεῖς ἔχον ... διαστάσεις, *In Phys.* 655.25–26), then void can be taken as that which is filled (τὸ πλῆρες) with a sensibly perceptible body (*In Phys.* 654.12). The second kind is the void interspersed with bodies, the interval within the bodies (*In Phys.* 645.30, 648.25–26, 663.15–17).[11] Simplicius then goes on to demonstrate through a number of arguments that the void does not exist either as an interval-διάστημα containing a body ("separated," τὸ κεχωρισμένον) or as filled with it ("unseparated," τὸ ἀχώριστον, *In Phys.* 657.20–21, 683.3, 684.16). What we can say about the void considered as a hollow interval or an empty place is ἄτοπον—literally, without and out of place.

Motion and void. Those who accept the existence of void provide several (four, by Simplicius' count but in fact five) arguments

---

[10] On Theophrastus' criticism of Aristotle's account of place, see Keimpe Algra. *Concepts of Space in Greek Thought*. Leiden: Brill, 1995, 231–48.

[11] So for the Atomists, when a body moves through the void, the empty intervals within the body move through the vacuum too.

in support of their position. These arguments are from (1) motion, (2) compression, (3) growth and nutrition, (4) ash (τέφρα), and (5) the Pythagorean cosmological argument (the heaven "inhales" the void) (*In Phys.* 649.4–652.19).

The first argument, from motion or change, suggests disjunctively that motion as the change of place in locomotion and growth occurs through a medium that is either filled or void. Yet, it is impossible to move through the filled. Therefore, the motion occurs through void. Hence, the void exists. In other words, if there is motion, there is void (*In Phys.* 649.7–11). Simplicius' response is that not every motion is change of place, such as the motion of alteration (ἀλλοίωσις) when, for example, a body becomes hot or cold (*In Phys.* 658.25–33).

As for locomotion through the void, it is impossible for a number of reasons, some of which will be mentioned below. The main reason, however, is that natural motion for Aristotle and Simplicius always has a reason or cause for moving in a particular direction (e.g., in a rectilinear motion toward the center of the Earth or in an uninterrupted circular motion in the skies)—but in the void there are *no distinctions* and hence a body in the void will not move in any direction. Here, Aristotle formulates the principle of sufficient reason long before Leibniz, which Simplicius in turn uses throughout his polemics against the existence of the void. In the void, there is *no sufficient reason* to move in any direction: why would a body move here rather than there? (*In Phys.* 649.26, 649.34, 664.3, 678.28). Nature-φύσις is the reason or the cause for change and motion, but the void cannot be either a cause (αἴτιον: paradigmatic, productive, or final) or an accompanying cause (συναίτιον: material, formal, or instrumental, *In Phys.* 26.5–7, 316.24–28, 663.30, 664.3 ff.).[12] Hence, motion and void are mutually exclusive: "If there is motion there is no void, and if there is

---

[12] See Lautner. "Introduction." In *On Aristotle on the Void*, 230n70.

void there is no motion" (*In Phys.* 658.29–30). In other words, void cannot be the (or a) cause of change or motion.

Most importantly, locomotion for Aristotle and Simplicius is possible without void, when bodies mutually replace each other, exchange places, or yield places to each other.[13] Such a motion does not require a presupposition of void as a separated interval. The motion of bodies in the *plenum* takes place as that of fish through water, where one part of the medium of motion is moved and mutually replaced by another one.

Negativity, non-being, privation, and void. So if a "what" can be established only if the "is" is ascertained and if the void does not have a demonstrable "is," then the void does not have a "what" and is therefore a non-concept. The void does not have any distinguishable properties and hence is an *empty* placeholder. Void is nothing that cannot be properly thought, and thus it cannot be a condition of the possibility of being in body or motion. The void as emptiness can only be referred to or reached by negation, by a logically void and vague "common concept."

The problem of the void thus implies a more general problem of negativity. Since "void" is commonly understood as a place or an interval without bodies, Aristotle and Simplicius treat it primarily within physics, with relation to natural things or bodies, their changes and motions. The void appears to be commonly but rather paradoxically understood as the being of non-being. As negativity, void is the negation of the existence of bodies there where the void is meant to *be* as the absence of a body but at the same time *not to be*, insofar as it is empty and devoid of any existence. For this reason—or, rather, for no reason that appears to be the reason—consideration of the void as negativity is also relevant to other theoretical disciplines, such as mathematics and ontology.

---

[13] ἀντιπερίστασις; ἀντιμετάστασις; ἀντιπεριίστασθαι; ἀντιμεθίστασθαι ἀλλήλοις τὰ σώματα; ὑποχώρησις; ὑπεξίσταται. Simplicius, *In Phys.* 659.5–15, 668.26, 681.6, 681.17, 682.29–30, 687.18; cf. Aristotle. *Phys.* 215a15.

As was said, non-being appears in Aristotle as privation and matter, and being and non-being are (1) in categories, (2) in potentiality and actuality, and (3) as (propositionally) true or false (*Met.* 1051a34–1052a11). The void, then, cannot be said to exist or to be considered being in any of these senses. Indeed, (1) void is not a category: it is not a substance, since it does not have either existence or being and is not any of the other nine categories. Most importantly, it is not the "where" (Aristotle. *Cat.* 2a1), since the void is not an interval or a place without the body. Besides, (2) void is not an actuality because it does not exist. But it is not a potentiality either, since, as Simplicius puts it, void is "impotent, being nothing" (ἀδρανὲς γὰρ τὸ κενόν, εἴπερ τὸ μηδέν ἐστιν, *In Phys.* 669.21–22).[14] Void cannot exercise any efficiency: as has been said, it cannot be a cause. It has nothing of its own, and hence it cannot be a potentiality *of* and *for* something. Finally, (3) void cannot be thought of in terms of truth and falsity. Since void does not have an essence, any statement about it of the kind "S is P" cannot be meaningfully formulated and so the statement is neither true nor false. But the existential claim "S is" is false, since the void does not exist and thus cannot be thought at all, either as composite (as having an essence and predicates) or as simple (as existent). Therefore, void can only be referred to or conceived of negatively as non-being.

Not having a concept and not being a thing, void is "non-being," τὸ μὴ ὄν, "altogether nothing," as Simplicius explicitly calls it (μηδὲν παντάπασιν ἔστι, *In Phys.* 667.30, 678.6, 681.18).[15] Following Aristotle, he argues at length that the void does not exist (οὐκ ἔστι κενόν) and there is nothing in the void (μηδενὸς ὄντος ἐν τῷ κενῷ, *In Phys.* 667.34, cf. *In Phys.* 669.16).[16] Nothing "is" in the void by not being there.

---

[14] See also Chrysippus, for whom the limitless void is nothing. Hans von Arnim, Ed. *Chrysippi fragments logica et physica.* Vol. 2 of *Stoicorum veterum fragmenta.* Stuttgart: Teubner, 1964. fr. 503.
[15] Cf. Melissus. DK 30B7: "τὸ μηδέν".
[16] See Aristotle. *Phys.* 215a11.

As noted, for Aristotle, *when* being is, it necessarily is, and *when* non-being is not, it necessarily is not. However, it does not mean that all being necessarily is when it is (such are physical things)[17] and that non-being necessarily is not when it is not (Aristotle. *De int.* 19a23–27). So, if void does not exist, it is not necessary that it does not exist. Void, then, is distinguished for Simplicius by *privation* (ἀφωρισμένος ... τὸ δὲ κενὸν στερήσει, *In Phys.* 647.3–4).

As was argued, however, void as privation differs for Aristotle from negation (ἀπόφασις), which is logically (predicatively) and ontologically a mere absence (ἀπουσία) of something, while privation is always referred to a being as an underlying nature (ὑποκειμένη τις φύσις) that can be deprived of something (*Met* 1004a14–16; cf. *Met.* 1056a15–16). As privation, void is that of a body that might occupy place. Yet, without a body as the substrate, void as privation does not exist on its own. Void is then the privation of being taken as substrate or substance (οὐσίας στέρησις, Aristotle. *Met.* 1011b18–19; *De gen. et corr.* 318b15–17) and is not an active act of a body's negation. Rather, it is a lack, a shadow that happens to "be," or rather not to be, there where the light does not penetrate.

Privation stands for the indeterminateness of non-being in the absence of anything that might be considered identically the same (substance or substrate). In this sense, privation is the *opposite* of being in the proper sense. As we have seen, privation in Aristotle "is" absolute non-being, non-being as such (καθ' αὑτήν, *Phys.* 192a5), and hence cannot exist on its own and have an active or final causality. This is the sense in which void is considered or, again, *seems to be* a non-being and privation (μὴ ὄν τι καὶ στέρησις δοκεῖ εἶναι, *In Phys.* 667.30).

Besides, void can also be considered to be the opposite to disposition (ἕξις) as the capacity to act or be in a certain way. As was already discussed, in the *Categories* Aristotle argues that privation is opposite to disposition, as "non-having" to "having" or "not being

---

[17] Cf. Aristotle. *Top.* 128b6–8.

able to" to "being able to," "incapacity" to "capacity" (*Cat.* 11b18). With respect to the void, this means the inability to contain a body in the absence of the body, as opposed to the place as capable of containing a body. Void thus cannot be a disposition or have a relation to anything, including a body.

The Eleatics and the Atomists on the void. Tradition preserves a number of arguments *pro et contra* void, are all of which Simplicius rejected on equally ontological grounds. Thus, the "ancient argument" (παλαιὸς ... ὁ λόγος, *In Phys.* 649.35) by Melissus is that if what is or being moves, it moves through the void; but only being is; being is one and does not change and hence does not move; therefore, there is no void (*In Phys.* 650.1–8).[18] Melissus follows the famous dictum of Parmenides: "It will never be proven that non-being is" (οὐ γὰρ μήποτε τοῦτο δαμῇ, εἶναι μὴ ἐόντα, Aristotle. *Met.* 1089a3–4), which is why we should not walk the way of non-being, as Parmenides explicitly warns us (*In Phys.* 650.13).[19] Only being is, whereas non-being is not, and since void is non-being, it is not or does not exist. Yet Simplicius does not accept this argument because for Melissus becoming is mixed with non-being, and therefore nothing physical exists in the proper sense and thus cannot be studied within physics.

But the Atomists, as was said, accept the void as necessary, even if they do so within an entirely different ontology. For Leucippus and Democritus, as well as for Epicurus, being is discrete and indivisible, although it is not one but rather multiple. Void, then, is the condition of the existence and motion of this multiple being, which leads the Atomists to conclude that void exists not only within the cosmos but also outside it (*In Phys.* 648.11–15).[20] Most of Simplicius' arguments and counterarguments regarding the void are derived from Aristotle but ultimately come from Democritus.

---

[18] Cf. Melissus. DK 30B1.
[19] Cf. Parmenides. DK 28B7.
[20] Cf. Leucippus. DK 67A20.

References to Aristotle are copious in Simplicius' works, especially in his commentary on Aristotle's *Physics*, which preserves many of Democritus' fragments. Clearly, Simplicius considered atomism a serious challenge and thus worthy of in-depth discussion.

For Parmenides and Melissus, being is one, while non-being (and void as non-being) is many and as such does not exist. For the Atomists, on the contrary, being as the atoms is many, mutually sealed off and impenetrable, while one as the opposite of many is non-being and is the void that can be occupied by pulverized being(s). Moreover, contrary to the Eleatics, for whom being is finite and limited, both being (atoms) and non-being (void) in atomism are *infinite*: being in number and non-being in extension.[21]

And if the void is to be considered outside of the cosmos, it should be *infinite* or indefinite. Yet, for Aristotle and Simplicius the infinite does not exist as an actual infinite, and such is also the void.

However, the Eleatics and the Atomists agree that becoming does not exist, since only being is, disagreeing only whether being is one (for the Eleatics) or many (for the Atomists). But for both there is no coming to be, no change or motion (*In Phys.* 679.13–22), which makes the whole of physics impossible. Neither Aristotle nor Simplicius can accept this notion, thus rejecting the arguments about the void from both schools of thought, which are based on entirely different ontologies that have nothing of the infinite at their core.

Matter, privation, and the void. As has been argued at length, matter in Aristotle appears under three guises: as substrate, as possibility, and as indefiniteness. Following Aristotle, in his earlier digression on matter in the commentary Simplicius takes matter as *indefinite* (ἀόριστος), appearing as "indefinite interval" (ἀόριστος διάστασις) or "indefinite quantity" (ἀόριστον ποσόν), in which

---

[21] Cf. David Konstan. "Epicurus on the Void." In *Space in Hellenistic Philosophy: Critical Studies in Ancient Physics*. Ed. Graziano Ranocchia, Christoph Helmig, and Christoph Horn. Berlin: De Gruyter, 2014, 90–91.

forms can be embodied (*In Phys.* 230.14).[22] Similarly, for Simplicius, as for Aristotle, such matter can be known only analogically, so that the thinking of matter is really a non-thinking, similar to Plato's "illegitimate reasoning" (ἡ περὶ αὐτῆς νόησις οὐ νόησις, ἀλλ' ἄνοια μᾶλλον, *In Phys.* 226.25; *Tim.* 52b).[23] The "learned knowledge" about matter, then, is ignorance (ἀγνωσία, *In Phys.* 227.5). But when Simplicius turns to the void, he shares and supports the Aristotelian position, taking matter not as a separable substance but as one substrate of opposites, in which only one of the opposites can exist or be actualized at any particular moment. For Simplicius, "Matter is the substrate (ὑποκείμενον) of opposites; thus, there is the same matter (ἡ αὐτὴ ὕλη) of hot and cold, and similarly of dry and wet and other opposites, being transformed from one to the other, since it is always actually one of the opposites and potentially the other (τὸ ἀεὶ ἐνεργείᾳ μὲν εἶναι τὸ ἕτερον τῶν ἐναντίων, δυνάμει δὲ τὸ ἕτερον). In existence (τῇ μὲν ὑποστάσει) matter is never separate from one of the opposites, but in its own definition and in concept (τῷ δὲ οἰκείῳ λόγῳ αὐτῆς καὶ τῇ ἐπινοίᾳ) it is something in addition to these. And it remains numerically identical while receiving each of the opposites (μένουσα κατὰ τὸν ἀριθμὸν ἡ αὐτὴ ἑκάτερον δέχεται τῶν ἐναντίων)" (*In Phys.* 688.7–14).

Matter is thus potentially *both* opposites (of hot or cold, rare, or dense, etc.) and is transformed into the opposites, but it can have only one of them actualized at a time (*In Phys.* 688.33–34).[24] This is the nature of matter (τῆς ὕλης φύσις): to receive opposites while remaining the same (ὡς ἡ αὐτὴ μένουσα δέχεται τὰ ἐναντία, *In Phys.* 689.15). In contradistinction to matter, void for Simplicius cannot be the same or receive the opposites because it is nothing,

---

[22] Cf. Simplicius. *In Phys.* 227.23–33.3.
[23] See Pantelis Golitsis. *Les Commentaires de Simplicius et de Jean Philopon.* Berlin: De Gruyter, 2008, 127–39.
[24] "The same matter (ἡ αὐτὴ ὕλη) becomes cold from hot and hot from cold, being potentially both (ὅτι ἦν ἄμφω δυνάμει)." Simplicius. *In Phys.* 689.2–3. "Matter is potentially both (opposites) and is transformed from potentiality to actuality." *In Phys.* 688.33–34. "The same matter is transformed into opposites." *In Phys.* 690.34–35.

non-being (τὸ μὴ ὄν), and thus impotent (ἀδρανές, *In Phys.* 667.30, 678.6, 669.21). Therefore, the hypothesis of the void is not needed for the explanation of the possibility of rarefaction and condensation in bodies as two opposite processes taking place in the same bodies.

As non-being, void lacks being or is a privation of being. As we remember, Aristotle argues that privation is the opposite of matter because privation is non-being as such, whereas matter is accidental non-being. And if void might be considered privation (of body in place), then it should be opposite to matter and hence is not matter in the Aristotelian sense.

As was said, the void cannot be the cause of change and motion because it does not exist and is nothing. "If, however, one treats the void as matter that is the cause of motion, he [Aristotle] agrees that in this way the void exists."[25] Thus, Simplicius concludes his detailed considerations on the void. Of three causes (paradigmatic, productive, and final) and three accompanying causes (material, formal, and instrumental), matter can be the material cause. Thus, if matter is the cause of rareness and density or of lightness and heaviness, then as such matter may be called void, since matter is not a definite something but is devoid of any qualities, and hence is conceived negatively by abstraction (κατὰ ἀφαίρεσιν), lacking in any forms or qualifications (*In Phys.* 692.18–23).[26]

So if one takes matter in this sense and identifies it with void because of the negativity of the two, then one can say that void exists—but only in this sense, contrary to the proponents of the void as empty interval without a body. One matter will suffice, making void obsolete and absent in the makeup of the world.

Thus, paradoxically void both is and is not matter. Or matter is and is not void. This conclusion, however, does not violate the

---

[25] εἰ μέντοι ὡς κινήσεως αἰτίαν τὴν ὕλην λέγοι τὸ κενόν, συγχωρεῖ κατὰ τοῦτον τὸν τρόπον εἶναι τὸ κενόν, Simplicius. *In Phys.* 693.9–10; see also *In Phys.* 646.11–12.
[26] Cf. Aristotle. *Met.* 1029a20–21.

principle of non-contradiction because, first, void here is taken in different respects (as privation and as the cause of change), and, second, void has no identity of being the same subject, since it is the absolute nothing of privation and is thus not a subject at all.

Mathematics, incommensurability, and the void. Although neither Aristotle nor Simplicius dedicate much attention to mathematical examples in the discussion of void, which mostly comes with reference to physics, both make a number of significant remarks about the impossibility of the void in mathematics. In the Pythagorean philosophical and scientific program, which is built on the pattern of mathematics, everything that is, is number, which is being.[27] And yet, the void makes its cryptic appearance, or rather disappearance, in mathematics to the extent that non-being still lurks on the margins of being, or rather *in-between* being. As Aristotle reports, for the Pythagoreans void exists as that which distinguishes natural things or "natures" (διορίζει τὰς φύσεις), appearing in and through their succession and separation (τῶν ἐφεξῆς καὶ τῆς διορίσεως). Such a succession primarily transpires in numbers, where the void sets them apart and distinguishes their nature (τὸ γὰρ κενὸν διορίζειν τὴν φύσιν αὐτῶν, *Phys.* 213b22–27).

As Simplicius further explains, in the Pythagorean cosmological doctrine (ἔνδοξον), a succession or series (τὰ ἐφεξῆς) presupposes that there is nothing *between* (μεταξύ) its members. In numbers as a succession of positive integers, then, there is nothing between the numbers. Therefore, void should be responsible for the separation and distinction between the members in the numerical series. Things are numerable and numbers are different because of the void that separates them. And since there is no substance (ὑπόστασις), no other being between the numbers, because numbers *are* being, it is the *power* of the void (τοῦ κενοῦ δύναμις) that distinguishes the monad from the dyad from the triad. Yet, "there" (ἐκεῖ), among beings, there is no void because in the intelligible there is no

---

[27] ἐκεῖνοι δὲ τὸν ἀριθμὸν τὰ ὄντα λέγουσιν, Aristotle. *Met.* 1083b17.

non-being but only being. Therefore, *there* the forms are separated and distinguished by *otherness* (ἑτερότης), which for Plato (as θάτερον, *Soph.* 259b) is the other of being, existing only to the extent that it participates in being, just as being participates in the other. Such otherness of and in being, then, is translated into, and becomes, the *cause* (αἴτιον) of void or emptiness *here*, among physical things in the cosmos, where separation (ὁ χωρισμός) is the result of the intervention of non-being (διὰ τὴν τοῦ μὴ ὄντος παρείσδυσιν, *In Phys.* 651.25–652.18). In this way, void for the Pythagoreans becomes the *principle of individuation* between things.

Simplicius agrees that otherness is always present in being, but he does not try to translate it into a void in the physical cosmos. Perhaps one might argue that among the causes (paradigmatic, productive, final) and accompanying causes (material, formal, instrumental) that he accepts, none can be considered the cause of nothing, since the produced effect is always something. But this possibility is left void.

A further problem for the Pythagorean approach is that, although the natural numbers, represented in and by physical discrete entities, are commensurable, the continuous magnitudes can be mutually incommensurable and therefore irrational (ἄλογα), such as the side and the diagonal of the square.[28] As we remember, the otherness of the infinite shows itself in two different ways in Aristotle: one in the discretely divisible numbers, which are limited in their divisibility by a discrete further indivisible unit—and the other in continuous magnitudes, which have no limit to their divisibility.

Number is thus unable to permeate and define the existent in its entirety because otherness is inescapably present in all the existent both "there" and "here," in being and becoming. For the Pythagoreans, in the physical it is matter that allows for the expansion and the void as being internalized, absorbed, or "inhaled" by

---

[28] Plato. *Theaet.* 147d; Aristotle. *An. priora* 41a26–27; Euclid. *Elem.* bk. X.

the cosmos. And in the geometrical as intermediary between the intelligible (numbers) and physical (bodies), the impossibility of establishing a common unit of measure between certain magnitudes comes with otherness as rooted in the aforementioned geometrical or intelligible matter as the source of incommensurability.[29]

Now it all comes back again to matter, the understanding of which always moves between that of *nothing* (as a relative non-being in Aristotle and absolute non-being in Plotinus) and a *principle* (in Plato [see *Tim.* 52a] and also equally in Aristotle), that of otherness. This double character of matter is further reflected in the ambiguous attitude to matter in Simplicius as both being and not being void. Incommensurability is even present among the numbers. In his commentary, Simplicius takes it that every number stands in relation or ratio (λόγος) to every number (*In Phys.* 673.10). And yet, he is quite aware from Aristotle's *Metaphysics* M 6–9 that Plato distinguishes ideal and mathematical numbers: ideal numbers are *forms* and thus are pure beings, while mathematical numbers are positive integers that allow for counting and as such are arithmetical entities. On this interpretation, ideal numbers are simple, indivisible, and finite in number, each one being distinct and different from every other ideal number. As such, they do not stand in a relation to each other, but their constituents or monads are incommensurable (ἀσύμβλητοι). In mathematical numbers, on the contrary, the monads are commensurable (συμβληταί), and their common measure is the indivisible monad.[30] Thus, the arithmetical number three is composed of three monads, while the number four is made up of four indivisible units or monads.[31] One could still say that even the incommensurable ideal numbers have a relation or λόγος to each other, that of the simultaneity of

---

[29] Aristotle. *Met.* 1036a9–12, 1036b35–1037a5, 1045a33–6; Plotinus. *Enn.* II.4 [12].1.14–18; Proclus. *In Eucl.* 93.18–19.
[30] Aristotle. *Met.* 1080b36–1081a1.
[31] τὰ σώματα ἐξ ἀριθμῶν εἶναι συγκείμενα, καὶ τὸν ἀριθμὸν τοῦτον εἶναι μαθηματικόν, Aristotle. *Met.* 1083b11–13; cf. *Met.* 1080a13–17.

the communication-κοινωνία discussed by Plato. This relation, however, is established very differently from the λόγος between the mathematical numbers, which is that of succession in counting and the addition of another arithmetical unit.

But for the Pythagoreans, according to Aristotle, the bodies themselves are composed of mathematical numbers, and these numbers are mathematical and hence commensurable. Yet for Aristotle this implies an impossible ontology that indiscriminately mixes being and becoming, the physical and mathematical. The two must be distinguished and kept separate because, as already said, mathematical numbers are divisible into a finite number of further indivisible units (monads), whereas physical bodies are infinitely divisible.

In contradistinction to the Pythagoreans, the "physiologists" or philosophers of nature, according to Simplicius, take point, line, and numbers to be void, since they all are non-corporeal (*In Phys.* 653.34–35). However, within Aristotelian physics, it is absurd—entirely out of place (ἄτοπον)—to call a point void because the point is unextended and thus cannot be a place of an extended body (*Phys.* 214a4–6). And, we could add, it is equally impossible that there be a place of and for a point, if place is the immediately surrounding extended body, which the point, being indivisible and thus unextended, does not have.

No relation to nothing. Mathematical entities—numbers—thus stand in a relation or λόγος to each other. Bodies and magnitudes have a proportion (ἀναλογία, *In Phys.* 672.38) to each other, even if they can be mutually incommensurable. Yet, as was said, void for Aristotle has *no relation* (λόγος) to a body, just as nothing (τὸ μηδέν) has no relation to number (*Phys.* 215b12–13). Simplicius accepts this claim, substituting, however, "body" for the "full" (τὸ πλῆρες, *In Phys.* 672.8–9, 13–14).[32] The assumed relation of void to

---

[32] See also Simplicius, *In Phys.* 675.23–25: τὸ κενὸν πρὸς τὸ πλῆρες οὐδένα ἔχει λόγον, ὡς οὐδὲ τὸ οὐδὲν πρὸς τὸν ἀριθμόν.

body, then, should be that of nothing to number. Yet, there is no relation of nothing to number, and hence there is no such relation of void to body, which therefore is utterly irrational and unthinkable (ἄλογον). For this reason, ancient mathematics does not have a *zero*, because mathematically and ontologically zero would stand for nothing. And since a (mathematical) number is composed of the constituents into which it is divided, then the excess of the number four to nothing is still four (*In Phys.* 672.19–27). Similarly, a line does not exceed a point, or there can be no common measure between a line and a point. Rather, points are the extremities or limits of a line that define that line. And even if the Pythagoreans famously consider the point as a unit that has position,[33] a line is nevertheless not composed of points, in contradistinction to mathematical numbers that are composed of monads. This suggests, once again, a fundamental ontological distinction between the discrete (numbers) and continuous (geometrical and physical magnitudes), none of which, however, allows for nothing or void within their ranks. Nothing is nothing that adds nothing.

For Simplicius, as well as for Philoponus, nothing (τὸ μηδέν, τὸ οὐδέν) therefore has no relation to being, number, or body,[34] since such a relation cannot be rationally understood and accounted for. Nothing and being have no λόγος. In mathematics and ontology, then, it is not nothing or a "zero" but rather the "indefinite dyad" (ἀόριστος δυάς) that stands for the otherness in being, since the indefinite dyad doubles or produces duality (δυοποιός, Aristotle. *Met.* 1083b36). This otherness in being appears as the aforementioned intelligible matter present in mathematical things (ὕλη νοητή), in opposition to the matter of sensible things.

---

[33] ἡ μὲν ἄθετος μονὰς ἡ δὲ θετὸς στιγμή, Aristotle. *Met.* 1016b30–31; ἡ γὰρ μονὰς στιγμὴ ἄθετός ἐστιν, *Met.* 1084b26–27; ἡ γὰρ στιγμὴ μονάς ἐστι θέσιν ἔχουσα, *De an.* 409a6. See also Simplicius. *In Phys.* 454.24.

[34] See Philoponus. *In Phys.* 676.18–19: "Nothing can have no relation to being" (οὐδένα γὰρ λόγον ἐνδέχεται ἔχειν τὸ μηδὲν πρὸς τὸ ὄν).

In the Platonic tradition, mentioned by both Aristotle and Simplicius with reference to Plato's Περὶ τἀγαθοῦ, the *material* aspect of being and mathematical objects, closely associated and often identified with the "indefinite dyad," is also expressed as "great and small" (τὸ μέγα καὶ τὸ μικρόν) or "more and less" (τὰ μᾶλλον καὶ ἧττον). This is also the principle of multiplicity in the intelligible objects (τὰ νοητά) or the forms (Aristotle. *Met.* 987b20; *Phys.* 207a29-30; cf. *Phys.* 192a6-7; *In Phys.* 454.19-455.14, 503.10-18). However, such otherness is considered the *principle* of multiplicity and otherness in all beings, and as such it is not nothing and therefore is not void.

Mathematical and physical volume. Criticizing the hypothesis of those who accept the void as interspersed within bodies in order to explain their increase and decrease in volume, Simplicius distinguishes intelligible or mathematical volume (ὄγκος νοητός or μαθηματικός), as well as perceived or sensible volume of the material substrate. The latter can become greater and smaller without void being added or subtracted to it but rather by the same form (e.g., of warmth) in matter being intensified or relaxed (ἀνίεται ἢ ἐπιτείνεται), which makes the perceived and enmattered (αἰσθητὸς καὶ ἔνυλος) volume increase and decrease, while the matter remains the same, transformed into opposites (*In Phys.* 690.8-11, 34-35).[35] In contradistinction to physical volume, the intelligible or mathematical volume always remains the same. But according to the doctrine of intensification and relaxation of the form in matter that allows for the increase and decrease of the volume, a (physical) magnitude (μέγεθος) appears as a kind of form (εἶδός τι) that, unlike the real form, can admit of "more and less." This allows us to consider "small and great as *formal* differences in magnitude"[36] rather than as the material distinction, which the "great and small" is in forms and numbers.

---

[35] Cf. Proclus. *In Tim.* II 25.3-4.
[36] τὸ μικρὸν καὶ μέγα μεγέθους εἰδητικὰς διαφοράς, Simplicius. *In Phys.* 690.12-13.

This is a curious transformation of the role of the indefinite dyad as the principle of otherness and materiality within the intelligible into the great and small as the formal principle that allows us to understand the form in matter as changing into greater and smaller in its effect in material magnitudes. Such an ambiguity of matter points, once again, to the inescapable duality of matter that appears both as utterly indefinite and as the principle of otherness. Applied reflectively to itself, the "indefinite dyad" is equally the "great and small" that makes itself other than itself, being *both* the material aspect in discrete intelligible objects (forms and numbers) and the formal aspect in continuous magnitudes (geometrical objects and physical bodies).

Physics and the void. This brings us finally to discussion of the void in physics, where the argument is to demonstrate that the existence of void makes motion impossible.[37] Simplicius' main thesis is this: "If there is motion, there is no void, and if there is void, there is no motion."[38] In other words, void is the *condition of the impossibility* of motion, and vice versa. Or, again, motion and void are mutually exclusive.

"How will something be (ἐνέσται) in a place or void?" asks Aristotle (*Phys.* 214b24). *To be* in the void for a body would mean to be in a place, to be placed or located, in nothing. Yet this is impossible because, as noted, place for Aristotle is the external limit of the body, equidimensional with the body and a kind of container or unmovable vessel in which the body *is* and which it can abandon when moving. A physical being in void as nothing, then, is impossible.

If nothing is (in the physical cosmos), if non-being exists (as void), and thus if a body *is* in nothing, then we run into a number of

---

[37] On motion in the void in Epicurus and the Stoics, and their corresponding accounts of void, see Richard Sorabji. *Matter, Space, and Motion.* London: Duckworth, 1988, 142–58; Algra, *Concepts of Space in Greek Thought,* 263–336.

[38] εἰ ἔστι κίνησις, οὐκ ἔστι κενόν, καὶ εἰ ἔστι κενόν, οὐκ ἔστι κίνησις, Simplicius. *In Phys.* 658.28–29.

absurdities and impossibilities, which appear as paradoxes that are contrary not only to perception and common opinion-δόξα, but also to rational argument or reason-λόγος. Quoted by Simplicius, Aristotle observes that the consideration of void inevitably leads to a self-contradictory, self-defeating, and self-canceling argument.[39] An attempt at thinking (physical) being in nothing is paradoxical and contradicts itself. Therefore, any claim about the *motion* of a body in a void should contain a contradiction, rendered explicit through a *reductio ad absurdum* that shows the utter impossibility of such motion. And when a statement contains contradiction, it is always not true, although when a statement contains no contradiction, it is not always true.[40]

(1) *The impossibility of motion.* For Simplicius, who closely follows yet expands Aristotle's arguments, there are two main reasons for distinctions in motion: the weight of bodies and the difference (density or resistance) of the medium (τὸ δι' οὗ) through which they move (*In Phys.* 671.24–36).[41] But in the void there is no resistance: void is yielding (τὸ ὑπεικτικόν, *In Phys.* 670.32), since it is nothing, and thus it is not a body that could deter or affect the motion of another body.

As Simplicius argues, "The void exceeds everything bodily in lightness by an *incommensurable excess.*"[42] The proportional relation of the density of the lightest and thinnest body to that of the void cannot be measured or expressed in terms of a proportion because void has *no* density. This means that void can have *no relation* (λόγος) to body, just as nothing cannot have a proportion to number (*In Phys.* 686.3–4, 671.21–23). Since void cannot be in a ratio or proportion to a body, it cannot affect or change the motion of the body. Therefore, void is *not a medium* for motion.

---

[39] αὐτὸς ἑαυτὸν ὁ λόγος ἐμποδίζει, Simplicius. *In Phys.* 661.24–25.
[40] Aristotle. *De int.* 21a24–25.
[41] Cf. Philoponus. *In Phys.* 676.4–6.
[42] κατὰ ἀσύμβλητον ὑπεροχήν, Simplicius. *In Phys.* 686.1.

Every place for Aristotle, as we know, has the up and the down, and every body by nature moves and rests in its proper place, which thus constitutes the up and down differentiation (*Phys.* 211a3-6). In other words, the physical cosmos has a system of distinctions that make motion possible. But in the void, as we have seen, there are *no distinctions*. Therefore, there is no up and down in the void and thus no natural or proper place for a body (*In Phys.* 670.6-11). This means that a body in void will neither move nor be at rest (*In Phys.* 664.21-22). In void, there is but a total disorientation.

Moreover, since there are no distinctions in the void, there is no (sufficient) reason for a body to move here rather than there (*In Phys.* 670.10, 20). Hence, a body will either move in all directions or nowhere at all (ἢ πανταχοῦ... ἢ οὐδαμοῦ, *In Phys.* 671.2-4). But moving simultaneously in all directions, it will either be torn into pieces or remain forever at rest, incapable of motion—or rather *not even at rest* (μᾶλλον δὲ οὐδὲ μονῆς) in the absence of any distinction between places (*In Phys.* 664.11-14). If nature is the source of motion, then void annihilates the very possibility of motion and thus cancels nature.

Void for Simplicius is τὸ ἀδιάφορον, indifferent and undifferentiated. But the indifferent and undifferentiated is the *uniform*, which does not have the up and down differentiation and hence does not allow for a system of natural places all of which are different from each other. Therefore, there can be no motion in the uniform (which is also Plato's argument),[43] which means that motion in the void is impossible.

Besides, if non-being (as void) exists as infinite (ἄπειρον) or indefinite, then it does not admit of a system of natural places because in the infinite too there is no differentiation, no above, below, or middle. Therefore, in the infinite there cannot be either a natural motion (κατὰ φύσιν) or a forced one (παρὰ φύσιν) as a deviation (ἐκτροπή) from natural motion (*In Phys.* 667.9-28).

---

[43] ἐν... ὁμαλότητι, Plato. *Tim.* 57e.

Furthermore, if one accepts the existence of the void, then other impossibilities follow, which literally lead the thought to a dead end and to be put out of place (ἄτοπα). In particular, there will be motion and locomotion (κίνησις καὶ φορά) of the void itself (*In Phys.* 685.4–6). Simplicius does not explain why this should be the case, but if one assumes that the void is interspersed in bodies, such a void will either move through void as place or will move through itself, in the case of the body's expansion or contraction. Yet, being nothing, void cannot move because motion is the motion of a moving body moved by a mover. Besides, if a body travels upward, it would be moving toward a place that is void. But then there will be a void in the void, which is equally absurd (*In Phys.* 685.6–8).

(2) *The impossibility of rest.* If void exists, then not only motion but also rest (μονή) is impossible because, again, there are no distinctions in the void and thus no natural places. For this reason, a body in the void will not move anywhere because there is no sufficient reason for a body to move in any particular direction, here rather than there. Therefore, it will not move at all (*In Phys.* 665.21–23). But at the same time, because nothing can be distinguished in the void, a body will not be at rest because there is no natural place for it to reside. Hence, there will be *endless* motion, unless something stronger stops the body (*In Phys.* 670.13–14). This is the inertial motion accepted in the modern infinite universe, which, however, is impossible in the finite Aristotelian cosmos. Paradoxically, in violation of the principle of non-contradiction, if the void exists, then a body will be *both* in motion and at rest but also will neither move nor be at rest. Therefore, in the void rest is impossible.

(3) *Same speed for all bodies.* Furthermore, if the void exists, then all bodies will be moving at the same speed. As said, the speed difference in Aristotelian physics is caused either by the resistance of the medium or by the weight of the moving body. But in the void, there is no resistance, which means that all bodies will move at the same speed (ἰσοταχῶς), even if there is a difference in their impulse

(ῥοπή) or weight (*In Phys.* 678.24–30). So the void is *not a medium*. One might take this assertion as anticipation of the principle of inertial motion, which requires recognition of the void as the condition of possibility of the *status movendi*. Yet, contra Galileo and Newton, and following Aristotle, Simplicius concludes that the heavier body will move faster.[44] Hence, again, motion through the void is impossible.

(4) *Timeless motion.* Finally, if there is void, motion will be timeless, non-temporal, or instantaneous (ἄχρονος) because a relation is between a time and a time or a motion and a motion, but not between void and full, which have no mutual relation or λόγος (*In Phys.* 671.21, 677.13).

In addition, Simplicius points to a paradox that results from accepting the void as evanescently or infinitesimally different in density from the thinnest possible medium (ἄχρι τοῦ λεπτοτάτου). Namely, in an *almost* empty or utmost rarefied air, a body will move very quickly and at a great speed, since such a medium will exercise almost no resistance. But in the void, which differs from such extremely thin air only by an infinitesimal degree, a body will move even faster. One should note that in this case the void and the thinnest medium are taken as commensurable, or the void is supposed to be the ultimate degree of thinness that evaporates into emptiness. The imperceptible—and unthinkable—relation here is similar to that of a curved line as coming not from the straight— for these have different forms—but from the *less curved* (*In Phys.* 689.22–25). Yet, the void and the medium, however rarefied, as was said, have no relation and thus no common measure. Besides, void is formless, and the form that defines the medium, even if very rarefied, cannot be understood in opposition to the void, in the way the form of a curve is understood as opposed to that of the straight line.

But at the same time, *if* a body moves at the greatest speed in the extremely fine medium and if, by an infinitesimal leap to the void,

---

[44] θᾶττον κινηθήσεται τὸ βαρύτερον, Simplicius. *In Phys.* 671.34–35.

it will move even faster in the void, then the speed in the void will be infinite. Correspondingly, the time of such a motion will be less than the least time of the body moving at the greatest speed. So the motion in the void will be in no time at all, or momentarily, which is impossible (*In Phys.* 676.21–30).

Therefore, void as a place of motion has no place in physics and has no place and is ruled out in the cosmos. From Simplicius' perspective, a theory of void is a-topian or absurd and self-defeating. Void is thus impossible and is a non-concept ontologically, mathematically, and physically.

Void is not. Void is nothing. Nothing is void. Nothing is voided from being and the order of existent. Void is powerless. It is devoid of any possibilities and cannot produce anything. It generates nothing. In its impossibility, void is non-being. In its "is," non-being is not. In its "what," non-being is void, and, literally, it is empty and absent from being, and thus is a privation of being.

With Simplicius, being finally wins its logical struggle against non-being: only being can be asserted to be, with its properties carefully and orderly laid out through a number of justified propositions, while non-being is reduced to a privative shadow of that which is. Except for a few daring attempts throughout the history of philosophy, non-being gets devoid of being a negative source and origin of being. Non-being is finally voided by the reasoning logos, which finds a proper place for non-being within a systematic account of being. Yet, demoted to a privative non-existence, non-being keeps making its surprising returns in many ways.

Conclusion

Even if at times vehemently contested, the approach to being as thinkable and as an object studied and described by thought has dominated philosophy until now. Non-being, then, is taken as a shadow of being, a lack of existence, as that which is not. And if non-being is not, then there is nothing we can properly say or think about it. Only being is and stands on its own and as such defines the thought. Being is thought, and in this way it is the beginning and the end of thought.

And yet, from its very inception, thinking about being stumbles up against non-being. If we look closely at ancient interpretations of being and non-being, we can discern two distinct and different ontological positions: one that asserts being while suspending non-being as a recess of being, and the other that takes non-being as original and thus as originating being. On the basis of our analysis throughout the long logos of this book, we can now further distinguish two different interpretations of non-being within this other, unrecognized negative ontology. One interpretation takes non-being as many or as the other of the one, and the other considers non-being as privation or as the other of being. In the first case, non-being acts as the constitutive element or principle of the *discrete*, which transpires in forms and numbers. In the second case, non-being resides within the *continuous*, which comes in magnitudes and the world, both physical and social. The proponents of the first view are Plato, Parmenides, and Plotinus (all in ontology), and advocates of the second are Democritus (in physics), Diogenes (in politics and social life), Aristotle (in logic, physics, and ontology), and Simplicius (in physics and the hermeneutics of the commentary).

In this way, the understanding of non-being separates the discrete (forms and numbers) and the continuous (geometrical and physical magnitudes) into two separate and distinct realms of being that coexist and meet but never merge or coincide—that is, until modernity. The insurmountable difference between the infinity of the natural numbers and that of the continuum thus remains an unprovable postulate for thought.

In both cases, however, non-being plays a central role in the constitution of being, either privatively, when being is what non-being is not in its absence, or as the origin of being that makes being be and be what it is by being one among many.

Bibliography

I. Primary Texts

Aetius. *De Placita Philosophorum.* Vols. 5.1–4 of *Aëtiana.* Edited by Jaap Mansfeld and D. T. Runia. Leiden: Brill, 2020.

Alexander of Aphrodisias. *Alexander of Aphrodisias on Stoic Physics: A Study of the De Mixtione with Preliminary Essays, Text, Translation and Commentary.* Translated and edited by Robert B. Todd. Leiden: Brill, 2018.

Alexander of Aphrodisias. *Alexandri Aphrodisiensis in Aristotelis Metaphysica commentaria.* Vol. I of *Commentaria in Aristotelem Graeca.* Edited by Michael Hayduck. Berlin: Reimer, 1891.

Alexander of Aphrodisias. *Alexandri in librum De sensu commentarium.* Vol. III.1 of *Commentaria in Aristotelem Graeca.* Edited by Paulus Wendland. Berlin: Reimer, 1901.

Aristotle. *Aristotelis fragmenta selecta.* Edited by W. D. Ross. Oxford: Oxford University Press, 1955.

Aristotle. *De anima.* Edited by W. D. Ross. Oxford: Oxford University Press, 1956.

Aristotle. *Ethica Nicomachea.* Edited by I. Bywater. Oxford: Oxford University Press, 1894.

Aristotle. *Metaphysica.* Edited by W. Jaeger. Oxford: Oxford University Press, 1957.

Aristotle. *Opera.* Edited by Immanuel Bekker. 5 vols. Berlin: Reimer, 1831–1870.

Aristotle. *Physica.* Edited by W. D. Ross. Oxford: Oxford University Press, 1950.

Aristophanes. *Clouds, Wasps, Peace.* Translated and edited by Jeffrey Henderson. Cambridge, MA: Harvard University Press, 1998.

Asclepius. *Asclepii in Aristotelis Metaphysicorum libros A-Z commentaria.* Vol. VI.2 of *Commentaria in Aristotelem Graeca.* Edited by Michael Hayduck. Berlin: Reimer, 1888.

Cicero, Marcus Tullius. *Academics.* In *On the Nature of the Gods/Academics.* Translated by H. Rackham. Cambridge, MA: Harvard University Press, 1933, 399–659.

Cicero, Marcus Tullius. *Letters to Friends.* Vol. 2. Translated by D. R. Shackleton Bailey. Cambridge, MA: Harvard University Press, 2001.

Cicero, Marcus Tullius. *On the Nature of Gods.* In *On the Nature of the Gods/Academics.* Translated by H. Rackham. Cambridge, MA: Harvard University Press, 1933, 2–398.

Cicero, Marcus Tullius. *On the Orator: Books 1–2.* Translated by E. W. Sutton and H. Rackham. Cambridge, MA: Harvard University Press, 1942.

Cicero, Marcus Tullius. *Orator.* In *Brutus/Orator.* Translated by G. L. Hendrickson and H. M. Hubbell. Cambridge, MA: Harvard University Press, 1939, 297–509.

Cicero, Marcus Tullius. *Tusculan Disputations.* Translated by J. E. King. Cambridge, MA: Harvard University Press, 1927.

Coxon, A. H, Ed. *The Fragments of Parmenides: A Critical Text with Introduction and Translation, the Ancient Testimonia and a Commentary*. Rev. ed. Edited and translated by Richard McKirahan. Las Vegas: Parmenides Publishing, 2009.

Diels, Hermann, and Walther Kranz, Trans. and ed. *Die Fragmente der Vorsokratiker*. 2 vols. 6th ed. Berlin: Weidmann, 1996.

Dio Chrysostom. *Discourses 1–11*. Translated by J. W. Cohoon. Cambridge, MA: Harvard University Press, 2002.

Diogenes Laertius. *Lives of Eminent Philosophers*. Translated by R. D. Hicks. 2 vols. Cambridge, MA: Harvard University Press, 2000.

Epicurus. *Epicuri epistulae tres et ratae sententiae a Laerto Diogene servatae*. Edited by P. von der Muehll. Berlin: Teubner, 1922.

Euclid. *The Thirteen Books of Euclid's Elements*. Vol. 1. 2nd rev. ed. Translated and edited by Thomas L. Heath. New York: Dover, 1956.

Eusebius. *Die Preparatio Evangelica: Books 11–15*. Edited by Karl Mras et al. Vol. 8 of *Eusebius Werke*. Berlin: Akademie Verlag, 1956.

Frommel, Wilhelm, Ed. *Scholia in Aelii Aristidis sophistae Orationes Panathenaicam et Platonicas*. Frankfurt: Broenneri, 1826.

Galen. *On the Elements According to Hippocrates*. Translated and edited by Phillip de Lacy. Berlin: Akademie Verlag, 1996.

Gellius, Aulus. *The Attic Nights of Aulus Gellius*. Translated by John C. Rolfe. 3 vols. Cambridge, MA: Harvard University Press, 1927.

Gemelli, Marciano, and M. Laura, Trans. and ed. *Die Vorsokratiker*. 3 vols. 2nd ed. Berlin: Akademie Verlag, 2013.

Graham, Daniel W., Trans. and ed. *The Texts of Early Greek Philosophy: The Complete Fragments and Selected Testimonies of the Major Presocratics*. Part 1. Cambridge, MA: Cambridge University Press, 2010.

Hard, Robin, Trans. and ed. *Diogenes the Cynic: Sayings and Anecdotes, with other Popular Moralists*. Oxford: Oxford University Press, 2012.

Heinze, Richard, Ed. *Xenocrates: Darstellung der Lehre und Sammlung der Fragmente*. Hildesheim, Germany: G. Olms, 1965.

Herodas. *Mimiambs*. Translated and edited by Graham Zanker. Liverpool: Liverpool University Press, 2009.

Hesiod. *Theogony*. In *Theogony, Works and Days, and Testimonia*. Translated and edited by Glenn W. Most. Cambridge, MA: Harvard University Press, 2018, 2–85.

[Iamblichus]. *Theologumena arithmeticae*. Edited by V. De Falco and U. Klein. Stuttgart: Teubner, 1975.

Jacoby, Felix, Ed. *Genealogie und Mythographie*. Part 1 of *Die Fragmente der griechischen Historiker von F. Jacoby*. Leiden: Brill, 1957.

Kindstrand, Jan Frederik, Ed. *Bion of Borysthenes: A Collection of the Fragments with Introduction and Commentary*. Uppsala: Acta Universitatis Upsaliensis, 1976.

Lurie, Solomon Yakovlevich, Ed. *Democritea: Collegit et emendavit interpretatus est Salomo Lvria*. Leningrad: Nauka, 1970.

Macleod, M. D., Ed. *Luciani Opera*. 4 vols. Oxford: Clarendon Press, 1972–1987.

Michael of Ephesus. *In libros de partibus animalium, de animalium motione, de animalium incessu commentaria*. Vol. XXII.2 of *Commentaria in Aristotelem Graeca*. Edited by Michael Hayduck. Berlin: Georg Reimer, 1904.

Nenci, Giuseppe, Ed. *Hecatei Milesii Fragmenta*. Firenze: La nuova Italia editrice, 1954.
Paquet, Léonce, Ed. *Les Cyniques grecs: Fragments et témoignages*. Ottawa: Les presses de l'Université d'Ottawa, 1988.
Philoponus. *Ioannis Philoponi in Aritotelis libros de generatione et corruptione commentaria*. Vol. XIV of *Commentaria in Aristotelem Graeca*. Edited by Hieronymus Vitelli. Berlin: Reimer, 1897.
Philoponus. *Ioannis Philoponi in Aristotelis de anima libros commentaria*. Vol. XV of Commentaria in Aristotelem Graeca. Edited by Michael Hayduck. Berlin: Reimer, 1897.
Philoponus. *Ioannis Philoponi in Aristotelis physicorum libros tres priores commentaria*. Vol. XVI of *Commentaria in Aristotelem Graeca*. Edited by Hieronymus Vitelli. Berlin: Reimer, 1887.
Philoponus. *Ioannis Philoponi in Aritotelis physicorum libros quinque posteriores commentaria*. Vol. XVII of *Commentaria in Aristotelem Graeca*. Edited by Hieronymus Vitelli. Berlin: Reimer, 1888.
Plato. *Fedon*. Translated by Alejandro G. Vigo. Buenos Aires: Colihue Clásica, 2009.
Plato. *Platonis opera*. Vol. 1. Edited by John Burnet. Oxford: Clarendon, 1900. Reprinted 1989.
Plotinus. *Enneads*. Vol. 1. Translated by A. H. Armstrong. Cambridge, MA: Harvard University Press, 1969.
Plotinus. *Plotini Opera*. Edited by Paul Henry and Hans-Rudolf Schwyzer. 3 vols. Oxford: Oxford University Press, 1964–1982.
Plutarch. "On Exile." In *Moralia*. Vol. 7. Translated by Phillip H. De Lacy and Benedict Einarson. Cambridge, MA: Harvard University Press, 1959, 513–74.
Plutarch. "On the Principle of Cold." In *Moralia*. Vol. 12. Translated by Harold Cherniss and W. C. Helmbold. Cambridge, MA: Harvard University Press, 1957, 227–87.
Plutarch. "Reply to Colotes in Defence of the Other Philosophers." In *Moralia*. Vol. 14. Translated by Benedict Einarson and Phillip H. De Lacy. Cambridge, MA: Harvard University Press, 1967.
Plutarch. *Table-Talk: Books 7–9*. Vol. 9 of *Moralia*. Translated by Edwin L. Minar, F. H. Sandbach, and W. C. Helmbold. Cambridge, MA: Harvard University Press, 1961.
Proclus. *In primum Euclidis elementorum librum commentarii*. Edited by Gottfried Friedlein. Leipzig: Teubner, 1873.
Proclus. *On the Existence of Evils*. Translated by Jan Opsomer and Carlos Steel. Ithaca, NY: Cornell University Press, 2003.
Proclus. *Procli in Platonis Parmenidem commentaria*. Edited by Carlos Steel. 3 vols. Oxford: Oxford University Press, 2007–2009.
Proclus. *Tria opuscula: De providentia, libertate, malo*. Edited by Helmut Boese. Berlin: De Gruyter, 1960.
Seneca. *De ira*. In *Moral Essays*. Vol. 1. Translated by John W. Basore. Cambridge, MA: Harvard University Press, 1928, 106–355.
Sextus Empiricus. *Against Physicists*. In *Against Physicists and Against Ethicists*, translated by R. G. Bury. Cambridge, MA: Harvard University Press, 1936, 2–383.

Sextus Empiricus. *Against the Professors*. Translated by R. G. Bury. Cambridge, MA: Harvard University Press, 1949.

Sextus Empiricus. *Outlines of Pyrrhonism*. Translated by R. G. Bury. Cambridge, MA: Harvard University Press, 1933.

Simplicius. *Corollaries on Place and Time*. Translated by J. O. Urmson. Ithaca, NY: Cornell University Press, 1992.

Simplicius. *On Aristotle on the Void*. Translated by J. O. Urmson. Edited by Peter Lautner. In *Philoponus: On Aristotle Physics 5-8 with Simplicius: On Aristotle on the Void*. Translated by Paul Lettinck and J. O. Urmson. London: Bloomsbury, 2013, 157-236.

Simplicius. *Simplicii in Aristotelis De caelo commentaria*. Vol VII of *Commentaria in Aristotelem Graeca*. Edited by Johann Ludwig Heiberg. Berlin: Reimer, 1894.

Simplicius. *Simplicii in Aristotelis Physicorum libros quattuor priores commentaria*. Vol IX of *Commentaria in Aristotelem Graeca*. Edited by Hermann Diels. Berlin: Reimer, 1882.

Sternbach, Leo, ed. *Gnomologium Vaticanum*. Vol. 2 of *Texte und Kommentare*. Berlin: De Gruyter, 1963.

Stobaeus. *Anthologium*. Edited by Curtius Wachsmuth and Otto Hence. 5 vols. Berlin: Weidmann, 1884-1927.

Strabo. *Geography*. Translated by Howard Leonard Jones. 8 vols. Cambridge, MA: Harvard University Press, 1917-1932.

Syrianus. *Syriani in Metaphysica commentaria*. Vol. VI.1 of *Commentaria in Aristotelem Graeca*. Edited by Guilelmus Kroll. Berlin: Reimer, 1902.

Tarán, Leonardo, Ed. *Speusippus of Athens: A Critical Study with a Collection of the Related Texts and Commentary*. Leiden: Brill, 1981.

Themistius. *Themistii in Aristotelis Physica paraphrasis*. Vol V.2 of *Commentaria in Aristotelem Graeca*. Edited by Henricus Schenkl. Berlin: Reimer, 1900.

Themistius. *Themistii in libros Aristotelis De caelo paraphrasis hebraicea et latine*. Vol. V.4 of *Commentaria in Aristotelem Graeca*. Edited by Samuel Landauer. Berlin: Reimer, 1902.

Theophrastus. *Metaphysics*. Translated and edited by Marlein van Raalte. Leiden: Brill, 1993.

Theophrastus. *Theophrasti Fragmentum De sensibus*. In *Doxographi Graeci*. Edited by Hermann Diels. Berlin: De Gruyter, 1965, 497-527.

von Arnim, Hans. Ed. *Chrysippi fragments logica et physica*. Vol. 2 of *Stoicorum Veterum Fragmenta*. Stuttgart: Teubner, 1964.

West, Martin L., Ed. *Iambi et elegi Graeci ante Alexandrum cantati*. Vol.1. 2nd ed. Oxford: Oxford University Press, 1989.

Westerink, L. G., Ed. *Anonymous Prolegomena to Plato's Philosophy*. Amsterdam: North-Holland Publishing, 1962.

Xenophon. *Memorabilia, Oeconomicus, Symposium, Apology*. Translated by E. C. Marchant and O. J. Todd. Revised by Jeffrey Henderson. Cambridge, MA: Harvard University Press, 2013.

II. Secondary Texts

Ackrill, J. L. "Plato and the Copula: *Sophist* 251-259." In *Essays on Plato and Aristotle*. Oxford: Oxford University Press, 1997, 80-92.

BIBLIOGRAPHY 263

Algra, Keimpe. *Concepts of Space in Greek Thought*. Leiden: Brill, 1995.

Algra, Keimpe. "On Generation and Corruption I. 3: Substantial Change and the Problem of Not Being." In *Aristotle: On Generation and Corruption, Book 1: Symposium Aristotelicum*. Edited by Frans A. J. de Haas and Jaap Mansfeld. Oxford: Oxford University Press, 2004, 91–121.

Ashton, Richard, and Stanley Ireland, Eds. *Bosporus-Aeolis*. Part 9 of *Ashhmolean Museum, Oxford*. Vol. 5 of *Sylloge Nummorum Graecorum*. Oxford: Oxford University Press, 2007.

Aubenque, Pierre. *Le problème de l'être chez Aristote: Essai sur la problématique aristotelicienne*. Paris: Presses Universitaires de France, 2013.

Austin, Scott. *Parmenides: Being, Bounds, and Logic*. New Haven, CT: Yale, 1986.

Barnes, Jonathan. "Parmenides and the Eleatic One." *Archiv für Geschichte der Philosophie* 61 (1979), 1–21.

Berryman, Sylvia. "Democritus and the Explanatory Power of the Void." In *Presocratic Philosophy: Essays in Honour of Alexander Mourelatos*. Edited by Victor Caston and Daniel W. Graham. New York: Routledge, 2016, 183–91.

Berti, Enrico. "Multiplicity and unity of being in Aristotle." *Proceedings of the Aristotelian Society* 101 (2001), 185–207.

Blumenberg, Hans. *Das Lachen der Thrakerin: Eine Urgeschichte der Theorie*. Frankfurt: Suhrkamp, 1987.

Brancacci, Aldo and Pierre-Marie Morel, Eds. *Democritus: Science, the Arts, and the Care of the Soul*. Leiden–Boston: Brill, 2007.

Branman, R. Bracht, and Marie-Odile Goulet-Cazé, Eds. *The Cynics: The Cynic Movement in Antiquity and Its Legacy*. Berkeley: University of California Press, 1996.

Bredlow, Luis Andrés. "Parmenides and the Grammar of Being." *Classical Philology* 106:4 (2011), 283–98.

Brown, Lesley. "Being in the *Sophist*: A Syntactical Enquiry." In *Plato 1: Metaphysics and Epistemology*. Edited by Gail Fine. Oxford: Oxford University Press, 1999, 455–78.

Bussanich, John. "Plotinus' Metaphysics of the One." In *The Cambridge Companion to Plotinus*. Edited by Lloyd P. Gerson. Cambridge: Cambridge University Press, 1996, 38–65.

Bussanich, John. *The One and Its Relation to Intellect in Plotinus*. Leiden: Brill, 1988.

Clarke, Timothy. *Aristotle and the Eleatic One*. Oxford: Oxford University Press, 2019.

Cordero, Néstor-Luis. *By Being, It Is*. Las Vegas: Parmenides Publishing, 2004.

Corrigan, Kevin. "Is There More than One Generation of Matter in the *Enneads*?" *Phronesis* 31:2 (1986), 167–81.

Corrigan, Kevin. *Plotinus' Theory of Matter-Evil and the Question of Substance in Plato, Aristotle, and Alexander of Aphrodisias*. Leuven: Peeters, 1996.

Crivelli, Paolo. *Plato's Account of Falsehood: A Study of the Sophist*. Cambridge: Cambridge University Press, 2012.

Curd, Patricia. *The Legacy of Parmenides: Eleatic Monism and Later Presocratic Thought*. Las Vegas: Parmenides Publishing, 2004.

Desmond, William. *Cynics*. Berkeley: University of California Press, 2008.

Desmond, William. *The Greek Poverty: Origins of Ancient Cynicism*. Notre Dame, IN: University of Notre Dame, 2006.
Emilsson, Eyjólfur Kjalar. *Plotinus on Intellect*. Oxford: Oxford University Press, 2007.
Fattal, Michel. *Platon et Plotin: Relation, Logos, Intuition*. Paris: L'Harmattan, 2013.
Foucault, Michel. *Fearless Speech*. Edited by Joseph Pearson. Los Angeles: Semiotext(e), 2001.
Franchi, Leonardo. "Parmenide a l'origine della nozione di nulla." *Giornale critico della filosofia italiana* 14:2 (2018), 247–74.
Franklin, Lee. "Dichotomy and Platonic Diairesis." *History of Philosophy Quarterly* 28 (2011), 1–20.
Fronterotta, Francesco. "Il non essere e la strategia dello straniero di Elea: deduzione o rimozione?" *Rivista di storia della filosofia* 70:1 (2015), 143–62.
Furley, David. *The Formation of the Atomic Theory and Its Earliest Critics*. Vol. 1 of *The Greek Cosmologists*. Cambridge: Cambridge University Press, 1987.
Galilei, Galileo. *Discoveries and Opinions of Galileo Galilei*. Translated by Stillman Drake. Garden City, NY: Doubleday, 1957.
Gavray, Marc-Antoine. *Simplicius lecteur du Sophiste: Contribution à l'étude de l'exégèse néoplatonicienne tardive*. Paris: Klincksieck, 2007.
Gersh, Stephen. Κίνησις ἀκίνητος: *A Study of Spiritual Motion in the Philosophy of Proclus*. Leiden: Brill, 1973.
Giannantoni, Gabriele, Ed. *Socratis et Socraticorum Reliquiae*. 4 vols. Naples, Italy: Bibliopolis, 1990.
Golitsis, Pantelis. *Les Commentaires de Simplicius et de Jean Philopon à la Physique d'Aristote*. Berlin: De Gruyter, 2008.
Goodwin, William. *A Greek Grammar*. Boston: Ginn and Company, 1892.
Gutiérrez, Raúl. *El arte de la conversión. Un estudio sobre la República de Platón*. Lima: Fondo Editorial PUC, 2017.
Hadot, Ilsetraut. *Simplicius the Neoplatonist in Light of Contemporary Research: A Critical Review*. With Philippe Vallat. Translated by Ian Drummond. Baden-Baden: Academia Verlag, 2020.
Happ, Heinz. *Hyle: Studien zum Aristotelischen Materie-Begriff*. Berlin: De Gruyter, 1971.
Heath, Thomas L. "Notes on the Common Notions." In Euclid, *The Thirteen Books of Euclid's Elements*. Translated and edited by Thomas L. Heath. Vol. 1. 2nd rev. ed. New York: Dover, 1956, 221–32.
Heidegger, Martin. *Die Grundbegriffe der Metaphysik: Welt, Endlichkeit, Einsamkeit*. Vols. 29–30 of *Gesamtausgabe*. Edited by Friedrich-Wilhelm von Herrmann. Frankfurt: Vittorio Klostermann, 1983.
Heidegger, Martin. *The Fundamental Concepts of Metaphysics: World, Finitude, Solitude*. Translated by William McNeill and Nicholas Walker. Bloomington: Indiana University Press, 1983.
Horn, Christoph, Daniela Patrizia Taormina, and Denis Walter, Eds. *Körperlichkeit in der Philosophie der Spätantike/Corporeità nella filosofia tardoantica*. Baden-Baden: Academia, 2020.
Kahn, Charles. *Essays on Being*. Oxford: Oxford University Press, 2009.

Kahn, Charles. *The Verb 'Be' in Ancient Greek: With a New Introductory Essay.* Indianapolis, IN: Hackett, 2003.

Kalligas, Paul. *The Enneads of Plotinus: A Commentary.* Vol. 1. Princeton, NJ: Princeton University Press, 2014.

Klein, Jacob. *Plato's Trilogy: Theaetetus, the Sophist, and the Statesman.* Chicago: University of Chicago Press, 1977.

Konstan, David. "Epicurus on the Void." In *Space in Hellenistic Philosophy: Critical Studies in Ancient Physics.* Edited by Graziano Ranocchia, Christoph Helmig, and Christoph Horn. Berlin: De Gruyter, 2014, 83–100.

Lanza, Diego. *Lo stolto: Di Socrate, Eulenspiegel, Pinocchio e altri trasgressori del senso comune.* Turin: Einaudi, 1997.

Lee, Edward N. "Plato on Negation and Non-Being in the *Sophist*." *The Philosophical Review* 81:3 (1972), 267–304.

Long, Anthony A. "The Socratic Tradition: Diogenes, Crates, and Hellenistic Ethics." In Branman and Goulet-Cazé, *The Cynics*, 28–46.

Luck, Georg, Ed. *Die Weisheit der Hunde: Texte der antiken Kyniker in deutscher Übersetzung mit Erläuterungen.* Stuttgart: Kröner, 1997.

Malherbe, Abraham J., Ed. *The Cynic Epistles: A Study Edition.* Missoula, MT: Scholars Press, 1977.

Marciano, M. Laura Gemelli. *Democrito e l'Accademia: Studi sulla transmissione dell'atomismo da Aristotele a Simplicio.* Berlin: De Gruyter, 2007.

Mazella, David. *The Making of Modern Cynicism.* Charlottesville: University of Virginia Press, 2007.

Mourelatos, Alexander P. D. *The Route of Parmenides.* Revised and Expanded Edition. Las Vegas: Parmenides Publishing, 2008.

Mueller, Ian. "What's the Matter? Some Neo-Platonist Answers." In *One Book: The Whole Universe: Plato's Timaeus Today.* Edited by Richard D. Mohr and Barbara M. Sattler. Las Vegas: Parmenides, 2010, 151–64.

Müseler, Eike, Ed. *Die Kynikerbriefe.* 2 vols. Paderborn, Germany: Schöningh, 1994.

Nails, Debra. *The People of Plato: A Prosopography of Plato and Other Socratics.* Indianapolis, IN: Hackett, 2002.

Nakhov, I. M., Ed. *Anthology of Cynicism.* Moscow: Nauka, 1984.

Narbonne, Jean-Marc. "La controverse à propos de la génération de la matière chez Plotin: l'énigme résolue?" *Questio* 7 (2007), 123–63.

Narbonne, Jean-Marc. "Le non-être chez Plotin et dans la tradition grecque." *Revue de la philosophie ancienne* 10:1 (1992), 115–33.

Narbonne, Jean-Marc. "Matter and Evil in the Neoplatonic Tradition." In *The Routledge Handbook of Neoplatonism.* Edited by Pauliina Remes and Svetla Slaveva-Griffin. London: Routledge, 2014, 231–44.

Nelson, T. G. A. *Comedy: An Introduction to Comedy in Literature, Drama, and Cinema.* Oxford: Oxford University Press, 1990.

Niehues-Pröbsting, Heinrich. *Der Kynismus des Diogenes und der Begriff des Zynismus.* 2nd ed. Frankfurt: Suhrkamp, 1988.

Niehues-Pröbsting, Heinrich. "The Modern Reception of Cynicism: Diogenes in the Enlightenment." In Branman and Goulet-Cazé, *The Cynics*, 329–65.

Nikulin, Dmitri. *Dialectic and Dialogue.* Stanford, CA: Stanford University Press, 2010.

Nikulin, Dmitri. *Matter, Imagination and Geometry: Ontology, Natural Philosophy and Mathematics in Plotinus, Proclus, and Descartes.* Aldershot: Ashgate, 2002.
Nikulin, Dmitri. *Neoplatonism in Late Antiquity.* Oxford: Oxford University Press, 2019.
Nikulin, Dmitri. *The Concept of History.* London: Bloomsbury, 2017.
O'Brien, Denis. *Plotinus on the Origin of Matter: An Exercise in the Interpretation of the Enneads.* Naples, Italy: Bibliopolis, 1991.
O'Meara, Dominic. *Plotinus: An Introduction to the Enneads.* Oxford: Oxford University Press, 1993.
Owen, G. E. L. "Plato on Non-Being." In *Plato 1: Metaphysics and Epistemology.* Edited by Gail Fine. Oxford: Oxford University Press, 1999, 416–54.
Palmer, John A. *Parmenides and Presocratic Philosophy.* Oxford: Oxford University Press, 2009.
Phillips, John. "Plotinus on the Generation of Matter." *The International Journal of the Platonic Tradition* 3 (2009), 103–17.
Rapp, Christoph. "Zeno and the Eleatic Anti-Pluralism." In *La costruzione del discorso filosofico nell'età dei Presocratici.* Edited by Michela Sassi. Pisa: Edizioni della Normale, 2006, 161–82.
Reeve, C. D. C. "Motion, Rest, and Dialectic in the *Sophist*." *Archiv für Geschichte der Philosophie* 67:1 (1985), 47–64.
Reichenberger, Andrea. "Zum Begriff des Leeren in der Philosophie der frühen Atomisten." *Göttinger Forum für Altertumswissenschaft* 5:1 (2002), 105–22.
Rist, John M. "The Problem of 'Otherness' in the *Enneads*." In *Le Néoplatonisme: Royaumont, 9–13 juin, 1969.* Edited by Pierre Maxime Schuhl and Pierre Hadot. Paris: Éditions du Centre national de la recherche scientifique, 1971, 77–87.
Robbiano, Chiara. "Being is Not an Object: An Interpretation of Parmenides' Fragment DK B2 and a Reflection on Assumptions." *Ancient Philosophy* 36:2 (2016), 263–301.
Rousseau, Jean-Jacque. *The Discourses and Other Early Political Writings.* Translated and edited by Victor Gourevitch. Cambridge: Cambridge University Press, 2002.
Schäfer, Christian. *Unde malum: Die Frage nach dem Woher des Bösen bei Plotin, Augustinus, und Dionysius.* Würzburg: Königshausen & Neumann, 2002.
Schofield, Malcolm. *The Stoic Idea of the City.* Cambridge: Cambridge University Press, 1991.
Sedley, David. "Atomism's Eleatic Roots." In *The Oxford Handbook of Presocratic Philosophy.* Edited by Patricia Curd and Daniel W. Graham. Oxford: Oxford University Press, 2008, 305–32.
Sedley, David. "Two Conceptions of Vacuum." *Phronesis* 27:2 (1982), 175–93.
Shea, Louisa. *The Cynic Enlightenment: Diogenes in the Salon.* Baltimore, MD: Johns Hopkins University Press, 2010.
Shields, Christopher. "Being qua Being." In *The Oxford Handbook of Aristotle.* Edited by Christopher Shields. Oxford: Oxford University Press, 2012, 343–71.
Sorabji, Richard. *Matter, Space, and Motion: Theories in Antiquity and Their Sequel.* London: Duckworth, 1988.

Tarán, Leonardo. *Parmenides: A Text with Translation, Commentary, and Critical Essays*. Princeton, NJ: Princeton University Press, 1965.

Theiler, Willy. "Einheit und unbegrenzte Zweiheit von Plato bis Plotin." In *Isonomia: Studien zur Gleichheitsvorstellung im griechischen Denken*. Edited by Jürgen Mau and Ernst Günther Schmidt. Berlin: Akademie, 1964, 89–110.

Tuominen, Miira. *The Ancient Commentators on Plato and Aristotle*. London-New York: Routledge, 2014.

Untersteiner, Mario. "L'essere di Parmenide è 'ΟΥΛΟΝ', non 'ΕΝ'." *Rivista Critica di Storia della Filosofia* 10:1 (1955), 5–23.

Van Eck, Job. "Non-Being and difference: On Plato's *Sophist* 256d5–258e3." *Oxford Studies in Ancient Philosophy* 23 (2002), 63–84.

Voelke, André-Jean. "Vide et non-être chez Leucippe et Démocrite." *Revue de Théologie et de Philosophie* 122:3 (1990), 341–52.

West, Martin L. *Studies in Greek Elegy and Iambus*. Berlin: De Gruyter, 1974.

Index

For the benefit of digital users, indexed terms that span two pages (e.g., 52–53) may, on occasion, appear on only one of those pages.

absence/ἀπουσία
  of form, 152–53
  and matter, 221, 226
  of mediation, 100
  and negation, 172–73, 240
  of non-being, 95
  present absence of non-being 50, 111–12
  and privation, 240
  and the negative, 161
  and the one, 190–91, 233
  of the other, 98
  and void, 238, 240–41
accident/συμβεβηκός, 160–61
  being, 21
  vs. essential, 175
  and non-being, 176, 244
activity/ἐνέργεια, 194, 200–1
  as actuality, 181–82, 203
antithesis, 21
apophatic, 25–26, 40–41
  apophatically, 120, 186, 225
  and cataphatic, 14
  and negative, 222
aporia
  and being as plural, 24–25
  and logos, 95
  and paradox, 112–13
  and puzzlement, 30
archetype/ἀρχέτυπον, 214–15, 227
argument
  and apophatic reasoning, 25, 26
  Diogenes on, 116, 117, 121–22
  and logos, 76–77
  making the weakest argument the strongest, 88
  vs. myth, 32–33
  and principle of isonomia, 61
  and the divine intellect, 219
Aristotle, 148–86
  on being, 151, 175–76
  and logos, 154–56
  on body, 67–68
    on the Pythagoreans on, 248
    the void as having no relation to, 248–49
  on comedy, 143
  as critic of the "other" ontology, 187
  on Democritus, 53–54, 55, 56–57
    and many worlds, 63–64
    and the full/being and the empty/non-being/void as principle of the existent, 45–46
    and the one and the many as co-original, 45–46
  on Diogenes
    as the dog (ὁ Κύων), 117
  on discursive and non-discursive thought, 170–73
  on *ergon*, 126
  on four kinds of what we search for, 148–50
  on knowledge, 148
  on logos, 14–15, 97
    as belonging to the essence of being human, 152
    as the sole way to the truth of being, 86–87
    and its limitations, 100
    and thinking logically about being and non-being, 36
  on matter, 180–85, 223, 242–44

Aristotle (*cont.*)
　on method, 49–50
　on motion, 67–68, 237–38
　on non-being, 149, 175, 176
　　two kinds: relative (matter) and absolute (privation), 172, 239
　　as what cannot be known, 186
　on nothing
　　and logos, 173
　　as a principle, ἀρχή, of everything that is, 174
　on opposites, 157–59
　on Parmenides on non-being, 12
　on place, 235–36, 251, 253
　on Plato
　　on nonbeing as "big and small", 113–14
　　on number, 91, 97–98
　　on the good as the one, 198–99
　　and the two principles of all opposites as one and many, 99, 113–14
　　on three elements, 101
　on privation, 159–61, 169, 171
　on sophistry, 80
　on the good as the object of desire towards which all things strive, 200–1
　on the principle of non-contradiction, 161–64, 169
　on the three principles for understanding what moves and changes, 153, 158
　on the void, 48, 60, 64, 66–67, 68, 232, 251–52
　　and the program of the study of the void, 232–33
　　as having no essence, 234
　　as logically a non-concept, 177
　　as not existing, 177–78
　　as the privation of being, 69
　　as different from negation, 240–41
　on the Pythagoreans on, 245
　on true and false, 164–65
askēsis/ἄσκησις
　Cynic askēsis, 143–44, 146
　Diogenes on, 128–29, 141

art/τέχνη, 85–86, 129
　vs. nature 149–50
asynonym(s)
　negations as, 8, 9–10
atoms, 44, 45, 72
　and being, 50–51, 52
　as beings, 47–48
　and infinity, 55–56, 57–59
　as indivisible, 52, 54
　as letters, 54–55
　as the many, 46, 177, 242
　and motion 107
　and void, 49, 65

beauty, 32–33, 49, 200
beginning
　and the principle of isonomia, 63
　as ἀρχή, principle/origin/source, 36, 152–53, 191–93
　of being, 32
　being as the beginning of everything, 1–2
　nature as beginning and cause of transformation and change, 156–57
　non being as, 174
　the one as, 192–93, 198–99
being
　as οὐσία, 114–15, 149–50, 166–67
　as τὸ ὄν, 21, 71, 92, 149–50, 153, 206
　being and history, 29
　being and thinking
　　being one, 22–23, 26, 105–6, 199
　　and being many 92
　　is/are the same, 19, 49, 208
　　the one as above, 197
　　as produced by the one, 210
　　as within the scope of the principle of non-contradiction, 161–62
　being as one/being as one-many, 22–23, 46, 93, 100, 101, 206
　being is, 187
　　and atoms, 52
　　and the one, 192
　　Parmenides on, 3–4, 10, 187
　　Plato on, 103
　　Aristotle on, 156

being is being, 10-12, 19-21, 23-24,
    95-96, 193
  beyond being, 7-8, 23-24, 34
    and the one, 188-89
    and the good, 189-90, 198-200
  modality of being, 5-6
  thinking being, 44, 116, 187
  univocity and plurivocity of being, 19
big and small/great and small/μέγα καὶ
    μικρόν
  and nonbeing, 113-14
  the infinite as, 212-13
  and the infinite dyad, 251
  as the material aspect of being and
    mathematical objects (Περὶ
    τἀγαθοῦ), 250
body
  as σῶμα, 72, 94, 120
  indivisible bodies/ἄτομα
    σώματα, 48-49
  atomists, contra Simplicius, on, 66-67
  ergon of the living body, 128-29
  soul as, 50-51
  and void 45, 65, 68, 177-78, 232, 236-
    45, 248-56

categories
  Aristotle's *Categories*, 158-59, 160-
    61, 169
  and being, 112-13
  deduction of, 102-3
  fundamental categories, 109
  of motion and rest, and same and
    other, 108
  as mutually participating in each
    other, 110
  and non-being, 115
    and logical categories, 161
  of one and many, 93
  as primary forms, 105-6
  system of, 110-11
  and the other, 113
  and void, 239
cause
  as αἴτιον, 196, 237-38, 245-46
  as ποιεῖν, 104
  being and non-being as
    being as, 104

nature as 149
productive cause, 39-40
Simplicius on, 244
and void, 68-69
combination
  as συμπλοκή, 47
  of atoms, 56, 61-62, 63-64
  and division, 165
  and separation, 70
comedy, 142-44, 145-46
communication
  and being, 105-6
  and νόησις, 219
  as κοινωνία, 101-2, 247-48
    of forms, 214-15, 217-18
  and the categories, 109
complexity
  vs. simplicity, 191-92
conception/ἔννοια
  as common conception (κοινὴ
    ἔννοια), 234
  and matter, 234-35
  as origin for inquiry/
    investigation, 234-35
  and the one as without conception
    (ἀνεννόητον), 204
  and void, 233-35
contradiction
  vs. contrariety, 158
  and discursive/nondiscursive
    thought, 165-66
  as immanent to logical discourse and
    reasoning, 85
  and impossibility, 36
  and logos vs. nous in thinking non-
    being, 168-69
  and opposition, 95
  and opposition/opposites, 12-13
  pragmatic contradiction, 124
  and privation and contrariety, 162
  and sophistry vs. philosophy, 79-81
  and the definition of true and false, 165
  and the self-correction of logos, 84-85
  and thinkability/unthinkability, 37
copula
  as ground of what can be called logical
    truth, 11, 17
  and logical propositions, 95-96, 167-68

copula (*cont.*)
 and logos, 14
 as mediating *is*, 21
 as the "downfall" of being, 10
 and the one, 188–89, 199
 and the principle of non-
  contradiction, 36
cosmos/κόσμος
 Aristotle on, 149, 165
 diacosmos, 38–40
 Diogenes on, 131
  cosmopolis, 121, 131, 136–37, 138, 140, 141
 Plato/Aristotle contra
  Democritus on, 64
 Plato on, 91, 92
  intelligible cosmos, 96–97, 99, 100, 104, 106–7
 Plotinus on, 206
  intelligible cosmos, 214–15, 217, 219
  and intelligible matter, 227
 physical cosmos, 228, 246, 251–52, 253
 and void
  Aristotle and Simplicius on, 236, 242
  Leucippus on, 241–42

darkness
 as description of both matter and
  evil, 229–30
 and intelligible reality, 227
 as life, 120
 and matter, 222
 as non-being, 80–81
 as source of being, 197–98
 as void, 65, 69
definition
 as based in logos as reasoning, 149
 Diogenes on, 123
 as disclosure of essence, 214–15
 and form, 152
 and logos, 79–80, 153
 and matter, 221, 242–43
 as supplying the 'what'/τί ἐστιν of a
  thing, 103, 149–50
 and the method of division, 85–86, 106, 153
 and the one, 190, 203

Democritus, 42–72
 and being and thinking as same, 51
 on imagination, 52, 65
 on intellect/νοῦς/νόος, 50–51
 on limit
  and atoms, 57–58
  of divisibility, 55
  of language, 72
  and magnitude, 46
  non-being as void and limit, 47
  of perception, 57
  and void, 61–62
 on motion, 63–64, 67–69
 on non-being, 42–43, 242
  as condition of possibility for
   being, 70, 72
  being is no more than non-being, 44
  cannot be understood on its own, 94
  and infinity, 59–60
  is no less than being, 45, 50, 52
  and its origin, 59, 63
  and thinkability, 51
   and the imagination, 52–53, 65
  as void, 47, 66, 69–70–
 on nothing
  and void, 46, 64–65, 68–72
 on number
  and atoms, 46, 55, 57–60, 67–68
  and worlds, 61–63
  and ontology, 51, 72
  and the imagination, 51
 on substance
  all beings/atoms, therefore, have the
   same substance, 47–48
  being bodily in its substance, 70
  one substance, 48
 on the many, 45–46
  as atoms, 46
   as being(s), 46, 52
 on thinking and being, 49, 50–51
 on the one
  as the void, 46
 on truth
  of being and non-being, 69
  and obscurity, 49–52
 on void, 42–72
Diogenes of Sinope, 116–47

on argument, 116, 117, 121–22
and *askēsis*/ἄσκησις, 128–29, 141
contra Plato, 116, 122–25, 135–36
on cosmos, 131
on definition, 123
on *ergon*, 125–29, 136–42
on free speech, 140, 142–43
on freedom
 as negative, 130–32
 as positive, 139–42
 and the political, 145–47
on limit
 and power and wealth, 146
 between private and public, 141
on logos, 121, 122–23
on motion
 contra Zeno, as established through *ergon*, 127–28
on nature, 116, 118–31, 133–38
on non-being, 116–17, 120–21, 142–43
 and life, 118, 120–21, 131–32
 and ἄσκησις, 128–29
 as convention and habit, 136–37, 145–46, 147
 polis as the seat of non-being, 130–31, 134
on nothing of non-being, 116–17, 120
on place, 118
 and the polis, 137
 as place of freedom, 140
on power/tyranny, 146–47
on praxis, 129
 vs. *ergon*, 126
 life as, 127
on simplicity, 139–40
on the good life, 116, 120–21, 124, 126–27, 128–29, 140
 according to nature, 136–37
 and comedy, 144
 and freedom, 139, 141–42
on thinking, 116, 126, 128
 and routine/habit/convention, 138, 143–44, 145
on truth, 141–42, 143–44
discursive thinking, 36–37, 165–66
logos as, 82
vs. reason-νοῦς, 87

as διάνοια, 81–83, 164, 166, 218
disposition/ἕξις
 as opposite to privation, 158–60, 240–41
 and void 240–41
division
 Aristotle on, 165
 and distinction, 80–81
 method of διαίρεσις, 85–87
duality
 and logos, 81, 82, 86
 of matter, 251
 of oneness and otherness joined synthetically in the intellect, 214
 produced by the indefinite dyad, 249
 of the one-many which constitutes being, 99–100

elements/στοιχεῖα
 atoms as elements, 54
 the four elements, 56
 the full and the void as foundational elements, 47
 Plato's three elements, 101
 two principles of the diacosmos as elements, 6
emptiness, 69, 70, 238, 245–46, 255
epic, 27–28, 34
 and narration/narrative, 40–41
ergon/ἔργον, 125–29, 136–42
error, 84–85, 87–88
essence
 and 'the what'/τί ἐστιν, 149–50, 151, 166
 and being, 179
 as being, 156
 and definition, 30
 and existence, 21
 and speech, 77, 80
 and substance, 152
Euclid
 Elements, 101–2, 219, 234–35
evil/κακόν
 Aristotle on
 evil and good as contraries, 158–59
 Parmenides on, 30

evil/κακόν (cont.)
  Plato on
    non being is not evil, 114–15
  Plotinus on
    and matter, 228–30
extension, 59–60
  continuous extension, 46
  empty extension, 48, 52, 70, 177
  imaginary extension, 51
  as διάστημα/interval, 65, 66, 178, 235, 236
  void as, 64–67, 69, 178

form, 10, 84, 86, 90, 92, 123, 152–53, 206, 210, 215–16, 227, 245–46, 250–51, 255
  as εἶδος, 94, 152, 157, 201, 225–26, 229–30
  as ἰδέα, 214
  as μορφή, 152, 156–57, 180, 181, 210
freedom
  as negative, 130–32
  as positive, 139–42
  and the political, 145–47
freedom of speech/παρρησία, 140, 141, 145–46
full, 45, 47–48
  and being, 52, 69
  and body, 248–49

glory/κλέος, 29, 135
the good
  Diogenes on
    the good life, 116, 120–21, 124, 126–27, 128–29, 140
      according to nature, 136–37
      and comedy, 144
      and freedom, 139, 141–42
  Plato on
    as beyond being, 114–15, 189–90
    cognition striving towards, 105–6
  Plotinus on
    and being, 207
    the one as, 198–201, 216–17, 229–30
    and the divine intellect, 209–10, 212
    ways of knowing the good, 201

image
  as εἴδωλον, 47–48, 223, 227
  gods as material images, 47–48
  of eternity, 91
  and non-being, 89
  of the logos, 218
  of the soul, 224–25
imagination
  and Democritus, 52, 65
  and Plato's theory of truth, 84
  as φαντασία, 81–82
  and the infinite, 58
  and void, 65
incommensurability, 244–45, 246–48
indefinite dyad/ἀόριστος δυάς, 45, 91, 212–13, 228
indefinite/indefiniteness
  and evil, 229–30
  indefinite dyad, 91, 212–13
  indefinite plurality, 97–98
  indefinite third, 94
  indefinite variety and non-being, 120
  intelligible matter as, 227–28
  and the intellect, 211
  matter as, 223–25, 235
  and non-being as an indefinite "beside itself", 8, 220
  and thinking, 19–20
  as one of four aspects of matter, 180, 184–86
  void as, 242
indifference/ἀδιαφορία, 61–62, 68–69, 131–32
indivisibility, 52–54, 57–58
ineffable/ἄρρητον, 40–41, 202
infinite/ἄπειρον, 59–60, 111–12, 179, 195, 211, 212–13, 221, 229–30, 253
infinity
  of atoms, 55–63
    of shapes and sizes, 57
  of causes, 176
  the infinite power of the one as not privative, 195
  of infinities, 58–59
  of natural numbers, 59
  as only potential and never actual, 185
  of the void, 59–60
  of worlds, 61–64
intellect/νοῦς/νόος
  Democritus on, 50–51

Plato on, 100, 106–7, 233–34
Plotinus on, 189, 208–20, 222, 228
intelligible matter/ὕλη νοητή, 226–28, 249

knowledge
  as action, 104–6
  and being, 41, 106
  as ἐπιστήμη, 30, 113, 149, 155–56
  and the divine intellect, 216
  διαλεκτικὴ ἐπιστήμη, 86
  as four kinds, 148–49
  of how things are, 50
  and non-being, 35, 185–86
  as non-theoretical, 121, 122, 127
  of matter, 222
  and the one, 205
  as universal human striving, 148
  and *via negativa*, 201

law
  moral laws, 138
  of non-contradiction, 18
  and self-reliance vs. self-legislation, 140
  as νόμος, 130, 131–32, 142–43
limit
  Aristotle on
    and time, 127
    of body 177–78
    and matter, 185
  Democritus on
    of divisibility, 55
    of perception, 57
    and atoms, 57–58
    and void, 61–62
    of language, 72
    and magnitude, 46
    non-being as void and limit, 47
  and being, 26, 48
  Diogenes on, 131–32, 134
    between private and public, 141
    and power and wealth, 146
  as πέρας, 26, 179, 214, 221, 225, 235, 236
  Plotinus on
    and the one, 190, 210
    of thought, 188–89
    as ὅρος, 175–76, 179, 210

limited/ὡρισμένον, 57–58, 63, 190, 212–13, 242
locomotion/φορά
  and the atomist view, 67–68
  Simplicius on, 237–38
logos/λόγος
  Aristotle on, 154–56, 161–62, 202
    and non-being, 174–75, 184–86
    and the principle of non-contradiction, 165
    and truth, 164, 166–67, 169
  Diogenes on, 121, 122–23
  ergon as, 140–41
  Parmenides on, 14–16
  Plato on, 76–87, 88, 90, 95, 100
  Plotinus on
    and matter, 221, 222
    and the intellect, 217, 218–20
    and *via negativa*, 201
  See also aporia; argument; assertion; contradiction; copula; definition; discursive thinking; duality; image; multiplicity; myth; negation; non-being; opposite(s); order; power; principle of non-contradiction; simplicity; thinking

magnitude/μέγεθος
  and atoms, 52–54
  and bodies, 248
  geometrical and physical magnitude, 249, 258
  infinitely divisible, 66–67
  matter as without, 223–24
  and number, 46
  physical magnitude, 250
  and the infinite, 179–80
the many
  as πολλά, 43–44, 45–46, 93, 188–89, 201, 206
  Democritus on, 45–46
    as atoms, 46
    as being(s), 46, 52
  Parmenides on
    the path of, 33–34
  Plato on
    with the Eleatic doctrine and contra Democritus, 44

the many (cont.)
　Plotinus on
　　and the one, 188–89, 201, 206
　　as without one, 228
　　the origin of, 205, 210
　Zeno on, 24–25
mathematics
　Diogenes on, 121–22, 123
　and infinite divisibility of
　　geometrical and physical
　　magnitudes, 53–54
　mathematical
　　entities, 248–49
　　vs. ideal numbers, 247–48
　　and intelligible matter, 180–
　　　81, 226–27
　　objects, 250
　　and physical volume, 250–51
　　volume, 250
　as model for ontology, 53
　in Plato, as propaedeutic to
　　philosophy, 74–75
　and the void, 238, 245–49
matter/ὕλη
　and non-being, 112–13, 185–86, 239
　Aristotle on, 159–60, 180–84
　　and privation, 155, 164, 172, 173–74
　　prime matter, 184–85
　　and non-being, 172
　Plotinus on, 220–30
　　and evil, 228, 229–30
　　and ἔννοια, 234–35
　Simplicius on, 39–40, 242–45, 247–48, 250–51
　See also indefinite/indefiniteness
mediation
　Aristotle on, 158, 160, 163–64, 169–70, 171–72
　Democritus on, 46
　Parmenides on
　　and logos, 16, 18, 19, 38–39
　　and being, 10–11
　Plato on, 99–100
　See also opposite(s)
mixture, 41, 101, 107–8
motion
　and void, Democritus on, 48

Aristotle on
　and the substrate, 151
　and change, both said in many
　　ways, 154–55
　and rest, 159–60
　of bodies, 177–78
Democritus on, 63–64, 67–69
Diogenes on
　contra Zeno, as established through
　　ergon, 127–28
Plato on, 107–8–
　and being, 99, 106
　as κίνησις; 105–6, 209, 254
　See also categories
multiplicity
　and being, 4, 10
　and logos, 14–15, 154–55
　and *via negativa*, 201
　of atomic monads, 46
　Plotinus on
　　and the one, 188, 191, 204, 206
　　and the good, 198–99
　　and the intellect, 189, 208–9, 210, 214–15
　　as unity in multiplicity, 216
　　and logos, 218
　　and matter, 228–29
myth
　and Plato's *Timeaus*, 94
　and the principle of non-
　　contradiction, 33
　of the way (μῦθος ὁδοῖο), 27–28, 32–33
　vs. logos, 76–78

name
　and being, 92
　and beings, 156
　and syntactic binding, 78
　and the one, 201–3, 204
　as ὄνομα, 5–6, 36, 203
　naming and non-being, 5–6, 89–90, 93, 95
nature
　and non-being, 114
　and obscurity/hiddenness, 49–51
　and void, 72

INDEX 277

Aristotle on, 156–57
   and matter, 180–81, 185–86
   and striving to knowledge, 148, 149
   and telos/purpose, 179
   as form, 181
   by nature, 155, 156, 158–61
   said in many ways, 154–55
   vs. through art, 149–50
book of, 55, 63–64
Diogenes on, 116, 118–31, 133–38
   and positive freedom, 139
   and free speech, 140, 142–43
   and power/tyranny, 146–47
of the cosmos, 91
as φύσις, 47–48, 104–5, 156–57
   as underlying 232, 237–38, 240
   of matter 243–44
necessity
   accident and, 61–62
   and modality, 5–6, 207–8
   and possibility, 132
   logical necessity, 207–8
   mighty necessity, 30, 31–32
   of becoming, 176
   of being, 1–2
   of producing being, 197
   of reason, 64
   vs. chance, 63–64
negatio negationis, 207–8
negation
   and affirmation, 169–70
   and assertion, 14, 79–80, 158–59, 163–64, 165, 169–70
   and knowing the good/the one, 204
   and logos, 94–95
   and nothing, 172–74
   and opposition, 169
   Aristotle on, 169–76
   as ἀπόφασις; 79, 95, 97, 158–59, 169–70, 172–73
   double negation, 5–6, 11–12, 14, 121, 171–73
   negation(s) as asynonyms, 8
   not graspable on its own, 8–9
   of a proposition, 171
   of the predicate, 171
   possibility of, 2

power of, 4, 37–38
pure negation, 9–10, 37–38
void as, 238
negativity
   and matter, 183–84, 186
   and non-being, privation, and void, 238–42
   and the one, 204, 207–8
   as essential for logos, 169
   as privation of being, 223–24
   as privation of being, 223–24
   as underlying the categories as forms, 109–10
   contradiction as, 165
   contradiction as, 165
   in the form of negation, 169
   otherness as, 109–10, 115
   radical, 204
noēma/νόημα, 17–18, 19, 20, 37
noēsis/νόησις, 100, 166–67, 213, 214, 216, 219
noēta/νοητά, 94, 96–97, 213, 214–15, 219, 250
non-being
   Aristotle on, 239
   absolute vs. relative non-being, 172, 180–86
   and logos, 155
   and principle of non-contradiction, 161–62, 163–64, 168–69
   and privation, 152–53, 159–60, 175, 240–41
   and what is false, 165
   as contradiction, 169
   as nothing, 173, 174–75
   as opposite of being, 156–58, 161, 175–76
   form as opposite of non-being as privation, 157
   generation of non-being, 175
   said in many ways, 148, 174–75
   Democritus on, 42–43, 242
   and infinity, 59–60
   and its origin, 59, 63
   and thinkability, 51
   and the imagination, 52–53, 65

non-being (*cont.*)
   as condition of possibility for being, 70, 72
   as void, 47, 66, 69–70–
   being is no more than non-being, 44
   cannot be understood on its own, 94
   is no less than being, 45, 50, 52
   Diogenes on, 116–17, 120–21, 142–43
     and life, 118, 120–21, 131–32
     and ἄσκησις, 128–29
     polis as the seat of non-being, 130–31, 134
     as convention and habit, 136–37, 145–46, 147
     vs. Plato, 136
   Parmenides on, 23–24, 242
     and speech, 41
     as precondition of truth and being, 41
     possibility of unconditional, direct, and simple generation of the existent from non-being, 175
     prohibition of thinking, 34–38
   Plato on, 73
     and logos, 95
     and discursive reasoning, 111–12
     and naming, 89–90
     and the categories, 111–12
     and the one and the many, 93
     and the truth of being, 88–89
     as existing, 113
     as negation of a form, 96–97
     as the other of being, 98
     impact on the existent, 87
     two main theses of the Sophist, 76
   Plotinus on
     and evil, 228–30
     as matter, 35–38
       and privation, 223–24
     as the one, 188, 189–90
     being and thinking as originating from non-being, 210
   Simplicius on
     as void, 232, 233–36, 238–39, 244, 256
   as μὴ ὄν
     Parmenides on, 3–4, 9–10, 12
   Democritus on
     and being/existing, 71–72, 88–89
     as void, 67
   Plato on
     and categories of being, 111–12
     and naming, 93
     and otherness, 114
     and the existence of, 112–13
   Aristotle on
     and accidental coming into being, 175
     and the need for non-being, 157
     as nothing, 173
     matter as non-being vs. privation as non-being, 184
     said in many ways, 148
   Plotinus on, 220
     and the one, 189, 220
     and the soul, 224–25
   Simplicius on
     void as, 239, 240, 243–44
not-being, 7, 19–20, 23–24, 38, 49, 98, 114–15, 164–65, 173, 187, 190, 191–92, 195
nothing
   Parmenides on, ch1Democritus on
     and void, 46, 64–65, 68–72
   Plato on, 93, 109, 111–12
     and logos, 83, 90
     as nonbeing, 102
   Diogenes on
     of non-being, 116–17, 120
   Aristotle on
     and logos, 161–62
     and void, 177–78, 232
     non-being and, 172–75
     non-being as, 148
     and negation, 171–72
   Plotinus on
     as matter, 225, 229
     as primary, 187
     the good as, 200
     the one as, 187–91
   Simplicius on,
     and mathematics, 248–50
     void as, 238–39, 244, 252, 254, 256

notion/ἐπίνοια, 235, 243–44
common notion/κοινὴ ἔννοια, 234–35
number
  and void, 245–47
  as being, 245
  Democritus on
    and atoms, 46, 55, 57–60, 67–68
    and worlds, 61–63
  Pythagoreans on, 45–46
  Plato on
    being and number, 90–91, 93, 96, 97–98, 113–14
    Diogenes contra, 123
    of fundamental categories, 109
  Aristotle on
    and infinity/the infinite, 179–80, 246
    and nothing, 173–74, 177–78
    the Pythagoreans on, 248
  Plotinus on
    and the indefinite dyad, 212–13
  Simplicius on, 247–48
  and nothing, 248–49, 252
  as ἀριθμός, 91, 212–13, 242–43, 245, 247–48

obscurity, 49
  and being and non-being, 51
  and matter, 221–22
  and nature, 50
  and truth, 49
one and many
  Aristotle on
    Plato on, 100, 101, 157
  Parmenides on
    relations between, 23
  Plato on
    and logical thought, 101–2
    and non-being, 93
    as not being opposite categories, 109
    being as a synthetic unity of, 92
    being as constituted by, 99, 103, 109, 114
    being as, 98
    contra Parmenides, 93
  Plotinus on, 189, 204
    and logos, 218, 220
    being as a synthesis of, 206

one/the one
  Aristotle on, 97
  as τὸ ἕν, 45, 89–90, 97, 211
  Democritus on
    as the void, 46
  Diogenes Laertius on the Eleatics on, 43–44
  Parmenides on
    of being, 27–28
  Plotinus on
    as beyond being, 188–89
    as transcendent to/other than being, 190–92
    as productive of being, 193–98
    as the good, 198–201
  Pythagoreans on, 45–46
  See also copula; definition; name; negativity
one-many, 205, 206
ontology
  and epistemology, 19, 105–6
  Aristotle's, 149, 158
  atomistic, 70
  Democritus', 51, 72
    and the imagination, 51
  mathematics and, 249
  mathematics as model for, 53
  Parmenides', 187
  Plato's, 97–98, 113
  Plotinus' understanding of, 189–90
  Pythagorean, 45–46, 248
  the "other," 187, 188, 257
opinion
  as δόξα, 29, 38, 81, 233–34, 251–52
  Aristotle on
    vs. justifiable rational account (ἐπιστήμη), 149
    as nothing, 177
    and void, 177, 178
  Democritus on
    sensible qualities as a matter of, 49–50
  Parmenides on
    the way/the path of, 33–34, 38–40, 41
    as shaky but also constant, 41
    and non-being, 35

opinion (*cont.*)
  Plato on
    expressive opinion/cognitive belief
      and the soul, 81
  Simplicius on
    and void, 233–36
opposite(s)
  Aristotle on, 158–61, 163–64
    and non-contradiction, 161–64
    and matter, 181–84
    and being, 100, 102, 108, 113, 114, 171, 223, 240–41
    and categories, 108–9
    and form, 152–53
    and habit, 133–34
    and logos, 79–80, 81, 95
    and mediation, 18
    unmediated, 11–12, 45, 70, 112, 162
    and nature, 133–34
    and negation, 97
    and non-being, 174
    and the one, 191–92
    as ἀντίθεσις, 158, 162
    as ἀντικείμενον, 151, 158, 161
    being and nonbeing as, 36–40
    being and non-being as, 156–57
    co-existence of, 33
    coincidence of, 14, 85
    contradiction and, 12–13
    distinction of, 7–8
    not the opposite of non-being, 4
    Plato on, 99–100, 107–9
    Simplicius on, 242–44
  opposition/ἐναντίωσις
    of is to is not, 3
    of and within being, 7
    See also contradiction; negation
order
  and cosmos, 99
  and logos, 14, 82, 84–85, 93, 103, 154–57, 164, 177
  and number, 98
  and the diacosmos, 5
  and the intellect, 215
  and the order of things
    and custom, 131–32, 142
    and nature, 156–57
  and the world, 39–40, 63–64
  as τάξις
    and atoms, 56
    and the world, 63–64
    and place, 236
  of being, 228–29
  of the existent, 64, 76, 194, 220, 256
the other/other
  Aristotle on, 149–50, 157
    and privation, 157
    as other to being, 173–74
    matter as other to being, 182
    of thought, 168–69
    reasoning- νοεῖν as the other
      of discursive thinking-
      λέγειν, 165–66
    the other of being as non-being, 149
    as ἕτερον, 39–40, 84, 97–98, 104, 108, 109–10, 111, 191–92, 198, 211, 223, 224, 245–46
    as θάτερον, 109–10, 207, 212–13, 245–46
  Democritus on
    of nothing, 72
  Diogenes on
    and logos, 140–41
    the comic slave as, 145
  Parmenides on
    and being, 1–2, 3–4, 6, 10, 12, 20–21, 23–24, 34, 40–41
    and nothing, 7–8
    and thinking, 18
  Plato on
    and being, 98, 99, 101, 109
      as constituted by the duality of the "one-many", 99–100, 103
    and dramatic doubling, 74–76
    and logos, 83, 84
    and the categories, 109–12
    and the philosopher vs. the Sophist, 80–81
    and the Sophist, 73
    motion as the other of rest, 108
    non-being as the other of being, ch3, 112–15, 245–46
    one and being as other to each other, 92

the dual number as representing the
  other of the one, 90
the other of the one as either
  duality, not-one, or indefinite
  plurality, 97–98
Plotinus on
  and the intellect, 216–17
  being as other to the one/the good,
    205, 206–8
  non-being as the other of the other
    of being, 220
  the other of being as constitutive of
    being, 187
    the other of being as one, 188
    and only one, 191
  and the one
    as other than being, 192
    as other to anything other
      before there is anything
      other, 191–92
    and no distinction in reference to
      the other, 202
    as productive of another as other
      to itself, 198
    as the good as other to every-
      thing that is, 198
    as the other of being and
      thought, 205
    as the other of everything that is
      in some way, 194–95
Simplicius on, 249

physics
  and Melissus, 241
  and the Eleatics, 242
  and the void, 238, 251–55, 256
  Aristotelian physics, 248
  Democritus on, 238
Parmenides, 1–41
  and ontology, 187
  and same
    and logos, 14–15
    thinking and thought as, 18
    being and thinking as, 19–20
    and itself, 22
    and being, 23, 26
    as substrate, 36
  and the other
    and being, 1–2, 3–4, 6, 10, 12, 20–21,
      23–24, 34, 40–41
    and nothing, 7–8
    and thinking, 18
  on evil, 30
  on logos, 14–16
  on mediation
    and logos, 16, 18, 19, 38–39
    and being, 10–11
  on non-being, 23–24, 242
    and speech, 41
    as precondition of truth and
      being, 41
  on opinion
    the way/the path of, 33–34, 38–
      40, 41
    as shaky but also constant, 41
    and non-being, 35
  on thinking
    logical thinking (λέγειν) vs. noetic
      thinking (νοεῖν), 16–19
    and being, 1–2
      being reflected as, 13
    as the same, 19–20
    and apophasis, 25–26, 40–41
    as poetic, 28
    and non-being, 34–41
    and logos, 22
  on truth, 4–5, 41
    of being, 29–34
    noetic vs. logical, 11–12, 15–16
    and logos, 16, 36
      and logical truth, 18
    reason- νόος as, 19
place
  Aristotle on, 163, 173, 177–78,
    251, 253
  and motion, 238
  as χώρα, 94
  as τόπος, 60, 235–39
  Diogenes on, 118
    and the polis, 137
  Plato on, 46, 47–48, 51, 64–69
  Simplicius on
    and void, 240–41, 253
    and interval, 235–37, 238–39

Plato, 73–115
  according to Eudemus
    on the plurivocity of being, 21
  on logos
    dianoetic logos as silent conversation of the soul with itself, 15
    the way of logos, 76–78
    weaving together, 78–79
    and non-contradiction as implicit regulating principle, 81
    and being, 81–83
    and truth, 83–85, 164–65
    and method, 85–88
      and dialectic, 87
    and non-being and negation, 95–97
    vs. noetic reasoning in thinking form, 101–2
    and grasping non-being in its elusive otherness, 115
  on the Sophist, 79–81
  on nous, 16
  on being, 92, 99–100, 112, 114–15, 135–36
    as the one-many, 23, 98, 99
    as thought through noetic reasoning, 100
    as having no opposite, 100
    and beings, 101–2
    as mediation, 101
  on Diotima, 30
  and the elenchic dialogue, 31
  on substrate, 36
  on Democritus, 43–44, 49
    and the infinity of worlds, 64
  on void, 64
  on mathematics as a propaedeutic to philosophy, 74–75
  on number, 91, 98
  on non-being, 94, 112–15, 220
  on the one and the many, 97
  on forms of plurality and opposition, 97–98
  on the categories, 102–12
  on the other, 113, 245–46
  on the good, 114–15, 198–99
  on Diogenes, 133
  on the one, 201–2, 204, 206, 207
  on matter, 221–22, 247–48
  and intellect vs. true opinion, 233–34

Plotinus, 187–230
  on cosmos, 206
    intelligible cosmos, 214–15, 217, 219
    and intelligible matter, 227
  on matter, 220–30
  on the divine intellect, 189, 208–20, 222, 228
  on limit
    and the one, 190, 210
    of thought, 188–89
  on logos
    and the intellect, 217, 218–20
    and matter, 221, 222
    and *via negativa*, 201
  on multiplicity
    and being, 4, 10
    and logos, 14–15, 154–55
    and *via negativa*, 201
    of atomic monads, 46
    Plotinus on
    and the one, 188, 191, 204, 206
    and the good, 198–99
    and the intellect, 189, 208–9, 210, 214–15
    as unity in multiplicity, 216
    and logos, 218
    and matter, 228–29
  on non-being
    as the one, 188, 189–90
    being and thinking as originating from non-being, 210
    as matter, 35–38
    and privation, 223–24
    and evil, 228–30
  on nothing
    the one as, 187–91
    as primary, 187
    the good as, 200
    as matter, 225, 229
  on the one
    as beyond being, 188–89
    as transcendent to/other than being, 190–92
    as productive of being, 193–98

as the good, 198–201
on privation
   matter as 223–25
   as evil, 230
on substance
   and the one, 190, 194–96
   and the good, 200
   and the intellect, 214–15
   and non-being, 220
on the good
   the one as, 198–201, 216–17, 229–30
   ways of knowing the good, 201
   and being, 207
   and the divine intellect, 209–10, 212
on the many
   and the one, 188–89, 201, 206
   the origin of, 205, 210
   as without one, 228
on thinking and being, 187, 193–94, 208–9
   and the one, 199, 201, 204–5, 209–10, 233
      as the source of, 196
      as above, 197, 203
      as unthinkable, 202
      and the divine intellect, 211–20
      and matter, 222
      and intelligible matter, 228
poet, 27–28, 41
poetic
   description/speech, 27, 197–98
   gift, 187
   journey, 31
   myth, 33
   narrative, 41
   prose, 28
   thinking, 28
poetry, 27–28, 143
poiēsis/ποίησις, 125–26, 193–94
polis, 118–20, 121, 123, 130–31, 133, 136–37, 138, 140
possibility
   and the one, 194–95
   as δύναμις, 181–83
   condition of, 48, 65, 68, 70, 232, 238
   (impossibility)
   of motion, 48, 252–54

of the coincidence of opposites, 163–64
of unmediated opposition of being and non-being, 169
of the void in mathematics, 245–46
conditions of, 68, 251
matter as, 181–83
of being, 10, 65
of liberation and freedom, 147
of motion, 68, 127, 253
of negation, 2
of truth, 87–89
of void, 70, 177
power
   and nothing, 69, 104
   and the good, 189–90
   and the one, 187, 194–96, 201–2, 226
   and the polis, 121
   and void, 66–67, 69
   as δύναμις, 194–95, 196, 226
   being as, 104
   freedom and, 145–47
   of contradictory opposites, 40–41
   of logos, 155–56, 174–75, 177
   of negation, 4, 37–38
   of non-being, 161–62, 187
   political power, 90, 130, 135–36
praxis/πρᾶξις
   and action, 78
   Diogenes on, 129
   life as, 127
   vs. *ergon*, 126
presence/παρουσία, 172–73
   absent presence, 29, 85
   and the one, 226
   of non-being, 85, 175–76
   of otherness, 179
   of the many, 227
principle of non-contradiction
   Aristotle on, 99, 100, 161–64, 169
   and logos, 36, 39–40, 81, 83, 86–87, 95
   and myth, 33
   and nothing, 23–24
   and ontological prohibition, 36
   and the one, 203
   and void, 244–45, 254

privation
　Aristotle on
　　and matter, 155
　　and non-being, 152
　　as a contrary to possession, 160-61
　　as distinct from contradiction, 162
　　as distinct from negation, 169
　　as either a contradiction or a
　　　contrariety, 161
　　as non-being, 161, 169
　　as one of the opposites, 158-60
　　as one of three principles, 164
　　as one of two kinds of non-being
　　　(with matter), 172
　　　matter and privation, 180-85, 223
　　　privation as absolute non-being,
　　　　172, 219
　　as opposite of form, 171
　　as privation of being, 69
　　and form
　　　as lack of form 152-53
　　　as somehow form, 160
　　as στέρησις, 153, 157, 158-59
　Plotinus on
　　matter as privation (contra
　　　Aristotle), 223-25
　　as evil, 230
　　and substance, 161
　　and void, 240
　Proclus, 40-41, 107, 158-59, 180-81,
　　212-13, 229, 231, 246-47, 250
prohibition
　of thinking non-being, 34-36, 37, 38
　social prohibition, 132-33
proportion(s)/proportional, 39-40,
　248, 252

reflexive/reflexivity, 6, 216
rest/μονή
　and place, 253
　and the divine intellect, 214
　and void, 253, 254
　and νοῦς, 106
　motion and, 99, 107-9, 111, 112, 160

same/ταὐτόν
　Aristotle on
　　and the principle of non-
　　　contradiction, 163, 169

　Democritus on
　　being and thinking as, 51
　Parmenides on
　　and being, 23, 26
　　and itself, 22
　　and logos, 14-15
　　and the opposing principles of Day
　　　and Night, 39-40
　　as substrate, 36
　　being and thinking as, 19-20
　　thinking and thought as, 18
　Plato on, 91
　　and being, 107
　　and logos, 81
　　and motion/rest, 108
　　and other as categories, 109-11
　　and the Sophist, 80-81
　Plotinus on
　　and the one and matter, 224
　　being and thinking as, 199,
　　　208, 215-16
　　same and other as two constitutive
　　　principles of being and the
　　　intellect, 207
　　the one as the principle of sameness
　　　in the constitution of numbers
　　　as the forms of being, 212-13
　Simplicius on
　　and matter, 242-44
　　and privation, 240
separation/χωρισμός
　and opposition as unmediated, 168-69
　and the thoughts of the intellect, as
　　being connected without
　　separation, 214-15
　as resulting from the intervention of
　　non-being, 245-46
　of beings and atoms, 70
　of the constituents of the said and
　　thought by logos, 165-66
simplicity
　and logos, 83, 154, 155-56, 166-67
　and the good, 199
　and the one, 191-92, 207
　Diogenes on, 139-40
　of being, 29, 33
Simplicius, ch7
　on cause, 244
　on cosmos, 236, 242

on place
    and void, 240–41, 253
    and interval, 235–37, 238–39
    on matter, 39–40, 242–45, 247–48, 250–51
    and non-being
        as void, 232, 233–36, 238–39, 244, 256
    on nothing
        void as, 238–39, 244, 252, 254, 256
    on number, 247–48
        and nothing, 248–49, 252
    on opinion
        and void, 233–36
    on opposites, 242–44
    on substance
        and void, 239, 240
        and matter, 242–43
    on thinking
        and matter, 242–43
    on truth
        and void, 239
    on void, 231–56
Socrates
    and dialectical truth, 30
    and Diogenes, 119–20, 121–22, 128–29, 133, 134–35
Sophists, 30, 74–75, 76, 88, 95, 113, 124, 133–34
subject, 10–11, 23–24
    and predicate, 5, 14, 18, 22, 106
    and the one, 199
    and void, 244–45
    Aristotle on, 150, 158–59
        and being, 167–68
        and truth, 166
        as substrate, 151, 156, 164
    logical subject, 24, 66–67, 90
substance
    Aristotle on
        as cause of being of each thing, 149–50
        substrate as, 150–51
        and form, 152
        and substrate, 153, 164
        and being, 156
        and privation, 161, 172–73
        and matter, 180–82, 184, 185–86
    as οὐσία, 153, 156, 190

Democritus on
    all beings/atoms, therefore, have the same substance, 47–48
    one substance, 48
    being bodily in its substance, 70
Plotinus on
    and the one, 190, 194–96
    and the good, 200
    and the intellect, 214–15
    and non-being, 220
Simplicius on
    and void, 239, 240
    and matter, 242–43
substrate
    Aristotle on, 150, 151–53, 190, 240
        and being, 156
        and negation as privation, 172–73
        and opposites, 158, 163, 181–82
        and change, 171
        and prime matter, 184–85
        and subject, 164
        as one of four aspects of matter, 180–81, 185–86, 223
        as ὑποκείμενον, 47–48, 150, 153, 190, 221–22, 242–43
    Democritus on, 47–48
    Parmenides on, 36
    Plotinus on, 227
    Simplicius on
        matter as, 242–43

telos, 179, 197
    as purpose, 126, 140, 149–50, 180
    Democritean infinity as a-telic, 63
theōria/θεωρία
    vs. ergon, πρᾶξις, and ποίησις, 126
thinking/νοεῖν
    Aristotle on
        according to Heidegger, 202
        and being, 155, 161–62
        and form, 153
        and logos, 154, 162–63, 165–66
        and truth, 166
        and the infinite, 180
        and νοῦς, 166–67
        void, according to Simplicius, 251–52
    Democritus on
        and being, 49, 50–51
    Diogenes on, 116, 126, 128

thinking/νοεῖν (cont.)
   and routine/habit/convention, 138, 143–44, 145
   Parmenides on
      and being, 1–2
         being reflected as, 13
         as the same, 19–20
         and apophasis, 25–26, 40–41
         and non-being, 34–41
         logical thinking (λέγειν) vs. noetic thinking (νοεῖν), 16–19
         and logos, 22
         as poetic, 28
   Plato on
      and being, 92, 106–7
      and form, 101–3
      and logos, 76–77
         as discursive (διάνοια), 82–83, 91, 93, 95
         as non-discursive (νοῦς), 87, 106
      of the philosopher, 77–81
   Plotinus on
      and being, 187, 193–94, 208–9
      and intelligible matter, 228
      and matter, 222
      and the divine intellect, 211–20
      and the one, 199, 201, 204–5, 209–10, 233
         as the source of, 196
         as above, 197, 203
         as unthinkable, 202
   Simplicius on
      and matter, 242–43
time/χρόνος
   Aristotle on
      and opposites, 243–44
      and the principle of non-contradiction, 163, 169, 202
      and zeno's paradox, 127–28
   Plato on
      and logos, 100
   Plotinus on
      and being, 208
      and the thinking of the divine intellect, 217
   Simplicius on
      and the void, 255–56
trace/ἴχνος, 189, 209–10
truth
   Aristotle on, 165–67, 202
      and logos, 150–51
      and contradiction, 169
   Democritus on
      obscurity and, 49–52
      of being and non-being, 69
   Diogenes on
      and being, 141–42, 143–44
      and *ergon*, 141
   Parmenides on, 4–5, 41
      of being, 29–34
      and logos, 16, 36
         and logical truth, 18
      noetic vs. logical, 11–12, 15–16
      reason- νόος as, 19
   Plato on
      and false, 164–65
      and lies, 87–88
      and logos, 76–77
      and method, 83–87
      and the narrated, 76–77
      of being, 88–89, 104
   Simplicius on
      and void, 239
two
   as first concrete plurality that is the other of one, 90
   as one half of the indefinite dyad, 90
   as one of two forms of otherness, 97–99

via negativa, 40–41, 201
via positiva, 40–41
void/κενόν
   Aristotle on, 177–81
   Democritus on, 42–72
   Simplicius on, 231–56
   See also absence; atoms; body; categories; cause; conception; cosmos; darkness; disposition; extension; imagination; indefinite/indefiniteness; limit; mathematics; nature; negation; number; physics; power; principle of non-contradiction; privation; rest
volume/ὄγκος
   mathematical and physical volume, 250
   of a cone and pyramid, 42–43

Zeno, 3, 24–25, 45, 127–28, 177